Borderland Families Always on the Edge

Journey of the Lykins, Peery, and Heiskell Families along the Missouri and Kansas Border

Rose Ann Findlen

March 2011

© Copyright 2011 by Rose Ann Findlen.

All rights reserved. Without permission in writing from the publisher, no part of this book may be reproduced or transmitted in any form or by any means, electronic or mechanical, including photocopying, recording, or by any information storage and retrieval system.

§The paper used in this publication meets the minimum requirements of American National Standard for Information Sciences—Permanence of Paper for Printed Library Materials, ANSI Z39.48-1984. This book is printed on recycled paper with at least 40% post-consumer materials.

Findlen, Rose Ann (Gard) (1942-)
    Borderland Families Always on the Edge: Journey of the Lykins, Peery, and Heiskell Families along the Missouri and Kansas Border
    by Rose Ann Findlen
        450 p.   cm.
    Includes bibliographical references and index.

    ISBN ISBN-13: 978-0615451565 (Generations Books)
    ISBN-10:   061545156X

1. Kansas–History–Civil War, 1861-1865–Social aspects. 2. Missouri History–Civil War, 1861-1865–Social aspects. 3. West (U.S.)–History–1848-1860. 4. United States–History–Civil War, 1861-1865–Biography. I. Findlen, Rose Ann. (1942-). II. Title.

Cover: "St. Louis from the River Below," 1832-33 by *George Catlin*

CONTENTS

Acknowledgments iii

Foreword: Where is Emeline? v

Sequence of Events 1

Chapter 1: The Lykins and a Vision for the
           Indian Territory of Kansas 11

Chapter 2: The Landscape of Emeline's World 57

Chapter 3: The Lykins and Heiskells in the Border War ... 99

Chapter 4: Friends and Family in the Civil War 149

Chapter 5: Missouri Families in the Civil War 171

Chapter 6: A Decade of Continuing Losses 219

Chapter 7: Along Came William F. Wallace 253

Chapter 8: Leslie Erle Wallace: A Kansan for All Seasons . 279

Chapter 9: Family Genealogical Charts 309

    David Lykins and Jemima Willis 311

    William A. Heiskell-Evalina Price-Emeline Peery 345

    William T. Wallace-Mary True-Lydia Waterman 353

Related Stories and Poems 359

    "Tecumseh's Tomahawk" (Referenced in Chapter 2) ... 361

    "The Mare Was Drugged" (Chapter 3) 365

    "The Lykins Mansion on Quality Hill" (Chapter 5) 369

    "Chief Joseph's Story" (Chapter 6) 375

    "Tales of Lost Spanish Gold": Baptiste Peoria
    and Patrick McNaughton (Chapter 6) 377

    "Memories of the Dead," by Sarah Lykins Russell
    (Chapter 6) 382

    "The Editor's Guests" (Chapter 7) 385

    "A Roaring Mob: How New York Appeared on
    Election Night" by Leslie Wallace (Chapter 8) 389

    "The Glory of Pawnee County," by Leslie Wallace
    (Chapter 8) 393

Selected Poems by Leslie Earle Wallace, Eunice Wallace
    Shore Rhea, and Ralph Wallace 395

Selected Bibliography 405

Illustrations 413

Index 419

About the Author 437

ACKNOWLEDGEMENTS

Many generous people have helped me with this book since it first became a glimmer in my eye. Betty Bendorf and other volunteers at the Ethel Hunt Library of the Miami County (Kansas) Historical and Genealogical Society dug through their archives and consistently went the extra mile—both in person and on the telephone—to help me find photographs and documents pertaining to the Lykins and Heiskells in Paola.

David W. Jackson, Archives and Education Director for the Jackson County Historical Society Archives in Independence, Jackson County, Missouri, found and shared important original documents related to these families in Kansas City and Independence, Missouri. At the Wisconsin Historical Archives and Library, Jim Hansen, Genealogy Reference Librarian, and Nancy Mulhern, Government Documents Librarian, provided expert guidance for researching arcane documents for the book. Indeed, archivists, librarians, genealogists and historical society officers from Kansas, Kentucky, Missouri, Wisconsin, New Hampshire, and Indiana used their professional expertise to enrich my knowledge of the lives led by families in the Borderland.

Descendants of the Owen and Wallace families, Leslie Zygmund of Montana, Robert Dewit Owen of New York City, and Karen Kimball Hull of New Hampshire, shared treasured family photographs, generously finding the time to help a complete stranger augment the pages of this book.

As the manuscript took shape, family, friends and colleagues read it and provided invaluable suggestions for helping bring to life Mattie, Emeline, Gen. Heiskell, W.F. Wallace, and the Lykins brothers. George Findlen, Sara Wallace and Pat Brunet spent countless hours reading the manuscript, making editorial suggestions and assisting with the creative process of weaving it all together.

Constructive criticism from Jim Hansen, Jean Lind, David W. Jackson, and Barbara Littlewood gave sharper focus and better organization to the book.

During the most arduous part of the birth of this book involving the formatting and organization of the references—my husband, George, took on the daunting task and stayed with it through hundreds of footnotes. That was truly an act of personal devotion and dedication to genealogical research standards. Without his help, the references could not have been cited so clearly and accurately for others to access. Tom Farrell graciously enhanced photographs which were often blurred and faded. David W. Jackson lent his expertise in editing, formatting, designing, and indexing. I feel I had my own personal community at my side through the book's long gestation and birth. Thank you to all who so kindly helped.

I am pleased to publish *Borderland Families Always on the Edge* in March, 2011, to commemorate the bicentennial of the birth of one of Missouri's most notable painters (and politicians) George Caleb Bingham, who married Mrs. Martha "Mattie" (Livingston) Lykins, a prominent figure in Kansas City in her own right...and an important subject of this historical sketch.

Enjoy skirting the borderland with one eye on the past!

Rose Ann Findlen
Madison, Wisconsin

FOREWORD

WHERE IS EMELINE?

One Saturday afternoon in my first semester in graduate school at the University of Kansas, I walked from downtown Lawrence at the base of Mount Oread to the Student Union to get a much-needed cup of coffee. As I sat in the Union I glanced occasionally outside the window to see red and gold leaves against the sapphire autumn sky. Suddenly a huge roaring sound shook the window next to my booth as I sat in the near-empty cafeteria. When I stepped outside to find out what was happening, I realized that the sound was coming from the football stadium. The stadium's walls formed the shape of an upside down bell or megaphone and the crowd's voices resonated upward and across the campus as Kansas football fans chanted, "Rock Chalk! Jayhawk!"

"Oh yes," I thought. "Today there is a game between Kansas and Missouri." Above my head a fierce sculptured bluejay, the university mascot, hovered menacingly.

In a few minutes, loud, excited undergraduates drove through the streets of fraternity row with cheerleaders and fraternity brothers perched on the backs of the convertibles' rear seats, their red sweatshirts emblazoned with the stylized image of the university mascot: a bluejay with an enormous yellow beak. Neither the boisterous students celebrating their team's victory nor I fully realized the profound brutality, lawlessness and vindictiveness that had given birth to the Jayhawk mascot.

As recently as November, 2007, a newspaper article remarked on the intense, historically rooted football rivalry between the University of Kansas and the University of Missouri:

> For 116 years an anger has coursed through Kansas-Missouri Rivalry. One Kansas coach used to tell his players that Quantrill graduated from Missouri. It wasn't true, but it would work the Kansas players into a frothing rage.... Only 26 years after the final shot was fired in the Civil War and less than 40 miles away from Lawrence, the Missouri-Kansas series began. Old soldiers and their children may well have been standing in that crowd when Kansas beat Missouri 22-8

in that historic first game in 1891. Still fresh in their minds would have been memories of dead bodies and burning homes and bloody border raids by both anti-slavery crusaders riding out of Kansas and pro-slavery zealots operating from Missouri.[1]

The mascot's image was originally based on "Red Legs" George Hoyt, one of the most brutal of the notorious Kansas Jayhawkers. Hoyt, who was John Brown's attorney, led a unit of the Seventh Kansas Cavalry called the "Red Legs" or "Red Legged Scouts."

An observer at a public meeting in Paola, Kansas, described Hoyt as "dressed in a suit of black velvet, red sheepskin leggings reaching to the knees, a red silk handkerchief carelessly thrown around his neck, and a military hat with a flowing black plume. At his waist was an embossed morocco belt carrying a pair of ivory-mounted revolvers."[2] Missouri painter George Caleb Bingham shows a similarly dressed man in Red Leg clothing killing an unarmed man in his painting, "Order No. 11."

The memory of the jubilant football victory came back to me years later when I was researching the story of Emeline Peery, a Civil War era woman who had intrigued me from the time I saw her photograph hanging on the walls of the public library in Paola, Kansas. As my research progressed, I discovered that not only was Emeline an engaging, courageous woman in her own right, but she was also part of the broader story of the intertwined Lykins-Heiskell-Wallace-Peoria families who embodied the early histories of the Missouri-Kansas Borderland.

Emeline Peery is the central focus of this book and, yet, she is hard to find within the following pages. Because her grandson, Leslie Wallace, was a writer and adored her, more glimpses of her remain than for most pioneer women of the nineteenth century. Charmed by her liveliness and story-telling, he had an interview of her published in the Sunday Edition of the Kansas City newspaper where he was editor. He wrote eloquently about her at the time of her death. Other members of her extended family also valued history and family stories, keeping letters and notes on the family's history which ended up in regional archives.

Another reason she has left a vague historical footprint is that she lived in a highly dramatic, pivotal time and place for the states of Kansas and Missouri. The men surrounding her played prominent roles in the early formation of the Kansas Territory, and were embroiled in the bitter border conflicts between Kansas and Missouri, and the Civil War. The players on the Borderland stage during Emeline's lifetime were, among many others: missionary visionaries, Isaac McCoy, and Johnston and David Lykins; Chief of the Five Tribes, Baptiste Peoria; insurgent fighter, William Quantrill; radical abolitionist, John Brown; Kansas governors Reeder and Geary; painters George Caleb Bingham and George Catlin; Kansas City founders, Johnston Lykins and John McCoy.

Emeline and her husband personally interacted with almost all of these historic figures.

Emeline was there but formal records detailing her life are elusive since she was hidden behind a veil of strict gender roles, as were the majority of women of her day. Family histories are replete with genealogical entries such as "Elizabeth X?" and "Spouse Unknown." Because most women were not involved in public affairs and large business enterprises, their names show up only in birth, marriage and death announcements with their surnames, and often even given names, replaced by phrases such as "daughter," "wife of the deceased," "his wife of the home." or, simply as "Mrs." followed by her husband's full name.

When historians and biographers of the time wrote about the eminent men of communities, they seldom made more than a one-sentence reference to their wives, mothers or sisters. The women were, obviously, present and deeply affected by the events around them, but discovering in print what they thought or did in a particular time is frequently not possible. What Emeline thought about slavery is not recorded; how she felt about the prominent men around her—both the infamous and the famous—is unknown. Emeline's story is defined through a consideration of negative space, aside from the few glimpses of her in a letter she wrote, an interview of her and obituaries, Emeline is found in the spaces between the lines of the social and political conditions and events of her time, and the actions of family members within that framework.

Another way in which "Emeline was there" is through the influence she had on her grandson, Leslie Wallace, and other family members. Because of the bare outlines of women in the shadows of male family members, their impact on historical and cultural events is often hard to discern. In her lifetime, Emeline's grandson, who was deeply inspired and influenced by her, became a central player in the journalism, arts and politics of Kansas. He lived with Emeline during his first two years of life and again during the summers when he learned the printing trade. His adventurous exploration of worlds and lives outside his own and his love for the written word were inspired, in part, by his grandmother, Emeline. These traits were later manifested by his publishing significant poets and creating a reputable poetry journal, advising state governors, and writing about pivotal people and events, both nationally and regionally.

Leslie's journalistic and political talents brought him as witness and participant at the center of important events and issues of his time, including the development of journalistic excellence in Kansas with prominent journalistic colleagues Lew Wallace and William Allen White.

Emeline's pride in her newly formed state of Kansas was passed on in the form of Leslie's nurturance of the region's history and art. Her grandson's poetry was published in journals encouraging regional artists and poets such as Paul Engle, long-time director of the prestigious Writers' Workshop at the University of Iowa, and artist John Steuart Curry. He created and published a national-level journal, *The Harp*, which had roots firmly planted in Kansas. In his news stories, he wrote about major events and issues of the time: the fall of Tammany Hall; progressive state and national politics (The Bull Moose Movement); the Kansas dust bowl and the Great Depression; the introduction of inter-continental air travel; and expanded globalization of markets and governments.

Emeline and her extended family in Kansas and Missouri played key roles in the development of the Borderland. Their stories bring into sharp relief the lives of men and women in Kansas and Missouri from 1800 to 1940.

In body and spirit, Emeline WAS there.

---

1. Doug Tucker, "Rivalry's Roots Deep," *The* (Madison, Wisconsin) *Capitol Times*, 23 Nov. 2007, A2.
2. Donald Gilmore, *Civil War on the Missouri-Kansas Border* (Gretna, La.: Pelican Publishing, 2006), 157.

SEQUENCE OF EVENTS

1800   Birth of **Johnston Lykins** in Virginia

1822   Baptism of **Johnston Lykins** by **Isaac McCoy** at mission in Michigan

1824   Birth of **Martha A. Livingston** in Kentucky (January)

1828   Removal of **Wea, Piankeshaw and Shawnee** to Kansas Territory

1828   Settlement of **Johnston and Delilah McCoy Lykins** and children at Shawnee Baptist Indian Mission in Kansas Territory

1830   Birth of **Emeline Peery** in Indiana

1830   Painting of Ke-mah-lan-eah (**Baptiste Peoria**'s son) by George Catlin

1832   Visit of **David Lykins, Sr., son David and daughter Eliza** to his son, **Johnston Lykins**, at Shawnee Mission, a suburb of present-day Kansas City, Kansas

1837   Marriage of **Claiborne Lykins** to **Nancy Johnson** near St. Joseph, Missouri

1841   **Johnston Lykins'** Publication of first Indian language newspaper/first newspaper in Kansas Territory

1

1843	Marriage of **David Lykins Jr.** and **Abigail Webster** at Shawnee Baptist Indian Mission
1844	Death of **Delilah McCoy Lykins,** Johnston Lykins' first wife
1844	Appointment of **David and Abigail Lykins** as missionaries at Wea Mission near present-day Paola, Kansas
1847	**Jonas Lykins'** construction of Pottawatomie Baptist Mission/School near present-day Topeka, Kansas
1849	Death of **Evalina Price Heiskell,** William Heiskell's first wife
1849	Death of **William Peery,** Emeline Peery's father
1851	Marriage of **Johnston Lykins** and **Martha Livingston**
1852	Death of **Abigail Webster Lykins** and son **Charles** (January)
1852	Arrival of newlyweds **Johnston and Mattie Lykins** in Westport (March)
1852	Arrival of **Emeline Peery** in the Kansas Territory (June 18)
1852	Arrival of **David Peery** (Emeline's brother) in the Kansas Territory (Autumn)
1852	Marriages of **Emeline Peery** and **William Heiskell;** **David Lykins** and **Sarah Tull**
1853	**Johnston Lykins'** election as first legally elected mayor of Kansas City, Missouri

1854 Passage of **Kansas-Nebraska Act** to open Kansas Indian Territory for Anglo-American settlement

1854-
1855 Staking of claims in Kansas: **W.H.R. Lykins** (Johnston's son), **Stephen J. Livingston** (Mattie Lykins' brother), **Claiborne Lykins and Joseph Lykins** (two of Emeline's uncles), **William Heiskell, David Lykins, Baptiste Peoria** (as part of treaty settlement), **John Brown and his sons**

1855 **William Jackson Livingston's** (Mattie Lykins' brother) rental of farm near Hannibal, Missouri

1855 Election of **William Heiskell and David Lykins** to First Territorial Kansas Legislature

1855 Establishment of town of **Paola** by **Baptiste Peoria, David Lykins, William Heiskell** and others

1856 Killing of five proslavery settlers at Pottawatomie Creek by **John Brown and associates** (May 24)

1856 Destruction of home of **Stephen J. Livingston** (Mattie Lykins' brother) by Free-state/Abolitionist forces (August)

1856 March on Lawrence, Kansas by proslavery forces, which included **William Heiskell's** army (September)

1857 Birth of **Sue Heiskell**, daughter of Emeline and William Heiskell (May)

1857 Arrival of **William Quantrill** in Kansas, near Paola, Kansas

1859 Death of **Jonas Lykins** (one of Emeline's five uncles in the Borderland)

1858-
1860 Relocation of **Ermina and Charles Keller** (Heiskell's former sister-in-law and her husband & foster parents to his children), **their children and Fanny Heiskell** from Cass County, Missouri to St. Louis; **Charles Heiskell** to Paola, Kansas

1860 Marriage of **David Peery** (Emeline's brother) and **Elizabeth Baptiste** (Baptiste Peoria's daughter)

1860 Birth of **Emeline and William Heiskell's** second daughter, **Alberta**

1860 Marriage of **David Lykins** and **Grace Tull** (sister of his deceased second wife)

1861 Death of **Alberta**, infant daughter of **Emeline and William Heiskell** (April)

1861 Arrest of **David Lykins** as a Southern Sympathizer by Captain Eli Snyder (June)

1861 **Kansas** statehood

1861 Renaming of **Lykins County** to **Miami County** (July)

1861 Departure of **David Lykins** from Paola; his death in Colorado

1862 Birth of **Emeline and William Heiskell's** third daughter, **Nellie** (February)

4

1862   Dispatch of **Baptiste Peoria** to Southeastern Kansas to persuade **Five Civilized Tribes** to remain loyal to Union

1861-1864 **Civil War Army Enlistments:**

<u>In the Union Army:</u>

Woodson D. Hoover (Joseph Lykins' son-in-law)
James Lykins (Joseph Lykins' son)

David Ferguson (Emeline's cousin)
Willis Earnest (Emeline's cousin)
Frank Betteys (Emeline's cousin)

Claiborne Lykins
Andrew C. Lykins (Claiborne Lykins' son)
David A. Lykins (Claiborne Lykins' son)

Charles Heiskell (William Heiskell's son)
Addison Madeira (William Heiskell's future son-in-law)

Egbert Freeland Russell (Johnston Lykins' son-in-law)
Theodore Case (Johnston Lykins' son-in-law)
George Caleb Bingham (Johnston Lykins' close friend)

William F. Wallace (Sue Heiskell's future husband)
William T. Wallace (William F. Wallace's father)
Dana Wallace (William F. Wallace's brother)

Judson Owen, Assistant Surgeon (Mattie Lykins' nephew)

In the Confederate Army:

William J. Livingston (Mattie Lykins' brother)
Spencer McCoy (Johnston Lykins' nephew)
E. C. Heiskell (William Heiskell's son)

1862 Deaths of **David Ferguson and Willis Earnest** of disease

1863 Arrest of **William J. Livingston,** Mattie Lykins' brother, for spying (May)

1863 Surrender at Vicksburg and imprisonment of **E.C. Heiskell**

1863 Death of **Spencer McCoy,** nephew of Johnston Lykins

1863 Raid of **Quantrill's band** on Lawrence, Kansas (August)

1863 Issuance of **Order No. 11** by Provost Marshall General Thomas Ewing (August)

1863 Banishment of **Mattie Lykins** from Kansas City (August)

1863 Desertion of **Charles Heiskell** from Union forces (October)

1863 Death of **Dana Wallace,** P.O.W. in Richmond, Virginia (November)

1864 Arrest of **Claiborne Lykins** near St. Joseph, Missouri (January)

1864 Return of **Mattie Lykins** to Kansas City (January)

1864 Execution of **William J. Livingston** for spying (August)

1864	Deaths of **Nellie and newborn Blanche Heiskell,** daughters of William and Emeline Heiskell (August/September)
1864	Death in battle of **David A. Lykins,** son of Claiborne Lykins (October)
1865	Convening of Peace Council Meeting resulting in establishment of Oklahoma Indian Territory and removal of tribes from Kansas (September)
1865	Deaths of **Mattie and Emily Case,** Johnston Lykins' Grand-daughters of sudden illness
1866	Campaign by **Mattie Lykins** to found Confederate Widows' and Orphans' Home (July)
1868	Preparation of **David Peery, Baptiste Peoria and Tribes** for removal to the Oklahoma Indian Territory
1868	Birth of **Minnie Heiskell,** fifth daughter of Emeline and William Heiskell
1869	Death of **Olive Case,** Johnston Lykins' granddaughter
1870	Deaths of **William Heiskell , Joseph Lykins' wife, Merb, and Mattie Lykins' nephew, Judson Owen**
1872-1874	Deaths of **Juliann Betteys** (Emeline's aunt), **James Lykins** (Joseph's son), **Juliana Case** (Johnston's daughter), **Effie and Willie Russell** (Johnston's grandchildren); and, **Baptiste Peoria**

1873 **The Panic of 1873** and following economic depression resulting in **Johnston Lykins'** loss of wealth

1874 Beginning of **Sue Heiskell's** teaching career

1875 Marriage of **Sue Heiskell and William F. Wallace**

1876 Death of **Johnston Lykins** (August 15)

1876 Birth of **Leslie Wallace,** son of **William F. and Sue Heiskell Wallace**

1877 Divorce of **Sue Heiskell Wallace and William F. Wallace**

1877 Death of **Claiborne Lykins**

1878 Death of **Price Heiskell Madeira,** William Heiskell's daughter

1878 Marriage of **Mattie Lykins and George Caleb Bingham** (June 18)

1879 Death of **George Caleb Bingham** (July 7)

1879 Marriage of **Sue Heiskell Wallace and Hiram Phillips.**

1880 Appointment of **Emeline Heiskell** as librarian at Paola Public Library

1882 Death of **Joseph Lykins,** last remaining of the Lykins brothers who migrated to Kansas

1883 Marriage of **William F. Wallace and Addie Gilman French**

1885	Death of **Hiram Phillips,** Sue Heiskell's second husband, leaving behind three young daughters and a stepson
1889	Marriage of **Sue Heiskell Phillips** and **Philip F. Latimer**
1890	Death of **Mattie Lykins Bingham** (September 20)
1893	Opening of Cherokee Strip to Anglo-American settlement in **Oklahoma Indian Territory**
1896	Death of **David Peery,** Emeline Heiskell's brother
1897	Retirement of **Emeline Heiskell** from Paola Public Library
1898	Hiring of **Leslie Wallace** as a reporter for *The Topeka Capitol*
1900	Newpaper correspondence by **Leslie Wallace** on failure of Richard Croker of **Tammany Hall** to carry New York City
1905	Marriage of **Leslie Wallace and Sara LeMaistre Johnson**
1905	Failure of Oklahoma Constitutional Convention to establish separate Indian state, **Sequoyah**
1906	Death of **William F. Wallace**
1907	Creation of **State of Oklahoma**
1910-1914	**Leslie Wallace**'s rise to Sunday Editor of *Kansas City Star*
1912	Founding of Progressive **Bull Moose Party**

1916   **Leslie Wallace's** acquisition as editor/owner of **The Tiller and Toiler**

1916   Death of **Emeline Heiskell** (August)

1918   Death of **Sue Heiskell Latimer**

1925   Establishment of **The Harp,** a national poetry journal, published by **Leslie Wallace**

1929   Beginning of the **Great Depression**

1930   Death of **Sara Johnson Wallace**

1932   Marriage of **Leslie Wallace and Bobbie Victor**

1935   **Black Sunday,** height of Dust Bowl

1935   First flight of **DC-3,** revolutionizing air transport

1939   Beginning of **World War II**

1940   Death of **Leslie Wallace**

CHAPTER 1

The Lykins and a Vision for the Indian Territory of Kansas

On June 19, 1852, when Emeline Peery woke up on her first morning in the Kansas Territory, the first person to come to the Indian mission to greet her was Baptiste Peoria, chief of the Peoria.[1] One of the earliest Anglo-American women to come to Kansas, Emeline arrived in the territory at the age of twenty-two. Years later, David's son Wayland wrote notes explaining Emeline's coming to the Kansas Territory:

> Emmaline Jamima Peery came to what became Lykins County Kansas Territory in 1849 [sic]. When her father, William Peery knew he was going to die. Her mother, Hannah Lykins Peery, being already dead. He wrote to his wife's brother, David Lykins started for Middle Town [Indiana] in the spring of 1852 and brought his niece to the Wea Mission. . . . The next morning after she got there she went to a window and looked out. She saw a man standing in the yard. He took off his hat, bowed to her in the politest manner. She was told that this man was Major Baptiste, a man of wonderful intellect, but no education.[2]

At the time of this meeting of tiny Emeline and rugged, gentlemanly Baptiste, neither of them knew that for the next twenty years, they would live as friends and neighbors, their destinies closely linked by family and events surrounding the development of the future state of Kansas.

The tall, courtly man understood new locations and beginnings well: in his lifetime, he had moved with his people to unknown lands three times. Baptiste was born in 1793 at the confluence of the Kankakee and Des Plaines Rivers in Illinois. A "man of large stature," he was a commanding presence, and had time and again been asked to use his language abilities to mediate conflicts among tribes and negotiate treaties with white men. Because he had assisted in the negotiation of the Treaty of Edwardsville in 1818, he had been called upon numerous times by both federal government officials and the other tribes of Illinois and Indiana to mediate and interpret.[3]

He was a fluent speaker of both French and English and had a working knowledge of the dialects of the Pottawatomie, Shawnee, Delaware, Miami, Illinois and Kickapoo tribes.[4] When he visited Baptiste sometime between 1859-1862, an anthropologist described him as a "half breed French and Peoria, with an intermixture of some African blood,"[5]…. [and] "is a man of note….He carries on a large farm well stocked, and is principal owner of the stage line from Ossawatomie to Kansas City.

Baptiste Peoria

He talks our language well, but slowly, has been among all the Kansas Indians and is well known throughout the territory as a man of large property. He and his households occupy several houses grouped near together about a mile from Paola."[6]

At the time Emeline and Baptiste met, Baptiste had his hands full. The Five Tribes--Miami, Wea, Peoria, Kaskaskia and Piankeshaw-- were at war with the Osage and Pottawatomie, because the two latter groups were intermarrying with young women from the Five Tribes. This situation was leading to skirmishes and bloodshed. In addition, the Five Tribes "were at war" with the Border Missourians who were "poaching on their reservations."[7] After a quarter of a century of enforced proximity in the Indian Territory of Kansas, the tribal groups were not one big happy family but remained, as they had been before, tribal rather than pan-Indian groups. These inter-tribal tensions constituted only one problem among many imported into the new territory with its artificially organized new settlements. The addition of European-American immigrants with their unresolved conflicts was the backdrop of Emeline and Baptiste's lives as they witnessed and participated in the history of the region.

Emeline and her brothers may have stayed with their widowed father until he died. However, in the 1850 Census, two years after the deaths of Emeline's father, William Peery, in 1848, and her brother, Albert, in 1850,[8] Emeline was living with her Aunt Eliza, her minister husband and their family.[9] Only a few months later, Aunt Eliza's husband died in San Francisco, having gone there to "scoop up gold." Eliza was left to raise their five sons on the farm in Illinois.[10] Emeline probably went from taking care of her brothers and father during his final days to assisting Aunt Eliza with her five sons to going to help Uncle David with his two little sons.

Forty-three years later, Emeline wrote to David's son, Edward about her arrival at Wea Mission and seeing him and Wayland for the first time:

Paola, KS, May 31st, 1895

My Dear Edward:--

As I want to give you something to remember "Cousin" by, I send you this sketch of my trip back to the old Mission days.

I have gone back with memory for guide and artist, and the pictures I see are unfading, and no mist from the years mar their tints.

I see again the old Mission buildings in the light of the setting sun of June 18th, 1852, and I see two little boys, one in dresses and long light curls, and one a little older, in his night dress ready for bed; and their father says: "Children, this is your cousin, you must be good to her, she, like you has no <u>mother</u> and no father either, and no one here to love her but you and I." Wayland clasped my neck and kissed me, but Edward stood back silent. How plain the picture is, my uncle, the little boys, Miss Tull, and I so tired and strange.

We had, my uncle and I, driven out from Kansas City that day. John Robideaux had met us at Dr. Johnston Lykins in Kansas City, that morning. He brought old Adrian and the buggy and led the pony which he was to ride back.

And memory, I thank thee for this picture I love, I have seen again their smiles and looks of love. Have again gone with the boys to the creek, gathered the wild verbena and roses, seen the dew on their leaves and inhaled their odor.

Again I hear the Chapel bell for prayer, and hear a soft voice singing: "There is a happy land far, far away."

I see again the little Indian boys and girls and hear their whispered replies.

I see the lone tree, the three trees in one, in all its vigor and perfect beauty. Beneath its shade the carved stones that told of the lives of the sleepers below. The stones are still there all tarnished and broken. But the picture of the tree is only a <u>picture</u> now. I *hear the soft rustle of its glistening leaves as they are tossed by each passing breeze, and the perfume of verbena and prairie pinks are borne on the wind that waves the soft grass like billows of the sea; and when the darkness has fallen over all, I see the spark of the cigar smoked by the bereaved father as he walks back and forth beneath the lone tree.*

I stand again beside the open grave where the fair mistress of the Mission home is being laid to rest. Her life was crowned with love and beauty, and while life was full of the beauty of living and loving, she laid it down.

I am with the boys and Sabo going to see the hole in the bank where they caught a groundhog, and I hear the story of Miss Osgood's bravery, when Sabo's life was about to be taken by a drunk Indian, who had raised his gun to shoot the dog, Miss Osgood sprang between the dog and danger. I see the boys pat Sabo's head as they both talk at once about the wonderful dog.

I see a small boy wading in the back water from Wea, I see the long table in the passage and Edward on it with the cow bell. I see the white head of Dr. Crochett and hear his wise words.

My brother [David L. Peery] stands in the walk between Dr. Lykins' room and the old passage. The sun glinting his curly hair. He stood a perfect picture of health and hope. I see him as if it were but yesterday.

I hear the boys call "Coy" [Eliza McCoy] and she answers, "Yes, my dears."

Through all the ups and downs of Mission life though I only looked on, I hear the echo of many voices, a part of a sentence or a reader's voice, or the loving glance of eyes that spoke of love to mine [William Heiskell's].

I see a little child [probably Edward] who has just learned to walk, walking back and forth in the old passage, hands clasped behind its back, in imitation of a grave man walking there. I smile proudly on the innocent darling.

I see the rough walls of the old passage and the split bottom chairs, and down the long vista to the east door, and I see the doors opening into the girl's room, the boy's room, the dining room, the kitchen and the little room beyond the kitchen which was called Dr. Findley's [missionary] room.

Some are coming, some are going, and all look happy. Dr. Findley comes to ask a question of the man walking there, and Grace, dear Grace, [David Lykins' third wife, Grace Tull], comes with a smile of love. The unselfish and loving Grace.

So goodbye dear old Mission days, to me you can never die, but crowned with youth and hallowed by the love and hopes that are immortal you will live forever.[11]

Emeline's Uncles and the Baptist Missions of Michigan

Emeline was born in 1830 near Terre Haute, Indiana where her destiny and the Lykins/Peery family story are intertwined with the Baptist missionary, Isaac McCoy, and the Shawnee, Wea, Piankeshaw, Miami and Pottawatomie peoples who were among those removed to today's State of Kansas as a result of the Act of May 26, 1830.[12] Having grown up in the place where missionary Isaac McCoy founded the Prairie Creek Baptist Church, visited frequently with frontiersman Daniel Boone as he passed through the settlement,[13] promoted the dream of the Indian Territory, and recruited Uncle Johnston to missionary work, Emeline was well-suited for life at Wea Mission. She had grown up as a second generation pioneer in Indiana and experienced the loss and hardship of that world; the challenges of frontier life in the Indian Territory would not have been alien to her.

Pioneering was in the blood of the Lykins' family. Emeline's grandparents, David Lykins and Jemima Willis Lykins and their children came to settle in Prairie Creek Township about 20 miles from Terre Haute, Indiana; they were among the first handful of pioneers venturing into the township in 1816.[14] When Emeline was a year old, in 1831, Jared Lykins had established Battlerow Settlement which had mills, a distillery, a hotel and a cotton gin.[15] The same year, Joseph Lykins built the second business in nearby Middletown, a framed building in which he established a store[16] and David Lykins, Sr. obtained a public land grant of eighty acres.[17]

Emeline's parents, Hannah Lykins Peery and William Peery, probably lived in a rustic log cabin in at least the early years of their marriage. Most of the early settlers lived in cabins which had begun as log rail pens that were later closed in as dwellings about fifteen feet square. This space served as parlor, dining room, kitchen and bedroom and on cold winter days the families shared the room with the weaker of their domestic animals. Many settlers were still living in these cramped cabins in 1830.[18]

Living on the frontier where sudden and untimely death had been a part of her life from childhood, Emeline resilience had been tested. Her Uncle Johnston's wife Delilah alluded to her deceased

A PIONEER DWELLING.

sister-in-law Hannah Lykins Peery's "poor motherless children," wishing they (Emeline and her brothers) were near enough for her to help. Three years later, Delilah's children were "motherless" as well, following her death from tuberculosis in 1844.[19] Of David and Jemima Lykins' twelve children, eight had children who lost one or both parents before they reached adulthood: Jared, Johnston, Joseph, David, Jonas, Eliza, Cynthia, and Hannah. Two of David and Jemima's daughters died in childhood.

In 1852, when she moved to Wea Mission, Emeline was again on the frontier and in the front lines of living with the hardships and infectious diseases that swept through both the white and Native American populations in this period of time. In addition, she was one of only a few Anglo-American women in the newly founded community. Her nephew, Edward, son of David and Abigail (Webster) Lykins, was the first Anglo-American child born in today's Miami County, Kansas.[20] A few years later, Emeline's daughter, Sue, would be the first Anglo-American child born in Paola.[21]

Although Emeline was a tiny woman, she had "an iron constitution" and a prodigious "nervous energy."[22] In later years, Emeline liked to tell her grandson and anyone else who would listen about those early pioneer days in Kansas Territory, enjoying the challenges of adapting to the new environment and creating innovative solutions to the daily problems of life in the wilderness.[23] She not only survived the difficult pioneer life—she thrived.

Living among and working with Native Americans was also a familiar concept. Six of Emeline's uncles had long been involved in Baptist mission work with these native groups. When Isaac and Christiana McCoy were granted permission to serve as Baptist missionaries to Native American groups in Michigan, McCoy recruited some of the young men living near Prairieton, Indiana. Three of David and Jemima Lykins' sons soon volunteered to work in Michigan: Emeline's Uncle Joseph Lykins taught Pottawatomie children at the Carey Mission near LaPorte, Indiana (then the

Michigan Territory);[24] and remained there as a farmer for a few years after the mission was closed. Her Uncle Jared went to Michigan to work, and he and fellow worker Charles Polke were baptized in the Michigan territory in 1822; McCoy wrote that they gained far more than wages from their time working at the missions.[25]

Uncle Johnston worked first as a teacher with Isaac McCoy in Michigan in 1819 and became committed to missionary work among Native Americans through his exposure to the visionary Baptist missionary. McCoy described Lykins' adult baptism:[26]

> On Lord's day, June 2d, 1822, immediately after the morning services, Mr. Johnston Lykins, our school teacher, related to us his exercises of mind on the subject of religion, which left us no doubt of his being a disciple of the Lord Jesus. He had obtained a hope in Christ while he taught our school on the Wabash river. At three o'clock in the afternoon, I preached on the subject of baptism, and baptized him in the Maumee river, in the presence of a considerable number of spectators, some of whom were Indians.[27]

Johnston married McCoy's daughter, Delilah,[28] and, in addition, the two men evolved a close, trusting partnership in their missionary efforts. During a dark, despairing time for McCoy in Michigan, fellow missionaries began to leave the missions, illness and isolation having frightened and discouraged them. McCoy wrote:

> In this time of severe trials, Mr. John Sears and Mrs. Sears gave evident signs of a disposition to quit the mission. Mr. And Mrs. Jackson had already gone. Mr. Benjamin Sears and Mrs. McCoy were both sick. Mr. Lykins alone remained to me a friend, whose circumstances enabled him to be a counselor and a comforter; and such he certainly was. Neither the performance of the most disagreeable services for the sick, whether they were missionaries, their children, or

Indian children, nor their peevishness and unreasonable demands, nor the deathlike discouragements which, in various forms, hovered around our abode, moved him from his noble determination to *do right*. He never became

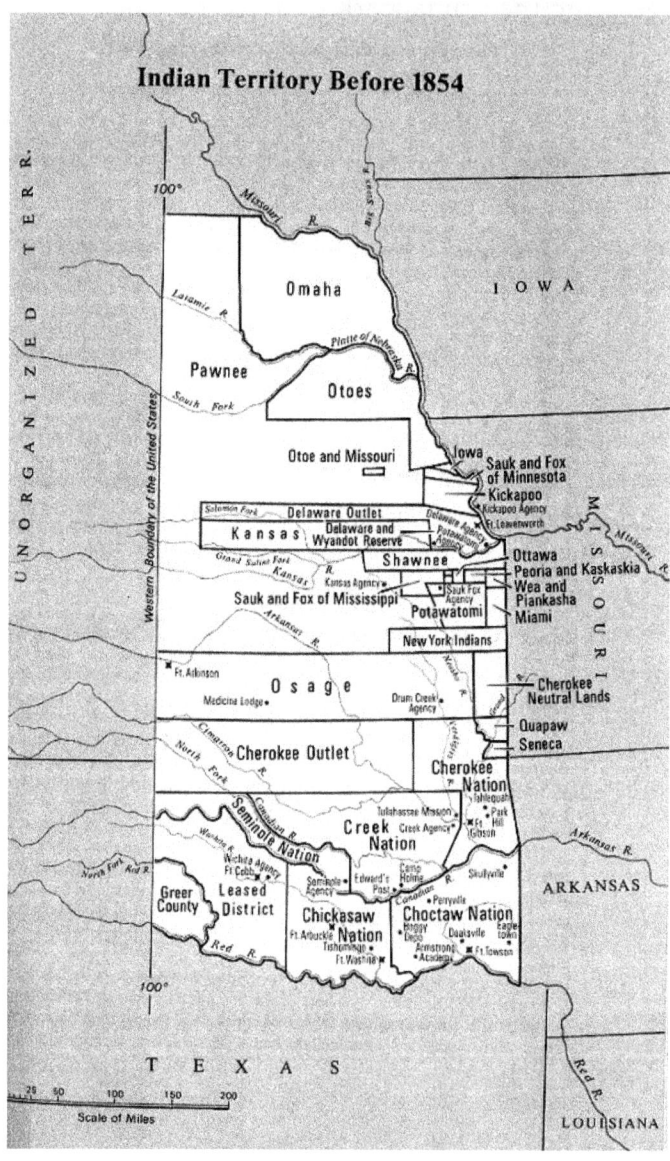

impatient, nor formed hasty conclusions, for the sake of getting out of a scene of distress. Seldom do circumstances occur so fully to attest what a *man is*. As those under which Mr. Lykins was at this time placed. It was not his amiable disposition alone by which we profited. His soundness of judgment in administering to the sick, and in relation to missionary affairs generally, was constantly developing."[29]

On one occasion, the two men were approaching an Indian village when an enraged man seized McCoy's horse by the bridle, swearing bitterly. As the attacking Indian reached for his knife, two other tribesmen intervened and helped McCoy and Lykins out-run the furious, drunken man and his friends. McCoy was well aware that this dangerous encounter would upset his wife, increasing her desire to leave the mission, so "to save Mrs. McCoy and others from anxiety, I requested Mr. L. not to inform them of the insolence of the Indians....After others had pretty generally lain down, I noted in my journal the adventures of the day, and carefully put my papers in my saddlebags, lest my wife should see them, and become acquainted with the unpleasantness of our circumstances. This was a night of great anxiety to me. Here lay my wife and our little ones, in this desert."[30] The danger and hardship did not deter McCoy from his vision. In his book, *History of Baptist Indian Missions*, McCoy states:

> At this time (June 4, 1823) I formed the resolution that I would, Providence permitting, thenceforward keep steadily in view and endeavor to promote a plan for colonizing the natives in a country to be made forever theirs, west of the state of Missouri and from that time until the present (1839) I have considered the promotion of this design as the most important business of my life."[31]

His rationale for the creation of an Indian Territory was that the Indians' proximity to "adventurers and worthless characters of the white settlements [who] were promptly on the frontiers with whiskey to sell, and demoralizing habits to bestow, as evidence of the kind of interest they felt in the future of the Red Man."[32] McCoy wrote in his journal that "The measure of allocating the Indians in a country of their own under suitable provisions of our government, is the only one in which we can discover grounds to hope for their preservation."[33]

Surveys of the proposed Indian territory took place in ensuing years and plans developed to move tribes native to Kansas further west to accommodate the groups from east of the Missouri River. In his report to the Secretary of War, P.B. Porter described the first westward migrations of Native American tribes into Kansas resulting from Indian removal actions of Congress: "It was during 1828 that these Indians first established villages in present Kansas. The exact time is unknown–a January 3, 1829, report on Indian tribes noted that 350 Shawnees 'with all the Weas and Piankeshaws' had removed from Missouri to lands assigned them."[34] Agreements with the federal government resulted in tribes native to the Indian Territory moving further west to make room for the displaced tribes from the other side of the Missouri River.

McCoy continued his efforts to promote the creation of an Indian Territory as white settlers encroached upon the Indian settlements in Indiana and Michigan. When the time finally came to remove the remnants of the tribes of this area to the Kansas Territory, the U.S. government asked Johnston to oversee the re-establishment of the tribes to this wild western reach beyond the Mississippi River.[35]

The Removal of the Tribes to the Kansas Territory

Emeline would have been familiar with a branch of the Miami who had a village "upon the beautiful prairie strip in the neighborhood of Terre Haute."[36] Chief Christmas Dazney [Dagenett] led the Mississineway band, the last group of Miamis to go westward in the fall of 1846 when Emeline was 16 years old and living in nearby Middleton. Emeline and the chief's wife, Mary Ann, were to become neighbors in Kansas after each woman established her home in Paola.

"St. Louis from the River Below," 1832-33 from
George Catlin and his Indian Gallery

The removal of the Mississineway band from the Terre Haute area to the Kansas Territory was traumatic. Mary Ann Dagenett described the 350 tribal members leaving farm houses and well-tended farms to go to Cincinnati. From there, they were placed on steamboats and taken down the Ohio River, up the Mississippi and Missouri Rivers where they finally landed in late fall at Westport Landing, near Kansas City:

Ragged men and nearly naked women and children, forming a motley group, were huddled upon the shore of a strange land, without food or friends, to relieve their wants and exposed to the bitter December winds that blew from the chilly plains of Kansas.

From Westport the Mississineways were conducted to a place near the present village of Lewisburg, Kansas, in the county since named Miami. They suffered greatly and nearly one-third of their number died the first year. Mrs. Mary Baptiste Peoria, then wife of Christmas Dazney, the agent having these unfortunate people in charge, and who accompanied her husband in this work stated to the writer "that strong men would actually cry when they thought of their old homes in Indiana, to which many of them would make journeys bare-footed, begging their way and submitting to the imprecations hurled upon them from the door of the white man as they asked for a crust of bread. I saw fathers and mothers give their little children away to others of the tribe for adoption, and then singing their funeral songs and joining in the solemn dance of death. Afterward go calmly away from the assemblage, never again to be seen alive."[37]

As he traveled near Fort Leavenworth in 1838, the painter George Catlin noted the miserable state of the Indians transported to the region. He saw firsthand the devastation brought to the Pawnee by smallpox:

> The present number of this tribe is ten or twelve thousand; about one half the number they had in 1832, when that most appalling disease, the small-pox, was accidentally introduced amongst them by the Fur Traders, and whiskey sellers; when ten thousand (or more) of them perished in the course of a few months....The destructive ravages of this most fatal disease amongst these poor people, who know of no specific for it, is beyond the knowledge, and almost beyond the belief, of the civilized world. Terror and dismay are carried

with it; and awful despair, in the midst of which they plunge into the river, when in the highest state of fever, and die in a moment; or dash themselves from precipices; or plunge their knives to their hearts, to rid themselves from the pangs of slow and disgusting death.[38]

Catlin drew, painted, and chronicled the Native Americans' ways of life, which he knew would be quickly lost in the years to come. Among the individuals he painted were Keokuk, Chief of the Sacs and Fox, who bought supplies at the trading post of Baptiste Peoria, a man who later figured greatly in the lives of Emeline, her brother and uncles.[39] Catlin and Baptiste hunted together and Catlin witnessed his first prairie fire with the him.[40] Baptiste's great-grandson proudly noted that Catlin also painted James Baptiste--Ke-mah-lan-e-ah--Baptiste Peoria's son.[41]

From 1828 through the 1850s, Uncle Johnston and other members of the Lykins and Peery families moved from Vigo County, Indiana, and missions in Michigan to the borderland of Kansas and Missouri. Most of them participated in the building and managing of missions and Indian lands in the Indian Territory that McCoy had worked with the Department of War to create.[42]

Ke-mah-lan-e-ah ("No English")

Uncle Johnston and his Family in the Kansas Territory

Johnston was the first Lykins family member to live in the Kansas Territory. He and his wife, Delilah, were well aware of the harsh, dangerous realities of frontier life. In a letter Johnston wrote to Delilah in 1838, he twice mentioned the possibility of his dying on his journey back to Indiana from the mission in the Territory:

Peoria, Illinois May 19, 1838

Dear Delilah

We arrived at this place in safety. While the Boat is preparing to return I drop you a line. I have had a passage somewhat lonely in the midst, as it were of masses of my race-But-they are not more Dear to me-mostly wicked Thoughtless men. My health has been Tolerably good-today feel somewhat unwell but hope I shall feel better when I get to land ____ if I am spared to do. We hope to leave here early in the morning for Pine on a boat now lying here.

The Indians are well–we have had some accidents by the way and I have reason to feel thankful that in the midst of dangers we have been preserved.

I have nothing to communicate now than the above and to ____ you of the most affectionate feelings of an absent husband. In the mean time let me entreat you to seek a change of heart and the favour of god as shall secure our reunion in another world if we should meet no more in this.

To gratify my little children I bought in St. Louis a willow waggon for them which Charles Findlay will take up. I miss the prattle of little Charly and the ____ of ____ very much.
Affectionate regards to all
Affectionately Your husband, J. Lykins
Please write to me at Logansport.

My Dear Willy and Sarah

I send by Mr. Findlay a little waggon for you all. I suppose little Charley will claim that he must let Sarah ride in it. I want you to tell Charles that Father sent it to him. Mother must put some kind of cover on it and Willy must draw Sarah and Charles about the streets. I wish you both to study your books well, to mind Your Mother & be kind to her.
I hope to come back to you all as soon as I can.
Your affectionate father, J. Lykins[43]

William was thirteen years old in 1841; already he was helping his father at the mission and, learning the Shawnee language, he was soon able to work at trading posts and teach Indian students using their Indian language textbooks.[44] He wrote to his aunt, Juliann Lykins Bettys in Illinois about their daily lives at the mission:[45]

West Port May 26th 1841

Dear Aunt

As I have not wrote to you for a long time I hope you will excuse me for this time. We are all well at present except I have had the chill and fever for a few days, but I am getting well. We have a school in West Port now and I have been going but I have had to stop a few days on account of not being well as I told you before. Mother and father are pretty well at present but they both had several severe spells of sickness. Little Charly was taken sick a few weeks ago and died on the 14 day of May what was the cause we cannot tell exactly but fathers thinks it was an abscess in the head. We have got a new house built with two rooms in it one father has for an office to write in and keep his books and medicine we have a good orchard and there is every prospect of having a good deal of fruit this year. We did have a good many peach trees but they have most all died but there a few left but the last frost has killed most all of the peaches. Our house is situated in the edge of the prairie on a hill and it is by fruit trees of most all kinds such as plum cherry and so forth. Our little town of West Port is improving but slowly and I am sorry to say that it is not a very flourishing town it is about 5 or 6 miles from the Missouri River there is but 14 stores in it there is several more store houses but they are shut up now it has got a good many dutch in it of all sorts and trades and in fact there is a good many groceries, that they put up. David is still living with us and he is in pretty good health. We have a great deal of butter and milk one milk 5 cents at present.

   I believe I have told you all the news and so I believe I will quit as mother wants to write a little in this letter-Please write as soon as you get this for I should like to hear from you we have not got any letters from you for a good while-give my love to Uncle Alonzo you must excuse me if this is not well written

Your affectionate nephew
William H R Lykins

P.S. We have a little girl named after you.

My dear sister

   William has written to you and left a blank for me to fill which I do with pleasure. Why is it that we do not often write to each other? I am sure it is not for want of affection and love for you that I have been so careless, neither am I willing to think it is the cause of our not receiving letters from you more frequently, and now dear sister let this be the beginning of a correspondence between you and me which will not soon be dropped. Of Eliza [Johnston's sister, Eliza Ferguson] *we know nothing.* David

[Johnston's brother] sometimes writes but receives no answers, perhaps, they never receive his letters, as we are not well informed as to where to direct them. Do they ever write to you, if so, please to let us know something about them. My heart often aches when thinking of Sister Hannah's poor motherless children. Oh how I wish they lived near to us that I might do something for them, we never hear from them, and Cynthia [Johnston's widowed sister, Cynthia Earnest] *too, how lonely must be her path, having none to help in raising her large family, may she put her trust in him who is more kind than any earthly friend could possibly be, and may she train up her children in the nurture and admonition of the Lord. Sarah,* [Sarah Kelso, Jonas Lykins' first wife] *Jonas writes, has gone he trusts to a better world, may he be enabled to do his duty to his children. And we too my dear Sister have been made to taste the cup of affliction. Our dear little Charles Rice has been taken from us. I thought I have known grief but it was nothing compared to what I have felt from the (loss) of dear little Charles. I pray that it may be to us all, and as he cannot return to us we may ...We have not heard from Claiborne* [Johnston's brother in St. Joseph, MO] *for...they were well last account we have...Andrew Chute, and Julian* [Claiborne's chidren]. *They live...from us, his wife*[Nancy Johnson], *I think a very amiable woman is still with us, what plan he has carved out fo....I know not, he is very steady and promises to ...his friends. Johnston is engaged in transla...scriptures into the Shawnee language, his h...is good. Sarah and Julian have the whoop...very badly. William is well, my own h...about as usual, sometimes poor and some...Hoping to hear from you soon I will clo...my warmest love to Joseph*[Johnston's brother] *and family an...and family.*

Your affectionate sister, Dehl.[46]

Losses and the fear of losses seemed to have dogged their consciousness daily, with the dread of loss balancing against the excitement of pioneering in a new land and discovering the cultural ways of the transplanted Native Americans.

Both Johnston and his son William learned as much as they could about the history and culture of the Native Americans they lived among. In 1851, when Johnston was working at the Pottawatomie Baptist Indian Mission, he made a business trip to see the Commissioner of Indian Affairs in Washington, DC, and some Pottawatomie entrusted him with taking a sacred relic with him for study there. *The New York Daily Times* (December 12, 1851) headline proclaimed, "Interesting Hebrew Relic." The article reported that:

> The relic consists of four small rolls or strips of parchment, closely packed in the small compartments of a little box or locket of about an inch cubical content. On these parchments are written, in a style of unsurpassed excellence and far more beautiful than print, portions of the Pentatench, to be worn as frontlets and intended as stimulants to the memory and moral sense....The wonder is, how this singular article came into their (the Pottawatomie family's) possession. When asked how long they can trace back its history, they reply

they cannot tell the time when they had it not. The question occurs here, does not this circumstance give some color to the idea, long and extensively entertained, that the Indians of our continent are more or less Jewish in their origin?[47]

Though anthropologists of today might shake their heads at this speculation, it was, at that time, a matter of serious scholarly interest. In William's later years, he pursued his own scientific study of Indian origins, reporting to the Board of Regents of the Smithsonian in 1877 regarding his discovery of very large skeletal remains in a cave in the Kansas City area.[48] Reprints of this report are still available today and quoted by people in search of Bigfoot. One example is W. H. R. Lykins, "Antiquities of Kansas City, Missouri," *Annual Report of the Board of Regents of the Smithsonian Institution showing the Operations, Expenditures, and Conditions for the year 1877* (Washington: Government Printing Office, 1978), 252-253. A facsimile reprint by Coyote Press, Salinas, California. http://www.coyotepress.com.

The missionaries in the Indian Territory made extreme sacrifices to establish and maintain the missions: the Baptist board expected the missions to become self-sustaining and often failed to provide adequate support to the families or to their missions; the missionaries were frequently on the road, leaving their wives and children to cope with sustaining themselves and the fledgling missions. A mission historian, Lyons writes:

Often, when McCoy had to be away from the mission, Mrs. McCoy managed the establishment herself. She kept house at the mission, as well as taught and directed the girls in work. She went into the wilderness with her husband and suffered privation and sickness because of the isolation from civilization and because of the insanitary conditions existing among an uncivilized people. McCoy said of her: *"none will be able to form an adequate idea of what she has borne."* The McCoys had fourteen children, eleven of whom died during the time their parents were missionaries.[49]

There was heart-wrenching loss of life among both the Anglo and Native American populations.[50]

One reason for the frequent absences of the missionaries from their missions was their having to travel back East to persuade indifferent religious and governmental agencies to provide support to the Native Americans they served and to their own families. In addition, intra-agency squabbles and competing groups involved in contracting to implement the re-location of the tribes consumed the missionaries' time and created a necessity to travel to meetings. The House of Ewing, Indian Traders on the "Middle Border," engaged in the business of Indian removal and contracting with the Indian Department to provide goods and services. Between 1848-1851, Lykins and John C. McCoy were involved in a savage dispute with the firm, with each claiming that the other was exploiting the Native Americans and defrauding the government. Lawsuits, character assassination, calls for Lykins' removal, and calls for removing Ewings' contract with the Pottawatomie ensued. Both sides looked bad.[51]

In addition, several Baptist missionaries departed from McCoy and Johnston's views on matters such as ordination of missionaries and independence of missions from each other.[52] Secret memos and allegations against Lykins and McCoy flew to the Baptist Board. Throughout the 1840s, Johnston was in the middle of a political stew. Some of his detractors demanded an investigation of his handling of funds; he was removed by the Baptist board in 1843 on the basis of the accusations in the secret memos of his colleagues; Johnston, however, had already tendered his resignation in November, 1842, but a political enemy delayed forwarding the resignation to the board in a timely manner so that Johnston would be "fired" in January. He was eventually exonerated in 1845 and his accusers reprimanded.⁵³ By this time, Johnston was disillusioned with the Baptist board and no longer sought to serve as a minister.

Yet another tribulation visited upon the Baptist missionary effort was competition from other Christian denominations. From the time the Indian Territory opened, a number of denominations established missions which competed for the loyalties of the Native American converts. In his journal of the Baptist missionaries, Jotham Meeker wrote that a Catholic missionary has "sprinkled" Meeker's prospective converts and that "the Indians are much confused by the two versions of Christianity. There is much drinking and rioting among the Indians and reversion to 'pagan' ceremonies."⁵⁴

Despite the rivalries among the missionaries, both within the Baptist missions and among the other denominations, Johnston had some successes. Isaac McCoy was elated at the development of a system of writing developed by Jotham Meeker which enabled the missionaries to teach their students to read. McCoy described the writing system:

On the new system, every sound is indicated by a character, [letter] which in Indian languages are usually about eight or ten, the greater parts of which, but not all, are vowel sounds. The other characters [letters] merely indicate the position of the organs of speech, preceding or following these sounds, by which the beginning or ending of sounds is modified. This modification, as we easily perceive, except in simple vowel sounds, is necessary to the articulation of a syllable.

Not more than twenty-three characters have yet been found necessary in writing any Indian language. A knowledge of the use of these can be acquired by the learner in as short a time, as he can learn the names of letters in the English alphabet. As soon as he has learned the use of the characters, he is capable of reading; because, by placing the organs of speech, as indicated by the characters severally as they occur, and uttering a sound, as is in like manner denoted by a character, he necessarily expresses a word.[55]

Using this system, Johnston translated and published "lessons and Bible stories into the Osage language, the Gospel of St. John in Creek, the Gospel of St. Matthew and the Acts of the Apostles in Potawatomie, and nine chapters of the Gospel of St. Matthew together with a number of hymn books in Shawnee."[56] He edited, and Meeker printed *The Shawnee Sun* (*Siwinowe Kesibwi*), the first newspaper published in the Indian Territory. Isaac McCoy identified the newspaper as the first printed exclusively in an Indian language.[57]

Proselytizing was the primary function of the newspaper. A translation of a surviving page shows the author of one of the articles–possibly a Shawnee convert to Christianity–exhorting the Shawnee to conform to Anglo-American values such as monogamy and patriarchal family structure as a means of reaching heaven. "In their attempts to promote permanent, patriarchal Shawnee households on the Kansas frontier, Baptists used *The Shawnee Sun* to underscore the sacredness of monogamous relationships and preach against sexual promiscuity." The newspaper attempted to bridge the cultural gap between the Baptists and the Shawnees by using language and imagery to transmit religious concepts such as "the afterlife" or "evil," which was personified as "the bad snake." The proselytizing was basically unsuccessful. In 1834, the Shawnee attempted to expel the missionaries from the Kansas Territory; at that time more than 80% of the tribe was non-Christian. Shawnee forms of ceremonial dance and prayer persisted into the 1840s despite the missionaries' efforts.[58]

THE FIRST PAPER PRINTED IN KANSAS.

[Fac Simile of one page of the "Shawnee Sun," a four page paper published at the Shawnee Baptist Mission, one mile south and three miles west of Westport, Mo., from 1836 to 1842.---The original, the only copy now extant, was given by the late Charles Bluejacket, late Chief of the Shawnees, to E. F. Heisler, of Kansas City, Kansas. Address, The Sun, Kansas City, Kansas.]

SIWINOWE
Kesibwi.

PALAKO WAHOSTOTA NAKOTE KESIBO.—WISELIBI, 1841.

J. LYKINS, EDITOR.   NOVEMBER, 1841.   BAPTIST MISSION PRESS.

Sietiwinoweakwa Nekinate, Sakimeki pahe eawibakence keketibomwi. Owanoke neketanbitolape, kwakwekeaphe Keahowaselapwipwi nawakawa noke wibakeata. Skiti Ketalalatimol ypwi howases mimowa, chena manwe laniwawewa Eieiweati.

HOXAKEKILIWIWA TAPALANMALIKWA SIWINOWITOWATOTA.

Siwinika sakimeka lanioake palako peace msalore, honenoce mtti, Mositiwe tipapakecike peace lauiwaweke. Hotipenekeke pilohe makecobec csice miti Koicomiwile Tapalamewalece Hoaenace milcahe Howase Eaweeitace cahtowawica litowabile. Sciti cieice wieieoticce mosi nacote weponiniwi. Eawecitace piese ceali netiwece cone wleioce namotace wiece manowitoce. Cieice pwiei ponicce comi eawecitace tipapaccice pipambace. Keciciceace macope wise hicwalamicwa Tapalamalicwa chena wise niebiwdace cetasetahawanani. Tipalamalicwa hewi; tbwalani selaniwace wanacisecce cocwalicw.se walaniwawete pwieceindcisece, wahiscime hicecchace.

Sciti lalatimowita, Siwinwice wesneitiwewa, chena manwelaniwawwewea wehmimaniwi eawecitace. Paceticce palocehe wamitlweabacesewece.

Eieiweati.

OPACECILIWEWA LABWIWELANE.

Sacinobece hipibsawa cwicweeasci na'kotebanwe weiwbe; wise bibieikeike elancle nole hkwale wehwewece. Tapalmakwe. Waki mukenhwahc nacepahe

weicowawa, pieaewa hiewe ciliwewa wiopasci weicowawa.

Hwscesaco Tapalamicwa mabhecea onama macice chene wawasice. Tapalamalikwa palowe hoce helipimihe wamita bele; picawi honinotiwihe camimitomakoce wabape laniwawelece.

Elane euscl aniwawece cahowaselapwi kakoce Tapalamalikwa wise howase nhilwalamakoce matalumakoce otilalamile.

Hiwekitiwe clane pocelakho skota chena miti einapoho?

Hiwnakote mkitailoke eipamba, chena miti einapobo?

Ene eiski weabi neahiti milikwihe wace kilakoce wewile tihipelece, kokwanabi kice wawesihile miti eibikieikebe.

Hene easeliweti nahilwiki ocicilikomile wahmeilobilile.

Lapwiti okwebemiw iwaselapwile, obile pleakwi wanitabeti okwebemi, mimicelapevile hokeale.

Sikealatika pakekilolatewa nhilwiki osekealamile ocicihkomile.

Neiswalanki kelike laniwawewewa waketamihe we.

Ealalatike ease kitanobota hipalobi camaoe kitamoee mili hotinikiti.

Wanitabeti hocicieikitoti otasetehawa waki lopwiwelane mieokwice eisetha.

WECHATEWA.

Enawaske Tapalamalikwa nakote mahe elanele hoshile chena nakote mahe hkwale. Chena Tapulamalikwa omelile elancle nole hkwale wehwewece. Tapalamahkwa miti notalalatimiwile elanele

1841 edition of "The Shawnee Sun"

Despite the Shawnees' reluctance to embrace Christianity, Johnston continued his work. In addition to attending the educational, religious, and medical needs of Native Americans recently displaced from their homelands, he advocated for them in various state governments and at the national level. He was saddened by the callous disinterest of Indian agents who exploited them further, and witnessed the starvation of the Indian tribes in their new environs.[59] In his 1851 report to the Commissioner of Indian Affairs, he reported that the Indians at Pottawatomie had:

> "...drunk to a greater extent, and have introduced ardent spirits more freely, and with less hesitation than previously known; added to this most disheartening circumstance, from Col. Sumner's regiment passing through their country they contracted the cholera, and many have fallen victims to this dreadful scourge. A few days since I met on the road an Indian wagon, containing a barrel of whiskey, accompanied by horses laden with kegs, all on the way to a village where the cholera was then raging. The result is not difficult to anticipate."[60]

He pleaded for the enforcement of laws governing the sale of liquor in the Indian Territory, seeing before him the destructive result of drinking on his people.

Johnston detailed the government's lack of financial support, indicating that only half the year's allowance had been received and the effect this shortfall had on the delivery of instruction. "The effect of this has been to paralyze and cripple our efforts, place us to bad advantage before our people, and greatly embarrass the superintendent of the school."[61] The family losses and the difficulty of his work in the Territory were taking their toll on him.

By the time Emeline came to the Territory, Isaac McCoy had moved back to Kentucky to administer an independent missionary agency, having despaired of the Baptist board's ever providing adequate support. Before he could complete his work, he died in 1848.[62] Johnston, though still in the region, had moved on to serving as mission physician, raising his motherless children and engaging in activities unrelated to the missions.[63] The two most influential proponents of a separate Indian Territory were out of the arena. In evaluating McCoy's plan for colonizing the Indians, Emory J. Lyons says:

> Never, at any one time in the history of the United States Indian policy of the first half of the nineteenth century, was all of McCoy's plan for colonization of the Indians completely carried out. Looking at the success or failure of McCoy's work from the standpoint of fulfillment of his plans for colonization, the answer would almost certainly have to be failure. It is true that parts of McCoy's plans were carried out by legislation of Congress but even those were not permanent. The two outstanding evils of the United States Indian policy, namely the treaty system and the great amount of fraud connected with the Indian agencies, were as prominent after the death of McCoy put an end to his work as they were before he began his work.[64]

Isaac McCoy's plan to secure permanent homes for the Indian people failed for a number of reasons: the complete opposition of the Indians and opposition from the Catholic Church, the white frontiersmen, and the Indian agents.[65]

Migrants to Kansas Indian Territory, 1830-1855

<u>Isaac McCoy & Christiana Polke's</u>
<u>Children</u>

<u>David Lykins & Jemima Willis'</u>
<u>Children</u>

John —— Eliza —— Delilah=Johnston Lykins —— *Hannah Lykins —— Jonas Lykins —— Joseph Lykins —— Claiborne Lykins —— David Lykins
                                            *Wm. Peery   =1) *Sarah Kelso =1) *M. Nixon   =Nancy Johnson   =Abigail Webster
                                                               =2) Priscilla

- Wm. H. R.   - *Albert   - James   -Charles
- Sarah   - Emeline   - Mary   -Wayland
- Charles   - David   - Andrew   -Edward
- Juliana
                                                =2) Merb Brown

Baptiste Peoria, Chief of the Five Tribes (Peoria, Wea, Piankeshaw, Kaskaskia and Miami) situated near today's Paola, KS

* = Deceased; did not migrate

Other Uncles Migrating to Kansas

The establishment of Baptist missions in Kansas was a family affair. David Lykins and several of Emeline's other uncles (Jonas, Joseph and Claiborne) eventually followed their oldest brother, Johnston, to the region of the Shawnee Baptist Indian Mission. Between 1830 and 1855, the Lykins brothers and a number of David and Jemima Lykins' grandchildren found their way to the Borderland.

Jonas Lykins

Johnston's brother Jonas gained an appointment as blacksmith at the Osage sub-agency in 1846.[66] It was part of the agreement with the Native American groups that the Indian Department provide each tribal reserve with particular land, services, and goods. The provision of a blacksmith was part of the agreement.[67] After living among the Pottawatomie on their Osage reservation, near present-day Osawatomie, Jonas became superintendent of the mission and set up a school for the children, employing Miss Elizabeth McCoy, Delilah McCoy's sister as one of the teachers.[68] Jonas, a widower, was married a second time to a Potawatomie woman and stayed with the Potawatomie when they were moved to a second location near Topeka, where he remained as a farmer until his death.[69] An early Shawnee County historian identified Jonas as Mission Township's first white settler:

> He moved from Osawatomie in the fall of 1847...and arrived here November 15th of the same year. He settled on the N E Of 17-12-15.... Mr. Lykins built a cabin that fall, and early in the spring commenced to make other improvements, such as fencing, etc. He broke twenty acres of land that season and raised a fair crop of corn. He married an educated Pottawatomie woman in 1846. Mrs Lykins greatly assisted

the Rev. Robert Simerwell in the translation of the scriptures into the Pottawatomie language. Mr. Lykins resided on this farm twelve years and died in 1859. Many of the old settlers remember him very distinctly.[70]

Jonas' widow, Prudence Lykins, married John Wilson and, in 1870, bequeathed a portion of Jonas' farm to Mary Burnett, Jonas' neighbor and widow of Pottawatomie Chief Abram Burnett, for use as a cemetery. Jonas is likely buried in this Burnett Cemetery. Among those buried in the plot are "An Indian named Lykins, buried sitting up with his grave walled with stone, and containing his personal effects. Done at his request." Near him is Prudence Lykins Wilson.[71]

Joseph, James and Claiborne Lykins

A former mission teacher for Isaac McCoy, Joseph Lykins became a teacher at the Wea Mission and an early owner of a drugstore in Paola, Kansas.[72] The last of the brothers to emigrate to the Kansas Territory, Joseph and his son, James, arrived in Lykins County in 1855.[73] He and his youngest brother Claiborne had claimed land in Shawnee County a year earlier.[74] Claiborne had arrived in the Borderland much earlier: in 1834, he was one of 33 signers of a petition to a Missouri congressman to establish a mail route between Fort Leavenworth and Fort Towson.[75] He married Nancy Johnson, a woman in the St. Joseph, Missouri area, in 1837.

David Lykins

The "David" William referred to in his letter to Aunt Juliana is his uncle, David Lykins, who had also come west to the Indian Territory. David appears to have initially stayed with Johnston and Delilah at Shawnee Baptist Indian Mission, where he met a teacher at the mission, Abigail Ann Webster; by January, 1843, his older brother Johnston had officiated at their wedding.[76] Eight years later, David (age 30), Abigail and their three small sons lived at the Wea Mission in the territorial county named for him, Lykins County.

The Indians living near David's mission regarded him highly, with tribal leaders asking him three times to come into the tribe. The leaders realized that they needed someone they trusted who was comfortable with the Anglo language and culture to protect them and advocate for them in treaty negotiations. David agreed to the adoption and was given the name Me-Cha-Co-Me-Yah.[77] In his 1851 annual report, David wrote eloquently to the U.S. [Indian] Agent to encourage financial support:

> When we contrast the present with the past condition of this people, we have good reason, I think, to hope for their advancement and prosperity in the future....It has long been the opinion of many that the ultimate destiny of the Indian race would be entire extinction; and such will doubtless be the case unless the religion, and some part, at least, of the laws and civilization of the white man be brought to bear upon them. The advancing waves of civilization have driven them already far towards the setting sun, and now they have but one alternative–to improve or perish.[78]

He described the thirty students' curriculum and summarized the teacher's assessment of their progress as exceeding last year's, commenting that the advanced students enjoyed their studies and conducted themselves in a manner that would satisfy the "most rigid preceptors."[79] David, Abigail, their three sons and the mission were thriving. In 1844, the Baptist Mission had sent David and Abigail Lykins to the Wea Baptist Mission near today's town of Paola, Kansas, where David became superintendent in 1848, overseeing a number of Indian agencies.[80] Only four months after David's upbeat report to the U.S. Indian agent, in January 1852, contagious disease wracked the missions.

A letter from Bishop Miege, written at St. Mary's Pottawatomie Catholic Mission on January 1, 1852, states, "Cholera, fevers of every kind, and smallpox...have made great ravages among our Indians this year."[81] Grieving the losses at Wea Mission, David Lykins wrote a poem about a child's death, perhaps that of the child who died at the mission school that January.

The poem, Requiem, on the facing page, was written on the death of a Kaskakia child member of the Wea Mission family in charge of Rev. D. Lykins.

Requiem

Gone down to the grave,
Gone down to thy rest;
As the star o'er the wave,
In the glorious West.
Gone up to thy home,
In the heavens on high;
No longer to roam,
No longer to sigh.

Thy people may move,
And their traces depart;
But thou art above,
With the faithful in heart.

No longer thine eye,
Will be turned to the sun;
When it sinks from the sky,
And the daylight is done.

No longer the dreams,
Of a dim, distant land,
With its bright flowing streams
And warrior band

Will haunt thee by night,
Nor cheer thee by day;
For those visions so bright
Have vanished away.

And though, though thy bed
Is here 'neath the tree;
And we speak of thee dead,
Yet thy spirit is free.

Thou livest, thou singest,
The bright choirs among;
And now thy ringest
Where Gabriel first sung.[82]

David's wife, Abigail, his son, Charles, his mission teacher, Sarah Ann Osgood, and an Indian student died within a week of each other. David, devastated by the deaths and resolving to leave the mission, wrote to William H. Finley to ask him to come to the mission in his place:

Mr. Wm. H. Finlay
January 27, 1852
My Dear Brother

I am in deep affliction. Sister Osgood died on seventh of this month. My wife on the 15th and Charles, my oldest child on the 16th.
I cannot tell you how much I have suffered. I have wept for days and nights, and still weep, and I believe you will weep with me.
I am determined to abandon the Station, God helping me, and I write to know if you would be willing to come again and assist me by taking charge of the farm the coming season and in other Mission work. If so, write to me–Quick, for things are suffering, and the Banner Cross must not go down where it has been raised in Indian Land.
Write immediately, and if possible come.

Your Brother in affliction,
D. Lykins[83]

Emeline's young uncle was inconsolable. In writing his 1852 annual report to A.M. Coffey, his pain was palpable:

Some twelve months ago, if I remember rightly, I received you at our door, in the midst of a heavy shower of rain, into the midst of a happy family. Where are they now? A much-loved wife, a promising child, and an esteemed teacher, are tenants of the quiet tomb. They sleep the untroubled sleep of death beneath the "Lone Tree's" shade, upon the edge Of the Great Western prairies, far from where their kindred rest, from the homes of their youth, and the friends of their earlier days. But a life well spent in the service of the Divine Master, and offered up as a sacrifice for the advancement of the cause and kingdom of the world's Redeemer, was their's....[84]

CEMETERY AT WEA MISSION STATION.

David's grieving and his sense of responsibility for his remaining family and mission continued to burden him in the following months. Emeline's description of the sad, lonely man wandering in the Indian cemetery resonates with the mood of the poem David wrote that fall:

Sunset Mound

Behold in the distance lies
Beneath the sunset's ruddy glow,
Rising to meet the evening sky
Like distant mountains tipt with snow.

And all beyond in shadow, lies
A wondrous region still unknown.
Vainly imagination tries
To make its secrets all its own.

And still that shadow region flies
Toward the Occidental sea,
And still the earthly pilgrim hies,
Still onward as the shadows flee.

Like many an earthly dream perchance,
As we near the long sought goal,
We see the dream forevermore advance
And cheat with care the anxious soul.

And such is life forevermore
Beneath hope's bright and shining sun,
We look forever on before,
And yet the goal is never won.

And as the sunlight sinks in the shade
Behind yon mount wild and lone,
So we at last shall be laid
In quiet, all our wanderings done.[85]

During that time, too, David must have made arrangements to bring Emeline to Wea Mission to help raise his sons. By June, she was there. Despite his resolve to leave the Indian Territory and the pain he had experienced there, David remained until the outbreak of the Civil War eight years later.

David Peery

Emeline's brother, David Peery, joined her a few months later, leaving Indiana in the fall of 1852, having run away from the family to whom he was indentured following his father's death:

> After his parents' deaths, as was the custom in those times, he was bound out. As soon as he was big enough he left for the west where his sister Emeline was. He did not like his place. The people gave him a round up over a cat one night (not his fault) and early next morning he was on his way for good. He had relatives there, which made no difference to him. He said he would not cross the road to speak to them. His brother, Albert Johnston Peery, started to California in 1849, never to return. He is supposed to have died in 1850.[86]

David Peery adjusted to life in the Borderland of Missouri and Kansas very quickly. His Uncle Johnston arranged a position for him as Deputy Postmaster at Westport, Jackson County, Missouri in 1853. Soon he moved to the Kansas Territory where he formed a life-long bond with the Peoria people. In 1854, he was adopted by the Confederated Peoria Tribe of Indians and given the Indian name, Me-shin-go-me-shia.[87] His cousin, Wayland Lykins, described the event:

> The old adoption ceremony partook in part of a religious nature. There was giving of gifts, dancing, feasting, naming of the adopted, and a good time was had. A person adopted

became a full member. There was no such thing as part member. John Charley or Pe-ke-nom-wak who was a Peoria Indian who was a grown man at this time and was present at this adoption told me about it years ago. He had no education and his command of English was limited, but his gestures and facial expressions were very suggestive.

At this late date I cannot describe it exactly as he did to me, but will give part of it. He was good at sign language, but somewhat mixed in English. John Charley said:

"They had it big crowd, big time, Beaver Creek 'Doption.' All people he good friend that time 'doption. After while big eat, dance it, good time, sing, whoop big, drum too. Pretty soon, hear it horse, hear it whoop, horse come close' and John put up his hand to shade his eyes as if to see who was coming so fast.

'We-non-ah, now he close some mans. He fix it up, paint, ribbon, feathers, shell, silver, sampum-old time.

Look it again, see Dave, Frank Valley (or Mac-o-se-tah), Sam Baptiste (Kil-son-sak), Ed Black (Me-cho-zah-ke-mah), Luther Paschall (She-kon-saac-quah). All go with Dave, his brother, have it heap big time, lots sing, dance, drum, whoop.'

This is what John Charley (Pe-ke-nom-wah) told me long years after this adoption took place.

At that time some of the Peorias still dressed old time, blankets, leggins, paint, moccasins, feathers, etc., and as Tom Rogers used to say, 'Tommyhawk, too.'

The people who were at this adoption and those who took an active part have passed on. Let us hope they arrived safely in Pho-Ne-Mah. The adopted person's name was placed on the tribal roll and he or she received an equal part from tribal land and money.[88]

Emeline and her brother, David Peery, arrived in the Territory near the end of its time as an embodiment of Isaac McCoy and other missionaries' hope for the Native Americans.

Their Uncle David Lykins re-opened the Wea Mission which had been closed down for a time after the epidemic killed his wife and son; Isaac McCoy's daughter, Eliza, came to Wea as a teacher for some 30 students and remained there until she retired from missionary work in June, 1853.[89]

Johnston and Delilah Lykins' son, William H.R. had been at his father's side, helping with the mission work, from early in his childhood. As the Indian Territory ceased to exist because of the passage of the Kansas-Nebraska Act, he wrote, under the pseudonym "Lucien," in the "Poet's Corner" for the *Occidental Messenger* :

The Last Indian

They are all gone! They all are gone!
the noble and the brave;
The white man's steel and pestilence,
have swept them to the grave.
No more I hear my brethren's shout,
as they wield the bow and lance.
No more I hear by brothers laugh
as they dance the festive dance
They all are gone–; me is left,
but the memory of our wrongs;
And I will bid adieu to earth,
with wild and mournful songs,
But the deer that bounds across the hills,
Knows where to find his mates.
And for her young, within her den,
the she-wolf calmly waits.

> I linger here like a summer bird,
> when all its mates have flown;
> To seek a far sunnier clime—
> why was I left alone?
> Would I had poured by life-blood out,
> by my brave brethrens side;
> Upon some fierce and well-fought field,
> Oh! I would that I had died.
> Like hunted wolf we had no home—
> the white man denied us rest;
> "Forever onward!" was his word
> there was no pity in his breast.
> He gained our bright and lordly streams,
> our fair and fertile plain.
> But we left them to his cursed hand,
> deep-dyed with bloody stains.
> Ay! their blood was mingled with our blood,
> on many a burning field.
> And though we fled before their strength,
> we never yet did yield!
> And I, the last of all my race,
> will thus unyielding die:
> And with my parting breath
> shout forth, a *last* defiant cry![90]

  The last Baptist mission closed in 1885, but the possibility of dedicated lands for Native Americans in Kansas was long gone.[91] With the end of the Indian Territory era in Kansas, the Lykins and Heiskells, whose lives had been so intimately tied to the missions and trading posts, had to adapt to white settlement and the issues which accompanied the settlers to their new lands.

1. Wayland Lykins notes, Lykins file, Miami County Historical and Genealogical Society, Paola, Kansas.
2. Hiram W. Beckwith, *The Illinois and Indiana Indians* (Chicago: Fergus Printing, 1884), 113.
3. Beckwith, *The Illinois and Indiana Indians*, 116.
4. Beckwith, *The Illinois and Indiana Indians*, 116.
5. Lewis Henry Morgan, *The Indian Journals, 1859-1962* (Ann Arbor, Michigan: University of Michigan Press, 1959), 41.
6. Morgan, *The Indian Journals*, 41.
7. Ely Moore, Jr., "The Story of Lecompton, an Address at an Old Settlers' Meeting, 1907," *Collections of the Kansas State Historical Society* (Topeka, Kansas: State Printing Office, 1910), 11:464.
8. Annie Lynch, editor, "Peery Families of Virginia," *Utah Genealogical and Historical Magazine* 8 (January 1917):25, and 8 (July 1917): 125.
9. 1850 U.S. Census, Lafayette Township, Ogle County, Illinois, p. 66 (stamped) [verso], line 20, Athol Ferguson household.
10. Eugene C. Ferguson to A.R. Markle, letter, Mar 1931, Lykins file; Vigo County Public Library, Terre Haute, Indiana.
11. Emeline Peery Heiskell to Edward W. Lykins, letter, 31 May 1895; Lykins File, Miami County Historical and Genealogical Society, Paola, Kansas.
12. Edward R. Roustio, Ben F. Keith, and Emory J. Lyons. *Early Indian Missions As Reflected in the Unpublished Manuscripts of Isaac McCoy* (Springfield, Missouri: Particular Baptist Press, 2000), 301.
13. Norah Johnson, *First Prairie Creek Baptist Church* (Fort Wayne, Indiana: First Prairie Creek Baptist Church, 1996), np. Leslie Wallace, "Miami Co's Oldest Citizen Dead," 1916, clipping, unidentified newspaper, Heiskell file; Miami County Historical and Genealogical Society, Paola, Kansas. The obituary was likely written by grandson Leslie Wallace, editor and owner of the Larned, Kansas, *Tiller and Toiler*
14. *Hiram W. Beckwith, History of Vigo and Parke Counties, Together with Historic Notes on the Wabash Valley* (Chicago: H.H. Hill and N. Iddings, Publishers, 1880), 490. Barry, Beginning of the West, 525.
15. Mike McCormick, "Ghost Towns in Vigo County? Yep, you bet," *Wabash Valley Generations*, 5 (Sept 2008): 11.
16. Beckwith, *History of Vigo and Parke Counties*, 494.
17. Bureau of Land Management, "Land Patent Search," database, General Land Office Records (http://www.glorecords.blm.gov/Patent Search : accessed 16 Mar 2007), David Lykins (Vigo County, Indiana), no. 2467.
18. Beckwith, *History of Vigo and Parke Counties*, 23.
19. Louise Barry, *The Beginning of the West: Annals of the Kansas Gateway to the American West, 1540-1854* (Topeka, Kansas: Kansas State Historical Society, 1972), 525.

20. *Paola, Kansas, A 150 Year Timeline: One Hundred and Fifty Years of History Events that Made Paola What it is Today* (Paola, Kansas: Miami County Historical Society, 2006), 17.
21. *Paola, Kansas, a 150 Year Timeline*, 49.
22. Wallace, "Miami Co's Oldest Citizen Dead," 1916.
23. Wallace, "Miami Co's Oldest Citizen Dead," 1916.
24. "Brief Survey of Religious Benevolent Societies and their Operations," *The Missionary Herald*, 26 (Boston: Crocker and Brewster, 1830): 33.
25. Mary Elizabeth Day Trowbridge, *History of Baptist Missions in Michigan* (Michigan Baptist State Convention, 1909), 27.
26. Isaac McCoy, *History of Baptist Indian Missions: Embracing Remarks on the Former and Present Condition of the Aboriginal Tribes and their Settlement within the Indian Territory, and Their Future Prospects* (Washington: William M. Morrison; New York: H. and S. Raynor; Utica: Bennett, Backus, and Hawley, 1840), 274.
27. McCoy, *History of Baptist Indian Missions*, 142.
28. McCoy, *History of Baptist Indian Missions*, 329.
29. McCoy, *History of Baptist Indian Missions*, 161-162.
30. McCoy, *History of Baptist Indian Missions*, 73.
31. McCoy, *History of Baptist Indian Missions*, 197.
32. Walter N. Wyeth, *Isaac McCoy; Early Indian Missions* (Philadelphia: American Baptist Publication Society [ca. 1895]), 101.
33. Isaac McCoy, Journal, 1808-1846, entry for 6 July 1828, manuscript, Kansas State Historical Society Library and Archives, Topeka, Kansas, as quoted in Roustio, *Early Indian Missions*, 285.
34. P. B. Porter, "Report from the Secretary of War, with a Detailed Statement of the Several Tribes of Indians within the U.S. and the Extent and Location of Certain Lands to which the Indian Title has been Extinguished," 20th Congress, 2d Session, Senate Document 27 (Washington, D.C.: Duff Green, 1829), Serial 181, p. 2.
35. McCoy, *History of Baptist Indian Missions*, 467.
36. Beckwith, *The Illinois and Indiana Indians*, 113.
37. Beckwith, *The Illinois and Indiana Indians*, 114-115.
38. George Catlin, "Letter no. 34, Ft. Leavenworth, Lower Missouri," *Letters and Notes on the Manners, Customs, and Conditions of North American Indians* (London: George Catlin [Tosswill and Myers], 1841; reprinted New York: Dover Publications, 1973), 2:24-25.
39. Mr. And Mrs. Albert E. Peery, 10402 Solo Street, Norwalk, California, to Mrs. Ethel Hunt, Clerk, District Court, Miami County, Paola, Kansas, letter, 2 Aug 1966; Lykins File, Miami County Historical and Genealogical Society, Paola, Kansas.
40. George Catlin, "Letter no. 33, Ft. Leavenworth, Lower Missouri," *Letters and Notes on the Manners, Customs, and Conditions of North American Indians* (1841; reprint, Minneapolis, Minnesota: Ross and Haines, 1965), 2:5-21.

41. Mr. And Mrs. Albert E. Peery to Mrs. Ethel Hunt, 2 Aug 1966.
42. Union Historical Company, *History of Buchanan County, Missouri: Containing a History of the County, Its Cities, Towns.* (Saint Joseph, Missouri, Union Historical Company, 1881; reprinted Cape Girardeau, Missouri: Ramfre Press, 1974), 817.
43. Johnston Lykins to Delilah McCoy Lykins, letter, 19 May 1838; Johnston Lykins Manuscripts, series 2, folder 58, Missouri Valley Special Collections; Central Library, Kansas City Public Library, Kansas City, Missouri.
44. Fred Lee, "Gone but Not Forgotten: William Hall Richardson Lykins," *Kansas City Genealogist* 36 (Winter 1996), 155.
45. William H. R. Lykins to Juliann Lykins Bettys, letter, 26 May 1841; Native Sons Archives, Western Historical Manuscript Collection, University of Missouri-Kansas City University Archives, Kansas City, Missouri.
46. Delilah McCoy Lykins to Juliann Lykins Bettys, letter, 26 May 1841; Native Sons Archives, Western Historical Manuscript Collection, University of Missouri-Kansas City University Archives, Kansas City, Missouri.
47. "Interesting Hebrew Relic," *The New York Daily Times,* 12 Dec. 1851.
48. W. H. R. Lykins, "Antiquities of Kansas City, Missouri," *Annual Report of the Board of Regents of the Smithsonian Institution for the Year 1877* (Washington, D.C.: Government Printing Office, 1878), 251-253.
49. Emory J. Lyons, "Isaac McCoy: His Plan of and Work for Indian Colonization," *Fort Hays Kansas State College Studies,* General Series, No. 9; History Series, No. 1 (Topeka, Kansas: Ferd Voiland, 1945), 18-19. The quote by McCoy comes from Isaac McCoy, *History of Baptist Indian Missions: Embracing Remarks on the Former and Present Condition of the Aboriginal Tribes and Their Settlement Within the Indian Territory, and Their Future Prospects* (Washington, D.C.: Wm. M. Morrison, 1840), 62.
50. "Missouri Marriages, 1851-1900," database, *Ancestry.com* (http://www.ancestry.com : accessed on 16 Mar 2008), Likens–Tull marriage, Cass County, 20 Mar 1853. Also, Miami County, marriage record 89, 21 Dec 1860, Likens–Tull, County Clerk's Office, Miami County Administration Building, Paola, Kansas.
51. Robert A. Trennert, Jr., *Indian Traders on the Middle Border: the House of Ewing, 1827-54* (Lincoln: University of Nebraska Press, 1981), 161-65.
52. Roustio, *Early Indian Missions*, 140.
53. Roustio, *Early Indian Missions*, 147-180.
54. Douglas McMurtrie and Albert Allen, *Jotham Meeker: Pioneer Printer of Kansas* (Chicago: Eyncourt Press, 1930), 88.
55. Isaac McCoy, *A Periodic Account of the Baptist Mission within the Indian Territory for the Year Ending December 31, 1836* (Shawanoe Baptist Mission, Indian Territory: Isaac McCoy, 1837), 17.

56. Kansas City Chapter, Daughters of the American Revolution, *Vital Historical Records of Jackson County, Missouri 1826-1876* (Kansas City, Missouri: Kansas City Chapter, Daughters of the American Revolution, 1933), 438-439.
57. Barry, *Beginning of the West*, 283.
58. James K. Beatty, "Interpreting the Shawnee Sun: Literacy and Cultural Persistence in Indian Country, 1833-1841," *Kansas History: A Journal of the Central Plains* 31 (Winter 2008-2009): 258-259.
59. Johnston Lykins, journal entry, undated; Johnston Lykins Collection #421, Box 1, Folder 1, Item no. 209994, Kansas State Historical Society, Topeka, Kansas.
60. Johnston Lykins report to Hon. Luke Lea, Commissioner of Indian Affairs, Document No. 11, 1 Sept 1851, Annual Report of the Commissioner of Indian Affairs, Transmitted with the Message of the President at the Opening of the First Session of the Thirty-Second Congress, 1851 (Washington, D.C.: Government Printing Office, 1851), 77.
61. Johnston Lykins report to Hon. Luke Lea, Commissioner of Indian Affairs, Document No. 11, 77.
62. Roustio, *Early Indian Missions*, 317.
63. Barry, Beginning of the West, 741.
64. Emory J. Lyons, "Isaac McCoy: His Plan of and Work for Indian Colonization," *Fort Hays Kansas State College Studies,* General Series, No. 9; History Series, No. 1 (Topeka, Kansas: Ferd Voiland, 1945), 57.
65. Lyons, "Isaac McCoy," 57.
66. Barry, *The Beginning of the West*, 661.
67. *Paola, Kansas, A 150 Year Timeline*, 11.
68. William E. Connelley, *History of Kansas. State and People* (Chicago: American Historical Society, 1928), 1:239.
69. Kansas State Board of Agriculture, First Biennial Report of the State Board of Agriculture to the Legislature of the State of Kansas, for the Years 1877-8 (Topeka, Kansas: Kansas State Board of Agriculture, 1878), 2.
70. William W. Cone, *Historical Sketch of Shawnee County, Kansas* (Topeka, Kansas: The Kansas Farmer Printing House, 1877), 9.
71. Louis Charles Laurent, "Reminiscences by the Son of a French Pioneer,*"* *Collections of the Kansas State Historical Society*, William E. Connelley, editor (Topeka: Kansas State Printing Plant, 1915), 13: 372-373.
72. Joseph Lykins obituary, 18 Feb 1882, clipping, unidentified newspaper, Lykins file, Miami County Historical and Genealogical Society, Paola, Kansas.
73. James F. Lykins obituary, "Died," *Miami Republic*, 3 Jan 1874.
74. James L. King, compiler, *History of Shawnee County Kansas, and Representative Citizens* (Chicago, Illinois: Richmond and Arnold, 1905), 52.
75. Barry, Beginning of the West, 281-83.
76. Fred Lee, "Genealogical Background of Dr. Johnston Lykins," *Kansas City Genealogist* 36 (Winter/Spring 1985), 125.

77. Notes on Lykins family, Lykins File, Miami County Historical and Genealogical Society, Paola, Kansas.
78. David Lykins, Report No. 14, Wea and Piankeshaw School, Osage river agency, submitted to Col. A. M Coffey, U.S. Agent, 3 Sept 1851; United States Office of Indian Affairs, *Annual Report of the Commissioner of Indian Affairs, Transmitted with the Message of the President at the Opening of the First Session of the Thirty-Second Congress, 1851* (Washington, D.C.: Government Publishing Office, 1851), 93.
79. David Lykins, Report No. 14 (1851), 93.
80. *Paola, Kansas, a 150 Year Timeline*, 17.
81. Barry, *Beginning of the West*, 1060.
82. David Lykins, "Requiem," Mattie Lykins' Scrapbook, Dr. Johnston Lykins (1800-1876) and Martha Lykins Bingham (1824-1890) Collection, KC0294; Native Sons Archives, Western Historical Manuscript Collection, University of Missouri-Kansas City University Archives, Kansas City, Missouri.
83. Lavita Lykins-Kettmann to Swan River Museum, letter, 30 Sept 2000, Lykins File, Collection Name; Miami County Historical and Genealogical Society, Paola, Kansas. (Lavita Lykins Kettman is Wayland Lykins' great-granddaughter.)
84. D. Lykins, Report No. 36, Wea and Piankashaw School, 20 Aug 1852 to Col. A.M. Coffey; United States Office of Indian Affairs, *Annual Report of the Commissioner of Indian Affairs Transmitted with the Message of the President at the Opening of the Second Session of the Thirty-Second Congress, 1852* (Washington, D.C.: Government Printing Office, 1852), 99.
85. David Lykins, "Sunset Mound," typescript, Lykins file, Miami County Historical and Genealogical Society, Paola, Kansas. The typescript was provided to the society by Lavita Lykins-Kettmann on 30 Sept 2000.
86. Notes on Lykins family, Lykins File, Miami County Historical and Genealogical Society, Paola, Kansas.
87. Notes on Lykins family.
88. Notes on Lykins family.
89. Barry, *Beginning the West*, 1060.
90. William H.R. Lykins (pen-name Lucien), "The Last Indian," Mattie Lykins' Scrapbook, Dr. Johnston Lykins (1800-1876) and Martha Lykins Bingham (1824-1890) Collection, KC 0294; Native Sons Archives, Western Historical Manuscript Collection, University of Missouri-Kansas City University Archives, Kansas City, Missouri.
91. Lyons, *Isaac McCoy*, 53.

CHAPTER 2

The Landscape of Emeline's World

Sights and Sounds at the Gateway to the Kansas Territory

Emeline's journey into Kansas began when the territory was rough and unsettled. To ensure her safe arrival, her newly widowed Uncle David went to get her and bring her to the Kansas Indian Territory where she would find few women and few amenities. They arrived at Westport Landing, where her Uncle Johnston had someone meet them with a wagon and horse to get them to Wea Mission before nightfall.[1] While it is not stated that Emeline and David came by steamboat, it is probable. Barry's *Beginning of the West* cites many reports of steamship arrivals from St. Louis.[2] Steamboat travel beyond St. Louis up to Kansas City was the major form of transportation until at least 1857. The railroad terminated in Jefferson City, Missouri as its most western stop. One of Barry's entries for 1851 describes the steamboat Clara: "The 'new and splendid steamer' Clara...having made her first voyage up the Missouri, left Kansas (City), Mo., on the 8th for St. Louis." Barry notes, "Advance notice had reported the Pittsburg-built Clara would have a 183-foot deck, a beam of 31 feet, three 40-inch boilers, 26 feet long; and that her cabin would be 'furnished in a style of comfort and elegance that will far excel that of any boat now plying above...(St. Louis)."[3]

Stephen L. Massey, who published *James's Traveler's Companion. Being a Complete Guide Through the Western States* in 1851, describes Kansas City as Emeline would have seen it:

This route (from the Kansas River to Oregon City) is generally considered as commencing at Independence, but the traveler does not actually take leave of civilization until he arrives at this point (Kansas River Landing). Hence we have given the route from this place....Kansas, situated near the mouth of Kansas river, in Jackson county, Missouri, is a pleasantly situated town, standing on a high bank of the river, and commanding a view of the surrounding country for many miles. It has been settled about four years....The business of the place is very extensive, there being an almost constant stream of travel passing through this region on their way to...[California]. Kansas contains 1 Methodist, 1 Baptist, and 1 Presbyterian church, large number of stores and about 800 inhabitants.[4]

Emeline's first sight of Kansas City would have been much like a visitor to the area had described it a year earlier. Paul Wilhelm, Duke of Wuerttemberg, who saw Kansas City, Missouri, in August, 1851, described it :

"Kansastown is quite picturesquely situated on some hills along the Kansas river near it in junction with the much bigger Missouri. The main street is about 30 feet above the water level. The houses are of both baked brick and boards, the latter called "frame" houses. It is a lively little place. Here most travelers bound for the West purchase what they require for their long overland journey of two to three months. Moreover, the neighboring hordes of semi-civilized Indians buy their supplies here....[5]

Mattie Lykins, Uncle Johnston's second wife, settled in Westport as a bride in the same year that Emeline came to Kansas, 1852.[6] The two women would have seen abundant wildlife outside their doors; Mattie later remembered the many birds and animals around them which would approach extinction within a few decades:

> *It was nothing unusual for prairie chickens in their flight from one field to another to light on the trees in our yard for rest. Flocks of quails in search for food would often come trooping into our gardens chattering their bird talk as fearlessly as if no man was near to dispute their right to the earth under their feet. When discovered, and hard pressed by boys and dogs, they did not hesitate to seek safety in our house. I have often caught them in my room under the sofa or bed and set them free that they might live to come again.*
>
> *Herds of buffalo were often seen on the prairie a few miles south of Westport cropping the tall grass without the least fear of a stray shot or the huntsman's lasso. Even in those days our village at the mouth of the Kaw was a stirring, bustling, busy place.*
>
> *In the Spring, just as early as the grass was sufficiently advanced to sustain life in oxen and mules, the loud whoop and the sharp crack of the unmerciful whip of Mexican peons and greasers could be heard from dawn until midnight. This point on the Missouri river certainly seemed destined by the hand of nature to be the great depot for all kinds of supplies for New Mexico and the Indian country. It was also the outfitting station and starting point for emigrants to California and Salt Lake City. I have known thousands of Mormons to be landed here in one season. Like weary cattle after a long drive, they pitched their tents over our hills for rest and recuperation before starting across the plains to the promised land of their hopes and faith. Poor things; discouraged, sick and feeble from their long sea and*

river voyage, many laid down in their tents never to rise again. To add to their afflictions notwithstanding, they were warned by our citizens, they cooked and ate poisonous weeds, the effects of which many died the victims of their own folly and ignorance.[7]

While Emeline feasted on the beauty and variety of Missouri's western border's physical setting, she saw, too, the energy of the people engaged in the settlement of the West. As the last outpost before entering the uncharted territories of the West, Westport Landing teemed with a diverse mix of enterprising residents whose primary business was preparing and supplying wagon trains to head west to the gold fields. One of the people in Westport at that time was Daniel Boone's grandson, Albert Gallatin Boone, owner of the general store and slave trader.[8] Harriet C. Frazier noted that local lore among descendants of Westport pioneers is that Boone chained slaves in the basement of his store as they awaited the slave auction nearby.[9] Slave traders, missionaries, realtors, wagon masters of the wagon trains bound for California and teachers were all interacting in Westport and, in many cases, embodied several of these roles simultaneously.

Drawing of Westport Road, Westport, Missouri (present-day Kansas City, Missouri) from the lid of a box owned by Mattie Lykins, circa 1852. Courtesy Westport Historical Society.

As pioneers moved westward, full of hope for their own and America's future, the institution of slavery came too, sowing the seeds for the anguish of the Border Wars to come. Alongside Isaac McCoy and Johnston's dream of finding a permanent home for the native tribes of America was the more nightmarish vision of a continuation of the enslavement of the African American. In fact, Johnston owned slaves,[10] though his father, David Lykins Sr., freed his slaves "for conscience's sake," in his will.[11]

Johnston, Mattie and other Kansas City pioneers embodied the complexities of the time and place. Johnston's daughter Sarah grew up at her father's Baptist Shawnee and Pottawatomie Baptist Indian Missions; in her teens, she took charge of Lykins' School's academic program and wrote religious poems.[12] One of the men walking the streets of little Westport was Col. William Henry Russell, grandson of Gen. William Henry Russell who fought in the battle at Chatham, Ontario, where the great chief of the Shawnee, Tecumseh, was killed. Missionaries' daughters and Indian fighters' grandsons lived side by side.

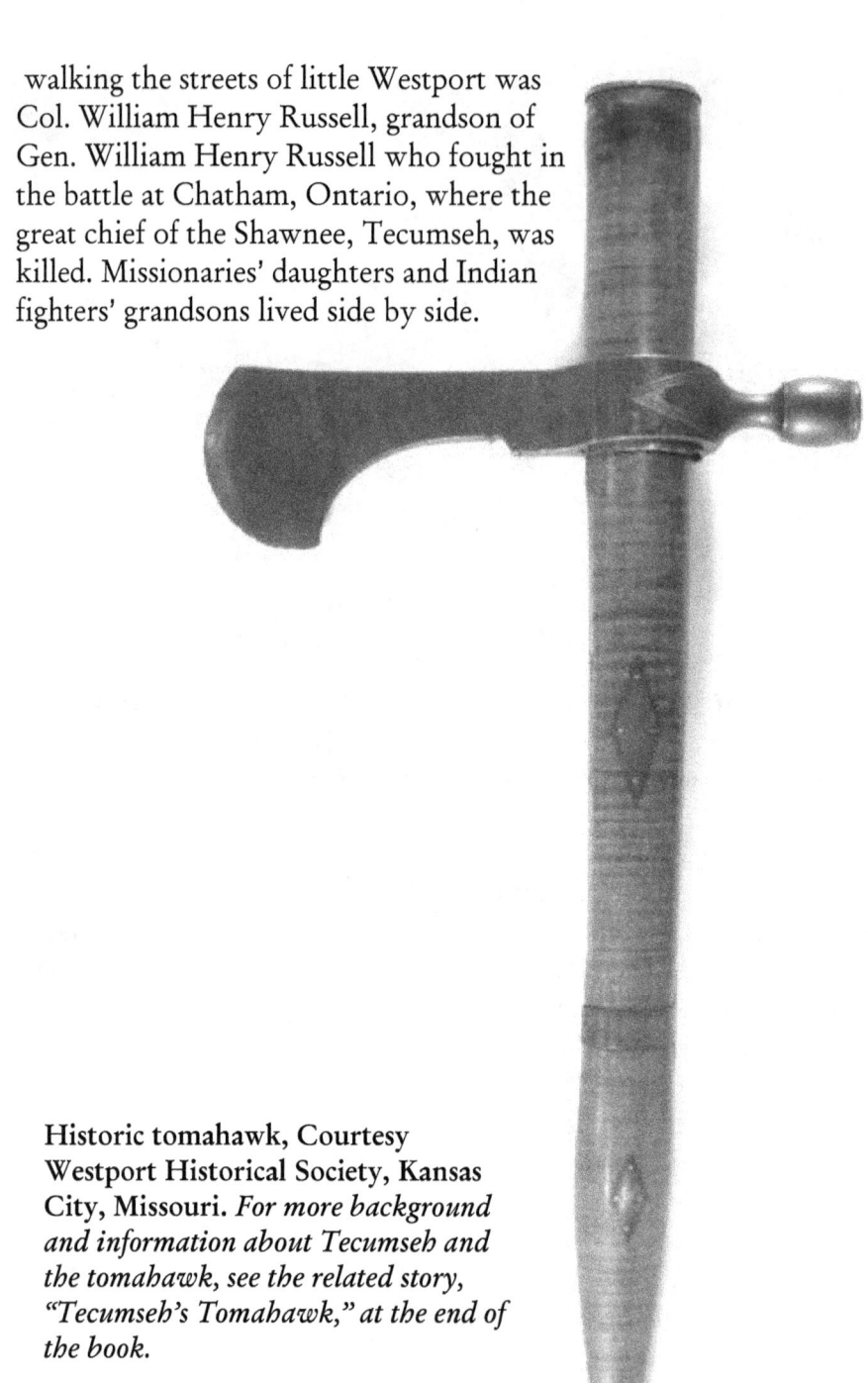

Historic tomahawk, Courtesy Westport Historical Society, Kansas City, Missouri. *For more background and information about Tecumseh and the tomahawk, see the related story, "Tecumseh's Tomahawk," at the end of the book.*

Col. William H. Russell was appointed United States Marshall of the District of Missouri, which included the Indian Territory in 1841.[13] His son Egbert established himself as a commercial photographer in Westport,[14] but he appears to have lived a wilder life as well. He nearly died from a wound he got during a gun fight in Harrisonville, a few miles south of Kansas City.[15] Egbert and Johnston Lykins' daughter, Sarah, married in 1850. By 1860, he was married with a number of children and a female slave.[16] His father, on the other hand, did not support the proslavery position, but aligned himself with Abraham Lincoln. At Lincoln's request, William went on to California and framed the constitution of the state of California.[17] The marriage of Sarah Lykins and Egbert was a metaphor for the complex moral and social frontier environment of Westport in the 1850s, the gateway to the west and a community simmering in the issues leading up to the Civil War.

On to Kansas

Immediately after leaving Westport Landing, Emeline entered the Kansas Territory and began her life there as a pioneer Kansas settler. The route and her experience of the trip to the mission at the edge of today's Paola, Kansas, likely paralleled that of a fellow pioneer, H.M. McLachlin, traveling in 1857, who described his journey from St. Louis to the two-year-old town of Paola, Kansas Territory as follows:

> *the writer, then a clerk in St. Louis, became imbued with the western fever and took advantage of the cheap rates furnished by the New England Emigration Co., to go to the then cynosure of all eyes–Kansas, firmly hoping that fame and fortune might be the reward."After his arrival in Kansas City, which he describes as a small city with its businesses on the waterfront, he learns that there are two roads leading "through the bluffs to the highland....I procured a stout cane, and swinging my store clothes*

in my valise over my shoulder, I walked to Westport, then a road through the timber...[during my journey] I enquired for Paola and no one knew it.[18]

The first stagecoach line passing through Paola was established in 1855.[19] In 1852, Emeline and her Uncle David made the trip in one day by wagon to Wea Mission from Westport, 42 miles to the north.
Wea Mission was located in one of the four original territorial counties, Lykins County, named for Uncle David, the first Anglo-American settler there.[20] As Emeline approached the mission she would have seen "an undulating prairie with a few bluffs and high lands on the streams. The valleys and creeks average one mile in width and aggregate twenty percent of the county area. The county is plentifully supplied with timber...walnut, oak, hickory, hackberry, ash, elm, maple, coffee bean, cotton wood, and box elder....Paola...(is) situated on high rolling ground between Bull and Wea creeks."[21]

Emeline's New Home: Wea Mission

When twenty-one year-old Emeline arrived at Wea Mission, the town of Paola had not yet been founded; rather there was a cluster of houses near Peoria Springs (misheard by English Speakers as Paolay Springs) inhabited by mission and trading post workers. Each mission had a few Anglo employees whose homes and a few supporting businesses were near the mission--an Indian agent, a blacksmith, one or more teachers, an interpreter, and a physician such as Johnston or David. Opportunists hovered at the edges of the reserves to sell whiskey, trinkets, and supplies to the Native Americans. If there were Anglo children, they attended school with the Native American children at the mission. A family member recalled that Johnston's father David Lykins "made him [Johnston] a visit [at the Indian mission he served] in 1832, traveling by wagon from Vigo co., [Indiana] and with him went my mother [Eliza Lykins Ferguson] and her brother David [Lykins], the latter being 16 years old. My G. Father staid there a year and the children went to school where there were mostly Indian children. He returned with my mother in 1833 in Oct."[22] As an adult, David followed in Johnston's footsteps as a missionary and physician.

According to B.J. Simpson, early resident, "At the close of the year 1854, the following persons were residing at or near the Agency: General W.A. Heiskell and family, the Shaw family, consisting of the four brothers, Cyrus, Isaac, Knowles and William, with their mother and sister, and D. L. Peery."[23] Knowles was one of Paola's first settlers and a blacksmith. She said that 'Cy Shaw' came to Paola in 1855 and credits him with running the first stagecoach line from "Kansas City to Fort Scott, by way of Paola and Ossawatomie."[24] In 1851, the Agency population would have been about the same–with about 30 children at the mission,[25] David and Abigail Lykins and their three sons, Sarah Ann Osgood, the teacher, a blacksmith, possibly an Indian Agent and an interpreter, and one or more traders in the Wea Indian community. Emeline told her grandson, Leslie Wallace, that in her first year in Kansas she made weekly horseback rides to Harrisonville, Missouri, to attend school.[26]

Late in her life, Emeline was revered as one of the surviving early pioneers in the Kansas Territory. When she visited family members in Kansas City in 1911, she met with an acquaintance who was a feature writer for the *Kansas City Star*, Nellie McCoy Harris. An early resident herself, Nellie was the daughter of the man who laid out the lots for Kansas City in 1839. When the two pioneer women talked, they must have had great memories to share. Nellie and Emeline's families were intertwined from the earliest days of the settlement of the borderland: Nellie's father was Johnston Lykins' brother-in-law. In the article which followed, Nellie referred to Emeline's memories of those early days:

"Old Baptist Mission founded 1842-1866 was a 4 room log house, 1 mile east of Paola on north side of Centennial Road. Later, the Robert & Alice McGrath homestead. It burned April 23, 1909.

Wea Mission, old Baptist Mission founded 1842

the curious makeshifts of those days which she personally used. Among them was an ear of corn which was used as a substitute for a rolling pin. It was crude, but effective.... This woman remembers that the first summer spent in Kansas it was necessary to wait until the prairie hay crop was harvested before 'filling' could be obtained for the mattresses, and they slept on blankets." Emeline said, "We were young and full of hope and it is a mistake to suppose that were are entitled to any sympathy because of our supposed hardships. Life stretched away before us. It was like a party eternally camping out. We enjoyed it all."[27]

Emeline's statement revealed some defining aspects of her character: her spunk and her optimism. In the decades to follow her arrival in the Kansas Territory, she would suffer both hardship and loss, but her strength and ability to see the beauty around her carried her forward to an esteemed place in the hearts of those who knew her.

To the contemporary reader, Emeline's sanguine view of the pioneer days may be hard to grasp. The constant presences of death and loss are difficult to understand in a society in which children may grow to adulthood without ever experiencing the death of a significant family member and the average life expectancy was 77.4 in 2000.[28] For Emeline's generation, the loss of parents, uncles, aunts, brothers and sisters at a young age was commonplace. White men and women born in the first decade of the nineteenth century had an average life expectancy of less than 40 years;[29] by 1850, the average life expectancy for a person born in 1850 was only 39.5 years.[30] The Lykins family fell well into the range of this statistic. Of the twelve children born to David Lykins and Jemima Willis, two died in childhood. The remaining ten children lived to adulthood and married, four of them more than once. In total, there were 15 marriages among this generation of the family. Of the ten, four had died or would die prior to age fifty (three of the four in their twenties or thirties): Jared, Hannah, Jonas and David. Of the fifteen spouses who had or would marry into this family, slightly over half (8) died at age 40 or below: Cynthia Peery, Delilah McCoy, probably Margaret Nixon, Lewis Earnest, Sarah Kelso, Athol Ferguson, Abigail Webster, and Sarah Tull.

As a result of the deaths in this generation, when Emeline arrived in the Borderland there were a number of new spousal and extended family relationships.

The Political Landscape, 1851-1855

Emeline's world, as she first encountered it at Wea Mission on arrival on June 18, 1852,[31] would be dramatically changed in four years. At that time, white settlers in Missouri were clamoring for the

Indian Territory to be opened to white settlement. During the month of September, 1851, the *St. Joseph* (Mo.) *Gazette* and the *Kansas* (Mo.) *Ledger* published the article quoted (in part) here:

> *As the season is advancing when the representatives of the people will again assemble at our national metropolis..., we deem it not amiss to direct their attention, as well as the attention of the people themselves, to the importance of trying early measures for bringing into market much, if not all, of the beautiful and fertile lands lying within the Territory of Nebraska* [which included the current State of Kansas]...*Congress should, at an early day at the next session, authorize a treaty to be held with the various Indian tribes inhabiting this territory, with a view to the extinguishment of Indian titles, & c....*"[82]

The lust for the Indians' land was a continuation of the relentless desire to advance white settlement across the continent. As poor agricultural practices and large population growth depleted the resources and opportunities to the East, the white settlers turned their eyes hungrily toward the fertile land they could see in the Territory. Many had seen the bounteous landscape as they crossed the Territory enroute to the purported fields of gold in California, and their reports caught the attention of farmers and European immigrants looking for land, the true gold standard in America.

In October, David D. Mitchell, head of the Indian superintendency in St. Louis, conveniently opined for the white settlement cause that:

> *the border tribes...are gradually advancing in civilization, and a large majority of the families are now as intelligent, comfortable and well informed as their white neighbors. They have become very mixed and amalgamated with the whites....The force of circumstances will soon compel the Government to adopt some plan by which the fine agricultural lands (of Nebraska and*

> Kansas) *will be thrown open to that class of citizens that have always been found on our extreme western frontiers, forming, as they do, a kind of connecting link between civilized and savage life. The State south of the Missouri river is densely populated all along the western border, being a continuous range of farms immediately on the line.*"[63]

In addition to the land-lust, the festering issues of slavery and economic/social practice were injected into the anticipated future statehood of Kansas and Nebraska lands. As settlers sought statehood, they brought with them their beliefs on slavery and the kind of agricultural patterns which should dominate in the new lands. Settlers who had migrated to Missouri and now eyed Kansas Territorial land had come primarily from Virginia, Kentucky, and Tennessee; they favored different social stratification and plantation farming practices from those of prospective settlers from Northern states where farmers worked on smaller tracts of land as individual farmers. The earlier, Southern settlers had farmed larger pieces of land using slave labor.

Many prospective settlers from the North favored the abolition of slavery, while many of their Southern counterparts fervently believed that abolitionists were violating their right to own property and preserve their way of life in the new territory. At the national level, congressional leaders knew that the future of the nation was at stake in the balance between increasingly divided Northern and Southern states. The unresolved issue of slavery had haunted the emerging nation from its beginning barely 75 years earlier.

The Nebraska Question

In Washington, D.C., Congressmen argued the issue of opening the Nebraska Territory (which encompassed the current state of Kansas and part of Colorado) to settlement. The debate had as its central issue not *whether* to take over the land for white settlement, but *how* it would be settled in the light of future states' admission into the union as states permitting or not permitting slavery.

"The Nebraska Question" was debated from 1852-54. On January 9-10, "at St. Joseph, Mo., several hundred persons (principally from northwest Missouri and western Iowa) attended a Nebraska delegate convention. Resolutions were passed, and a petition to Congress was adopted, calling for immediate organization of the Nebraska territory, extinguishment of Indian land titles, therein, and 'liberal encouragement' to settlement." On January 18, 1854, "The *St. Joseph Gazette* reported that congress was considering the organization of the large Nebraska territory into three territories, to be named 'Cherokee,' 'Kansas,' and 'Nebraska.'"[34]

Throughout the United States, people prepared for the rush to the new territories, not waiting for congress to sign the proposed Kansas-Nebraska Act into law. *The Missouri Statesman* in Columbia, Missouri, reported on March 3, 1854, "Mules, Nebraska, and cattle, and cattle, Nebraska and mules are the topics of the day."[35] Some settlers did not wait for the passage of the act, but rushed ahead into Indian Territory in 1853-54. Jotham Meeker reported in his diary: "Learn that many White families are breaking over the rules of the Government, and are actually settling and opening farms within from 12 to 15 and 25 miles from us." He noted visits from Indiana families intent on "settling on the Peoria lands, some 5 or 6 miles S.E. of us."[36]

The New England Emigrant Aid Society was formed for two purposes: (1) to make a profit by encouraging large numbers of northern settlers to build and develop land in Kansas, and (2) to ensure that sufficient numbers of abolitionists and Free-state proponents went to the territory to vote for Kansas' admission to the Union as a Free-state. Prominent east coast journalists and writers such as Horace Greeley of *The New York Tribune*, William

Cullen Bryant of *The New York Evening Post,* and Sara Robinson, author of *Kansas: Its Exterior and Interior Life,* used their popularity and influence to promote the settlement.[37] The famous Quaker poet, John Greenleaf Whittier, even wrote a poem to be sung to the tune of "Auld Lang Syne," which settlers sang again and again on their way to Kansas:

The Kansas Emigrants

We cross the prairie as of old
The pilgrims crossed the sea,
To make the West, as they the East,
The homestead of the free!

We go to rear a wall of men
On Freedom's southern line,
And plant beside the cotton-tree
The rugged Northern pine!

We're flowing from our native hills
As our free rivers flow;
The blessing of our Mother-land
Is on us as we go.

We go to plan her common schools
On distant prairie swells,
And give the Sabbaths of the wild
The music of her bells.

Upbearing, like the Ark of old,
The Bible in our van,
We go to test the truth of God
Against the fraud of man.

> No pause, nor rest, save where the streams
> That feed the Kansas run,
> Save where our Pilgrim gonfalon
> Shall flout the setting sun!
>
> We'll tread the prairie as of old
> Our fathers sailed the sea,
> And make the West, as they the East,
> The homestead of the free![38]

Fortified with the passion of the abolitionist rhetoric and the promise of an abundant future, the settlers marched into the Kansas Territory full of righteous zeal and a feeling that God had surely smiled on them. The earlier emigrants from the Mid-South shared their enthusiasm for land and, from their perspective, believed that they also were protecting their constitutional and historical rights from the intrusions of interlopers.

The Missourians lost no time in staking their claims. In today's Doniphan County, Kansas, directly across the Missouri River from St. Joseph, a series of meetings related to Kansas squatters' claims were held to endorse Stephen Douglas' Nebraska bill and to adopt rules and resolutions to protect squatters' claims.[39] A stridently proslavery newspaper, *Squatters' Sovereignty*, published in Atchison, Kansas, near St. Joseph, Missouri, stirred up Missourians to vote in Kansas as a way to dominate the land settlement. An Indiana visitor at Fort Leavenworth, Kansas, A. H. Johnston, observed: "To-day, and for several days past, persons from Missouri have been landing from steamboats, and with their hatchets are marking off their claims in the Indian country, not knowing whether the 'bill' has passed Congress or not."[40]

The Missourians had the advantage of knowing where the best land was and moved in early to claim those parcels. Because the Missourians had had easy access to the Kansas Territory and had traded, traveled and hunted there for years, they believed the land was a natural extension for settlement from western Missouri.[41]

By mid-1854, many Indian communities had acquiesced to the inevitability of the settlers' onslaught and to the end of the Indian Territory and its isolated settlements of Native Americans, missionaries, and traders–the world that Emeline had come to only two years earlier. In the case of Baptiste Peoria, he had lived long enough to be removed from Indian-held lands three times prior to the passage of the Kansas-Nebraska Act. This new legislative decision to open the Indian Territory to white settlement ushered in the prospect of still another removal to a place the white settlers from the East did not yet desire. The Wea, Piankeshaw, Kaskaskia and Peoria nations were en route to Washington, D.C.., with Baptiste Peoria (her brother David's future father-in-law) as interpreter, to negotiate the cessation of their lands by May 11, 1854.[42] The bill was signed on May 30 of that year.

Within two and a half weeks of the signing of the Kansas-Nebraska Act, The Independence, Missouri newspaper, *The Occidental Messenger,* reported, "We learn that since the passage of the bill opening this (Kansas) territory for settlement, some three thousand claims have been staked off, to be occupied by virtue of the bill. We are also informed that many difficulties and furious quarrels are arising among the claimants."[43] "Philos", a correspondent wrote from Claiborne Lykins' place of residence in St. Joseph, Missouri, that two deaths resulted from an argument over a claim with the claim jumper and the original claimant, a man from Weston, Missouri, killing each other with axes.[44]

As passions rose and the opportunity to get land and wealth dangled before settlers from both North and South, the families who were inter-twined with the Lykins were swept headlong into the Border War.

The Lykins as Land Developers

As the territory changed almost overnight from Indian Territory to the white man's land for settlement, Emeline's family was caught up in the unstoppable torrent of land lust. The family adjusted to the new reality and vigorously entered the fray to claim land in the newly established territory of Kansas. The Lykins family had claims near Lawrence, Kansas, where Johnston's son, William, was deputy postmaster and the owner of a log building. As noted earlier, both Joseph and Claiborne accessioned land near Topeka, not far from their brother Jonas' farm. By the end of 1855, several of Emeline's family members had embraced the business opportunities afforded by the white settlement of Kansas. In addition to her husband's and Uncle David's part in incorporating Paola as a town, Uncle Joseph Lykins moved to Paola and eventually established a pharmacy there.[45] Heiskell, Baptiste Peoria and others planned for the development of real estate opportunities by creating plots of land in the new town. [46]

Native Americans in the Paola area had known of "tar springs" early on; white settlers learned of them around 1855 and soon formed a company to drill for oil; Dr. David Lykins was part of that company, which ceased its oil exploration at the beginning of the Civil War.[47] Johnston's son, William H.R. Lykins was part of the Kansas Valley Railroad Company, of which his father, Johnston, was a founding director. The company's purpose was to "build a road on the south side of the Kaw river to Fort Riley."[48]

Johnston Lykins had come to the Indian Territory to further the dream of establishing a haven for Native American peoples; in this time, he embraced the vision of Kansas City emerging as a commercial center of importance. He was a member of an elite group of decision-makers who shared the desire to build Kansas City into a city.[49] In 1855-56, Johnston wrote a series of letters in the city newspaper, *The Enterprise*, which was designed to build public support for Kansas City as a railroad and commercial center. "Commerce," wrote Lykins, "like the star of empire wends its way to the West; and commerce creates at given distances commercial centres." Lykins suggested the awe-inspiring consequences of

New Family Connections / New Marriages: 1851-1854

| McCoy Livingston | Lykins/Peery | Heiskells Price/Kellers |

*Delilah(1) Martha (2) = Johnston   *Abigail(1) = David=(2)Sarah   Claiborne Joseph Jonas *Hannah/*Wm   Ermine = Charles
McCoy   Livingston   Lykins   Webster   Lykins Tull   Lykins   Lykins Lykins   Lykins Peery   Price   Keller

-William H.R. Lykins   -Emeline   William   *Evalina
                                                                   Peery(2) = Heiskell = Price (1)
                                                                   -David   -E.C. Heiskell
                                                                    Peery   -Price Heiskell
-Sarah Lykins = Egbert F. Russell   -Charles Heiskell
                                                                                           -Fannie Heiskell

Charles and Ermine Keller:
William Heiskell's in-laws by marriage to Evalina Price;
foster parents to Heiskell's children after Evalina's death

Baptiste Peoria: William Heiskell and David Peery's employer at trading post/Chief of the Five Tribes
John C. McCoy: Delilah McCoy's brother (both were children of Isaac McCoy, a founding father of Kansas City
Nellie McCoy: John C. McCoy's daughter

* deceased by 1852
= marriage
- child of

completing these projects. The tropical South and the temperate North, the agricultural fertility of the West, and the industrial power of the East–all would meet in this great central emporium. Nature had made it potentially the hub of direct trade with an area which stretched away over a thousand miles in every direction.[50]

Johnston Lykins became the first legally elected mayor of the gateway to the new territory, Kansas City: "In her diary under date of 'Wednesday, April 6, (1853)' Oregon-bound Celinda E. Hines wrote: '*On Tuesday, Kansas was made a city and Dr. Lykins mayor.*'"[51] After the incorporation of the Town of Kansas Johnston platted two additions, and built a large brick warehouse opposite the Missouri Pacific Railway tracks. He was president of the Mechanics Bank of Kansas City.[52] In five years, he was wealthy enough to build a palatial home at Twelfth and Broadway in Kansas City,[53] but Johnston's vision of the region as a center of commerce and industry was threatened by chaos and violence in the following years.

Emeline's cousin, William H.R. Lykins, was the founder of today's Lawrence, Kansas, based on his early squatter residence at that site. His first land claim was dated on May 26, 1854, the day that Wyandot claims were "extinguished" and the land was legally open to white settlement.[54] He and another settler, each unaware of the other's presence, staked a claim to the same property. Lykins laid a foundation and left the area--it was assumed that he had vacated his claim; the other settler sold the land to the Emigrant Aid Society. When Lykins and other Missouri "squatters" returned they claimed ownership; the Lawrence Association disputed their claim, saying that the first Emigrant Aid settlers had arrived and claimed the land on the day that the Wyandots' title to the land was officially extinguished and the first day the land was legally open to white settlers. The Society further argued that the land was claimed as a town site, which exempted it from pre-emptive claims. To make their position clear, Lykins and Robotaille posted the property with a warning sign:

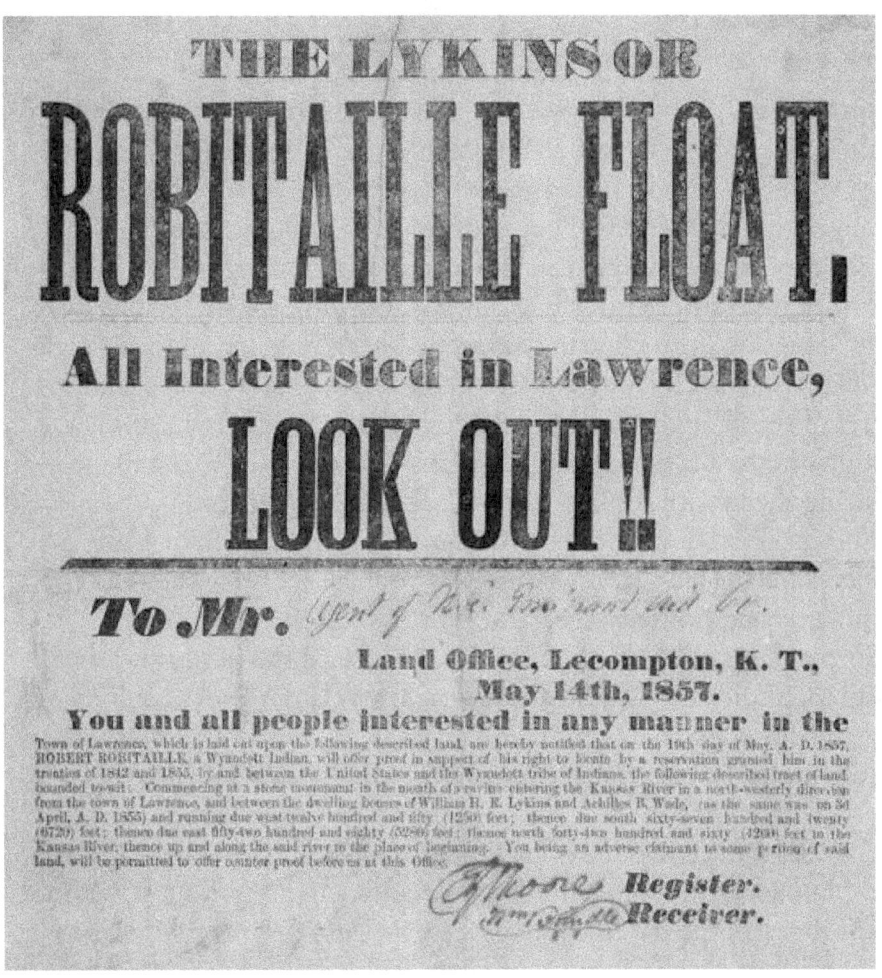

The original claimants and their sympathizers began to gather to protect the tent erected by Lykins' co-claimant; likewise, subsequent settlers banded together. For a few days, it seemed that violence could erupt at any moment; then Lykins and his associates appealed to Governor Reeder, Judge Lecompte, and U.S. Land Commissioner Wilson to intervene. They effected a compromise: the town site should comprise one-mile square and be divided into

220 shares, with 100 going to Lykins and the other three claimants in equal parts, 110 to the Land Association, and 10 to the Emigrant Aid Society. Two of the Society's shares were reserved for the site of the future college to be built there, today's University of Kansas.[55]

Thus William was situated in a cabin in today's Lawrence, Kansas, in August 1854, shortly before the Emigrant Aid Society colonists arrived and named the community "Lawrence" in honor of abolitionist settler Amos Lawrence. Johnston Lykins' brother-in-law, Stephen J. Livingston, had settled near William on the Lykins Float.[56] When Livingston petitioned to have patent to this land as part of the claim dispute, his claim was not upheld. Livingston had built a house on the Lykins Float in November 1854, and moved in during the month of July 1855. He abandoned the claim a few months later because he "was driven from his claim by fear of personal danger—that his house was robbed, &c." He then moved into a second house to the east of his first claim. The Land Commission ruled that because he abandoned the house and land and then sold the plot, he lost the right to claim the property as part of the dispute settlement.[57] William H. R. Lykins was soon to be surrounded by settlers recruited by the Emigrant Aid Society.

In anticipation of the signing of the Kansas-Nebraska Act, The Emigrant Aid Society had incorporated on February 21, 1854, in Massachusetts, so it could recruit settlers to go to Kansas. Samuel A. Johnson describes its aims as follows:

> *The New England Emigrant Aid Company, incorporated as a stock company after the first few months of its operation, was a queer combination of philanthropic venture and money-making scheme. Its promoters and managers were genuinely anxious to make Kansas a Free-state, and believed that everything they did would contribute to that end. At the same time they expected to capitalize the rise in land-values which would come with the growth of settlement, and from this source to repay the capital invested with a considerable profit. The plan of operation was,*

> *first, to disseminate information and encourage migration to Kansas; second, to assist eastern emigrants by securing reduced railway and steamboat fares and by organizing them into conducted parties; third, to invest all the capital that could be raised in mills, hotels and other local improvements in Kansas in order to attract settlers from all parts of the North.*[58]

Although the company never fully realized its stated goals, it had a great impact on the lives of both the current residents and the new Free-state settlers. Three communities founded by the Aid Company colonists figured largely in the Free-state movement: Lawrence (known in territorial days as "the Yankee settlement"); Topeka; and Ossawatomie.[59] Lawrence became the primary symbol of abolitionist and Free-state sentiments and a focal point for the growing anger of the settlers originating from Missouri, Kentucky, and Tennessee, who saw the new state as legitimately theirs based on traditional westward settlement patterns.[60]

Among the "local improvements" envisioned by the Emigrant Aid Company was the establishment of universities. In the fall of 1854, Amos Lawrence, a primary figure in founding Lawrence, wrote to fellow Emigrant Aid activist Robinson proposing the establishment of a boys' academy in Lawrence. By the end of that year, Lawrence had given $10,000 to the Aid Company trustees to found an institution of higher learning on Mount Oread;[61] after several years of faltering attempts to establish this college, the state of Kansas finally succeeded in founding and developing its flagship university, the University of Kansas on Mount Oread, the hilltop originally named for an educational site in Worcester, Massachusetts.[62]

The community development and land ownership opportunities afforded settlers from all regions of the country through the passage of the Kansas-Nebraska Act brought with them another issue that engulfed Emeline, her family, and other Kansas and Missouri residents in ensuing years: slavery. "On May 30, 1854, with a stroke of the pen, The Kansas-Nebraska Bill was signed into life, and the Missouri Compromise was declared null and void. Henceforth, the law of the land would lay with the settlers themselves–should a majority in a new territory vote for slavery, then, upon admission to the Union, a slave state would join the ranks of the South. If free-soil was their choice, then the North would gain. The first test of this theory in 'popular sovereignty' would come on the virgin plains of Kansas and Nebraska."[63]

The fertility of the land and its economic potential drew settlers in droves. A Free-state proponent, Samuel N. Wood brought his family from Ohio to settle. On June 27, 1854, he wrote from Independence, Missouri, to the *Columbian* in Cincinnati:

We have made one short trip over into the Indian country, and satisfied ourselves that a man can get almost just such a home as he pleases. I never saw richer land in my life; and it appears inexhaustible....The only drawback is this slavery question. Missourians have already flocked to this Territory by hundred; many slaves are already in the Territory. A few missionaries thought in the start that they would regulate the settlement of this whole Territory. Northern men were ordered off; lynching was freely talked of, even by United States officers at Fort Leavenworth, merely because they happened to be born North of Mason and Dixon's line. Some Northern men were actually driven off; others were frightened away. All manner of lies were told and misrepresentations made, in order to keep Northern men away. But now the charm is broken. A dozen families of Free Settlers drove ahead, and have commenced a settlement upon Kansas river.(Wood settled three miles south of Lawrence on 'the California Road.'). A meeting is called on July 8, of those friendly to making Kansas a Free-state. Emigrants from Iowa, Illinois and Indiana are arriving daily. Two days will not pass until the cabins of at least two hundred opponents of slavery will be in progress of construction. A few more, and we shall be invincible. All we want is, for every Northern man—every Northern family, who have their minds on this Territory, to come on at once. This slavery question must be met and decided now.[64]

Theodore Brown notes that "the most important effect of the local agitation upon Kansas Cadence was probably not so much economic as cultural. Geographically bracketed by Westport and Independence, Kansas City, too, was at least sympathetically proslavery. Southern-minded though the city may have been, however, its opportunities were Western, and there lay the crucial influence in the conduct of its citizens."[65] Brown's observation is dramatically illustrated in the stances toward slavery and secessionist sentiments in Emeline's family. Johnston Lykins, who was the first legally elected mayor of Kansas City in April 1853,[66] no longer supported the Southern Cause by the time the first shots of the Civil War were fired. His arguments were based in his conviction that the well-being of his city lay in maintaining the Union and in looking westward economically, though he owned slaves and his wife, Mattie, strongly and vociferously supported the South. Emeline's uncle, David Lykins, made a speech advocating the admission of Cuba to statehood as a slave state;[67] her cousin William Lykins evolved from living in Lawrence as a squatter to townsman and

William H. R. Lykins

twice-elected mayor of the abolitionist stronghold of Lawrence. In 1868, when Lykins moved to Kansas City; his sentiments, like his father's, were more "Westward-looking" than "Southern."

Emeline's Marriage

As the large national issues of slavery and western expansion roiled the Borderland, Emeline's personal life flowered. In her first few months at Wea Mission, Emeline met a widower, William A. Heiskell, twenty-three years her senior. William and his first wife, Evalina Price, married in 1831.[68] In the 1840 census, they lived in their county of birth, Hampshire County, West Virginia; William, his wife, and a young son were on a farm next to his father, Christopher Heiskell.[69] William's wife Evalina Price Heiskell died in Westport in 1849[70] at about the age of 37. Her sister, Ermina Keller, lived in Cass County, Missouri, at the time and took in the children. Judging by the age of a young Heiskell girl, Fanny, born in 1844 in Virginia and living in the household of Eveline's married sister, Ermina Keller, in 1850, the Heiskells had left Virginia between 1845 and 1849. Four of Heiskell's children lived with the Kellers in 1850: Charles, Edmund, Elizabeth, and Fanny.[71]

It is not known what caused Evalina's died; however, in June and July, 1849, "Cholera, in a form as virulent as before (earlier in the year), returned to the Town of Kansas, late in June. By July 12 the second epidemic...had resulted in 20 deaths there; and across the Kansas river, on the Wyandot reserve, four Indians had died," and it spread to Westport and Independence, taking many lives there.[72] Connie Price, a descendant living on the Silas Price Homestead in 2006, hypothesized that Evalina died of diphtheria because a family traveling westward came across the farm and all died of the disease and were buried on the Price farm. Evalina and William's son Frederick died as well and is buried in the Price-Willet Cemetery on the Price family farm in Cass County.[73]

Heiskell worked as assistant clerk to J.M. Chouteau who traded with the Wea, Piankeshaw, and Miami, across the Cass County, Missouri border, in the Kansas Territory.[74] He traded in furs with Chouteau and learned some Indian languages in the course of his work, sometimes serving as interpreter.[75] Heiskell would have met Emeline while doing this work; they were married at Wea Mission on March 20, 1853 by Johnston Lykins, who also married David Lykins to his second wife, Sarah D. Tull on the same date.[76]

W.A. Heiskell

Heiskell's work as a trader required him to travel periodically, and Emeline "often spoke of the terror she felt as a mere child (sic) at the strange, isolated surroundings, the sight of so many Indians, and there were days of terror for her, she said, after her marriage when her husband made periodical trips to Westport for supplies, leaving her practically alone and unprotected, as was necessary in those pioneer times."[77] During an interview in later years, Emeline said that her husband, William, gained access to some Native American groups for trading through John Brown,[78] ultimate symbol of Bloody Kansas; Emeline considered herself a friend of John Brown's. His home was a little over seven miles from hers.

The Lykins and Heiskell Family and the Territorial Elections

Heiskell, too, was heavily involved in the events surrounding the passage of the Kansas-Nebraska Act and its aftermath. A little over a year after Emeline and William Heiskell's marriage, the ferocious struggle over whether Kansas would be a Free-state or a proslavery state was a war on the ground, the Kansas-Nebraska Act having been signed in May of 1854. Real estate developers, social and religious visionaries, farmers, merchants, and politicians engaged in feverish activity to have the Kansas-Nebraska question settled in their favor.

William Heiskell's loyalties were firmly planted with the southern settlers. He was born and raised in Hampshire County, West Virginia, where at least three Heiskells in the area owned slaves.[79] In Missouri, his former brothers-in-law, Silas Price and Charles Keller owned slaves.[80] Emeline Heiskell's uncle, Johnston Lykins, and his Kentucky-born wife, Mattie, owned slaves in Westport.[81] Emeline's Uncle David Lykins at Wea Mission was a member of the proslavery first Kansas Legislature.[82] W.H.R. Lykins, "the squatter" in Lawrence, hosted the first Territorial election in Lawrence.[83] William had numerous Missouri family ties in a nearby hotbed of proslavery sentiment, Cass County, 15 miles from Paola, where his sister-in-law, Ermina Price Keller, his own children, and a former brother-in-law, Silas Price, lived.[84] Silas and Ermina Price's husband, Charles Keller, co-owned a mercantile business in Harrisonville. In addition, they had some interest in the local hotel and Silas owned a 400-acre farm near there.[85]

In the spring of 1855, elections to the first Kansas Territorial legislature were to be held. A major player in the election debacle to follow was David Atchison, the first U.S. Senator from Missouri to be elected from the western side of the state and President Pro Tem of the United States Senate. Realizing that he needed to protect his senate seat in the Missouri General Assembly and fight for Kansas to be admitted to the Union as a Slave State, he resigned early from his office as President Pro Tem in December, 1854. He needed to be back in the Borderland, meeting the voters face to face. Atchison was the "moving force" in getting the repeal of the Missouri Compromise to be part of the Kansas-Nebraska Act. A man named Ben Stringfellow worked as Atchison's representative when he was away from the state. During the summer of 1854, Stringfellow organized the Platte County Self-Defense Association, a secret organization of Missourians planning to win Kansas for the South. Several "Blue Lodges" with the same agenda sprung up in western Missouri towns. Stringfellow and Atchison went from town to town to organize the "Kansas" election. In the six western Missouri counties along the Missouri River between Lexington and Saint Joseph, there were 78,875 whites and 19,097 slaves in the 1860 US census; in Kansas, however, there were 8409 whites and 192 slaves in the 1855 territorial census.[86]

    Several Lykins family members who lived in Missouri or had close family ties there voted in the Kansas Territory elections of 1855. A visitor to W.H.R. Lykins' cabin shortly before the March election (of the Kansas legislature) recalled having heard unusual activity in an unoccupied part of Lykins' building and upon inquiry, learned that young Lykins was storing bacon, corn, and other provisions for the use of the Missourians who were expected in great numbers on election day.

W. H. R. Lykins' cabin in Lawrence, Kansas

With his son operating a commissary for the 'border ruffians,' it is not surprising that Dr. Johnston Lykins, at a meeting of a squatter association, publicly argued his contention that he had a right to vote in Kansas. The Free-state candidate attempted to refute Lykins, denying that resident Missourians could claim franchise in Kansas."[87] Emeline's Uncle Claiborne was apparently successful in his attempt to vote in Kansas. In the Kansas Voter Registration Lists, 1854-56, Claiborne is shown as registered in Brownsville, District 3, to vote in the election on December 15, 1855.[88] At the time he lived across the Missouri River, near St. Joseph, Missouri.

One of the early Free-state inhabitants of Lawrence, Sara Robinson, wrote inflamed, eye-witness accounts of the March election:

> *Before the time of the election in March, the border papers were again rife with their [the Missourians'] threats of outrage. The following, from the Leavenworth Herald will suffice to show the character of the leaders of the pro-slavery party, and their intentions regarding the manner in which Kansas was to be made a slave state. The plan of operation was laid down in an address to a crowd at St. Joseph, Missouri, by Stringfellow. "I tell you to mark every scoundrel among you that is the least tainted with free-soilism, or abolitionism, and exterminate him. Neither give nor take quarter from the d–d rascals. ... To those having qualms of conscience, as to violating laws, state or national, the time has come when such impositions must be disregarded, as your lives and property are in danger, and I advise you one and all to enter every election district in Kansas...and vote at the point of the bowie-knife and revolver...."*
>
> *[The Missouri voters] were rough, brutal looking men, of most nondescript appearance. They had, however, one mark upon them, a white or blue ribbon to distinguish them from the settlers. This was wholly unnecessary, no one ever mistaking one of these men for an intelligent, educated settler in the territory. Those Missourians who did not feel the interest to come over to vote, paid their money, or contributed provisions and wagons for the new raid. The expenses of the vandal horde were paid, and they were en route again to overrun the fair country, with drunkenness, and fraud, and murder, if the cause demanded it....Provisions were sent ahead of the parties, and those intended for the invaders at Lawrence were stored in the house of W. Lykins. The polls were also opened at the same place.[89]*

Robinson related that a judge was appointed by the governor to oversee the election, but after being threatened with hanging, he declined to show up on election day. A new judge was appointed who "claimed that a man had a right to vote if he had been in the territory but one hour."[90] Robinson describes Missourians coming to the polls from their campsite in a nearby ditch in "crowds so great around the log cabin, that many of the voters, having voted, were hoisted on the roof of the building, thus making room for others."

Out of consideration for the elderly among them, the Missourians allowed its weary older voters, who had come long distances, to vote first, with many Missourians "leaving for home as soon as they had voted." Those who stayed overnight freely and unceremoniously entered the houses of the citizens of Lawrence, sometimes even inviting themselves to share the Free-state residents' dinners! Of the 1034 people who voted, Robinson reported, 802 were non-residents and illegal voters.

In Paola, the scene was likely similar, except that Paola was known to be a stronghold of proslavery settlers–provided that "forty active residents" constitute a "stronghold." "At the close of the year 1855, there were about twenty rough plank and log houses in Paola and the town contained about forty active residents" 28 men were "about all the actual bona fide (white, male) residents here.[91] Among those she identified were Emeline's husband, W.A. Heiskell (business manager for Baptiste Peoria) , her brother, D. L. Peery (Baptiste's employee at the Trading Post where all the early settlers bought their supplies), her uncle, Joseph Lykins, and her cousin, James Lykins. At an election for a delegate to Congress on October 1, 1855, the proslavery candidate received 220 votes. Seventy legal voters resided in the Paola precinct at the time; 150 of the votes were illegal. Free-state men would have remembered the March 30 election at Baptiste Peoria's house at which there were 20 legal voters in the precinct. Over 300 men (mostly Missourians) were at the election, armed, drunk and threatening.[92] It is not hard to imagine Emeline staying in her cabin behind a barred door on these election days when bullets might fly at any moment.

William Chesnut, a Connecticut emigrant, was at the March 30 election, having been appointed by Governor Reeder to serve as a judge for the Pottawatomie precinct. He testified before the U.S. House of Representatives regarding that election day:

> *I was appointed by Governor Reeder as one of the judges of the election at the Pottawatomie precinct. I got there about eight o'clock or a little after, in the morning of the election. The other two judges except Wilkinson, who was a candidate, and therefore unqualified, were not there. I claimed the privilege of appointing two to fill the vacancies, when a stranger came forward and told me he was from Missouri. He was armed with a revolver and a knife, and had a rifle in his hand. He told me his party would appoint the judges. I remonstrated with him, and named two persons for judges that I thought were qualified. He told me that if I made any trouble with them they would dispose of me with very little ceremony then asked with a kind of sneer in what manner I would like to have the election conducted, and I said, in conformity with the instructions contained in the governor's proclamation.*
>
> *He said the governor had no right to impose such conditions and restrictions upon them; that their being there that day constituted them legal voters; that they had come on purpose to vote, and I could see they had come well prepared, and would vote, let the consequences be what they might....*
>
> *Over four-fifths of the votes were handed in by armed men, strangers to me. I knew at that time most every legal voter in the precinct. I objected to several when they offered to vote, believing they were not legal voters, and the other two that acted as judges would immediately take the ballot without taking any notice at all of my remonstrance, except to say by way of reply, that they*

> *knew the gentleman, that he lived up the creek and had a claim there....*
>
> *Those strangers voted for Lykins and Coffee for councilmen. I am pretty confident Coffee did not live in the district at that time. It was generally understood that he lived in Missouri. They voted for Younger, Wilkinson, Haskell, and Scott, for representatives....*
>
> *I should think there were not over fifty or sixty legal votes polled there; not over seventy-five, at all events....I thought there were from one hundred and fifty to two hundred illegal votes polled at that election.*[93]

Many free-soilers either boycotted these elections or were too intimidated to go to the polls; it is reasonable, too, to assume that Lykins County's proximity to one of the hotbeds of southern sentiment, Cass County, Missouri, assured that a fair number of voters would have crossed over into the Territory to cast their votes, and, of course, Heiskell had family connections in Cass County, including his son, E.C. Heiskell and the foster father for his children, Charles Keller. Both E.C. Heiskell and Charles Keller were on the voter lists for elections investigated by the Special Committee.[94]

Not surprisingly, William A. Heiskell was elected to be a member of the House of Representatives and David Lykins had been elected to the Council in the March election. Thirty-eight pro-slavery legislators met at the Shawnee Baptist Indian Mission between July 16 and August 30, 1855.[95] This group immediately set about establishing governance structures for the new Kansas Territory. Among the structures the legislators established was the Kansas militia. Heiskell was given the rank of Brigadier General of the Southern Division: suddenly, Emeline was married to a military man.

One of the first actions of the legislators was to incorporate or charter cities. As Charles Clark put it, "Selling town lots was one of the quickest ways to wealth in territorial Kansas. . . . Town companies with a legislative charter had assurance that their title to the town site and right to sell lots had legal sanction....Cities had no legal existence without legislative incorporation and therefore had no power to tax or enforce ordinances."[96] William A. Heiskell, David Lykins, Baptiste Peoria, and Isaac Jacobs had formed a town company to lay out Paola in the spring of 1855.[97] At the legislative session that year, Heiskell put forth a bill to incorporate the town; Heiskell then became a member of the Paola Board of Trustees.[98] He and David Peery had worked closely with Baptiste Peoria at Peoria's trading post, William as manager and David as clerk. Peoria, who owned the land on which Paola was built, "ran a trading post at his home, located at a clearwater spring on a hill...."[99] Peoria supplied the trading post by taking furs to the firm of Ewing Clymer of Westport and exchanging them for goods to sell near Wea Mission. According to an old trading post ledger book, he was one of two of Clymer's foremost customers in terms of volume of good purchased.[100]

The newly incorporated town was named "Paola" in honor of Baptiste Peoria. Members of Peoria's tribe pronounced his name as "Batice Paolay," with a soft or "liquid r"; English speakers heard and wrote the "soft r" in the Miami Indians' language as an "l", so the name of the town, "Peoria," came to be pronounced and spelled as "Paola." [101] With the birth of Paola, the men whose former occupations had been that of trader and missionary devoted their energies to land development, government, and political and military action in this new era of Kansas. When Emeline came to Kansas and for the following ten years, she and her family were caught up in a set of opposing contradictions which would whipsaw them back and forth as these contradictions fought for dominance and brought the nation to war with itself. Family members embodied the contradictions which lay at the center of the American psyche in the mid-nineteenth century. They lived in a time when many Americans' grandparents had carved out the new nation and religion was still central to the social fabric. Paradoxically, many Americans embraced both democracy and inequality; a longing for social justice co-existed with racial and ethnic prejudice and intolerance. Emeline's family members could champion the cause of Indians on one hand and benefit from their removal on the other; they could speak up for their Indian neighbors, work for them and marry them while ardently trying to preserve the Southern way of life with its continuation of slave ownership and plantations. Several were loyal to their Southern roots, but drew the line at fueling sentiments which could lead to the dissolution of the fledgling nation. They, like so many other Americans of their time, were capable both of greatness and of condoning grievous injustice and cruelty.

At this point in their lives, Emeline and her family were on the edge of the American frontier, among the men and women in love with the limitless potential of a land brimming with resources for the taking. Those very resources undermined Isaac McCoy's vision for the Indian, leading to ever more white trespassers wanting ever more of the Indians' land for themselves. Before the Indians were overwhelmed, Emeline, William and her brother David lived among them, served them, and grew to love them. All of them, white settlers and Indians, were soon caught up in

the compelling crosswinds of their time and place. Emeline and her family's journey to Kansas mirrored the unfolding history of the nation as it struggled with the contradictions deeply embedded in its psyche.

---

1. Emeline Heiskell to Edward W. Lykins, letter, 31 May 1895; Lykins File, Biography Collection, Miami County Historical and Genealogical Society, Paola, Kansas.
2. Louise Barry, *The Beginning of the West*, 81-86, 116. Berenice Boyd Wallace, compiler, *History of Paola, Kansas, 1855-1955* (Paola, Kansas: Miami County Genealogy and Historical Societies, [1955] 1.
3. Barry, *The Beginning of the West*, 1034.
4. Barry, *The Beginning of the West*, 1053-1054.
5. Barry, *The Beginning of the West*, 1054.
6. Martha A. (Livingston) Lykins Bingham, "Recollections of Old Times in Kansas City," 67-page, handwritten manuscript, ca 1883 - 1890. Jackson County Historical Society Archives, Independence, Missouri, Gift of Robert Dewit Owen, in memory of his grandmother, Mrs. Dewit Livingston (Ada Campbell) Owen, Document ID 110F7. Adrienne Tinker Christopher transcribed a portion of this manuscript in *The Kansas City Genealogist* 25 (Winter & Spring, 1985):116.
7. Martha Lykins Bingham, "Recollections of Old Times in Kansas City," 4-5.
8. Albert Gallatin Boone entry, "Movers and Shakers: The People of Westport"; (www.westporthistorical.org/people, accessed on 2 Sept 2007).
9. Harriet C. Frazier, *Runaway and Freed Missouri Slaves and Those Who Helped Them, 1763-1865* (Jefferson, North Carolina: McFarland and Company, 2004), 175.
10. 1860 US Census, Kansas City Division 35, Jackson County, Missouri, slave schedule, Division 35, p. 1 [p. 367 stamped], lines 13-15.
11. Eugene Ferguson, "To my niece" [recipient unidentified], undated, letter; typescript, Union Cemetery Historical Society files, Union Cemetery, Kansas City, Missouri.
12. Nettie Thompson Grove and Walter Wayne Smith, "Notes on the Pioneer School of Kansas City, Part One," *Annals of Kansas City*, 1 (Dec 1922): 6-25.
13. W. J. Ghent, "Russell, William Henry," *Dictionary of American Biography*, Dumas Malone, editor (New York, Charles Scribner's, 1935), 16: 251.
14. David Boutros, "A Preliminary Survey of Photographers and Arts in Kansas City, Missouri 1850 to 1882;" on-line article, Western Historical Manuscript Collection, University of Missouri at Kansas City Library, Kansas City, Kansas, (http://www.umkc.edu/whmckc/Scrapbook/Articles/KCPhotographers.pdf : accessed 21 Oct 2008).
15. "Fatal Affray in Harrisonville," *The Liberty* (Mo.) *Tribune*, 29 Apr 1859, 2:f.
16. 1860 US Census, Kansas City Division 35, Jackson County, Missouri, population schedule, p. 28, dwelling 253, E. F. Russell household. 1860 US Census, Kansas

City Division 35, Jackson County, Missouri, slave schedule, p. 1 [p. 367 stamped], line 34.
17. *Dictionary of American Biography*, 16: 252.
18. H. M. McLachlin, *The Story of Paola, Kansas, 1857-1950* ([Paola, Kansas: Miami County Historical Society, 1951?]), 1-2.
19. McLachlin, *The Story of Paola, Kansas*, 90.
20. Wallace, *History of Paola*, 90.
21. Wallace, *History of Paola*, 90.
22. Eugene Ferguson, Bloomington, Illinois to A.R. Markle, Terre Haute, Indiana, letter, Feb. 13, 1931, Lykins family file; Vigo County Public Library, Terre Haute, Indiana. Information in the brackets was added by Rose Ann Findlen.
23. Miami County Historical Society, *Paola, Kansas, a 150 Year Timeline: One Hundred and Fifty Years of History Events That Made Paola What It Is Today* (Paola, Kansas: Miami County Historical Society, 2006), 17-18.
24. Wallace, *History of Paola*, 94.
25. Barry, *The Beginning of the West*, 1060.
26. Leslie Wallace, "Miami-Co's Oldest Citizen Dead", undated clipping from unidentified newspaper, Heiskell file; Swan River Museum, Miami County Genealogy and Historical Society, Paola, Kansas. The obituary was likely written by grandson Leslie Wallace, editor and owner of the Larned, Kansas, *Tiller and Toiler*.
27. Nellie McCoy Harris, "Pioneer Reminescenses of Early Kansas City," *Kansas City Star*, 12 Dec 1911, 1, typescript; Missouri Valley Room, Kansas City Public Library, Kansas City, Missouri.
28. Haines, Michael, "Fertility and Mortality in the United States," EH.Net Encyclopedia, editor, Robert Whaples, 19 Mar 2008, (http://eh.net/encyclopedia/article/haines/demography; accessed 21 July 2010).
29. Haines, "Fertility and Mortality in the United States."
30. Haines, "Fertility and Mortality in the United States."
31. Emeline Heiskell, to E.W.W. Lykins, letter, 31 May 1895.
32. Barry, *The Beginning of the West*, 1041-1042.
33. D. D. Mitchel, Superintendent, Office of Indian Affairs, to Hon. L. Lea, Commissioner, Indian Affairs, report, 25 Oct 1851; *Annual Report of the Commissioner of Indian Affairs Transmitted with the Message of the President* (Washington, DC: Government Printing Office, 1851), 60-64.
34. Barry, *The Beginning of the West*, 1191.
35. Barry, *The Beginning of the West*, 1195.
36. Barry, *The Beginning of the West*, 1212.
37. Donald Gilmore, *Civil War on the Missouri-Kansas Border* (Gretna, Louisiana: Pelican Publishing Company, 2006), 24.
38. John Greenleaf Whittier, "The Kansas Emigrants," *Poems of American History*, Burton Egbert Stevenson, editor (Boston: Houghton Mifflin, 1908), 389.
39. Barry, *The Beginning of the West*, 1202.

40. "Webb Scrapbooks," Thomas H. Webb, compiler, v. 1, p. 42; Kansas State Historical Society, Topeka, Kansas; cited in Barry, *The Beginning of the West*, 1217.
41. Jeremy Neely, *The Border Between Them: Violence and Reconciliation on the Kansas-Missouri Line* (Columbia, Missouri: University of Missouri Press, 2007), 43.
42. Barry, *The Beginning of the West*, 1213.
43. (Independence) *Occidental Messenger*, 17 June 1854, reprinted in (*Liberty*) *Weekly Tribune*, 23 June 1854, quoted in Barry, *The Beginning of the West*, p. 1229.
44. *The Missouri Republican*, 12 July 1854, as cited in Barry, *The Beginning of the West*, 1232.
45. H. M. McLachlin, *The Story of Paola, Kansas*, 21.
46. *Paola, Kansas, a 150 Year Timeline*, 22.
47. *Paola, Kansas, a 150 Year Timeline*, 22.
48. Union Historical Society, *History of Jackson County, Missouri: Containing a History of the County, Its Cities, Towns, etc., Biographical Sketches of its Citizens . . .* (Kansas City, Missouri: Union Historical Society, 1881), 444.
49. Theodore Brown, *Frontier Community: Kansas City to 1870* (Columbia, Missouri: University of Missouri Press, 1963), 132-133.
50. Theodore Brown, *Frontier Community*, 118-119.
51. Barry, *The Beginning of the West*, 1143.
52. Fred L. Lee, "Dr. Johnston Lykins: Baptist Missionary, Realtor, Doctor, First Legal Mayor of Kansas City," *Kansas City Genealogist* 36 (Winter 1996):21.
53. Daniel Geary, "Looking Backward," *Annals of Kansas City*, 1 (Dec 1922), 227.
54. Cutler, *History of the State of Kansas, Containing a Full Account of its Growth from an Uninhabited Territory to a Wealthy and Important State, of its Early Settlements, its Rapid Increase in Population and the Marvelous Development of its Great Natural Resources. Also, A Supplementary History and Description of its Counties, Cities, Towns and Villages, their Advantages, Industries, Manufactures and Commerce, to which are added Biographical Sketches and Portraits of Prominent Men and Early Settlers*, (Chicago: A. T. Andreas, 1883), 308.
55. Cutler, *History of the State of Kansas*, 315.
56. House Committee of Claims, "Kansas Claims," House Report 104, *Reports of Committees of the House of Representatives, Made during the Second Session of the Thirty-Sixth Congress, 1860-61* (Washington: Government Printing Office, 1861), Serial 1106, pt. 1, p. 800-801, Claim No. 187 (Stephen J. Livingston), affidavit of Martin Young, 22 Apr 1859.
57. William Weer, "Brief for Applicant in the Matter of the 'Wyandott Robitaille Float,'" [1856?], 16-17; Kansas State Historical Society Library and Archives, Topeka, Kansas; digital images, *Territorial Kansas Online, 1854-1861* (http://www.territorialkansasonline.org : accessed Nov 2009).
58. Samuel A. Johnson, "The Emigrant Aid Company in Kansas," *Kansas Historical Quarterly*, 1 (Nov1932), 429-430.
59. Johnson, "The Emigrant Aid Company in Kansas," 432.

60. Charles Clark, "Missourians," *Kansas Bogus Legislature* (www.kansasboguslegislature.org/mo/index.html : accessed 19 June 2008).
61. W. M. Backus to Samuel A. Johnson, letter, 27 Nov 1930; privately held by Samuel A. Johnson and cited in Johnson, "The Emigrant Aid Company in Kansas," 438.
62. Johnson, "The Emigrant Aid Company in Kansas," 438.
63. Thomas Goodrich, *War to the Knife: Bleeding Kansas 1854-1861* (Lincoln, Nebraska: University of Nebraska Press, 1988), 5.
64. Barry, *The Beginning of the West*, 123.
65. Brown, *Frontier Community*, 98.
66. Barry, *The Beginning of the West*, 1143.
67. Daniel Webster Wilder, *Annals of Kansas* (Topeka, Kansas: George W. Marten, 1875), 67.
68. Ira D. Hyskell, *Early Heiskells and Hyskells, with a Genealogical Table of the First Seven Generations in America* (New York: np, 1958), 42.
69. 1840 US Census, Hampshire County, Virginia, p. 151, William A. Heiskell household.
70. The Church of Jesus Christ of Latter-day Saints [LDS], "Pedigree Resource File," database, *FamilySearch* (http://www.familysearch.org : 20 Oct 2008), entry for Evalina Price (AFN: 228P-6XQ); submitted by William E. Price, 18603 Whitewing Drive, Rio Verde, Arizona, 85263, Microfilm 1512713, Submission: AF 97-000240.
71. 1850 US Census, Sixteenth District, Cass County, Missouri, p. 244, Dwelling number 881, Charles Keller household.
72. Barry, *The Beginning of the West*, 878.
73. Connie Price, interview by Rose Ann Findlen, 24 Oct 2006.
74. Barry, *The Beginning of the West*, 1016, 1025.
75. National Historical Company. *The History of Cass and Bates Counties* (St. Joseph, Missouri, 1983), 169.
76. "Missouri Marriage Records, 1805-2002," database, *Ancestry.com* (http://www.ancestry.com : accessed 19 Jan 2008), entry for David Likens and Sarah D. Tull, 20 Mar 1853, Cass County.
77. "Miami-Co's Oldest Citizen Dead."
78. "Pioneer Kansan Dies Here," *Kansas City Times*, 4 Aug 1916, 2.
79. 1850 US Census, District 24, Hampshire County, Virginia, slave schedule, p. 27-28, F. W., Isaac N., & C. Heiskell.
80. 1850 US Census, District 16, Cass County, Missouri, slave schedule, p. 339, Charles Keller & Silas Price.
81. Union Cemetery Historical Society, "Mrs. Mattie A. Bingham," Obituaries and Biographical Sketches, *Union Cemetery* (Kansas City: Union Cemetery Historical Society, 1990), 8: 22.
82. Charles Clark, "Members," *Kansas Bogus Legislature* (http://www.boguslegislature.org : accessed 15 Feb 2008).

83. Cutler, *History of the State of Kansas,* 308.
84. 1850 U.S. Census, Sixteenth District, Cass County, Missouri, p. 243, line 38, household 889.
85. Connie Price, interview, Oct. 24, 2006.
86. J. C. G. Kennedy, *Population of the United States in 1860 Compiled from the Original Returns of the Eighth Census Under the Direction of the Secretary of the Interior* (Washington, D.C.: Government Publishing Office, 1864), 286-287.
"Missouri Waltz," *Kansas History Online,* Henry J. Fortunato, editor, Hall Center for the Humanities, University of Kansas, Lawrence, Kansas (www.kansashistoryonline.com : accessed 22 Oct 2008).
87. Brown, *Frontier Community,* 98.
88. U.S. Congress, "Report of the Special Committee Appointed to Investigate the Troubles in Kansas, with the views of the minority of said committee," 34th Congress, 1st Session, House Document 200 (Washington, D.C.: Cornelius Wendell, 1856), serial 869, p. 727.
89. Sara T. L. Robinson, *Kansas: its interior and exterior life: including a full view of its settlement, political history, social life, climate, soil, productions, scenery, etc.* (Boston: Crosby, Nichols, 1856), 14-15.
90. Robinson, *Kansas: its interior and exterior life,* 15.
91. Wallace, *History of Paola,* 94, 96, 107.
92. Cutler, *History of the State of Kansas,* 880.
93. U.S. Congress, Report of the Special Committee, p. 229-231, testimony of William Chesnut, 9 May 1856.
86. U.S. Congress, Report of the Special Committee, p. 596, Lykins County voters' list, voters 13 & 48.
95. U.S. Congress, Report of the Special Committee, p. 229, testimony of Joseph M. Gearhart, 9 May 1856.
96. Charles Clark, "Legislation," Kansas Bogus Legislature (http://www.boguslegislature.org : accessed 15 Feb 2008).
97. Paola City Council Journal, p. 228, as cited in Elmer LeRoy Craik, *Southern Interest in Territorial Kansas, 1854-1858* ([Topeka, Kansas: State Printer, 1923]), 334-450.
98. *Paola, Kansas: a 150-Year Timeline,* 22.
99. Jack Morris, "Old Ledgers Reflect Local History," 1976, clipping from unnamed newspaper, Peoria file, Miami County Historical Society, Paola, Kansas.
100. Morris, "Old Ledgers Reflect Local History."
101. Hiram W. Beckwith, *The Illinois and Indiana Indians* (Chicago: Fergus Printing, 1884), 116.

CHAPTER 3

The Lykins and Heiskells in the Border War

Emeline, her family, and neighbors lived during an extremely difficult time in the years of 1855-1857 as they struggled to preserve their safety and guarantee their places in the newly opened territory. The situation was charged with competition as settlers with sharply different visions for the region attempted to prevail. A high school history teacher might construct a multiple choice exam question about Kansas and Missouri in this period:

Question: Which factor or factors contributed to the Borderland conflict of 1855-1857?

A. The national struggle over the institution of slavery;
B. Competition for the land;
C. Economic opportunities for land speculators and investors;
D. Regional differences/culture clash;
E. Fear and terrorist acts;
F. National politics;
G. All of the above;
H. None of the above.

The various players' motivations were intertwined and complex. Historians from the end of the nineteenth century to the present have argued for the primacy of one or the other of these causal factors. Attentive students would mark "G. All of the Above" for the best answer among the seven; all were contributing causes. The distinct but overlapping impact of each is hard to determine. The Emigrant Aid Society, for example, was motivated by abolitionist sentiment as well as by a desire to profit from sending colonists from the East to settle there.[1] Many of the Lykins were Southerners in sympathy but also quick to see business opportunities in the Kansas Territory. Some wanted the beautiful farm land; others resented Northerners coming to take what the Borderland settlers from the South saw as rightly, historically theirs.[2]

Borderland historian Thomas Goodrich described the feverish rush to obtain the rich farm land now available to them: "Thousands of small farmers, merchants and mechanics were unceremoniously packing family and furniture, setting their sights on Kansas. For most of these immigrants the opening of the Kansas Territory to settlers did not represent a way to resolve the Free-state/Slave State issue; rather, it was an opportunity for them to better themselves."[3] Later, some members of the militias and raiders who committed atrocities were these family men, farmers, and shopkeepers caught up in the environment of terror and revenge. The border conflicts and the fighting that took place along the Missouri-Kansas border were qualitatively different from Civil War battles in most states; it was a particularly wrenching, intimate war which commonly took place as skirmishes and raids at the family and community levels–families against neighboring families, adjacent communities against one another. The combatants knew one another personally and had, perhaps, even been friends. Emeline called John Brown a friend, saying that he had opened up trading for her husband among the Native Americans living near Ossawatomie,[4] even though her husband would be called upon to pursue Brown and his sons after the Pottawatomie Massacre.

The Livingston, Heiskell/Price, and Lykins settlers in Missouri and Kansas held within their own ranks widely different views: there were Unionists, Free-state farmers, proslavery advocates and neutralists and co-mingled with those diverse views were deep ties of marriage and blood.

The Borderland, along the Kansas Territory and Missouri border, extended from a little north of St. Joseph, Missouri, on the Missouri River, to Fort Scott, 150 miles south in the Kansas Territory. From East to West, the primary action took place along this line for about 50-60 miles on either side. Events which took place in those relatively few square miles reverberated nationwide, bringing to a boil the conflict of agricultural, human rights, and economic visions which had bubbled among American settlers before the country had its name. A number of inter-related families—the Lykins, the Livingstons, the Heiskells, and relatives of the three families—were right in the middle of the conflict, both ideologically and geographically.

The election rigged by Missourians in March 1855, caused the mix of motivations and perspectives in Borderland residents to begin to boil over. The Missourians' roughshod take-over of the electoral process and the subsequent legislative actions were important factors inciting the violent actions and counter-actions that followed.[5] In Paola, an election was held at Baptiste Peoria's house on Monday, October 1, 1855, with William A. Heiskell taking an oath as one of three official clerks. Among the men voting to select delegates to the U.S. Congress were Charles Keller and E.C. Heiskell, William's former brother-in-law and his son, both residents of Cass County, Missouri.[6] Among the laws passed by the territorial legislature were severe restrictions on and punishments for aiding fugitive slaves. They also challenged the legitimacy of Free-state delegates.[7]

Border War Relationships 1855-1860

Livingston Family

Wm. J. Stephen J. Mattie & Johnston
(Mattie's brothers)

Lykins Family

Joseph Jonas David

- Wm. H.R.
  - Mary=W. D. Lykins Hoover
  - James Hoover

Heiskell Family

Emeline & William
- Sue Heiskell

Keller Family

With Kellers in Missouri after death of mother, Evalina (Price) Heiskell
- E.C. Heiskell
- Price Heiskell
- Charles Heiskell
- Fannie Heiskell

Charles Keller=Ermine Price
- Susan Keller=Wm. Austin
- Wm. Keller=Jennie Hill
- Florence Keller

Baptiste Peoria, land grantor for founding of Paola, Kansas

John Brown, radical abolitionist at Osawatomie, Kansas, 8 miles from Paola

William Quantrill, leader of proslavery insurgent band at Stanton, Kansas, 12 miles from Paola

Governor Geary, second territorial governor of Kansas in Lawrence, 52 miles from Paola

Harrisonville, Cass County, Missouri, home of Keller family, 35 miles from Paola

The free-soil and abolitionist settlers were enraged; proslavery elements were jubilant, unabashedly proud of what they had pulled off. The northerners reacted . . . sometimes violently, sometimes strategically; name-calling and labeling abounded on both sides: the first legislative session held by the Missouri-elected voters was called "The Bogus Legislature"; Missourians were "Border Ruffians," characterized as murderous, ignorant brutes. Northern and Eastern farmers were seen as interlopers and the Abolitionists as wild-eyed radicals and rascals.

In addition to the involvement of Emeline's family in making land claims, voting, and holding office, family members were involved in events surrounding the removal of Governor Andrew Reeder, the first governor of the Kansas Territory. Reeder challenged the results of the first territorial election, by which David Lykins and William Heiskell were selected as legislative members, and enraged the proslavery forces when he called for a new election. The first legislature responded by petitioning President Franklin Pierce to fire him. Pierce did. Free-state advocates then elected him to become a U.S. senator causing a proslavery grand jury to indict him for high treason.[8] To avoid being hanged, Reeder needed to get out of the Kansas Territory, and at that point Emeline's Uncle Johnston became part of the picture.

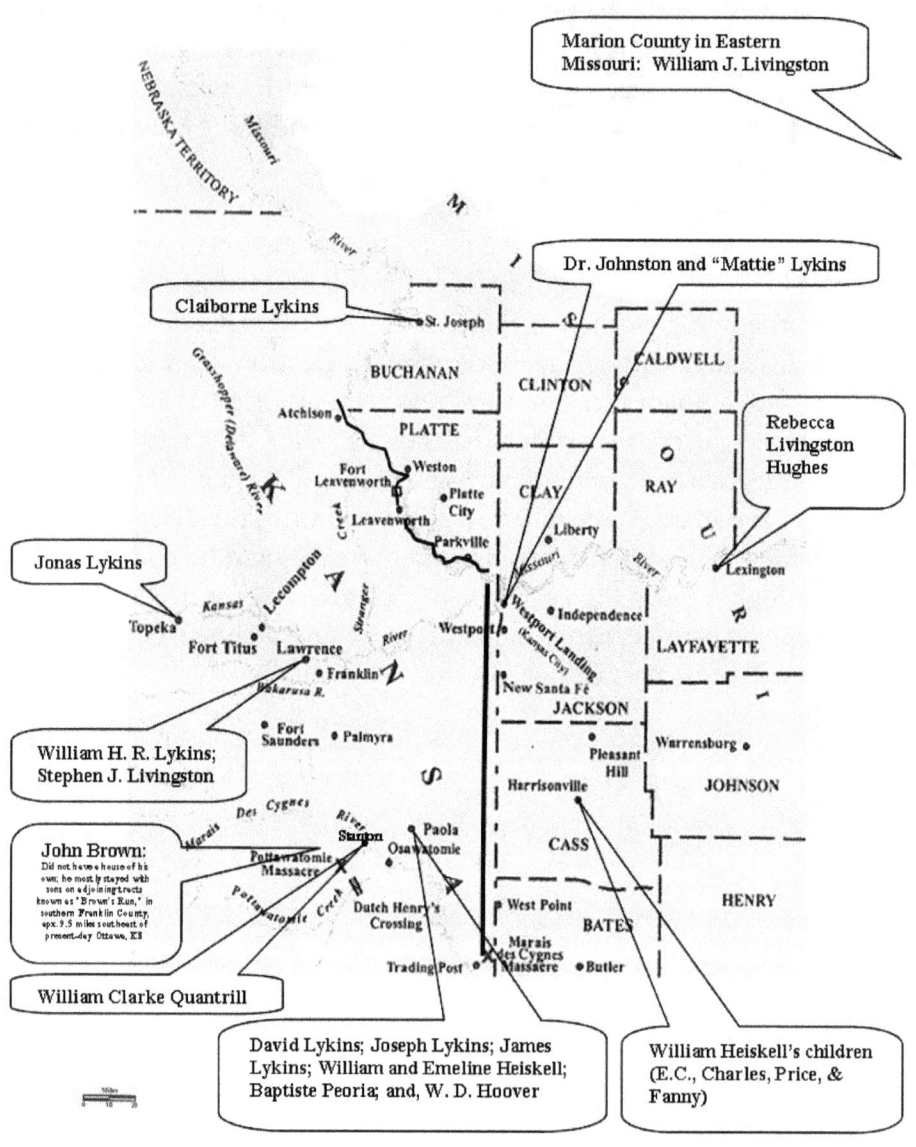

Mattie, Johnston and Governor Reeder

Johnston Lykins, Col. Eldridge and Kersey Coates, all Kansas City residents, agreed to help get Reeder safely out of their city and on to St. Louis where he could escape the irate proslavery forces in the Borderland. Johnston's own son had assisted in arrangements for the fraudulent election in Lawrence and both Johnston and his son had been hotly engaged in William's contested squatter's rights there. Nonetheless, Johnston eschewed the violence and foresaw the necessity for keeping the Borderland from disintegrating into civil war. He and William also had a strong economic interest in the future of the region, so their cultural identity as Southerners was not over-riding. One of their contemporaries in the region, Ely Moore Jr., who had come to the Kansas Territory in 1853 with his father, wrote:

> *Upon our arrival at Westport...we found great political strife existing, not between the proslavery and Free-state men–the Free-state men were not yet in evidence–but between the men of the South proper, and border slave states; many, even though slave owners themselves, advocating in the strongest language against the extension of slavery. Not one of the histories of Kansas mentions this fact, but still the advocacy of extension or non-extension of slavery into Kansas severed political and social fellowship between many old friends, thus showing that the South was not a unit in making Kansas a slave state.*[9]

Mattie wrote that hot-headed proslavery pickets hoped to intercept Reeder as he left Kansas and had posted themselves at the landing. A single picket was on duty on the night that Reeder was rowed across the river and darted into the Eldridge Hotel (aka. the Gilliss House Hotel on Kansas City's riverfront). The picket was suspicious, but his comrades would not take him seriously when he reported seeing a man he thought was Reeder entering the hotel.

The next morning the picket, a friend of Johnston's, was still suspicious and told Johnston when he dropped by the Lykins house at breakfast that he was going to have the Eldridge Hotel searched. Johnston did not react to this information, but shortly excused himself to visit patients. "He was not long in reaching the Eldridge House and in imparting to Colonel Coates and Mr. Eldridge the information he had gained from Mr. Lawton."[10]

The men took Reeder to a house west of Broadway Street where he remained for three weeks. During his time there, Mattie sent him clean handkerchiefs and changes of underwear. Because Reeder was ill and suffering from anxiety, Johnston arranged for a woman at the hiding place to feign illness so that Johnston could be summoned there to attend Reeder. Coates, Lykins and Eldridge arranged for Reeder's escape on a boat disguised as a woodchopper.[11] The plan succeeded and Reeder went to Pennsylvania never to return to the vortex swirling in Kansas.[12]

When Mattie's Southern-leaning friends in Kansas City found out about the concealment and care the Lykins gave Reeder, they felt betrayed by them and "bitterly denounced" Mattie for her part in his escape.[13]

Emeline's New Neighbors: Free-State and Abolitionist

In both Kansas City and Paola, people of opposing views lived side by side as neighbors and even as relatives. Emeline and William had neighbors such as abolitionists, Samuel and Florella Adair. Samuel Adair may even have shopped for supplies at Baptiste Peoria's trading house and interacted with William Heiskell and David Peery or his wife, Florella (John Brown's half-sister) could have chatted with Emeline, one of a small number of women in the region. The Adairs had come to Kansas with the second New England Emigrant Aid Company to organize the Osawatomie Congregational Church. Samuel strongly supported the Free-state movement and funneled money to John Brown and the abolitionist cause from Eastern supporters. Samuel and Florella also staked a claim, building a log cabin northwest of Osawatomie which served as an Underground Railroad stop, and, later, as a refuge for John Brown, activist abolitionist.[14] The Free-state, "Yankee settlement" of Osawatomie was situated about seven miles to the southwest of Paola. Another resident not far from Paola was Martin White, a strong proslavery Baptist minister, who settled near Stanton. In two years, the Adairs, the Browns, and the Whites would intersect in a deadly clash of preacherly extremes. Following the Pottawatomie Massacre, Martin White shot Frederick Brown, John's son, in front of the Adair cabin.[15]

In May 1855, John Brown's sons joined other Free-state settlers in claiming farms near Osawatomie. After a series of frightening and harassing events aimed at driving Free-staters out of the territory, the Browns wrote to their father and asked him to send them guns so they could protect themselves from violent proslavery advocates. Brown made his way to Kansas, stopping to go to an anti-slavery convention in New York State in June, 1855. There he asked for and received money for guns, ammunition, and swords from Free-state supporters.[16] He arrived in Kansas in October, 1855.[17] According to historian Thomas Goodrich,

> One old man [John Brown] was not happy with the quiet situation [in the Lawrence area]....As he sat shivering in his cold cabin near Osawatomie, waiting out the winter, biding his time, John Brown warmed his soul with sweet visions of what was to come: of Missouri cities wrapped in flames; of streets, littered with slaughtered men, women, and children; of a torch-lit army of pike-wielding slaves marching from there throughout the South to repeat the bloody process a thousand times over. As an instrument of God's will, the old man had come west to do everything in his power to ensure that this terrifying specter came to pass. "It is ultimately better that this generation should be swept away from the

face of the earth," he declared, "than that slavery shall continue to exist."[18]

Brown was not alone in his calls for war. Newspapers such as the *New York Times* called for armed resistance to the proslavery forces: "The provocation of our forefathers to Revolution was trifling compared with that which these Kansas settlers have experienced....[Free-state men of Kansas] should not hesitate an instant to take up arms...against the dastardly tyrants."[19] An alternative strategy to violence, however, was beginning to develop in the Kansas Territory. Charles Robinson of the Emigrant Aid Society settlement in Lawrence took leadership in formulating the idea of using civil disobedience, "repudiation," to overcome the misbegotten legislature. Robinson knew that an enormous tide of settlers was coming to the territory: the population of the Kansas Territory in March, 1855 was 8000; exactly one year later, the Territory had 45,000 residents.[20] The Free-state settlers would prevail by their numbers alone, so he advised Free-state settlers to ignore the Kansas Legislature resulting from the March 1855 election and go about holding a legitimate election and writing a new state constitution.

Both impulses, calls to arms and civil disobedience, influenced the actions of Free-state settlers in the coming months. The Free-state convention met in Lawrence that summer and called for the election of delegates to a Free-state constitutional convention. By October, they elected Charles Robinson governor.[21] The meetings were held in Lawrence and Charles Robinson was an important member of the Emigrant Aid Society, so the town of Lawrence became identified in southern settlers' minds as the focal point of abolitionist activity and Free-state supporters refusal to accept the first territorial legislature as legitimate.

Proslavery forces, in addition, were frightened and enraged by the building of a fortress, thinly disguised as the Free State Hotel, in Lawrence. The Free State Hotel, owned by the Emigrant Aid

Society, was described in a Free-state newspaper, *The Herald of Freedom:* "[There are] stairs leading to roof, which is flat, and affords a fine promenade and a splendid view of the surrounding scenery. There are thirty or forty port-holes in the walls, which rise above the room, plugged up now with stones, which can be knocked out with a blow of the butt of a Sharp's rifle."[22] A correspondent for *The Boston Traveler* wrote from the Free State Hotel,

> *As I write, the heavy and measured tread of the sentinel, as he paces his beat on the roof above my head in the midst of a blinding snow storm, reminds me that I am at the very focus towards which all eyes are now turned....General Robinson does not sleep at his own house, but takes his quarters here in the fortress, and sleeps sometimes in my room, while a company of soldiers are quartered in another near by. The roof of the building, three stories in height, has a parapet running all around it, pierced with loop holes, from which in a street fight there could be poured a most destructive volley of rifle balls....The thorough look-out which is being kept, will, we think, prevent us from being taken by surprise and...hacked to pieces by demons with wood hatchets...*[23]

This fortress-hotel became the symbol of the threat posed to the proslavery settlers who then used Sheriff Jones' posse to ride into Lawrence and burn the hotel to the ground.

National politicians seized upon the Kansas drama to unite a divided Republican party to defeat President Franklin Pierce.[24] Malin explains:

> In order to justify the action of Jones [in burning the hotel and destroying two presses], the Proslavery newspapers alleged that Jones was executing the orders of the grand jury or of the United States District Court.... This claim of right under law, played directly into the hands of the Free-state

party, in Kansas, and the newly organized Republican party in federal politics, which were engaged, for political purposes in the midst of the presidential campaign, in pinning all Kansas troubles upon the federal government, as represented by the Democratic party and the Pierce administration. In fact, the excesses of the presidential campaign are the major explanation of the so-called Kansas Civil War of 1856, with Bleeding Kansas as the principal stock in trade of the newly launched Republican party, composed of discordant elements whose only point of coherence was this one issue of opposition to the extension of slavery into the territories, epitomized by Kansas.[25]

This event, the Sack of Lawrence, was one of several violent events which led John Brown to believe that the proslavery forces would commit any act of violence in order to prevail. When Brown heard that Charles Sumner, Massachusetts congressman, had been severely beaten after giving a speech, "The Crimes in Kansas," Brown became irate; in the words of his son, "crazy." Brown's son, John Brown, Jr., reported that his father said, "Something must be done to show these barbarians that we, too, have rights."[26] In November of 1855, two Free-state men were killed by proslavery supporters. Brown was disgusted by what he viewed as Free-state settlers' anemic response to the violence and, according to his sons Jason and John Jr., "did not go on an unsystematic murder spree but instead chose his victims, who were active in proslavery politics and had challenged the Browns personally."[27]

In late May, Brown, John Brown gathered together his sons and closest followers to discuss making a retaliatory attack. His son, John Brown, Jr., recalled the meeting:

It was now and here resolved that they, their aiders and abettors who sought to kill our suffering people should themselves be killed, and in such a manner as should be likely to cause a

> *restraining fear. Father...proposed to return with several of my men....I assisted in the sharpening of his navy cutlasses....No man of our entire number could fail to understand that a retaliatory blow would fall.*[28]

One of the group objected to the plan and Brown stared at him, saying "I have no choice....It has been ordained by the Almighty God, ordained from eternity, that I should make an example of these men."[29] On Saturday, May 24, 1856, Brown, five of his family members and two other Free-state settlers pulled five proslavery settlers from their cabins on Pottawatomie Creek and hacked them to death with broadswords. "John Brown not only wanted to kill proslavery people, he wanted to do it in a way that insurrectionary slaves or embittered Indians would have done it."[30] The Brown company's choice of weapon for these killings was particularly grisly, aimed at creating terror. The Scottish Claymore Broadsword, a common sword at the time of the Pottawatomie Massacre, was a double-edged carbon steel sword about 32 inches long and weighing about two and a half pounds, conjuring up images of butchery and dismemberment.

The violence escalated from there. Both regional and national newspapers sensationalized the event, calling for blood. Some lauded John Brown and his band heroes and patriots; others screamed that they were crazed devils.

News of the slaughter spread quickly among the terrified men, women and

John Steuart Curry's rendition of John Brown

children of Kansas. "Within hours," stated Goodrich, "horror-struck proslavery settlers had cleared the valley 'almost entirely,' fleeing the midnight monsters moving in their midst—monsters who not only massacred innocent men and boys before the eyes of their screaming families but who also 'chopped them into inches.' "[31] Many settlers—southern and northern—immediately left the Kansas territory, and, for those who stayed behind, life became nightmarish. Goodrich quotes a proslavery man as saying, "I never lie down without taking the precaution to fasten my door, and fix it in such a way that if it is forced open, it can be opened only wide enough for one person to come in at a time. I have my rifle, revolver, and...pistol where I can lay my hand on them in an instant, besides a hatchet & axe."[32]

"'Ossawatomie is in much fear & excitement...," reported a resident from that New England colony. "All work is nearly suspended, the women are in constant fear.'....

'All here is excitement and confusion,' echoed a dweller in Paola to the north."[33] William Heiskell was, overnight, catapulted into active military duty. A Westport newspaper, *Border Times*, reported:

WAR!   WAR!
Eight Pro-Slavery men murdered by the Abolitionists in Franklin County, K.T.

LET SLIP THE DOGS OF WAR!

We learn from a despatch just received by Col. A.G. Boone, dated at Paola, K.T., May 26, 1856, and signed by Gens. Heiskell and Barbee, that the reported murder of eight pro-slavery men in Franklin County, K.T., is but too true.[34]

William Heiskell amid the Battle for Kansas

One of the ironies of this Kansas Civil War was that two prominent players, John Brown and William Heiskell, were grandsons of Revolutionary war heroes. John Brown's grandfather, John, born in 1728 in Connecticut died in the Revolutionary War while serving as captain of "Train Band 9" of the 18th Connecticut Regiment.[35] William's grandfather fought at Bunker Hill.[36] Perhaps both grandsons had some predisposition for military engagement from having heard the tales about their heroic grandfathers as they were growing up. Now, on the prairies of Kansas, the two men were on opposing sides in a precursor to the Civil War.

The pursuit of Brown and his company began shortly after the massacre at Ossawatomie. Captain Henry Clay Pate took about 25 militiamen to Paola to assist a United States Marshall in arresting Brown and his company. On June 2, 1856, Pate and his militiamen were camped beside the Santa Fe Trail near Black Jack Creek. John Brown rushed from where he was encamped to attack Pate's men. The two forces fought from defensive positions behind the Santa Fe wagon train ruts and along creek beds. After three hours, Brown outwitted Pate and his men fell into Brown's hands.

"For the first time, an Abolitionist made proslavery ruffians cower. If, as some say, 'Bleeding Kansas' was the opening episode of the Civil War, then Black Jack was its first real battle."[37] Following the battle, Brown and Pate, with their respective officers, made an agreement on the conditions for Pate and his men's release. One copy of the agreement was retained by Brown, but Pate managed to get a duplicate of his copy to "United States Marshal Hays, Colonel Coffey, General Heiskell, or Judge Cato, or friends at Baptiste Paola, K.T." according to F. B. Sanborn, an early biographer of John Brown. In writing his biography of John Brown, Sanborn used the copy Emeline Heiskell sent to the Kansas Historical Society some years later, citing the address written on the back of it as evidence that Pate's letter was given to Heiskell, who then contacted Fort

Leavenworth to send Federal dragoons to liberate Pate and his men.[38]

Brown intended to use the agreement to negotiate the release of two of Brown's sons (ironically, the two innocent ones) held captive by Missourians. The agreement was not kept by either side because of intervening events; however, both of Brown's sons were eventually released after a harrowing captivity by a lynch mob. Brown's son Jason described being taken by the Missourians to Paola:

> *As the fever* [a malarial fever plaguing settlers at that time] *came on they put me on a horse, tied my feet beneath him and my arms behind me and took me, with a guard of twenty men, to Paola, where there were about three hundred armed pro-slavery men. One flourished a coil of new hemp rope over his head as we rode up. 'Swing him up! Swing him up!' he shouted. They hustled me over to a tree and that man flung his rope end over a limb and stood ready. I sat down on the grass by the tree. I didn't suppose I had a friend in that crowd. Then came what changed my whole mind and life as to my feeling toward slave-holders. I can't see a Southerner or a Southern soldier, now, whatever he thinks of me, without wanting to grasp his two hands.*
>
> *As I sat there waiting under the dangling rope, I saw three men aside from the yelling crowd, differently dressed from the rest. One of them came quietly, tapped me on the shoulder and showed me a scrap of paper in the palm of his hand. "Whose writing is that?" asked he. "My father's." "Is old John Brown your father?" "Yes." Never another word did he say, but went around and spoke to the crowd, who made so much noise that I could not hear what he said. Then he came back, (he was Judge Jacobs, of Lexington, Kentucky, and one of his companions was Judge Cato)" and quietly said to me: "come with me to my house and I will treat you like my own son, but we must hold you prisoner....*

There I was, one lone coward, and about forty pro-slavery men in the house that night....On the third night, John [Jason's brother] *was brought in. We lay together and I slept soundly on the front side of the bed. In the night there was a sudden commotion and a crowd of men rushed in. One brandished a bowie knife over me as if to drive it into my right side. I slept on. John* [who was insane at that time] *bared my heart, and, pointing to it, said, "Strike there." They took me away, two men holding my tied arms, in the middle of the night, leaving John, up to the Shawnee Mission. But they were afraid to keep me there and the same night brought me back again....*"[39]

There is no way of determining whether members of the Lykins/ Heiskell family who lived in Paola--William Heiskell, David Lykins, David Peery, Joseph Lykins, and his son James--were part of that frenzied lynching mob, but even if they were not participants, they were likely in Paola at the time. There were only about twenty houses in Paola at that time, so the anger and fear-driven events of those days would have been hard to miss.

General Heiskell had plenty to worry about in the weeks and months following the massacre. Kansas Citians hearing reports of the massacre were "whipped to madness with each new report."[40] J. W. Stringfellow of Atchison called for proslavery forces to go to war: "Let not the knives of the Pro-slavery men be sheathed while there is one Abolitionist in the Territory. As they have shown no quarter to our men, they deserve none from us. Let our motto be written in blood upon our flags, 'Death to all Yankees and Traitors in Kansas!' "[41] Federal troops from Fort Leavenworth and Fort Riley were called out to prevent civil war, but both Free-state and Proslavery guerrillas continued pursuing each other's bands, fighting skirmishes, throwing around inflammatory rhetoric, and looting and harassing farmers and townspeople caught in the middle of it all.[42] Both proslavery and Free-state settlers sent pleas to Governor Geary. One plea was from thirty-one citizens of Anderson and Coffey counties asking for troops to protect them: "We have been forcibly ejected and driven from our homes, our houses burned, robbed and our crops destroyed and our lives threatened by organized bands of Abolitionists...."[43]

During this time, Emeline was probably staying with Heiskell's relatives in Harrisonville, just across the Missouri line near Paola. Heiskell wrote the governor from Harrisonville alluding to frightened settlers who had left the territory to escape "this midnight assassin:"

> *I have been informed by parties upon whom I can rely, that the self-styled Capt. John Brown Sen/r is in the Marais des Cygnes and Pottawatomie Creek country not far from Osawatomie, with a company of fifty or sixty men. He has within the past week giving notice to law and order* [proslavery] *men who had returned to their homes, that they must leave the territory immediately, and also that he was commissioned by your excellency and ordered upon the service of keeping peace in the southern portion of the territory. His mode of peace, being I suppose to drive all law and order men from the country. He is no doubt sustained by the Ottawa Creek Rangers..., a company of about a hundred and ten men.*
>
> *The settlers are afraid to return to their homes until something is done to relieve them from the presence of this midnight assassin, the author and executor of the Pottawatomie Creek murders and second only to Lane in importance of those who have set themselves up in opposition to the laws of the United States and of the Kansas Territory.*
>
> *I submit this plain statement of facts for your excellency's consideration, hoping that you will send such aid as is necessary to that portion of the territory, at your earliest convenience.*[44]

Malin cited a second letter that Heiskell wrote a few days later on October 1st. He informed the governor that "a company of forty mounted riflemen had been organized in Lykins county for the protection of public peace under Martin White as captain." Heiskell again asked for Geary's support: "They offer their services to your excellency as you will see by the enclosed rather informal paper, and ask that their officers may be commissioned." He repeated that John Brown had a group of 60 men on Pottawatomie Creek who were inactive only for lack of arms and that proslavery men were afraid "to return to the Territory whilst this band of outlaws is permitted to remain organized in their midst."[45]

Martin White wrote to Geary from Paola four days later again asking for authorization to move on Brown's band [misspellings retained]:

> Sir I have ritten 2 letters to you and have received no ansure from you the first was asking purmision to rase a Cumpaney to be stationed at Stanton to protect the inhabitants and thare property subject at all times to your order and the mintanance of the law the 2 was informing you of Brown and his Cumpaney who ware still marching through the country takin every thing that tha could that tha could make money out of even plows and driving every boddy back that did not suit thare purpus and destroying the crops for which I asked you to fore a detachment of the forces under your command to arrest these high way robbers and murders I went on the 30 of last month expecting to git help from you but received no ansur and found no help and finding that I was in danger I shal leive to day. There is a bought 110 Fameileys wating for protection to go back. We have rased a Cumpaney of 80 men and elected our officers and will report imediately and we asked to be mustered in to the united states survices.

> *The names of our officers will be reported to you imediately please rite to me and oblige yours direct yours to peoly Lykans Co. K.T. yours with mutch respect references to my carector Col. Boon westport Col. Titus Lecompton Genral Calhoon Wyandot.*[46]

On October 7, Geary wrote to White that he "would muster in the company when occasion required and that he would visit southeastern Kansas when some least expected it. To General Heiskell he gave assurances that he would afford protection."[47]

Possibly Geary responded to Martin White's letter as he did because he did not trust White: White was the same rabidly proslavery minister who shot John Brown's slow-witted son Frederick on sight at the Adair cabin. Also, the low level of literacy in the letter must have conjured up the characterization of proslavery settlers as "Border Ruffians," uncouth and blood-thirsty illiterates. He may have been wary of Heiskell as well, recognizing him as the man who was able to muster over 800 proslavery militiamen about six weeks earlier. He may not have wanted such an armed force outside his immediate environment (LeCompton and Lawrence); his goal was, after all, the demilitarization of the Kansas Territory. Because Geary responded to Paola and southeastern Kansas calls for help differently from the way he handled similar requests in Lawrence and Lecompton, Free-state settlers in southeastern Kansas took up the call for help and for equitable treatment. According to Malin, "Geary had not only refused but warned them, quoting the [New York] *Tribune* of October 31, 1856 that 'if he found any of them under arms that he would hang them.' " In reaction, Free-state advocates formed the National Kansas Committee to stockpile arms in Tabor, Iowa, for transmission into Kansas.[48]

The Free-staters' Response

In "*How Bloody was Bleeding Kansas: Political Killings in Kansas Territory, 1854-1861*" historian Dale Watts wrote that narratives about Bleeding Kansas were exaggerated in their reports of murder and violence. For example, he reported that eight people were killed in Lykins County in 1856, the worst year of the conflict and that, in the territory as a whole, the two sides were about equally responsible for the killings. His analysis does not, however, take into account the proportion of the population the murders represented or the traumatic effect of repeated reports of lawlessness, violence and threat on people living in the county. The number "eight" sounds small; in that time and place, it would have felt very large as one side and then the other exacted revenge:

> No angels lived in Kansas Territory. The Pottawatomie Massacre constituted the bloodiest single atrocity, but these murders were balanced by the killings of peaceful antislavery men....Tit for tat, killing for killing, each side fought to revenge supposed crimes by its enemies while striving to convince the world that it did so only with the purest of motives...Both sides often placed human life below ideology and personal gain.[49]

Nationally newspaper accounts of violence sensationalized the conflict and galvanized the moral indignation of Northern and Eastern readers to increase their efforts to prevail in Kansas. Watching politicians and newsmen fanning the flames ever higher, the editor of the *Leavenworth Kansas Weekly Herald* read the tales of rape, murder and torture in disbelief:

> What voracious and blood-thirsty barbarians these reporters must be. Still, we suppose, they are not so much to be blamed, after all. The Chicago folks want lies and nothing

but the most transcendent mendacity will satisfy them. A respectable, reasonable hoax would be no more to them than a slice of meat to a hungry hyena.[50]

Goodrich noted that "in their all-consuming hatred of slavery and zeal to win Kansas, many were ready, willing, and able to invent almost any story that would help them win it. Unfortunately, too many in the East were ready, willing, and able to accept any tale issuing from Kansas. Meanwhile, with each apocryphal report, the gulf splitting the nation yawned wider and wider, making compromise increasingly more difficult and national civil war increasingly more likely."[51]

The Eastern press did not report the violent excesses of the abolitionists and Free-state men as frequently as it published accounts of proslavery violence. Bands led by John Brown, Jim Lane, and others ransacked, robbed and murdered with little notice from the press.[52] Donald Gilmore, a former editor of the press of the Combat Studies Institute of the U.S. Army Command and General Staff College at Fort Leavenworth, Kansas, observed, "The Civil War and Border War were really two wars, one fought with bullets and guns, the other fought with words and propaganda. The South lost both wars, the propaganda one most thoroughly. And although the shooting war largely ended in 1865, the propaganda war, to some extent, is still being prosecuted today as it was 140 years ago."[53]

Hearing lurid, outrageous reports from speakers such as Free-state Governor Robinson's wife, Sara, and General Jim Lane of the Free-state militia, enraged crowds in Chicago, Wisconsin, and points eastward. The North mobilized for war.[54] Hundreds of Free-state men, thirsting for battle, headed toward the Kansas Territory, equipped by "Christian Armies," church groups who saw it as their Christian duty to supply arms and munitions. In his biography of John Brown, Reynolds discussed Brown's appeal to New England descendants of the Puritans:

By mid-May 1856 the events in Kansas and on the national scene made the Old Testament God of Battles seem more relevant to him (Brown) than the New Testament's Prince of Peace. In this sense he followed the example of his greatest hero among white Christians, Oliver Cromwell....(Brown) matches Cromwell more closely than he does any other historical figure. Both were devout Calvinists who ascribed their deeds to God.... Despite Cromwell's obvious shortcomings, many nineteenth-century Americans, especially New Englanders like those who funded John Brown's raid on Virginia, idolized him.[55]

In the face of all this righteous zeal and the lust for land, General Atchison set up barricades all along the border, boarding incoming steamships and dumping the dreaded Sharps rifles into the river, but the free-soilers would not be deterred. They soon discovered that they could reach the Territory without going through Missouri. At first, only a small number of emigrants made it into the territory, but by midsummer, hundreds were on their way through Iowa.[56] The Kansas militiamen and Federal troops who rushed to turn back the Free-state horde were over-extended and unable to turn back the incoming Free-staters at the Nebraska line.[57]

Although the communities near the Missouri line remained in proslavery hands, those further west began to be dominated by the settlers from the east and midwest.[58] One after another, communities such as Indianola and Council Grove were inundated with free-soil settlers and its original residents "cast to the wind."[59] William and Emeline would have been well aware of the Free-staters' raid on Indian traders' wagon train of supplies near Palmyra a few miles northwest of Paola. The proslavery settlers established fortified blockhouses, arsenals, and places of protection for the proslavery settlers. And while the Free-staters insisted that the forts were occupied by 'brigands," they appear to have been used only for defensive purposes and not as locations from which assaults were being launched. As there were no corresponding forts used by Free-staters in the hinterlands outside Lawrence, it seems clear that the proslavery settlers were the ones under siege....As well as seizing proslavery settlements during the Wakarusa War (from August 12-19, 1856) the Free-staters burned a number of homes in the general area, took numerous prisoners, and in general terrorized the proslavery settlers of the Lawrence area. In short they were committing the same depredations that their supporters in the Eastern press establishment were claiming that proslavery bands were committing.[60]

Among the settlers terrorized, for a second time within a year, were Mattie Lykins' brother, Stephen J. Livingston, and his family. Livingston's brother-in-law, his mother-in-law, his hired hand and his family all lived about one to two miles northwest of Lawrence in August, 1856.[61] Around August 21, 1856, Stephen Livingston went to Missouri on business, leaving his wife, who was ill, in the care of his mother-in-law, Ann Hopper. In her claim for restitution of losses, Mrs. Hopper testified that "her house was visited by a band of armed men, who acted very rudely and carried off two guns; there was so much excitement and danger, that the Doctor ceased to attend upon the sick persons at her house, in consequence of which she was compelled to abandon her house in company with the sick persons then at her house and seek safety and medical aid for them at the city of Lecompton."[62]

Livingston and his family's troubles continued. After fleeing Jim Lane's Free-staters, Livingston was accosted in Lecompton by General Marshall's proslavery forces, who demanded that he give them his wagon and team of horses to transport the army's cannon. When Livingston refused, he was taken prisoner for two days. Because of the military upheaval and his wife's illness, he was unable to return to his home for four weeks after his release. When he returned to his house, it had been "almost entirely stripped of its furniture and contents and a family had taken possession of it....The woman who was then occupying the house said there was nothing in the house when she moved in, except a clothes-press, two bedsteads and a few chairs. The house had been set on fire, but not consumed."[63]

The Livingstons, Hoppers and Youngs vacated their homes near Lawrence, hotbed of contention, and wisely relocated further away from the turmoil swirling around the town. When Livingston made a claim seeking damages in 1859, he testified that he was in the crosshairs of both the Free-staters and the proslavery advocates because he would not ally himself with either faction. In 1855, he served as "a justice of the peace in Lawrence under the territorial laws of 1855, which gave great offence to many of the people at that place; he was afterwards, and while holding said office of justice of the peace, a candidate for representative in the legislature under the [opposing Free-state] Topeka constitution. This gave equal offence to the other party and [he] was denounced as a traitor by both factions."[64] In the Kansas Territory in 1856, there could be no neutrality: in that time, individuals had to choose sides. Tolerance and peaceful co-existence were crushed beneath the wagon wheels of two factions, each seeking to win dominance by destroying the other.

STEPHEN J. LIVINGSTON
Lost in the year of 1856, during the troubles in Kansas

One wagon and harness	$125.00
One hundred pounds of feathers, in pillows, bolsters, and sacks, at 50 cents per pound	50.00
One lot of cupboard ware	30.00
Six chairs, not recovered, at $1 each	6.00
One lot of cooking utensils, pots and kettles	5.00
Wife's clothing	30.00
My own clothing, coats, pants, boots, vests &c.	30.00
Fifty pounds of soap, at 10 cents per pound	5.00
Bacon, one barrel, 150 pounds, at 10 cents per pound	15.00
Coffee	3.00
Two or three crocks, two or three jars, and churn, worth	5.00
Farming utensils, hoes, rakes, and forks	3.00
Rails taken from around garden. Say 500 rails, at $5 per hundred	25.00
Gardening all taken; vegetables, &c.	25.00
Twelve acres of corn; field all destroyed; new ground; at $10 per acre	120.00

Nine head of hogs, one sow and eight shoats, at $3 each	27.00
One hundred chickens	25.00
Crowbar, spade, shovel, pick, and stone hauler	10.00
Old corn in the crib, five bushels	5.00
Four blankets; home-made bed blankets	12.00
Four quilts	8.00
One coverlet, woolen	5.00
Nine sheets, at 75 cents each	6.75
Eight pairs of pillow-slips	4.00
Other bed clothing to the amount of	10.00
One sifter	.75
Two trunks	5.00
Three barrels and three boxes, at 50 cents each	3.00
One rag-carpet, at 25 cents per yard	12.00
Two axes	2.00
Yarn	1.00
Two wash-tubs and board	3.00
One cedar bucket	1.00
Two wooden buckets	.60
Two tin pans, at 75 cents each	1.50
One wash-pan	.40
Two coffee pots	.80
Clothes and work basket	1.50
One coffee-mill	1.00
Two candlesticks	1.50
Salaratus, spice, pepper &c., say	.50
Two large butcher knives	1.50
One hand-saw	1.25
Three augers	1.50
One drawing-knife	.75
Two iron wedges	2.00
Six tablecloths	6.00
Twelve towels	1.50
One hatchet	1.00
Two hammers	1.50
One looking-glass	1.25
One plough	5.00
One grindstone	2.00
Two chisels	1.00
One pair of plough gears	3.00
Three mattresses, at $2 each	6.00
Two hats	5.00
One pair of coarse boots	3.00
One pair of steelyards	1.25
One pair of scales	.60
One lot of books	<u>5.00</u>
	573.20[65]

By then Kansas Territorial General David Atchison knew that the proslavery effort would fail. He and his generals decided to gather their forces and attack Lawrence in a last-ditch effort to win the Kansas Territory for the South. By September, 1856, a new territorial governor was on his way to the Borderland. As he made his way into the area by steamboat and then by coach, he was sobered by the severity of the situation and of the difficulty of the task of bringing peace to the territory. Matters were far worse than he had known. In his report to Washington, D.C., Governor Geary wrote:

> *It is no exaggeration to say that the existing difficulties are of a far more complicated character than I had anticipated....The actual proslavery settlers of the territory are generally as well-disposed persons as are to be found in most communities. But there are among them a few troublesome agitators...who labor assiduously to keep alive the prevailing sentiment. It is also true that among the free-soil residents are many peacable and useful citizens; and if uninfluenced by aspiring demagogues, would commit no unlawful act. But many of these, too have been rendered turbulent by officious meddlers from abroad....The roads are filled with armed robbers and murders for mere plunder are of daily occurrence. Almost every farm-house is deserted, and no traveller has the temerity to venture upon the highway without an escort. Such is the condition of Kansas faintly pictured. It can be no worse.*[66]

Geary decided on a strategy for handling the explosive situation, and after having arrived in the Territory only 36 hours earlier, he acted. Geary concluded that both sides were wrong, and he decided on a middle course between them. While he removed restrictions barring the free settlement of the territory, he also insisted on upholding existing territorial laws.[67] As Geary saw guerrilla bands and troops on both sides amassing from Iowa, South Carolina, Missouri, the Kansas Territorial militias, and the Free-state Militias, his first and most important task had to be the demilitarization of the Territory. He issued proclamations to disband all voluntary militias and to require "all free male citizens qualified to bear arms" to enlist in the regular Territorial militia.[68] To ensure that the proslavery forces were quickly informed of the proclamations, he ordered these proclamations to be immediately printed for hand-delivery to Kansas both to the proslavery forces gathering at Franklin and to the Free-state citizens of Lawrence.

After delivering the proclamations, his emissary, Theodore Adams, reported to the Governor that a thousand Missourians were poised to attack Lawrence. The Lawrence citizens were paralyzed by dread and engulfed by one rumor after another. A military officer stationed at Lawrence at the time described the town in his journal on September 3:

> *[The town of Lawrence was at this time a strange mixture of] stone houses, log cabins, frame buildings, shake shanties and other nondescript erections...Lawrence presents a sad picture of the evils this partizan warfare is bringing over us. Buildings half finished or deserted are now occupied as quarters for the small army of devoted men who are fighting the battle of Freedom. Trade is at a standstill. Work is not thought of, and the street is full of the eager, anxious citizens who cluster eagerly around every new-comer, drinking in greedily the news, which generally is exaggerated by the fears or imagination of those who tell it. To a stranger, it seems a wild confusion, and however much they may desire, the incidents come in so fast that it is morally impossible to form a just estimate of the true conditions of things.*[69]

With proslavery militia surrounding the town, the trapped citizens of Lawrence waited for the new Governor's intervention while, Geary, who had been in the territory fewer than 48 hours tried to grasp the political and military situation and respond to the crisis at hand.

He [Geary] was puzzling over a communique from one William Heiskell, who signed himself, 'Brigadier General Commanding First Brigade, Southern Division, Kansas Militia.' Writing from his headquarters on Mission Creek, Heiskill said, "In obedience to the call of Acting Governor Woodson, I have organized a militia force of about eight hundred men, who are now in the field, ready for duty and impatient to act. Hearing of your arrival, I beg leave to report to you for orders."

The new governor was bewildered. Heiskill obviously had not heard his proclamations, and this was the first the governor had heard of Woodson's call to arms against the Free-state guerrillas who had been raiding proslavery towns. He began to suspect that Woodson had not delivered his papers to General Strickler, a suspicion soon confirmed by a dispatch from Special Agent Adams. Strickler had not received the governor's orders and his army was being augmented daily by companies of Missourians....Adams estimated that 2700 men were encamped at Franklin and in the more than 300 tents a mile away on the Wakarusa. An attack on Lawrence was imminent.[70]

Geary rode to Lawrence with 400 federal troops under the command of Lieutenant Colonel Joseph E. Johnston, who later served as a distinguished Confederate general. When he arrived, Geary found the Missourians and their leaders--Atchison, Reid, Heiskell, Stringfellow, and Whitfield–assembled in Franklin, determined to make a final effort to conquer the Territory through military force. Many of their cavalrymen and infantry soldiers wore uniforms and were well-equipped with arms, including a six-pounder battery. They had gathered a formidable force."[71]

With Johnston's troops setting up camp on Mount Oread during the night of September 14, the citizens felt somewhat safer. The three hundred men currently in the town stood at the barricades, arming their women and children as well. Old John

Brown, standing on a dry goods box, advised the citizens on how to defend themselves:

> *Gentlemen–It is said there are twenty-five hundred Missourians down at Franklin, and that they will be here in two hours. You can see for yourselves the smoke they are making by setting fire to the houses in that town. This is probably the last opportunity you will have of seeing a fight, so that you had better do your best. If they should come up and attack us, don't yell and make a great noise, but remain perfectly silent and still. Wait till they get within twenty-five yards of you, get a good object, be sure you see the hind sight of your gun, then fire. A great deal of powder and lead and very precious time is wasted by shooting too high. You had better aim at their legs than at their heads. In either case, be sure of the hind sight of your gun. It is for this reason that I myself have so many times escaped, for, if all the bullets which have ever been aimed at me had hit me I would have been as full of holes as a riddle.*[72]

Geary sent the citizens away from the barricades and back into their homes, assuring them that Johnston's troops would protect them. Hearing from a scout that the territorial forces, led by General and Legislator John Reid, were forming to attack, Geary rode out to the proslavery camp. He was escorted to camp headquarters where he immediately met with the generals, including General Heiskell (also a legislator) and his own Supreme Court Justice, Sterling Cato. His words to the generals were as follows:

> *Though held in a board house, the present is the most important meeting since the days of the Revolution, as its issues involve the fate of the Union then formed."* Then he looked squarely at David Atchison, *"When I saw You last, you were acting as vice-president of the nation and president of the most dignified body of men in the world, the Senate of the United States,"* he said. *"It*

is with sorrow and pain that I see you now, leading on to a civil and disastrous war an army of men, with uncontrollable passions and determined upon wholesale slaughter and destruction.[73]

Geary repeated his order that the volunteer militia disband and said he would handle the "Northern rebels" himself.[74] The generals did not at first in agree on whether to obey Geary's directive. Some felt that the moment to defeat the northerners was at hand; others had heard Geary's assurances that he would moderate and ameliorate the situation in the Territory. Finally, the generals obeyed their governor's orders.   Geary's bold actions at that hour probably averted for a few years the outbreak of the "Second" more broadly based Civil War, saved hundreds of lives, and the town of Lawrence from burning to the ground. Emeline saw her husband and, doubtless, other family members, return alive, but demoralized, to their homes in Paola. David Atchison's comments to southern colleagues acknowledged "At one time we had high hopes that in Kansas we should soon have another outpost protecting the institutions of the south, but we are no longer laboring under any such flattering illusion."[75] After the stand-down of the Kansas Militia and the departure of many out-of-state mercenaries and partisans such as John Brown and Jim Lane, the governor was able to bring relative, if temporary, quiet to the Kansas Territory.

Paola in 1857

Bloody Kansas left a bloody mess, but within months, the people in the territory energetically began to build and develop its communities. When Emeline's first child, Sue Heiskell, was born in May 1857, Paola and the Kansas Territory were ugly, rough, war-ravaged outposts. With the energies of citizens of both the free-soil and proslavery communities directed toward survival and warfare in prior years, the building of the towns languished. The armed bands of each had repeatedly burned houses, barns, and crops, stolen livestock, and torn down fences; when a crop reached harvest, the farmers were not there to harvest it; instead, they and their families were fighting or fleeing. The stores had hardly any inventory because of disruptions in trade and the well-founded fear that any inventory on hand would be stolen or destroyed by raiders. Goodrich wrote, "Few communities in Kansas could qualify for the title of 'town' much less 'city.' Many places…were little better than pig sties–low, muddy, foul, 'reeking with filth and heavy with malaria. Even Lawrence, for all its notoriety and vaunted 'New England tidiness' was hardly more than a squalid collection of cabins, shacks, and 'hen coops.' "[76]

During Sue's first year, increasing numbers of settlers were moving into the area, and the demographic mix of the population in the Kansas Territory was rapidly changing from that of her parents to farmers from states north of the Ohio River:

> During the early territorial period, most of the children born in southeastern Kansas came from families in which both parents were born in a slave state. If one includes households of mixed nativity (in which one parent was born in a slave state and the other in a Free-state), the proportion of at least partial southern ancestry rises to nearly 75 percent. Almost all of these southern parents had come directly from Missouri or the Upper South slave states of Kentucky or Tennessee. Only one in four Kansas-born children came from families in which both parents had been born in free states. In the late territorial period a strikingly different pattern emerged. More than half of the children born then came from Free-state parents, while the ratio of children with southern-born parents slipped to 28 percent. The balance of power in Kansas Territory, as these figures reveal, was steadily shifting from proslavery to free-soil settlers.[77]

A settler who arrived in Paola in the year that Sue was born described the town as he first saw it:

> *It was with feelings of exultation that I reached the crest of the hill north of Paola and beheld the few houses below. That hill was then a forest, the only house being a long one about where W. H. Browne's residence now stands, and was occupied by Luther Paschall, an Indian. Taking a drink at the Mitchler Spring, which was then open and constituted the water works for the town, I brought up at the frame hotel on the northwest corner of the park....There were a couple of small dwellings west on the same block, and opposite a store run by Cy Shaw and a dwelling occupied by Arbuckle. About where Grimes' drug store now stands was a frame one story, which was occupied by Baptiste's store [where brothers-in-law D.L. Peery and W.A. Heiskel worked]. On the northeast corner...was the dwelling of Tom Hedges, and in the same block one occupied by Knowles Shaw. Opposite...was Mrs. Baptiste's, and on the east side was the small building owned by Jno. Eisle and then occupied by Jim Scott. Cannot recollect of any buildings on the south side. There were other small houses scattered around, but they were not very numerous.*[78]

In 1857, the total population of Lykins County was 1, 352.[79] One of the settlers coming to Lykins County in Sue's first month of life was William C. Quantrill, a man whose name became synonymous with "Bushwhacker" and "terror" in future years. When Quantrill first arrived in the Kansas Territory he paid $2.25 an acre at Paola's public land sale on June 29, 1857.[80] He was a middle class Ohioan, a "handsome boy, who from the time he was sixteen, worked off and on as a schoolteacher. Wanderlust and the persuasion of friends, however, convinced him in 1857, when he was twenty, to go to Kansas to stake a claim....For the next six months, Quantrill did minor farming and developed his claim, which was located close to the Marais des Cygnes River near Stanton in Miami [Lykins] County."[81] His home there was probably a dug-out near the river. According to Kansas historian Elizabeth Barnes, "The early settler often selected a spot for his home near a timbered stream, where he could cut logs. Homes were made from the earth and were called dugouts. They were rectangular holes cut in the side of a bank of suitable size and depth, roofed with poles over which were heaped cornstalks and dried grasses, and then topped with strips of sod. They were warm, dry and windproof. Walls were plastered with a mixture of clay and sand."[82]

Lumber and shingles were practically the same as legal tender in 1857 as the settlers rushed to build their homes. With the county now relatively peaceful, settlers could look around them and see the beauty and promise of the countryside. As the settlers planted and harvested, the beaten down towns began to use the lumber and shingles to build and grow their communities. Some stayed to become venerated founding fathers; others, like Quantrill, were motivated more by the adventure of the west than by the settling of it, moved on to other places and pastimes, leaving the growing and building to others. Quantrill's friend and mentor from Ohio, Colonel Torrey, addressed the lodging shortages brought about by the emigrants pouring in by building a hotel in Paola and the first non-Indian school was established by subscription in 1857. "It was a one story, board structure, about twenty feet square with three windows and a door at 114 South Pearl," about a block from the home where Sue spent her childhood.[83] In 1857, too, the Paola Town Company had a house built on the north side of the square to serve as city hall.

Paola did not have meat shops until the Winter of 1860. Prior to that time, one of the settlers recalled, "There were no meat shops nor ice, and bacon was to dear to be wholesome. By the winter of 1860, the meat shops came, and more varied victuals. Even the mysterious hash came into existence."[84] An advertisement in *The Miami Republican* for 1866 announced, "Stages leave this house daily for all points."[85] Students researching the history of Paola in 1929 reported that:

> Food and supplies were brought to Paola by means of covered wagons. Many of the supplies came from Leavenworth, Kansas....There was a saloon in the building where The Republican printing office now is. A brewery stood where the junk yards on West Peoria now are. ...In those early days, whiskey was sold over the counter at the store as freely as vinegar is today [in 1929]. Fathers warned their little daughters and told them it was not nice to walk along the west side of the square because of the drunkenness of many there. Later the liquor was taken to the basement to be sold. This was called "Basement Liquor.[86]

The daily presence of the Indian residents would have been integral sights and sounds to the world Sue experienced as a little girl in Paola. When the junior high school students interviewed old-time residents of Paola, one of the town's early residents, Mrs. James Neylon, recalled a childhood in which the Indian families still lived in Paola:

> The land for the spacious City Park Sue played in was granted to the city by Chief Baptiste Peoria who specified that the town square must always remain free of buildings and open to all for recreation. One of the most popular activities of the time, an early settler recalled was horse racing: "The Indians were then in force, and life with them was sport galore. Horse racing was the event of the time. A straight track (north of Wilson's sales barn) about a quarter of a mile long was cleared. The Indians were great traders and every horse they got was tried on the track. Saturday was always fete day, and all congregated at the track, and races filled out the time."[87]

Paola Town Square

Sue's childhood was filled with the excitement of diverse populations mingling, an energized population building its community and many family members sharing her days. As Sue was growing up, she might have seen the horse races and Indian dances at the square, and probably looked for her Uncle David Peery in the crowd or Uncle David Lykins' boys, William and Edward, all of whom interacted comfortably with their Peoria neighbors.

Sue was surrounded by family–Uncles Joseph and David Lykins and their children, Cousin Mary Lykins Hoover and her family, Cousin James Lykins on the farm right outside Paola, and, by 1860, her teenage half-brother, Charles Heiskell.[88]

> **For more information about the passion of horse racing in Paola, turn to "*The Mare was Drugged*," in the Related Stories and Poems section at the end of the book.**

As the Kansas towns went about the business of building themselves, people who had been proslavery understood that if they were going to stay in Kansas, they needed to adapt themselves to the new circumstances. Economic opportunity buoyed up townsmen and farmers and moved them forward with developing their communities. Old wounds and memories, though, were right below the surface, punctuated by news of the bandits and marauders roaming in the southern borderland of Kansas and Missouri.

Sue Heiskell

The awful events that had taken place and the vituperation of the newspapers, made names and labels stick and southerners suspect. As Sue was growing up she may have caught snatches of conversation or playmates' catcalls referring to her father, uncles, and cousins as "Border Ruffians." If so, she might have wondered about that term suggesting dirty, ignorant rubes who knew of nothing but violence and brutality.

"Could this be true?" she might have thought. Uncle David, Uncle Johnston and his son W.H.R. wrote poetry from time to time; her father was often turned to for writing official communications and was the county's first registrar of deeds; Uncle Joseph had been a missionary and was now a Paola businessman; cousin Mary's husband was a physician; Uncle Johnston was a mayor and real estate developer and his son a banker. Johnston's wife Mattie wrote stories, books, and newspaper columns and taught school. The woman for whom she appeared to have been named, Susan Keller Austin, was her cousin in Cass County, Missouri. Susan had recently moved to St. Louis with her extended family, probably to escape the violence and destruction overwhelming the Harrisonville area.[89]

Gilmore contends that the southern sympathizers lost the propaganda war, not only at the time, but for decades to come. At the height of the Kansas Territorial conflict, Horace Greeley, editor of the *New York Tribune*, coined the term "Border Ruffian," "describing them as swaggering drunkenly around Kansas with Bowie knives hanging from their waists." Contrary to the usual impressions left by historians, these proslavery units were composed mostly of people generally more affluent and prominent than typical Missourians; that is, many of them were members of the affluent, slave-owning families of Missouri . . . .These maligned men certainly had no monopoly over Kansas when it came to wearing Bowie knives and acting pugnaciously."[90] The broadsword, the heavy sword used for up-close hand-to-hand combat, was, remember, the weapon of choice of John Brown, darling of Eastern intellectuals and journalists at that time. Josiah Grinnell, for example, was a fervent abolitionist and founder of the historically active Grinnell College. Grinnell hid John Brown as the old man fled across Iowa toward Harper's Ferry and, ultimately, the hangman's noose.[91] People of all social classes and backgrounds participated, in both heroic and self-serving ways, in the events of those days, but, as is the case in any war, the story that is told after the war is shaped by the victors.[92]

Although the level of violence in Kansas decreased after the slavery question was settled, there was a desire for revenge against Missourians and proslavery advocates. With their close family ties to

St. Joseph, Westport and Cass County, Missouri, Heiskell and David Lykins must have been deeply concerned for their relatives: Claiborne and his family in St. Joseph, Johnston and Mattie in Kansas City, David's sister-in-law, Grace Tull, near Harrisonville, and Heiskell's children and his first wife's family in Cass County. They likely felt personally threatened as well, having been so closely associated with the legislative body resulting from the election bootlegged by Missourians. In 1858, angry Free-state bands attempted to drive proslavery settlers from the Borderland. Self-appointed "Colonel" James Montgomery, actually a preacher and school teacher, established the policy of Jayhawking. According to Gilmore, "The term Jayhawking is said to have originated with the activities of a marauder named Pat Devlin who, when he rode into Linn County (Kansas) one day loaded down with plunder from Missouri, was asked where he obtained it. He said he 'Jayhawked' it. When asked what that meant, he explained that in Ireland, his homeland, there was a bird that 'worries his prey before it devours it.' He claimed that's what he was doing. Others believed Jayhawking was just 'a fancy name for horse stealing.' . . . By May 1858, Montgomery began an aggressive campaign against the Missourians by leading large groups of armed Linn County raiders into Missouri to rob and murder."[93] Jayhawkers and other outlaw bands roamed the countryside, taking what they wanted:

> Many Kansans wanted more than a mere purge of slavers from the territory; many actively sought a way to punish Missouri for its acts of the past. Among a goodly number of Kansans there was an added incentive. From 1859 to 1860 a severe drought seared the territory, ruining crops and impoverishing farmers and merchants alike. By the eve of statehood, early in 1861, Kansas was on the brink of starvation. Western Missouri, on the other hand, because of a stable, long-rooted society, remained a region of peace and plenty. With no small amount of envy mingled with an

already potent hatred, the eyes of Kansas were locked on the land over the line during the spring of Secession.[94]

William Heiskell's children and the Price relatives with whom they stayed after their mother's death dispersed in the decade leading up to the Civil War, Cass County having become a battleground for the Border wars of the time. Between 1855 and 1858, Heiskell's former brother-in-law, Charles Keller, moved from Cass County with his wife, daughter Florence, and Heiskell's youngest daughter Fanny to St. Louis. His son William married Jennie Hill in St. Louis in 1858.[95] He, his wife and baby son lived in St. Louis in 1860. In the 1860 census, the two Keller households were next door to Charles and Ermina's daughter Susan and her husband, William Austin. When E.C. Heiskell enlisted in the Confederate army, he named his place of residence as Independence, Missouri.[96] Heiskell's daughter, Price, age 18, was living in the Edmond Price household in Westport, Missouri.[97] Charles Keller's business partner and brother-in-law, Silas Price, died in 1858,[98] and his family remained in Cass County. Connie Price, Price family researcher, quoted Silas' grandson as saying that Silas' early death to disease left his wife and children alone on their plantation near Harrisonville. They moved into town during this time because of the violence around them.

To prepare a report to Missouri Governor Stewart, General Parsons traveled to western Missouri in May 1858 to review the destruction caused by the Jayhawkers. He reported that:

A large strip of country within our state is almost entirely depopulated, our citizens driven from their homes, and in many instances property taken, and they are threatened with death should they return. Many of these men we saw in and about Butler and Harrisonville. Parsons warned Stewart that the local units he was organizing would be insufficient to meet the challenge. The local farmers were so involved in farming and

> located in such widely separated locations that when Montgomery (and the Jayhawkers) crossed the line into Missouri, it would take the men too long to respond to be effective. According to Parsons, "depredations" in these areas had been "going on to a greater or lesser degree for 4 years."[99]

Because they lived so close to the Missouri line, the citizens of Paola were confronted with the lawlessness of the time. As a four year old, Sue Heiskell may have heard her parents worrying about their friends and family in Cass County and their own safety in Paola. Former Lawrence Kansas newspaper editor, G. W. Brown, wrote in later years of his intervention in a Jayhawking incident in Paola. He heard that Captain Snyder and his Jayhawkers had crossed into Missouri and stolen around 100 head of cattle. They announced to residents of Paola that they planned to butcher the cattle and that "all who favored Jayhawking were welcome to all the meat they should want."[100] Brown reported them to the local sheriff, demanding that the men be arrested for theft. The sheriff arrested 16 of the men but later released them all without penalty on their own recognizance. These model citizens then joined the Union Army to continue their activities.[101]

Goodrich described the pervasiveness of carousing and intimidation in the Borderland at this time:

> When a company of Kansas troops paused in Paola before resuming their trek south, the stay more resembled a bushwhacker raid than a visit by U.S. soldiers. According to a local editor: 'Their conduct was disgraceful in the extreme- they were drunken, ruffianly and brutal.-They beat citizens over the heads with revolvers whenever they happened to see one and were near enough to strike. They . . . presented revolvers at the breasts of several of our merchants, fired off their pistols on the streets and in the saloons, insulted grossly an old lady in one of the stores, and, in fact, did every mean

act their brutal and ruffianly natures suggested. The captain either could not or would not, or at least did not, control them or attempt to do so–in fact he indulged largely in the indiscriminate abuse . . . God save us from another visit . . . ,"102

The fledgling frontier town did not have the resources or ready access to protection from the poorly controlled soldiers. The residents lived at the beginning of the wild west.

For the next few years, little Sue Heiskell's family and neighbors in Paola experienced both the famine and the danger posed by Jayhawkers. Paola citizen McLachlin noted, "During the exciting times between 1856 and 1860, Miami County was the scene of bloody warfare between the Free-state and the proslavery men, which later on during the Civil War was engendered by the horrors of guerrillas and jayhawkers in almost daily conflict . . . ." He continued, "With the year 1860 came the famine, and hustlers for Pomeroy's beans and old clothes showed up in force. Aid was given from the room on the northeast corner and was quite a help to some although like all charities it was greatly abused."[103]

Another source of tension in Paola that year was William Quantrill's arrest. Quantrill had come to the Kansas Territory from Ohio to farm, later securing a teaching post in Stanton, 11 miles from Paola. In 1858, Quantrill wrote his mother expressing outrage at the high-jacked Lecompton election, but in two years, his ideas had changed dramatically. He wrote his mother in January, 1860,

> *You have undoubtedly heard of the wrongs committed in this territory by the southern people, or proslavery party, but when one knows the facts they can easily see that it has been the opposite party that have been the main movers in the troubles and by far the most lawless set of people in the country. They are all sympathetic for old J. Brown, who should have been hung years ago, indeed hanging was too good for him. May I never see*

a more contemptible people than those who sympathize for him. A murderer and a robber made a martyr of, just think of it.[104]

Gilmore notes that historians' views of Quantrill are, to this day, divided between those seeing him as a thief and murderer and those seeing him as a guerrilla fighter motivated by protecting Missouri residents against jayhawkers.[105] In 1929, junior high school students in Paola interviewed an "early pioneer" of the town about Quantrill. The pioneer settler responded with a description of a disturbed, violent boy:

Quantrill was a homeless waif who was taken to raise by Mrs. Wagstaff who at one time was Mrs. Torrey. Many of our citizens know of the old Wagstaff Place just west of the south bridge. Quantrill became so unruly that Mrs. Wagstaff could not control him. When just a lad he is said to have pinned live snakes to trees with nails. He went into Missouri, collected a group of border ruffians and then often came into Kansas to raid. Some one squealled on him and he was arrested and placed in jail in Paola. As they did not have enough evidence to hold him, he was released.[106]

The settler's memory of Quantrill stands out in stark contrast to Gilmore's description as well as the description of Quantrill's release from jail in Stanton. The terror his name must have engendered for her as a child fearing his raids and violence created the myth of his being an incorrigible orphan.

Certainly Quantrill's actions in 1860 were confusing. As he moved between and seemed to befriend both jayhawk and southern-sympathizing groups, he took part in raids into Missouri but also warned Missourians and proslavery citizens in Kansas of impending raids on them. His one-time friends from both groups reported to Quantrill biographers that Quantrill was involved as an agent and counter-spy for proslavery advocates. One of them, W.I. Potter, who held positions as deputy U.S. marshal, deputy sheriff and jailer near Paola, said that "in the fall of 1860, he (Quantrill) was involved in a meeting held at the Union Hotel in Paola in which only men opposed to Jayhawking attended 'by special invitation.'"[107] Quantrill told the group that a raid on Paola was in the works and that the plan was to rob a gold shipment on the Kansas City, Paola, and Fort Scott stage destined for Col. Seth Clover, agent to the Miami Indians. The Paola men then arranged for the gold shipment to be guarded by a company of U.S. infantrymen.

Later, Quantrill was detained in Stanton by Capt. Snyder, the same Kansas militiaman—jayhawker—who arrested David Lykins a few months later. A posse from Paola raced to Stanton to Quantrill's rescue. One of the rescuing posse members was Dr. W.D. Hoover, the husband of Emeline Heiskell's cousin Mary and a respected member of the Paola community.[108] Family members in Paola and Missouri had chosen, or were thrown into, complex and dangerous alliances in a border conflict soon to be expanded to national warfare.

As the country teetered on the edge of the Civil War, the events in the Borderland foreshadowed the national trauma of the Civil War. When Walt Whitman heard of John Brown's capture after his raid on Harper's Ferry, he worried that the militancy of the abolitionists would lead the nation into civil war. "If things go on at this rate," he jotted in his notebook, "the Union is threatened with a destiny horrible as it is altogether a novelty, something that never happened to any nation before–it is likely to be saved to death."[109]

Charles Sumner, Republican senator, predicted that the Civil War which would have "an accumulated wickedness beyond that of any war in human annals." Looking at it retrospectively, he was right: the Civil War would be the "bloodiest conflict in history (in which more Americans died than in all the nation's other wars *combined*.)"[110] The Union armies had between 2,500,000-2,750,000 soldiers; their loss would be: 110,070 on the battlefield and 251,152 from disease for a combined total of 360,222 or more than 13% of all

Union soldiers. Of roughly 750,000 -1,250,000 Confederates, 94,000 would die in battle and 164,000 of disease with a combined total of 258,000 or more than 20% of all Confederate soldiers.[111]

Men in the Lykins and Heiskell families—David Lykins, Dr. Hoover, Johnston, William Heiskell and his sons, Joseph and his sons, Claiborne and his sons and their nephews and cousins in other states—were about to be thrown into the teeth of a horrific war. The allegiances they held and the decisions they made changed their lives forever. Of the nineteen men in the Lykins/Heiskell extended family who enlisted in the Civil War armies, five of them died by the end of the war (26%) with several others suffering life-long effects of disease, wounds, and alienation from their families.

---

1. Nicole Etcheson, *Bleeding Kansas: Contested Liberty in the Civil War Era* (Lawrence, Kansas: University Press of Kansas, 2004), 36-37.
2. Thomas Goodrich, *War to the Knife: Bleeding Kansas, 1854-1861* (Mechanicsburg, Pennsylvania: Stackpole Books, 1998), 12.
3. Goodrich, *War to the Knife*, 13.
4. "Pioneer Kansan Dies Here: Emmaline Heiskell Was Niece of Kansas City's First Mayor," *Kansas City Times*, 4 Aug 1916, p. 2.
5. Etcheson, *Bleeding Kansas*, 68-70.
6. U.S. Congress, *Report of the United States Congress House Special Committee Appointed to Investigate the Troubles in Kansas*, 34th Congress, 1st session, House Report 200 (Washington, D.C.: Cornelius Wendell, 1856), serial 869, p. 596-597.
7.. Etcheson, *Bleeding Kansas*, 222, 62.
8. William E. Connelley, *History of Kansas, State and People* (Chicago: American Historical Society, 1928), 1: 410, 466-469.
9. Ely Moore, Jr., "The Story of Lecompton, An Address at an Old Settlers' Meeting in Lecompton, 1907," *Collections of the Kansas State Historical Society, 1909-1910*, editor, George W. Martin (Topeka: State Printing Office, 1910), 11: 464.
10. Martha A. (Livingston) Lykins Bingham, "Recollections of Old Times in Kansas City," 67-page, handwritten manuscript, ca 1883 - 1890. Jackson County Historical Society Archives, Independence, Missouri, Gift of Robert Dewit Owen, in memory of his grandmother, Mrs. Dewit Livingston (Ada Campbell) Owen, Document ID 110F7.
11. Mattie Livingston Lykins Bingham, "Recollections of Old Times in Kansas City."

12. Wendell H. Stephenson, "Reeder, Andrew Horatio," *Dictionary of American Biography*, Dumas Malone, editor (New York: Charles Scribner's Sons, 1935), 15: 463.
13. "M.A. Bingham is Dead," *Kansas City Times*, 21 Sept 1890, 6:1.
14. "Samuel Lyle Adair 1811-1898," Personalities, *Territorial Kansas Online, 1854-1861: a Virtual Repository for Territorial Kansas History* (www.territorialkansasonline.org: accessed 14 Apr 2008).
15. David S. Reynolds, *John Brown, Abolitionist: The Man Who Killed Slavery, Sparked the Civil War and Seeded Civil Rights* (New York, Alfred A. Knopf, 2005), 152.
16. Reynolds, *John Brown, Abolitionist*, 135.
17. Reynolds, *John Brown, Abolitionist*, 145.
18. Goodrich, *War to the Knife*, 96.
19. "The Crisis in Kansas," *New York Daily Times*, 11 Sept 1855, 4:a.
20. C. W. Dana, *The Garden of the World or the Great West; Its History, Its Wealth, Its Natural Advantages, and Its Future. Also Comprising a Complete Guide to Emigrants, with a Full Description of the Different Routes Westward* (Boston: Wentworth and Company, 1856), 198.
21. William E. Connelley, *History of Kansas, State and People*, 1: 410, 466-469.
22. Correspondent "W," clipping from Boston *Daily Evening Traveller*, 13 Feb 1857; Webb Scrapbooks, vol. 9, p. 115, Kansas State Historical Society Library and Archives, Topeka, Kansas; as cited by James C. Malin, "Judge Lecompte and the 'Sack of Lawrence,' May 21, 1856," *Kansas Historical Quarterly* 10 (Aug 1953), 478.
23. Correspondent "W," clipping from *Boston Daily Evening Traveller*, as cited in Malin, "Judge Lecompte," 478.
24. Malin, "Judge Lecompte and the 'Sack of Lawrence,' " 465.
25. Malin, "Judge Lecompte and the 'Sack of Lawrence,' " 1-2.
26. Goodrich, *War to the Knife*, 123.
27. Reynolds, *John Brown, Abolitionist*, 166.
28. Goodrich, *War to the Knife*, 123.
29. Goodrich, *War to the Knife*, 123.
30. Reynolds, *John Brown, Abolitionist*, 167.
31. Goodrich, *War to the Knife*, 128.
32. Goodrich, *War to the Knife*, 128.
33. Goodrich, *War to the Knife*, 128.
34. Oswald Garrison Villard, *John Brown, 1800-1859, A Biography Fifty Years After* (New York: Alfred A. Knopf, 1943), 255.
35. Marilyn Getty, Barbara Rentenbach, and Dick Taylor, "The Browns," Biographies, Resource Articles, *The Kansas Collection: Letting the Voices of the Past Be Heard*, (www.KanCol.org: accessed on 22 Feb 2008).

36. "Another Revolutionary Patriot Gone," *Winchester* [Virginia] *Gazette*, 3 Aug 1822. Heiskell, Adam: obituary transcript, MMF-39 THL; Stewart Bell Archives, Handley Regional Library, Winchester, Virginia.
37. Reynolds, *John Brown, Abolitionist*, 186-187. See also "The Battle of Black Jack, Kansas Territory, June 2, 1856," The Black Jack Battlefield Trust, *Black Jack Battlefield and Nature Park* (http://www.blackjackbattlefield.org/battle.html : accessed 15 Mar 2007).
38. F. B. Sanborn, *The Life and Letters of John Brown: Liberator of Kansas, and Martyr of Virginia* (1885; reprinted New York: Negro Universities Press, 1969), 300-301.
39. Villard, *John Brown*, 194-195.
40. Goodrich, *War to the Knife*, 128.
41. Cutler, *History of the State of Kansas*, 135.
42. Goodrich, *War to the Knife*, 129.
43. Probate Judge George Wilson to Governor John W. Geary, petition, Correspondence of Kansas Governors, Kansas State Historical Society, Topeka, Kansas; quoted in James C. Malin, "Judge Lecompte and the 'Sack of Lawrence,' May 21, 1856," *Kansas Historical Quarterly* 10 (Aug 1953), 478.
44. General William A. Heiskell to Governor John W. Geary, letter, 25 Sept 1856; Correspondence of Kansas Governors; Malin, *John Brown*, 647-648.
45. Malin, *John Brown*, 648.
46. Malin, *John Brown*, 649.
47. Malin, *John Brown*, 649.
48. Malin, *John Brown*, 650.
49. Dale Watts, "How Bloody was Bleeding Kansas? Political Killings in Kansas Territory, 1854-1861," *Kansas History: a Journal of the Central Plains* 18 (Summer, 1995):25.
50. *Leavenworth Kansas Weekly Herald,* 4 Oct 1856, np, cited in Goodrich, *War to the Knife*, 165-166.
51. Goodrich, *War to the Knife*, 166.
52. Goodrich, *War to the Knife*, 166.
53. Donald Gilmore, *Civil War on the Missouri-Kansas Border* (Gretna, Louisiana: Pelican Publishing, 2006), 9.
54. Goodrich, *War to the Knife*, 135.
55. Reynolds, *John Brown, Abolitionist*, 164-165.
56. Goodrich, *War to the Knife*, 135-136.
57. Goodrich, *War to the Knife*, 145.
58. Goodrich, *War to the Knife*, 168.
59. Goodrich, *War to the Knife*, 171.
60. Gilmore, *Civil War*, 76-78.
61. House Committee of Claims, "Kansas Claims," House Report 104, *Reports of Committees of the House of Representatives, Made during the Second Session of the*

Thirty-Sixth Congress, 1860-'61. (Washington, D.C.: Government Printing Office, 1861), serial 1106, pt. 1, p. 797-803, Claim No. 187 (Stephen J. Livingston), and Claim No. 188 (Martin Young), both 22 Apr 1859.
62. House Committee of Claims, "Kansas Claims," p. 794-797, Claim No. 186 (Ann Hopper), 22 Apr 1859.
63. House Committee of Claims, "Kansas Claims," p. 800, Claim No. 187 (Stephen J. Livingston), 22 Apr 1859.
64. House Committee of Claims, "Kansas Claims," p. 798, Claim No. 187 (Stephen J. Livingston), 22 Apr 1859, deposition of Stephen J. Livingston.
65. House Committee of Claims, "Kansas Claims," p. 798-799, Claim No. 187 (Stephen J. Livingston), 22 Apr 1859, list of losses.
66. John H. Gihon, *Geary and Kansas–Governor Geary's Administration in Kansas with complete History of the Territory until June 1857* (Philadelphia: J. H. C. Whiting, 1857), 120.
67. Alice Nichols, *Bleeding Kansas* (New York: Oxford University Press, 1954), 152-153.
68. Nichols, *Bleeding Kansas*, 153.
69. Colonel Richard J. Hinton, Journal, entry for 3 Sept 1857; Kansas State Historical Society; Topeka, Kansas, quoted in Villard, *John Brown*, 258.
70. Nichols, *Bleeding Kansas*,155.
71. Villard, *John Brown*, 257.
72. Richard J. Hinton, *John Brown and His Men, with Some Account of the Roads They Traveled to Reach Harper's Ferry* (New York: Funk and Wagnalls, 1894), 49-50. Villard, in *John Brown*, 259n, wrote, "Hinton wrote to W. E. Connelley, June 9, 1900, that the account given of Brown's speech 'is accurate. I took it down in shorthand. I am a stenographer. I was by his side.'"
73. Quoted in Nichols, *Bleeding Kansas*, 157. Nichols supplies no sources for her quotations.
74. Nichols, *Bleeding Kansas*, 157.
75. David R. Atchison, in Richmond *Enquirer*, 26 June 1857, np; quoted in Kenneth M. Stampp, *America in 1857–A Nation on the Brink* (New York: Oxford University Press, 1990), 148.
76. Goodrich, *War to the Knife*, 197-198.
77. Jeremy Neely, *The Border Between Them: Violence and Reconciliation on the Kansas-Missoui Line* (Columbia, Missouri: University of Missouri Press, 2007), 63-64.
78. Henry Marshall McLachlin, "Retrospect," *The Story of Paola, Kansas, 1857-1950*, Berenice Boyd Wallace, compiler, (Paola, Kansas?: np, 1951?), 2-3.
79. Miami County Historical Society, *Paola, Kansas, a 150 Year Timeline: One Hundred and Fifty Years of History Events That Made Paola What It Is Today* (Paola, Kansas: Miami County Historical Society, 2006), 24.
80. *Paola Kansas*, 23.

81. Gilmore, *Civil War*, 164-66.
82. Elizabeth E. Barnes, "Historic Johnson County," 1969, cited in *Paola Kansas*, 21.
83. Gilmore, *Civil War*, 164; *Paola Kansas*, 23.
84. McLachlin, "Retrospect," 97.
85. "History of Paola," undated clipping from unidentified newspaper name, History of Paola file, Paola Free Library, Paola, Kansas.
86. "History of Paola."
87. H. M. McLachlin as cited in Berenice Wallace, *History of Paola, Kansas, 1855-1955* (Paola, Kansas: Miami County Historical and Genealogical Society, [1955?]), 97.
88. 1860 US Census, Paola, Lykins County, Kansas, p. 40, dwelling 284, Wm. A. Haskell household.
89. 1860 US Census, St. Louis, Missouri, p.135, dwelling 630, Charles Keller household, William Austin household and William Keller household.
90. Gilmore, *Civil War*, 53.
91. Kenneth L. Lyftogt, "Grinnell, Josiah Bushnell (1822-1891): Iowa Abolitionist, Republican Congressman," *Encyclopedia of the American Civil War: a Political, Social, and Military History*, eds. David S. Heidler and Jeanne T. Heidler (Santa Barbara, California: ABC-CLIO, 2000), 2: 896.
92. Gilmore, *Civil War*, 9.
93. Gilmore, *Civil War*, 90-91.
94. Thomas Goodrich, *Black Flag: Guerrilla Warfare on the Western Border, 1861-1865: A Riveting Account of a Bloody Chapter in Civil War History* (Bloomington, Indiana: Indiana University Press, 1999), 7.
95. 1860 U.S. Census, Ward 3, Saint Louis (Independent City), Missouri, p. 135, dwelling 630, Charles Keller household.
96. Office of Adjutant General, Index of Service Records, Confederate, 1861-1865, Box 103, Reel s732, Missouri Soldiers (1861-1865) War Between the States; Missouri State Archives' Soldiers Database: War of 1812–World War I (http:www.sos.mo.gov/archives/ : accessed on 12 Oct 2008).
97. 1860 US Census, Fourth Ward, Westport, Jackson County, Missouri, p. 134, dwelling 1138, Ed Price household.
98. Connie Price, interview by Rose Ann Findlen, 24 Oct 2006; interview notes in possession of author.
99. Gilmore, *Civil War*, 93.
100. G. W. Brown to Mr. Field, letter, 7 Sept 1903; Box 2, MS Collection 297, Box 2; Kansas State Historical Society, Topeka Kansas.
101. G. W. Brown to Mr. Field, 7 Sept 1903.
102. Goodrich, *Black Flag*, 118.
103. McLachlin, "A Retrospect," 98.

104. William C. Quantrill to Caroline Cornelia Clark, letter, 26 Jan 1860; Quantrill Papers, Kansas State Historical Society, Topeka, Kansas; cited in Donald L. Gilmore, *Civil War on the Missouri-Kansas Border* (Gretna, Louisiana: Pelican Publishing, 2006), 168.
105. Gilmore, *Civil War*, 303.
106. "History of Paola," undated clipping, unidentified newspaper, Paola vertical file; Paola Free Library, Paola, Kansas.
107. William Elsey Connelly, *Quantrill and the Border Wars* (Cedar Rapids, Iowa: Torch Press, 1910), 191.
108. Connelly, *Quantrill and the Border Wars*, 187.
109. Catherine Reef, *Walt Whitman* (New York: Clarion Books, 2002), 62.
110. Reynolds, *John Brown, Abolitionist*, 95-96.
111. "The Price in Blood! Casualties in the Civil War," Civil War Potpourri, Shotgun's Home of the Civil War (http://www.civilwarhome.com/casualties: accessed on 17 Feb 2008).

CHAPTER 4

Friends and Family in the Civil War

For Emeline and her cousins, the moment after which nothing would ever be the same would surely have been the opening of hostilities at Fort Sumter. In November, 1860, Abraham Lincoln was narrowly elected, having received only 40% of the popular vote and by the end of the year, South Carolina had seceded from the Union and six other states followed within six months, selecting Jefferson Davis as their president. Emeline's relatives in Kansas and her cousins in Illinois and Indiana were sucked into the violent vortex of the war, whether on the battlefield or in the politics and violence of their home towns.

In addition to the secession of several states from the Union and the ensuing Civil War, other life-changing events were taking place in the lives of Emeline and her Paola relatives. As she and other Paola residents coped with rampant jayhawking and famine, Emeline again became pregnant. On August 13, 1860, she gave birth to a second daughter, Alberta.[1] Her brother, David Peery, married Baptiste Peoria's daughter in that same year.[2] Her Uncle David's second wife, Sarah Tull, had apparently died, because he married her sister, Grace, in December, 1860.[3] William's son Charles was living with Emeline and William in Paola.[4]

Emeline Heiskell's Relatives during Civil War 1861-1865

Lykins

Eliza L. Ferguson (Illinois)	Cynthia L. Earnest (Indiana)	Julia L. Betteys (Iowa)	Claiborne Lykins (Missouri)	David Lykins (Kansas)	Joseph Lykins (Kansas)
-David Ferguson	-Willis Earnest	-Frank Betteys	-Andrew Lykins	-Wayland Lykins	-James Lykins
			-David A. Lykins	-Edward Lykins	-W.D. Hoover (son-in-law)

Wm. Heiskell

- E. C. Heiskell
- Charles Heiskell
- Sue Austin = -William F. Heiskell (Wallace)

William T. Wallace

- Dana Wallace
- William F. Wallace

Baptiste Peoria, Chief of the Five Tribes (Peoria, Wea, Piankeshaw, Kaskaskia and Miami), near Paola

Five Civilized Tribes: Choctaw and Chickasaw (predominantly pro-Confederacy); Creek and Seminole (predominantly pro-Union); Cherokee (divided loyalties), located in Southeastern Kansas Territory

Captain Ely Snyder, Free State militia leader

William T. Wallace and sons Dana and William F. (future in-laws of Emeline Heiskell) located in New Hampshire

Ongoing Border Conflict

The ongoing border conflicts provided tangible evidence of the devastation Johnston Lykins feared would rain down on Missouri if the state seceded. Jayhawker and bushwhacker actions were frequent and violent in 1861. Each group identified people they deemed enemies, attacking and harassing them: along the border, Missourians wanted Unionist farmers to leave; Kansans wanted to see the last of southern sympathizers. Among smaller towns in Southeastern Kansas, Paola stood out as a "Southern Stronghold" and the place where Jason Brown was almost hanged; the town's proximity to Cass County made it a prime target for violent and intimidating tactics as the war broke out. Paradoxically, the proximity of Paola to the Missouri border also made it a place of refuge for Unionist farmers fleeing Missouri. The year before, Unionists had begun to leave Cass County to find safer places; many arrived in eastern Kansas with only the personal items they could carry. "Struck by the poignant situations of Missouri Unionists filtering into the town of Paola, one correspondent noted, 'Our town is full to overflowing of poor miserable wretches begging for food to keep them alive.'"[5] Similarly, Jayhawkers targeted southern sympathizers in Paola and attempted to drive them out of Kansas.

David Lykins and His Family Flee Kansas

Even as Johnston graphically described the suffering and destruction that secession would bring to Missouri, his brother on the Kansas side of the Borderland was drawn into the conflict. In June, 1861, an associate of John Brown's, Captain Eli Snyder, and his band went to Wea Mission where David Lykins lived a mile outside Paola and arrested him as a Southern sympathizer. "Captain" Snyder was a blacksmith and Jayhawk leader of a band chasing down and fighting proslavery guerrillas such as the notorious Charles Hamilton of Georgia.⁶ In those times, guerrilla bands of both Free-state and Southern sympathies roamed the countryside gathering the names of suspected perpetrators of violence and theft on the opposing side. Snyder and his men marched Lykins into Paola. Behind the scenes, Lykins' oil-prospecting colleague from Lawrence, G.W. Brown, quietly interceded in Lykins' behalf. Because of Brown's earlier intervention in the butchering of stolen cattle from Missouri, Snyder's men disliked him and it was only by talking quietly with the sheriff that Brown could get David released. In his letter describing the incident in 1903, Brown wrote that Lykins had been addicted to opium for some time and was "hardly responsible for his actions." He cited an event in which Lykins, unable to obtain opium at that time, went into a frenzy, demanding to be baptized into the Catholic Church, a surprising action by a Baptist missionary.⁷ The 1929 chronicling of the History of Paola stated that because David Lykins was Southern sympathizer, the land he lived on at Wea Mission was taken from him.⁸

    Lykins realized that his life was in danger. The Free-state settlers, who were now in the majority in Paola, lost no time in re-naming the county originally named for him, the first white settler. "Lykins County" became "Miami County" in July 1861, when Kansas became a state. A 1937 interview with Florence Wade, daughter of one of Baptiste's closest friends suggests additional detail about David's departure and the difficulties the boys experienced: "Dr. Lykins, (who) was a Baptist Minister preached among the Peoria in Kansas but a difference arose between him and Peoria Baptiste over a negro that Lykins tried to get into the Chief's home, so Dr. Lykins took his two sons, Wyland [sic.] . . . and Ed, and started to California.⁹ David's loss of loved ones, his earlier good name, his political viewpoint, his Wea Mission, and his increasingly problematic handling of his loss and pain by opium use left no good reasons for him to stay around Paola. He had to leave.

Shortly after his release from jail, Lykins and his son Wayland left Kansas for California. David became ill on his way there and died in Colorado.[10] David's death may have been caused, directly or indirectly, by his addiction. As a physician, David had easy access to opiates and, in the mid-nineteenth century, doctors prescribed it liberally for ailments ranging from babies' teething to insomnia to emotional and physical pain.

Opium addiction was so prevalent among Civil War soldiers that it was called "the soldier's disease."

Physicians in blue and gray prescribed opium for diarrhea and dysentery, arguably the two greatest causes of death in the war. One Confederate surgeon revealed just how freely opium was dispensed for intestinal ailments. While on his march he carried in one pocket a ball of a laxative called blue mass, and in the other a ball of opium. Each morning at sick call he would first ask each soldier: "How are your bowels? If they were open, I administered a plug of opium, if they were shut I gave a plug of blue mass." Given the commonplace occurrence of malaria, dysentery, and the "Tennessee Trots" and the cavalier issuance of opium, one can understand the ease with which troops on both sides of the conflict contracted the "soldier's disease."… There are also references to women and men committing suicide during the war by taking overdoses of laudanum.[11]

An 1859 cartoon in the *Harper's Weekly* pictured a sedated baby being tended by a big bottle of opium with the caption, "The Poor Child's Nurse."[12]

When David died at 40 of an unidentified illness, his thirteen-year old son Wayland, eight-year-old son Edward and his wife of eight months had to fend for themselves. What became of Grace Tull, Wayland and Edward's step-mother of only eight months, and whether she and David's sons were together in the Colorado Territory is unknown; there is no mention of her in family stories and notes about that time period. If Emeline knew of the plight of the little boys she had helped raise and her tormented

OPIUM—THE POOR CHILD'S NURSE.

young Uncle's untimely death, the situation must have caused her and other family members a great deal of heartache and many sleepless nights. Where were the boys? What was happening to them?

In 1863, Wayland, who had accompanied his father to the Colorado Territory, joined a surveying party for a preliminary survey of the United States Railroad; from there, he went to the Arkansas River where he herded sheep one winter. He began a survey from Pueblo to Canyon City, Colorado, before returning to

Paola to learn the retail business.[13] According to Wayland's death announcement, he even served for a time under General Custer (long before the Battle of Little Big Horn).

Florence Wade's recollection of the boys' return to Kansas suggested that the entire family started out for California. She recalled that the two boys in their early teens made their way on foot back to the friendly Peorias and when they arrived, they were barefoot and destitute. They were taken in and cared for; one was given a job in a store and the younger sent to school. Both were later adopted by the tribe.[14] Some of this detail is corroborated by Gideon's biographical sketch of Wayland Lykins, which indicates that Wayland stayed in Paola for a time with W.D. Hoover (a cousin's husband) and tried to study law, which he did not like, and turned to the retail business.[15]

It seems that Edward may have lived with his cousin, David Peery, after returning to Paola, because there was a lifelong bond between the two. When Peery moved to the Oklahoma Territory after the war, Edward was sent ahead of the family to prepare for their arrival.[16] After a six-month stint in the "Indian Wars" in the 19th Kansas Cavalry,[17] Edward established his roots in the Oklahoma Indian Territory, farming land originally owned by Peery and marrying Sara Whitefeather, a woman of the Miami Tribe.[18]

The Heiskells in Paola

Heaped on top of David's notoriety, arrest, departure, and death were other frightening, sad events in 1861. Emeline and William's second daughter, Alberta, died at the age of eight months that April[19] and, a few weeks later, Emeline was again pregnant. The family's anxiety level must have been high: because of Heiskell's prominence in the First Kansas Legislature and the march on Lawrence, he would need to be *unobtrusive* to the Jayhawkers feverishly hunting down Southern sympathizers. The famine and the chaos around Paola could not have contributed to either Emeline's or her daughters' health. To lose a baby then have another child on the way must have anguished and frightened them.

In February 1862, Sue Heiskell had a new baby sister, Nellie,[20] as violence from all sides escalated around them. Military leaders along the border were frustrated at their inability to contain the guerrilla fighters and instituted an Oath of Loyalty aimed at identifying those suspected of supporting Quantrill and other guerrillas.[21] A former Jackson County magistrate, Robert Smart, hid from federal troops for several weeks to avoid taking the oath. Elvira Scott, writing from Miami County in the summer of that year described 50-100 federal troops chasing him down and shooting him to death: "The men [i.e., citizens] seemed so horror stricken that they dared not go to him. And then these 'brave soldiers' of their great nation formed in line by the dying man. He was old, helpless, & unarmed. What a victory on this bright sabbath day!"[22]

Roundups and murders were common on both the Kansas and Missouri sides of the Borderland. "Southern sympathizers and proslavery holdouts from the territorial days were... ready targets in Kansas."[23] Julia Lovejoy's son Charles, a Federal officer stationed at Paola, was awakened one night by two men who determined that "he was not the man they wanted." In an adjacent room they found two men and forced them to accompany them. The next morning a soldier walking in the woods "saw a human hand protruding from a hastily dug grave, and there was one of the men dead, shot through the head."[24] Emeline's Uncle David had narrowly escaped a similar fate when he was arrested the previous year. As well-known proslavery advocates, other family members such as her husband and her cousin's husband, W.D. Hoover, would have been in constant danger.

Baptiste Peoria's Involvement with Native American Unionists and Secessionists

Native Americans living in the Kansas Territory were dragged into the Civil War. The Kansas-Nebraska Act had divided the Kansas Indian Territory into two parts. The northern tribes were part of the Kansas and Nebraska territories. These tribes of the Old Northwest were weak and disorganized; federal agents could easily talk them into "surrendering their communally owned reservations and accepting individual allotments."[25] Unionist Jim Lane envisioned recruiting men from the tribes to join bands of jayhawkers;[26] the Confederates, meanwhile, wanted to create a home guard among the groups inhabiting the southern portion of the Kansas Territory,[27] where the Indian inhabitants were more sympathetic with Confederates' views on slavery. Trying to avoid violent encounters, owners of trading posts sold arms and food to both sides.[28] *The Daily Conservative* reported that the "Wea, Piankeshaws, Peorias and Miamies wanted to enlist in the Union Army because "the Missourians would not leave them alone."[29] Indian agents in southern counties reported that Indian traders of southern sympathy were telling Indians that the northern armies would drive them from their homes and take away their slaves[30]. The tribes who had emigrated from the northern parts of the U.S., such as the Miami tribes, often identified with the Union while those who had come to the Kansas Territory from the southern states, such as the Cherokee and Creek, followed the cultural practices of their white counterparts.[31]

In the southwestern corner of the state, Indian traders of southern sympathy worked hard to recruit the "Five Civilized Tribes" (the Cherokee, Choctaw, Chickasaw, Creek and Seminole tribes originating in the Southeastern United States) to fight alongside them. One of these traders was Asbury M. Coffey, a man who had joined with David Lykins, Baptiste Peoria and Isaac Jacobs to incorporate the town of Paola six years earlier.[32] Coffey had been an Indian agent for the Miamis, Wea, Piankeshaw, Kaskaskia and Peorias at the Osage River Agency, so Baptiste knew him well.[33] The Confederate and Indian secessionist forces took control of the five tribes' allotted lands and demanded that all tribal members supporting the Union leave. An elderly chief of the Muskegee band of the Creek nation, Opothleyaholo, refused to secede and the Muskegee were expelled from their land. They began to make their way north to federal protection in Kansas in November, 1861.[34] Political wrangling in Washington and bureaucratic incompetence resulted in horrific loss and suffering for this loyal band.

A group of Sac and Fox buffalo hunters came across the Muskegee refugees two months later. They had traveled over 250 miles from North Fork Town in the Creek Nation.

The group of several hundred men, women and children were a small part of the survivors of three battles against the Confederate forces of Colonels Douglas Cooper, Stand Watie and James McIntosh in Indian Territory. In each battle they had lost possessions, food, cattle and ponies until they were destitute, bereft of any sustenance. The Indians' trail to freedom had been marked with bloody footprints and strewn with unburied bodies. Many had frozen to death and were left to be devoured by the wolves that paralleled their path. Babies were born and died in the snow.[35]

The Sac and Fox hunters gave the refugees as much food as they could and told settlers all along the trail ahead of them that the Muskegee were coming that way, but there was not enough to feed them all. By the time the group reached the Verdigris River in Wilson County, Kansas, many more had suffered frostbite, amputations, disease, starvation and exposure to rotting carcasses of their remaining horses. In all, more than 8,000 refugees struggled northward from the Indian Territory seeking protection.[36]

Officers at the area's federal forts sent contaminated bacon. It was not good enough for their troops, but good enough for the Indians. While the Indians sickened and died, the Indian agents dithered in Leavenworth, waiting for the arrival of William Dole, the Commissioner of Indian Affairs. In the first month after their arrival in Wilson County, 240 more Creeks died. Opothleyaholo asked Washington to let General Lane lead them back to their homeland and to let them fight their way home while officials in the War Department competed and postured over whether the loyal Indians could be recruited to fight in the Union Army. One official said yes, then another no; one was in charge one week only to be supplanted and his decision overturned the next week.[37]

In February, 1862, Dole appointed Baptiste Peoria, whom he knew and trusted, to be a U.S. Agent charged with visiting the tribes he could safely reach. Dole wanted Baptiste to tell the Indians that the federal government and the U.S. citizens held them in esteem and would protect those who remained loyal; he also asked Baptiste to assess the condition of the tribes and their loyalty or disloyalty to the Union. Their allegiance, he was to say, would result in the "Great Father" sending his army to protect them.[38] That month Dole was disappointed to receive word from the War Department's newly appointed Secretary of War, Edwin Stanton, that the loyal Indians would not be allowed to enlist in the Union Army and that General Lane would not lead them back to their homeland.[39] The suffering of the Muskegee Creeks would drag on and despite their suffering through remaining loyal to the federal government, they would not be entrusted with arms to defend themselves and recover their farms.

The political backdrop for the decision not to allow loyal Indians to enlist in the U.S. Army was the Battle of Pea Ridge. In March, 1862, three regiments of Cherokee and Creek were engaged in the battle;[40] General Pike of the Confederacy gave the First Cherokee Mounted Rifles the orders to fight as they knew how; they proceeded to do that with a vengeance, fighting guerrilla-style effectively, killing wounded men and mutilating (scalping) prisoners.[41] Commanders of the opposing armies were equally appalled by the brutality of the Cherokee warriors and their defiance (or possibly lack of knowledge) of the white man's conventions of war. The Confederate command realized that the untrained Indians were "quite equal to making their own plans in fighting and were to be relied upon to do things decently and in order."[42] From that point on, Indians were relegated to fighting skirmishes and serving as scouts, instead of engaging in white men's "civilized" war practices.[43]

After returning from his dangerous trip into the Indian Territory, Baptiste sent his report to Dole from Paola on May 1, 1862, giving secessionist numbers and troop locations. He had done what he could to convince the Black Dog and Clamos bands of the Osage that the Rebels would never be able to follow through on their promises to them. "I found the whole country," he reported, "as might have been expected, in a very troublous, disturbed condition—in fact, a reign of lawlessness, violence and terror existing. Suspicion had taken the place of confidence. Spies were watching during daytime, and hired assassins during night, to pick off those whom neither money could buy nor threats silence."[44] Baptiste had returned to Paola unharmed, but the war continued to take its toll on Emeline's family and friends, proslavery and unionist, white and Indian, for three more long years.

Joseph Lykins' Son and Son-in-Law

Two of Emeline's Kansas relatives who enlisted, James F. Lykins and his sister's husband, Woodson D. Hoover, were among the earliest settlers in Paola. James had come to the area with his father, Joseph, in 1855;[45] Dr. W.D. Hoover was Assistant Physician and Surgeon at the Wea Mission under David Lykins in 1856.[46] James initially signed up with Company B of the Second Colorado Cavalry as a volunteer for the New Mexico Campaign to subdue Indians and Confederate guerrillas in that area.[47] Until 1861, Colorado and parts of New Mexico were part of the Kansas Territory, so it is not so unlikely that borderland men would have been recruited to go to what had so recently been the western part of Kansas.⁴⁸ Like Claiborne Lykins' son, David, James F. Lykins served in the Second Colorado Cavalry and would have been engaged in the pursuit of General Price along with his cousin. James was among the veterans of the Colorado Volunteers of the New Mexico Campaign (1862) whose infantry company was merged with another to form the Second Colorado Cavalry in November, 1863. By the beginning of the new year, the Cavalry was ordered to the Borderland to engage bushwhackers in Jackson, Cass and Bates counties in Missouri. The Governor of the Colorado Territory desperately needed these troops to quell Indian fighters, but the Cavalry's return to Colorado was interrupted by General Price's invasion of Missouri. The Second Colorado Cavalry was attached to Union forces and engaged in the battles of the Little Blue, Westport, Marais des Cygnes, and Mine Creek in October 1864, not far from James' hometown.⁴⁹

During the war, Joseph's son-in-law, W. D. Hoover served as Post Physician in Paola. His enlistment is particularly interesting because of his involvement in Proslavery activities in the years leading up to the war and his having been in Captain Arbuckle's (proslavery) Lykins County Militia.⁵⁰ Writing in 1895-96, W. L. Potter described Quantrill's meeting in Paola with a select number of officials, among them W.D. Hoover:

> It was in the fall of 1860 That a meeting was held up stairs of the Union Hotel in Paola Kan. I was there as well as every one then Present by special invitation. None but those who were known to be opposed to the Jay Hawking carried on by Montgomenry Jennison & Ossawatomie Brown, or John Brown & their followers, were admitted, or know of our Meeting. The following citizens of Paola to my certain knowledge were Present some of whom are still living Dr. W.D. Hoover now in Paola and Geo W. Miller Ex circuit Judge of denver Colorado....Wm C. Quantrell was I introduced him to the citizens. He stated to us that he was at

Lawrence or Topeka Kansas in Nov 1860...Quantrell said that he wanted to get Jennison in a Place where he could either capture or Lawfully kill him...Quantrell stated, at the meeting that the Jayhawkers, while in camp near Osawatomi had contemplated a Raid on Paola, intending to rob the stores and the Town, and also contemplated the Robbing of the Kansas City, Paola & Fort Scott Stage with the money that was expected to be sent to Gen. Clover the agent for the Miami Indians some $30000.[51]

 The following spring, Potter reported that the Hon. George W. Miller "called to me as I was passing Col Torreys Hotel one morning early and handed me a letter from Quantrell stating that he was at Mr. Bannings House, & Surrounded by some 14 Jayhawkers, who were trying to take him a Prisoner on a Fic(ti)tious charge..." Potter gathered W.D. Hoover and a number of other Paola men. "We went there in a sweeping trot in Hacks, Buggies & on Horseback. No one else in town knew where we were going or any thing about our business, until we came back with Quantrell in triumph. We were all armed with Revolvers, Rifles & shot guns, & Plenty of ammunition."[52]

 One explanation for Hoover's subsequent enlistment in the Union Army might be that while he engaged in anti-jayhawker activities, he did not favor secession. A second possibility is that he and his family were in a town now predominantly populated by Free-state settlers and practicing medicine for the post was expedient, both financially and politically. W.D. Hoover remained in Paola following the war, but his brother-in-law, James Lykins, did not. After living a few years in the newly opened Cherokee lands in southern Kansas and in Joplin, Missouri, James returned home to stay with the Hoovers and died there of typhoid-pneumonia eight years after the war's end.

Cousins Back East

Two of Emeline's cousins in Illinois and Indiana enlisted in 1861, a few months after Lincoln's call to arms. Emeline knew one of them, David Ferguson, well, because she stayed with the Ferguson family in 1850, shortly after her father's and brother's deaths.[53] David, the cousin whom Emeline knew as a little boy of 11, signed up in 1861 and marched with his unit to the regiment's winter quarters at Camp Nevin, Kentucky. In two months, he was dead, having succumbed to typhoid malaria.[54] The disease ravaged the soldiers existing there in unsanitary conditions.[55]

Another cousin, Willis Earnest, responded to the call at about the same time and was mustered into Company E, "The Vigo Tigers," 31st Volunteer Indiana Infantry, in September, 1861.[56] Like his cousin David Ferguson, he marched to Kentucky. That fall, the regiment headquartered for the winter in filthy, rat-infested Camp Calhoun, Kentucky. Indiana visitors to the camp returned to their home state and reported the conditions there [misspellings retained]:

> *Morris House*
> *Opposite the Union Depot,*
> *Indianapolis, Ind....Jan. 10....1862*
>
> *To the honorable (Governor, I have been visiting my friends in the 31ˢᵗ reg. At calhoun kentky to my sorrow they are in bad condition of health caused by imprudence incompatincy or neglect of the officers there health is so very bad only near half of the reg is able to turnout to service.... many of the sick and feeble have spent there last money and there friends money to procure some little nourishing food.... we have given our neighbors our friends our sons to our Cuntrys call to put down the rebellion but to see them sick suffer and wast away be negligence or incompatency is more than we are willing to bear.*

The Sanitation Commission made an investigatory trip to the camp that month and wrote an extensive report.[57] Unfortunately, the letter and the report were too late for Willis Earnest. He died of disease at the camp on January 3, 1862, leaving a young wife and two little daughters to fend for themselves back in Indiana.[58]

Disease: the Common Enemy

The Heiskell and Lykins families experienced enormous losses during the war. Over half the men fighting in the Civil War with family connections to Emeline Heiskell or Johnston Lykins were significantly affected by disease or disability; two died in battle. A standard treatment of disease during the Civil War tells us:

> While the average soldier believed the bullet was his most nefarious foe, disease was the biggest killer of the war. Of the Federal dead, roughly three out of five died of disease, and of the Confederate, perhaps two out of three....About half of

the deaths from disease during the Civil War were caused by intestinal disorders, mainly typhoid fever, diarrhea, and dysentery. The remainder died from pneumonia and tuberculosis....

The culprit in most cases of wartime illness, however, was the shocking filth of the army camp itself. An inspector in late 1861 found most Federal camps "littered with refuse, food, and other rubbish, sometimes in an offensive state of decomposition, slops deposited in pits within the camp limits or thrown out of broadcast; heaps of manure and offal close to the camp....

Typhoid fever was even more devastating. Perhaps one-quarter of noncombat deaths in the Confederacy resulted from this disease, caused by the consumption of food or water contaminated by *salmonella* bacteria. Epidemics of malaria spread through camps next to stagnant swamps teeming with *anopheles* mosquito. Although treatment with quinine reduced fatalities, malaria nevertheless struck approximately one quarter of all servicemen; the Union army alone reported one million cases of it during the course of the war....A simple cold often developed into pneumonia, which was the third leading killer disease of the war, after typhoid and dysentery.[59]

The long and short term effects of the war on the soldiers in Emeline's family represent a microcosm of the devastation that the war brought to the nation. The extent of illness and death the family suffered is represented by the chart below.

Whether they lived in Kansas or across the river in Missouri, suffering was the common denominator.

Civil War Soldiers in Emeline Heiskell's Family

Name	Relation	Unit	Condition	Fate
Willis Earnest	Emeline's cousin	31st Vol. Indiana Infantry	disease	died at Camp Calhoun, KY
David Ferguson	(Emeline's cousin)	34th Vol. Illinois Infantry	typhoid fever	died at Camp Nevin, KY
Andrew C. Lykins	(Emeline's cousin)	12th Missouri Cavalry	chronic diarrhea	invalid pension
F. M. Lykins Betteys	(Emeline's cousin)	12th Missouri Cavalry	unknown condition	
Claiborne Lykins	(Emeline's uncle)	1st Missouri Militia Cavalry	"Mania"	arrested & jailed
David A. Lykins	(Emeline's cousin)	2nd Colorado Cavalry	killed in action	
Charles F. Heiskell	(Emeline's stepson)	2nd Bttn. Cav., Missouri St. Mil.	deserted	fate unknown
E.C. Heiskell	Emeline's stepson	3rd Missouri Batt., L. A. (CSA)	POW, Vicksburg	fate unknown
James F. Lykins	(Emeline's cousin)	2nd Colorado Cavalry	typhoid pneumonia	died before age 40, 1873
W.D. Hoover	(Emeline's cousin's Husband)	Kansas militia, Paola post physician	unknown condition	received invalid pension
William T. Wallace	(Emeline's daughter's father-in-law)	2nd New Hampshire Infantry & 1st New Hampshire Cavalry	tuberculosis	died in 1868
William F. Wallace	(Emeline's daughter's first husband)	18th New Hampshire Infantry	malaria, rheumatism	invalid pension
Dana Wallace	(Emeline's daughter's half-brother-in-law)	2nd New Hampshire Infantry	POW, Gettysburg	died in Confederate prison
Judson Owen				

1. Annie Lynch, "Peery Families of Virginia," *Utah Genealogical and Historical Magazine* 3 (July 1917): 125.
2. "Kin of Baptiste Peoria is a Visitor," (Paola, Kansas) *Western Spirit,* 20 June 1966, np, transcription of newspaper clipping, Lykins File, Miami County Historical Society, Paola Kansas.
3. Miami County, Kansas, Record of Marriage Certificate no. 89 (1860), Lykins-Tull; Office of County Clerk, Miami County Courthouse, Paola, Kansas.
4. 1860 US Census, Paola, Lykins County, Kansas, p. 40, dwelling 284, family 278; William A. Haskell household.
5. Jeremy Neely, *The Border Between Them: Violence and Reconciliation on the Kansas-Missoui Line* (Columbia, Missouri: University of Missouri Press, 2007), 108.
6. Leverett Wilson Spring, *Kansas: The Prelude to the War for the Union* (Boston: Houghton Mifflin, 1885), 245-246.
7. G.W. Brown to Mr. Field, letter, Sept 7, 1903; box 2, MS Coll. 297, Kansas State Historical Society Library and Archives, Topeka, Kansas.
8. 1929 clipping from unidentified newspaper, Paola History files, Miami County Historical and Genealogical Society, Paola, Kansas.
9. Florence Wade, interview by Nannie Lee Burns, 21 July 1937; Interview S-149, Indian-Pioneer History, North American Thought and Culture (http://www.alexanderstreet.com : accessed 25 July 2008).
10. Notes on early Paola families, Lykins file, Miami County Historical and Genealogical Society, Paola, Kansas.
11. James B. Jones, "The Use and Abuse of Drugs in Nineteenth-Century Tennessee History*,"* *Every Day in Tennessee History*, *Historical Findings* (www.netowne.com/historical/tennessee/drugs.htm; accessed 12 Mar 2008).
12. "Opium–the Poor Child's Nurse," cartoon, *Harper's Weekly*, 29 Jan 1859 (http://www.harpweek.com/09Cartoon/RelatedCartoon.asp?Month=January&Date= 29; accessed 28 June 2008).
13. Cutler, *History of the state of Kansas*, 1158.
14. Florence Wade, interview, 21 July 1937.
15. D.C. Gideon, *Indian Territory, Descriptive, Biographical and Genealogical . . . with a General History of the Territory* (New York: Lewis Publishing Company, 1901), 444-446.
16. Willis Lykins interview, interview by Nannie Lee Burns, 28 Oct 1937; Indian Pioneer Collection, vol.56, Interview 12029; Manuscript Division, Western History Collections, University of Oklahoma Library, Norman, Oklahoma.
17. Edward W. W. Lykins, (Pvt., Co. L, 19th Cavalry, Indian Wars), certificate 7977; "Civil War Pension Index: General Index to Pension Files, 1861-1934," database, Ancestry.com (http://www.ancestry.com : accessed 12 July 2008).

18. Notes on early Paola families, Lykins file, Miami County Historical and Genealogical Society, Paola, Kansas.
19. Annie Lynch, "Peery Families of Virginia," *Utah Genealogical and Historical Magazine* 3 (July 1917): 125.
20. Lynch, "Peery Families of Virginia," *Utah Genealogical and Historical Magazine* 3 (July 1917): 125.
21. Thomas Goodrich, *Black flag: guerrilla warfare on the western border, 1861-1865* (Bloomington: Indiana University Press, 1995), 44.
22. Goodrich, *Black Flag*, 45.
23. Goodrich, *Black Flag*, 45.
24. Goodrich, *Black Flag*, 45.
25. Arrell Morgan Gibson, *The American Indian: Prehistory to the Present* (Lexington, Massachussetts: D.C. Heath, 1980), 359.
26. Annie Heloise Abel, *The American Indian as Participant in the Civil War* (Cleveland, Ohio: Arthur H. Clark, 1919), 56.
27. Abel, *The American Indian as Participant in the Civil War*, 23.
28. Florence Wade, interview, 21 July 1937.
29. *The* [Leavenworth] *Daily Conservative*, 9 Feb, 1862, np, cited in Abel, *The American Indian as Participant in the Civil War*, 77.
30. Baptiste Peoria, Letter to G. A. Colton, Indian Agent, 1 May 1862; Document No. 34, *Report of the Commissioner of Indian Affairs for the Year 1862* (Washington, D.C.: Government Printing Office, 1863), 173.
31. Gibson, *The American Indian*, 367.
32. Miami County Historical Society, *Paola, Kansas, a 150 Year Timeline: One Hundred and Fifty Years of History Events That Made Paola What It Is Today* (Paola, Kansas: Miami County Historical Society, 2006), 22.
33. Lela J. McBride, *Opothleyaholo and the Loyal Muskogee: Their Flight to Kansas in the Civil War* (Jefferson, North Carolina, McFarland and Company, 2000), 179.
34. McBride, *Opothleyaholo and the Loyal Muskogee*, 7.
35. McBride, *Opothleyaholo and the Loyal Muskogee*, 7-8.
36. McBride, *Opothleyaholo and the Loyal Muskogee*, 8.
37. McBride, *Opothleyaholo and the Loyal Muskogee*, 179.
38. William P. Dole, Commissioner of Indian Affairs, to Baptiste Peoria, letter no. 33, 10 Feb 1862; Document No. 33, *Report of the Commissioner of Indian Affairs for the Year 1862* (Washington, D.C.: Government Printing Office, 1863), 171.
39. Caleb B. Smith, Interior Secretary, to William P. Dole, Commissioner of Indian Affairs, telegram, 6 Feb 1862, 11 Feb 1862, and 14 Feb 1862, Document No. 201, Southern Superintendency; Special Files, 1833-1907, Records of the Indian Division, Office of the Secretary of the Interior, Record Group 48; National

Archives, Washington, D.C; cited in Abel, *The American Indian as Participant in the Civil War*, 76.
40. Abel, *The American Indian as Participant in the Civil War*, 30.
41. Abel, *The American Indian as Participant in the Civil War*, 34.
42. Abel, *The American Indian as Participant in the Civil War*, 33.
43. Abel, *The American Indian as Participant in the Civil War*, 36.
44. Letter from Baptiste Peoria to William Dole, 1 May 1862, *Report of the Commissioner of Indian Affairs for the Year 1862,* Washington: Government Printing Office, 1863, 178.
45. "Died / LYKINS," undated clipping, ca. Jan 1874, from unidentified newspaper, Lykins file; Miami County Historical and Genealogical Society, Paola, Kansas.
46. Cutler, *History of the State of Kansas*, 883.
47. Columbine Genealogical and Historical Society *Colorado Territory Civil War Volunteer Records* (Centenniel, Colorado: Columbine Genealogical and Historical Society, Inc. 1994), 217.
48. "When Pike's Peak was in Kansas," *Kansas City Star*, 4 Feb 1912, 6B.
49. *Colorado Territory Civil War VolunteerRecords*, 217.
50. Cutler, *History of the State of Kansas*, 883.
51. William Elsey Connelley, *Quantrill and the Border Wars* (New York: Pageant Book Company, 1956), 150.
52. Connelley, *Quantrill and the Border Wars*,187.
53. Athol Ferguson household, 1850 U.S. Census, Lafayette, Ogle County, Illinois, p. 66 [verso] (stamped), dwelling 3.
54. Fred Delap, Illinois Civil War Muster and Descriptive Rolls Database, Illinois State Archives (http://www.ilsos.gov/genealogy: accessed 10 Mar 2008), David Ferguson, Pvt., Co. F, 34th Illinois Infantry.
55. Edwin W. Payne, *History of the Thirty-Fourth Regiment of Illinois Volunteer Infantry, September 7, 1861, July 12, 1865* (Clinton, Iowa: Allen Printing, 1903), 8.
56. John Thomas Smith, *A History of the Thirty-First Regiment of Indiana Volunteer Infantry in the War of the Rebellion* (Cincinnati: Western Methodist Book Concern, 1900), 162.
57. Dennis Hutchinson, A Short History of the 31st Indiana Volunteer Infantry, *31st Indiana Volunteer Infantry* (http://www.psci.net/hutch/31hist.html: accessed on 28 Mar 2008).
58. Indiana Adjutant General's Office *Report of the Adjutant General of the State of Indiana* (Indianapolis: A.H. Connor, 1869), 8: 498. 1860 U. S. Census, Fairbanks Township, Sullivan County, Indiana, p. 99, dwelling 682, Willis Earnest household.
59. Civil War Society, *The Civil War Society's Encyclopedia of the Civil War* (New York: Wings Books, 1997), 237-238.

CHAPTER 5

Missouri Family Members in the Civil War

Emeline's friends and family members in Missouri were also caught up in the war machine. To distinguish between those loyal to the Union and those who were "disloyal," the Missouri enrollment act of 1862 required all men between the ages of eighteen and forty-five to join the Emergency Military Militia (EMM).[1] All able-bodied men not already enlisted in either the Union Army or the Missouri State Militia were ordered to report for service in the EMM "to exterminate the guerrillas." Several Civil War enlistments among Sue Heiskell's Missouri step-brothers, uncles and cousins took place in that year. Their enlistments may not have been entirely motivated by Union fervor. Among those who enlisted with Union forces that year were Sue's uncle, Claiborne Lykins, age 49, in March, 1862,[2] and William Heiskell's son, Charles, in April, 1862.[3] Charles' brother, Edmund C. Heiskell, joined Sterling Price's Confederate Army of the West in Cross Hollows, Arkansas, in February 1862.[4]

The formation of the EMM was Union Army General Schofield's attempt to address the complaints of Missouri citizens that the use of Kansas and other northern state military units in Missouri caused the poor treatment they received from the these troops. The general hoped that using local militia would deter the federal troops from thieving and foraging. As a result, Egbert Freeland Russell, Johnston's son-in-law, age 38, enlisted in the 77th Regiment E.M.M. in August, 1862;[5] it is not clear what further involvement, if any, he had in the war.

Missouri Family Members during Civil War 1861-1865

John C. McCoy	Johnston Lykins	Mattie Livingston Lykins	Claiborne Lykins	Wm. Heiskell
-Spencer McCoy (Johnston's nephew)	-Egbert Russell (Johnston's son-in-law) — Wm. J. (Mattie's brother)	-Rebecca Hughes* (Mattie's sister)	Andrew Lykins	-E.C. Heiskell
-Nellie McCoy (Johnston's niece)	-Theodore Case (Johnston's son-in-law)	-Alphonse Hughes (Mattie's nephews)	David A. Lykins	-Charles Heiskell
	-Wm. H.R. Lykins	-Judson Owen		-Addison Madeira (future son-in-law)
		-Elizabeth Owen (Mattie's sister)		

George Caleb Bingham, painter and friend of Johnston and Mattie Lykins

William C. Quantrill, insurgent leader who led raid on Lawrence, Kansas

General Thomas Ewing, Brigadier General, overseeing military occupation of Missouri's Borderland

*Deceased before beginning of war

One of the unanticipated outcomes of this order was that thousands of Missouri men fled the state or joined the guerrillas to avoid signing up in the EMM.[6] William Keller (Heiskell's nephew by marriage) had gone with the Keller family to St. Louis, probably to escape the violence and hardship in Cass County before 1860. It is likely that he fled to the Colorado Territory after Schofield's order. The 1870 census shows that he had one son born in Missouri in 1859, then two daughters born in the Colorado Territory between 1862 and 1865. A third daughter was born back in Missouri in 1868.[7]

Mattie's nephew, Judson Owen, who was living with the Lykins in 1860 as a medical student, used his medical training as a contract surgeon for the U.S. Army Medical Department.[8] The grisly business of the war created an overwhelming demand for physicians. At the beginning of the War, the Union Army had only 90 surgeons.[9] To address the need for large numbers of physicians to treat the wounded and diseased, large numbers of physicians were recruited for service (12,500 for the Union and 3,000 for the Confederacy) with large numbers of additional medical volunteers.[10]

The Army Medical Department created the contract surgeon category in order to have a ready pool of qualified surgeons to treat the wounded. Prior to the creation of this corps, volunteers of all stripes hurried to the battlefields to "help." These volunteers "might include quacks, cultists and practitioners of questionable ethics" and "they often performed unnecessary operations or wrought havoc as they dug about for bullets." To ensure better quality medical care, the Army called on a corps of reserve surgeons initially vetted by the governors of various states.[11]

As a contract surgeon, Judson held no commission but was paid at the rank of first lieutenant when he worked for the Army and, if he purchased it for himself, he would have worn that uniform.[12] Most of the 5,532 Union contract surgeons, also called Acting Assistant Surgeons, worked primarily in general hospitals and continued their own practices in their home cities. Some contract surgeons were sent to field hospitals in times of emergency or after high-casualty battles.[13] Judson is cited in a "Summary of Nineteen Hundred and Fourteen Cases of Primary Amputations in the Lower Third of the Femur for Shot Fracture," as the Acting Assistant Surgeon performing "an anterior posterior flap amputation of the left leg of Pvt. W. Dooley, Washington Artillery, age 29 on Dec. 7-8, 1864."[14] This record suggests that Mattie's nephew may have gone to field hospitals where immediate amputations took place before the patient was moved to a facility for recovery. As a medical student or newly minted physician at the age of 24, he had to develop his surgical skills on the field under intense conditions. If the Army Department permitted him to perform this surgery as an Acting Assistant Surgeon, he was deemed to be among the more skilled of his group. At this point in the war, seasoned doctors were put in charge of amputation cases and determined who among their corps at the facility had the competence to perform the operation.[15]

Judson Owen

Johnston's brother Claiborne enlisted with the Missouri Militia and was briefly assigned to medical duties. Two of Claiborne's sons later enlisted in the Union Army: his son Andrew C. Lykins, a farmer in the St. Joseph, Missouri area, enlisted in 1863;[16] and his 19-year old son David A. Lykins enrolled in the Colorado Cavalry in 1864.[17]

The Mystery of Claiborne Lykins

At the end of the war, only a few of the Missouri men returned to their homes to resume the lives they led before enlisting. The oldest member of the Lykins/Heiskell families to sign up was Emeline's Uncle Claiborne, an established pioneer farmer, a physician, and the father of 12 children. His actions during the war years, as puzzling now as they were to the newspaper readers of the time, were troubling and erratic from the beginning of the war to the end. Two months after his enlistment as a cavalryman, he was assigned extra duty in the army hospital from May 12-May 26, 1862. From November 1862, until April 1863, he was absent from duty because of illness, and during that time, in January 1863, he was mustered out because of "old age and infirmity." His Certificate of Disability for Discharge indicates that, beginning in January 1863, he was "unfit for duty" and "subject to loss of mind." The examining doctor knew "nothing of the cause" but later noted that he was "unfit for the invalid corps" and that the diagnosis was "partial mania brought on by intoxication."[18]

A year later, his life and reputation disintegrated further. Platte and Buchanan Counties, north of Kansas City, were strongholds of southern sympathizers during the war. As anti-Union activity increased in the two counties, the military government attempted to stem the recruitment of Confederate soldiers, guerrilla activities, and jayhawking from across the Missouri River by forming two Enrolled Military Militia regiments in the two counties. These units, known as the Paw-Paw Militia, were composed of "disloyal citizens" (those who had neither joined the militia nor taken a loyalty oath) and former Confederate soldiers who had returned to Missouri.[19]

As such, they were highly suspect and controversial, with local observers noting that they appeared to pursue jayhawkers energetically while failing to accost the Missouri guerrillas and recruiters working right under their noses.[20] Some federal military officers went so far as to conclude that the Paw Paws and the guerrillas had, in fact, agreed to "let each other alone."[21]

That may have been the case with Claiborne who ran afoul of the law after his return to St. Joseph, although it is not clear what his motives and loyalties were. St. Joseph's "Morning Herald" reported the arrest of Dr. Claiborne Lykins in its January 21, 1864 edition:

HORSE STEALING

One of the unmistakable signs of revolution and anarchy is the readiness, and almost eagerness with which men engage in lawless enterprises. In a new country, before the legal machinery gets fairly in operation, plundering is indulged in to an alarming extent; but the wholesome spirit of Judge Lynch soon quiets all such disturbances.

North Missouri has been infested with robbers and horse thieves ever since the rebellion opened. It has been customary to lay all crimes of this character to the door of our neighbors across the Missouri. Every man who loses a horse invariably turns his longing eyes towards Kansas. We have long suspected that our Missouri thieves were doing a business on the credit of the Jayhawker. Monday-night our theory was tested. James Karnes and John Johnson, who live but three or four miles from this city, on the Rochester road, were visited by a company of "Jayhawkers." The thieves stole all of their horses and took enough from their neighbors to make a baker's dozen. Johnson started after the party, fired into them and brought to the ground–*his nearest neighbor and brother-in-law,* Dr. Lykins. The Doctor was taken up and lodged in jail, where he now lies with two bullets in his rebel carcass. The horses and thieves were chased down through town at an early hour Tuesday morning, and two of the animals were captured.

By close watching, it will be seen that the thieving is not all done by the Kansans. A Constitutional butternut is not averse to horse-stealing, when there are chances of escaping merited punishment.[22]

In addition to calling Claiborne a "rebel," the editor called him a "Constitutional butternut." In the Civil War era, a "butternut" was a generic term for a person who grew up in southern Illinois, Indiana or Ohio and tended to have Confederate leanings. (The term originally derived from the homespun dyed with walnut, buckeye, or butternut tree oil which the farmers of the southern parts of those states wore.) As a native of Indiana with parents from Kentucky, Claiborne would have fit the description of a butternut, who had an interest in agricultural crops of corn, hogs and whiskey and a distrust of Yankees, railroads and banks.[23] In calling Claiborne a "Constitutional butternut" the editor was likely suggesting that he declared himself a loyal Unionist in the daytime and worked as a guerrilla at night. The day after the news article, thieves took Claiborne's own horses in a demonstration of the tit-for-tat lawlessness in Northwest Missouri in 1864.[24]

Throughout the Spring and early Summer of 1864, a rash of incidents occurred in the St. Joseph area. One of the Paw Paw militia units were "slipping into the brush" and joining the rebels; when they were ordered to disband and their arms were enroute to the St. Joseph Armory, the arms were stolen overnight. Right after local Unionists petitioned to form home guards to protect themselves, twenty-three kegs and 150 cans of gunpowder were found on the land of four of St. Joseph's most prominent families. The gunpowder had been stolen from Camp Jackson in 1861 and had since been concealed in the outbuildings of the men who professed loyalty to the Union and were leaders in the Paw Paw militia.

By June, 1864, the Paw Paws on duty at New Market, Missouri, surrendered to guerrillas and then joined their ranks.[25] In that month, too, Paw Paws allowed seven guerrillas to escape from jail in St. Joseph and, in a guerrilla skirmish a few days later, eleven guerrillas were identified as Paw Paws, active duty members of the Platte County Enrolled Missouri Militia. Other Platte County reports noted that Paw Paws were assisting guerrillas in horse theft. Claiborne was arrested in St. Joseph on suspicion of "subversive activity." In June, Claiborne was ordered appear, under guard, before the Provost Marshall.[26]

Claiborne's case was in the courts for over three years. After raising a hefty bail, he was released from jail and successfully argued for a change of venue for the trial to neighboring Andrew County. Following his release, he went to live with his sister in Iowa; his nephew Eugene Ferguson recalled that Claiborne came riding up to the house on a pony in 1865-66 and spent the winter there.[27]

After three years of seeking court delays, the trial occurred in April 1867, with the jury finding him, amazingly, not guilty, after having been shot at the scene of the crime and testified against by his brother-in-law. With his Andrew County cousin, Archibald Lykins, testifying in his behalf, it is not a stretch to imagine that the jury was influenced locally and by the need to move beyond the lawless time of divided loyalties they had recently endured. Claiborne left the region and spent the remainder of his life apart from his family in the territory vacated by the Indians in Southeastern Kansas. In 1870, Claiborne was a boarder and physician in Labette County, Kansas, while his wife, Nancy, remained in the St. Joseph, Missouri area.[28] In the *History of Buchanan County*, written in 1881, Nancy Lykins' biography described her as an area farm owner and early settler.

There was only a vague reference to her husband.[29] Neither the Provost Marshall's records nor the subsequent trial record reveals the actual testimonies, so it is difficult to know where he really stood during the Civil War. The actions and statements of his sons further complicate an understanding of his loyalties: in his son William's biography years later, William stoutly maintained that Claiborne was a Unionist through and through, and the fact that two of his sons enlisted in the Union Army further confounds an understanding of what really occurred in his fateful actions between 1862-1864.

Claiborne's Sons, Andrew and David

Claiborne Lykins' oldest son, Andrew, returned from the war with ruined health. After a stint with the volunteer Missouri militia, Andrew enlisted in the 12th Missouri Cavalry in 1864; however, his nearly illegible civil war service record suggests that he was hospitalized in May of 1865 when the regiment returned to Fort Leavenworth from campaigns in Tennessee and Mississippi. A treatment note from the post hospital at Fort Leavenworth states, "this man has deserted the hospital or may…[illegible]."[30] This regiment lost 36 men in battle and 227 to disease.[31]

Andrew Lykins' Civil War Pension file documents Andrew's ruined health. His bunkmate and cousin, F. M. Betteys, described Andrew as "unfit to perform manual labor" upon his discharge from the army. He remembered that Andrew fell ill in 1864 in Tennessee with a bout of dysentery that became chronic for the remaining 19 years of his life.[32] His brother-in-law, who also served with him in Company B, reported that a month after the devastating onset of the chronic diarrhea, Andrew had a sunstroke which "caused him to fall down" and a severe attack of arthritis from exposure to the elements in Evansport, Mississippi. He was hospitalized in Fort Leavenworth until the war ended.[33]

Betteys describes seeing Andrew in 1884, "I saw him the last time in 1884. He seemed to be in a much worse condition and still suffering from the said chronic diarrhea and rheumatism. He was in 1884 thin and emaciated in flesh and appeared like a sick man. He was scarcely able to walk or get around."[34] He was so disabled by these two chronic conditions that he had been declared "half-disabled" by a physician in 1878; however, he did not receive a pension because he could not demonstrate that these two conditions were a result of his military service.[35]

He was crushed to death by a train in 1884, leaving a wife and three children. When his wife died two years later, their youngest child, Sylvia, was four years old. After the older children reached adulthood they re-opened Andrew's case in behalf of Sylvia, who was still a minor, and the bureaucratic process of documenting the claim went on and on until 1904, and, in the end, was not resolved in favor of his children.[36]

Claiborne and Nancy's son, David A. Lykins, was killed at Newtonia, near Joplin, Missouri, as the Second Colorado Cavalry pursued General Sterling Price's army southward.[37] David was involved in heavy fighting in the borderland of western Missouri from January 1864, through October 28, 1864, when he was killed during the last Missouri engagement with Price. When he died on October 28, he was in southwest Missouri, about 160 miles from Emeline's home.

William Heiskell's Sons, Charles and Edmund

Charles Heiskell deserted after six months in the Second Battalion State Militia Cavalry. The battalion was fighting near Independence from May 15-17, 1863, and was at Grand Prairie on October 24, six days before Charles was reported as a deserter.[38] From March 1862, until March 31, 1863, when the battalion was mustered out, it lost "three officers and 48 enlisted men killed and mortally wounded and 1 officer and 109 enlisted men by disease."[39]

His name does not appear in subsequent military records for either the North or South or in census records. The cavalry headed toward Arkansas in pursuit of Sterling Price's army a few days after Charles deserted. According to Thomas Goodrich, "The Missouri enrollment act of 1862 "not only failed to achieve its goals but in fact greatly exacerbated an already existing situation. Most 'fence-sitters' who were forced into the militia were half-hearted soldiers at best– 'about as effective as Falstaff's recruits,' sneered one Unionist–and the vast majority of Secessionists who joined saw enlistment as the only alternative to imprisonment or death. A great many, of course, chose the second option (not enlisting) and either fled south to the Confederate army or slipped quietly into the brush with the guerrillas."[40]

Edmund Heiskell's residence before the war was Independence, Missouri. He entered the CSA in the Sixth Missouri Infantry and transferred to Lowe's Company, Jackson's 3rd Missouri Battery Volunteers at Cove Creek, Arkansas, in June of 1862, serving as an artilleryman. He engaged in battles in Arkansas, Louisiana and Mississippi: Elk Horn, Farmington, Iuka, Corinth, Hatchie Bridge, Port Gibson, Baker's Creek, Big Black and Vicksburg. His brigade's first major battle was at Pea Ridge, where the Missouri Confederates lost their chance to win Missouri for the South.[41]

The men foraging for food and supplies near Pea Ridge were grossly under-supported by their government. According to Albert Castel, Civil War historian, Heiskell's brigade began as a tatterdemalion "hodge-podge of ill-trained, often untrained, militia outfits. Far from having distinctive uniforms, most of its men began the war without any uniforms at all and the first uniforms they eventually did receive were more bizarre than impressive! As for weapons, they fought for nearly a year and a half before being issued rifled muskets; prior to then, those who were equipped with a semi-obsolete smoothbore considered themselves fortunate."[42] Despite their lack of support, the soldiers performed highly because they were motivated by a strong desire to fend off Unionist dominance of their state. In their eyes, they had originally enlisted to save their home state from "Yankee-abolitionist domination." By the time they had joined the CSA in 1862, Missouri had been overrun by Northern troops and "their sole hope of liberating it was to fight, and fight hard, for Southern victory on the battlefields." As the men of this brigade fought their way across six states, "their exploits gave them a reputation for bravery, determination, and fighting skill...." Major Dabney H. Maury, who saw them fight on two occasions stated that the soldiers of the First Missouri "were not surpassed by any troops in the world."[43]

During the siege of Vicksburg in 1863, "The Missouri brigade suffered more casualties than any Confederate brigade at Vicksburg, except for Hebert's Louisianians."[44] Colonel Cockrell's report of the Missourians at Vicksburg stated:

> This is a loss in killed and wounded of over one-third of the whole brigade, and shows that this brigade was almost continuously during the entire siege exposed to the enemy's fire, and at no time during this eventful siege did these troops ever waver or fail to go to or occupy any point, regardless of its exposure, and had to and did occupy points on the line so exposed that other troops, although on their own line, would give them up for these troops to occupy. They endured all the dangers, fatigues, exposures, and the weakness consequent on the insufficient rations, with a most commendable cheerfulness and soldierly bearing, willing to endure all things for the safety of the garrison, and desirous of holding out and fighting as long as there was a cartridge or a ration of mule or horse, and when the garrison capitulated they felt, and were, disarmed, but in no wise whipped, conquered or subjugated.[45]

After the fall of Vicksburg and the surrender of Lowe's company there, the Union imprisoned the soldiers who did not agree to take an oath to stop fighting:

> During this period, Federal authorities had 'used every argument imaginable to induce the men whose homes were in their lines, to return there and take the oath when they could remain on parole without being disturbed until the close of the war....All the Missourians had opportunities of going home upon the most favorable terms; but it is honorable to their proud name and high character that they turned aside from the alluring temptation presented to them, and, with noble fortitude and courageous devotion, determined to stand by the waning fortunes of the Southern cause. Only a few left–perhaps a dozen from our regiment and about in this proportion from the other regiments of the division.[46]

E. C. Heiskell did not take the oath and was sent to a camp in Citronelle, Alabama, where he was listed as a soldier in the last organized Confederate forces on May 4, 1865. Of the entire brigade, fewer than 300 men remained at the end of the war.[47] He was paroled six days later at Meridian, Mississippi.[48] Like his brother Charles, his name has not been uncovered in any subsequent records. William Heiskell may never have seen his two sons again after the war.

Mattie Lykins' Brother, William Jackson Livingston

Mattie Lykins' brother, William Jackson Livingston, lived across the state in Marion County. At the outbreak of the war, Marion County was considered one of the most secessionist counties in the state. The county "was declared to be the South Carolina of Missouri" and one of its towns, Palmyra, "a miniature Charleston."[49]

When news of South Carolina's secession from the union arrived at Palmyra, the town went into high gear, organizing Confederate military units, stitching uniforms, and charging around the streets with great fervor. Livingston rented a farm near West Ely, 12 miles from Palmyra, and as a veteran of the Mexican War, was named Captain of a local Missouri State Guard unit. Soon he achieved great notoriety as "Hawkeye Livingston," leader of a band of Confederate insurgents which numbered up to 50 men [50] On one occasion, he climbed to the top of a roof in Hannibal to determine the number of Federal troops in the town. He and leaders of some of other insurgent bands considered an attack on these troops to regain control of Hannibal; Livingston's observation, however, was that there were too many Federal troops in town and advised the bands not to attack.[51]

The St. Joseph-Hannibal Railroad line was one of his chief military targets. Throughout 1861, Livingston's band harried trains making their way to Hannibal or St. Louis. During one of these episodes, two federal soldiers were killed.[52]

In August 1861, Livingston's band captured and killed Reverend Josiah Wheat, whom they suspected was a Federal spy. The old man was hung by Livingston's men and his body mutilated.[53] Eleven months later, Livingston was captured near Branson, Missouri, and detained at the military prison at Alton, Illinois.[54] Livingston was found "not guilty" of three of the four charges, including the murder of Josiah Wheat, but was sentenced to be shot for violating acts of war. President Abraham Lincoln, however, declined to approve his death sentence, citing lack of evidence.[55] In May 1863, Livingston was arrested a second time in Hannibal and charged with spying.[56] A few months later, Livingston wrote to the Provost Marshall requesting that his trial date be set as soon as possible.[57] His trial was conducted in the Summer of 1864, and, on August 26, 1864, a Lowell, Massachusetts newspaper reported that his sentence had been carried out:

Execution of a Spy.—Mr. Jackson Livingston of Marion county, Missouri, was hung last Friday in the jail yard of St. Louis as a spy. He protested his innocence to the last. He joined the Catholic Church shortly before his execution and met his fate with as much apparent composure as if he was starting on a pleasant journey. He left a wife and four children. His wife was present at the execution.[58]

Johnston and Mattie at the Beginning of the War

1861 was an unkind year of decision for Missouri and the Lykins/Heiskell families living in the state. Lincoln issued a call to arms in July, 1861. Throughout the early part of 1861, Missourians debated whether to secede. Johnston Lykins, his wife Mattie, and their good friend George Caleb Bingham, important civic leaders in the Kansas City area, entered the debate.[59] The Lykins' house, well-known for entertaining Kansas City's most influential and well-connected leaders would have buzzed with discussion.

The Lykins Mansion on Quality Hill

The beautiful house that Johnston and Mattie had built in 1857 was a hub of the intellectual, political and social exchanges of the time; considered the finest house west of the Mississippi, the house was a 2 1/2 story brick structure at Twelfth Street between Broadway and Washington.[60] The Director of the Johnson County Kansas Archives, Gerald Motsinger, described the house on Quality Hill:

The home, designed in the classic revival style and strongly reminiscent of a southern mansion, belonged to Dr. and Mrs. Johnston Lykins. Finished in 1857, it became the focal point of the community because both the building and its inhabitants provided a display of reassuring good taste not customarily found on the local scene.

Construction presented many obstacles. A lack of skilled craftsmen forced Lykins to look elsewhere for his builder, and he ultimately hired the Alexander Brothers of Cincinnati. In addition, most of the specialized building materials had to be shipped from the East....The unusual building duo, one an architect and the other a carpenter, succeeded in creating what many claimed was the "Handsomest mansion west of St. Louis."

The exterior boasted such refinements as intricately detailed shutters and columned porches on front and side, thus providing inviting embellishments to the brick finish. The interior, with its 14 rooms, 10 fireplaces, wide staircases and crystal chandeliers equaled the best to be found in eastern cities. Located in a community often depicted as consisting of gullies and shanties, it sparkled like a jewel.[61]

The "handsomest mansion west of St. Louis" came to a sad end. By the 1970s the Lykins' mansion had been relocated and altered to become the Hotel Roslin; passersby would not have noticed it as anything other than a down-at-the-heels old hotel "of no historical interest" as the urban re-developers later claimed, and would have driven past it with no more than a quick glance. After historical and architectural preservationists waged and lost the battle to preserve the house, it was bulldozed to make room for the complex of buildings in the vicinity of Kansas City's Convention and Entertainment facilities.

Besides her social position as Johnston's wife, Mattie was an intellectual and activist in her own right who did not hesitate to use the pen to support proslavery and states' rights stances. In her columns sent under the pseudonym of Debby Doolittle, she mocked the Missouri legislature; she wrote serialized novels for the *Kansas City Star*.[62]

Lykins' mansion on Quality Hill

Johnston took a more pragmatic approach, writing an open letter to Missourians describing in graphic terms what secession would mean to the state.[63] Theodore Brown noted that although Johnston was "Southern by birth and sympathy" and his wife favored the Confederacy vocally, Lykins had devoted twenty years of his life to the growth of Kansas City and wrote passionately for the preservation of the Union:

> War meant not only the destruction of the beautiful American idea, as Lykins painted it, of a land "where under his own vine and fig trees, the citizen may enjoy the fruits of his labor, with none to molest him or make him afraid...." War would also bring anarchy and pillage "and subject us to the rule of the tyrant, the robber, the pirate–and our wives, daughters, and mothers to the brutality and lust of fiends in human shape. *Do not say this cannot be–that this is far off–that*

we shall not see it..." Lykins spared his readers nothing: towns would be sacked, cities destroyed, farms burned, banks robbed. Already, he computed conservatively, the very threat of secession had cost Missourians about $100,000,000 in the decline of property values. Calling attention to his status as an old citizen, Lykins concluded with a strong pro-Union appeal.[64]

Johnston knew that both he and Kansas City had much to lose if Missouri seceded. He was well aware of Missouri's geographic location surrounded on three sides by the free states of Iowa, Kansas, and Illinois. C.C. Spalding used the Lykins Addition as an example of the business opportunities the city held in its hand:

Of seventeen acres, has sixty rods of river front, and runs south, fronting on the east line of Broadway, for a distance of 750 feet. This land was bought by Dr. Lykins over twenty years ago, and held over, as he informs us, during this long period, in anticipation of a large city being one day built on the great bend of the Missouri River. All the solid and substantial elements and interests of the Doctor's "large city on the bend" are now here, and in a few more years the mere process of building walls, walk, and Pavement will be completed.....For five more years of improvements like those of this year will give us a city half as large again as Memphis, Tennessee, where five daily and three weekly papers are published. Or in eight years...we shall be equal to Savannah, Georgia, with her twenty-six wards, court house, jail, custom house, exchange, arsenal, United States barracks, city hall, market house, hospitals, asylums, theatres, gigantic railroads, machine buildings, &c.,&c.[65]

Quantrill and Aunt Mattie

Though Mattie Lykins (Mrs. Johnston Lykins) and Quantrill may or may not have known each other personally or have ever interacted with each other, Mattie's fate during the war was linked to actions surrounding his attack on Lawrence, Kansas, in 1863. Pressure on guerrilla bands in Missouri escalated when General Ewing assumed command of the forces garrisoned in the Kansas City area to control the pro-secessionist citizenry and guerrilla bands. At the beginning of the summer of 1863, Gilmore wrote, "Much of the power within the western Missouri guerrillas was concentrated in the guerrilla chiefs, who operated under Quantrill's direction in large operations, but acted more or less independently the rest of the time."[66]

Prior to this summer, Brigadier General Ewing, who was in charge of federal forces in the Borderland, announced that all guerrillas captured were to be summarily executed.[67] In addition, Ewing "began a policy of arresting and imprisoning the sisters of known guerrillas. He used their alleged 'spying' as a pretext for these illegal arrests, and the women were held without trial, bail, or legal recourse."[68] Among those held were the sisters of Bill Anderson, one of the most notoriously vicious of the guerrillas; when the building that Ewing commandeered from George Caleb Bingham (unbeknownst to Bingham who was out of town) collapsed, five of the young women prisoners were killed, one of them was Anderson's sister. Another sister sustained injuries which made her an invalid for life.[69] In addition to her indignation of the detention and imprisonment of the women, Mattie must have envisioned that she could be put in that prison. Her brother William had been arrested for spying only six weeks earlier. Mattie Lykins was at the scene of the horrific collapse:

One hot day (August 13), about two o'clock, this prison fell, burying beneath its walls a number of its inmates, four of whom were dreadfully mangled and crushed. In less than an hour after the building fell, I was informed by some of the women prisoners that they had been told repeatedly by the guards that this house was giving away and would eventually fall. "But," they said, "we had so often been told during our imprisonment equally as alarming stories which proved false that we paid no attention to this one: yet every few days, we heard the building crack, which was invariably followed by the falling of pieces of plastering from the ceiling." Doctor Joshua Thorne...was at that time chief surgeon of the hospital at this place. While I stood beside him near the building, watching the removal of the living and the dead from the debris, someone remarked to him that they supposed some of the soldiers on guard would be found buried beneath the ruins. "No," replied Doctor Thorne, "not a bluecoat will be found; every man who has been detailed to stand guard at the prison for the last few days and weeks knew the house to be unsafe and have kept themselves at a safe distance from the trembling walls. I knew the building to be unsafe," he continued, "and notified the military authorities of the fact, and suggested the removal of the women prisoners, but my suggestion was not heeded and before you is the result."[70]

Mattie would have known, too, that Ewing's General Orders 9 and 10 called for the forcible removal to distant locations further south of wives of known guerrillas and others identified as having aided guerrillas, enraged the guerrilla forces. These events were among those which culminated in the attack on Lawrence that August. Quantrill called together his captains, Bill Anderson among them, to agree on a plan to attack Lawrence, a site where he believed the most property stolen from Missourians was taken and where the greatest revenge could be exacted.[71] Quantrill and 194 men rode into Lawrence at dawn on August 20; by the end of their massacre, "some 150 male inhabitants of Lawrence were killed in the raid, and much of the town was burned to the ground. On August 23, 1863, *The Leavenworth Daily Conservative* reported the loss to the town as two million dollars in property and two hundred thousand dollars in cash. It described Massachusetts Street, the main business artery, as 'one mass of smouldering ruins and crumbling walls....Only two business houses were left upon the street–one known as the Armory and the other the old Miller block....About one hundred and twenty-five houses in all were burned, and only one or two escaped being ransacked, and everything of value carried away or destroyed.'"[72]

W.H. R. Lykins' house was not touched. In the anger and confusion that followed the raid, he and his step-mother, Mattie, came under suspicion as being involved in orchestrating the raid. Burton Williams explored an accusation against them made by Rev. Hugh D. Fisher, Methodist Minister, a man of questionable credibility. As a Free-stater, Fisher quickly got an appointment as the Chaplain of James H. Lane's Fifth Kansas cavalry, freeing slaves and helping himself to Missourians' property; further, he got into difficulty with other clergy, mishandled church funds and was "cited as a fraud and a liar."[73] In his papers, Fisher claimed:

> *Spies were in town all night...indeed it is placed beyond peradventure that the mother of a certain Banker of Lawrence, who secured all his valuables the night before the raid, spent weeks with his family in Lawrence, and made a map of the town giving the names, residences, and location of those who were to be killed and their homes burned, marking them thus–"Kill and Burn," or "Burn" as if the property belonged to a sympathizer only "Kill." This map was taken by this heinous woman to Kansas City, and Quantrall and his lieutenants entertained day and night in the greatest seclusion in her parlor, where they had the maps explained preparatory to the sacking of Lawrence.*[74]

When this claim appeared in published form, Fisher went further: "An old Mrs. L-----, of Kansas City, was the spy who furnished the necessary information and map of Lawrence...the torch was applied to every house that had been marked on the traitoress' map."[75] Williams cited other historians' claims that Lykins and his home were passed over because Sallie Young, a resident of Lawrence, asked that specific persons not be touched, some saying Sallie was a conspirator and others claiming that she was heroically saving others on that day. Williams concluded that the evidence against Lykins and his step-mother was circumstantial, citing Lykins southern background, his Kansas City roots, and Lykins' own acknowledgment that he knew some of the raiders, but Williams also raised questions regarding the survival of Lykins' home and the sparing of his life in the neighborhood where the worst destruction occurred. Finally he noted that Lykins received restitution for losses suffered during the raid, wondering whether the "destruction of property [was] brought on by his own complicity or that of his mother."[76]

Mattie wrote her own account of that day in Lawrence in a journal which remained in the family until it was donated to the Jackson County (Missouri) Historical Society in 2009 by Robert D. Owen, the grandson of Ada (Campbell) Owen, a niece of Mattie's by marriage. Mattie took her three-year old grand-daughter with her to visit her step-son and his family in Lawrence, arriving on the evening before the raid. When she asked W.H.R. about the news of the day, he reported that the commander at Fort Leavenworth had announced that Quantrill had left the Borderland and gone South. As a result, the men of Lawrence had been directed to stack their arms in the arsenal and get some rest. "We have had a hard time of it this summer," William said. "We have stood our guard every night for months and we were beginning to feel pretty well used up for want of rest from drill and guard duties."

As Mattie prepared for bed she heard gunfire and when she asked about it, William told her that Captain Jennison had been forming a new regiment and that the troops who were camping near the town drilled in the late evening and early morning to avoid the heat and then concluded their drills by firing their rifles. As a result, when Mattie heard gunfire and saw men riding in the streets at dawn, she was not alarmed. When she saw a man running away from men on horseback, she awakened her daughter-in-law, who sleepily responded, "Oh, those fellows belong to Jennison's regiment. They are just riding about in the cool of the morning for fun." Then Mattie saw the horsemen kill a man going to work and she awakened William:

> *Mr. Lykins, (Wm), who was asleep in another room, was about the last person in the house to be made acquainted with the appalling situation. Throwing on his clothes he started for the door with the hope of making an escape into a cornfield near by. By this time the guerrillas had surrounded his house and were guarding every avenue of escape. I told him that escape was impossible and that his safety depended on his remaining in the house. Still, he insisted on making the attempt, fearing he would do so, with all the physical strength I had, I held him back and by dint force and argument succeeded in getting him back and then I locked the door and put the key in my pocket. It was thus that he escaped death.*[77]

Were Mattie and William involved in the planning of the raid on Lawrence? Anything is possible, of course; however, it defies the imagination that a grandmother would be so irresponsible and ghoulish as to knowingly bring a three-year-old grandchild into such a dangerous and ugly situation. Indeed, she would have stayed away herself both for her safety and, if she were indeed a co-conspirator, to avoid suspicion. Further, Fisher's accusation does not match up with what is known of other aspects of their characters. Although Mattie was an articulate Southern sympathizer, she spent her life taking up the causes of children, whether through educating them or through establishing a home for Confederate orphans. An orphan herself, she would not likely have wanted to see other children made orphans.[78] The prominence of her husband and his good friend George Caleb Bingham, and their ardent stances against secession and having the Borderland devastated by violence make it unlikely, too, that she would have been plotting the raid while entertaining Quantrill in her parlor. The historian, Williams, pointed out that C.E. Lewis, writing to his brother from Franklin, Kansas, a few days after the raid stated that there was a map and that "Names and houses were marked prior to their coming in."[79] Lewis did not assert, however, that Mrs. Lykins was the creator of this map as Fisher had intimated.

An assertion by Mattie's nephew, Alphonse Hughes, however, does muddy the waters. Alphonse told Eugene Ferguson that he lived with Mattie and Johnston at the time of the raid and that they were nearly hanged following the raid because Mattie had told Quantrill to avoid bringing harm to particular homes and individuals in Lawrence.[80] It is possible that in the feverish rage of the moment, Mattie knew that guerrillas were threatening to attack Lawrence in reprisal and that she asked them not to harm people she cared about there; that is different from saying that she was part of a plot or was aware of the date or plan of attack.

Not long after the circulation of accusations and innuendo about Mattie and her stepson, the Lawrence community moved on in its thinking. The Borderland in this time was both immersed in the sectional and cultural battles of the time and committed to developing the economy and the region's future. The times and the people's motivations were too complex to fit into a single issue or perspective. In the 1860s, William became a trusted leader in the Lawrence community though memories of the raid were still painfully fresh. During the next five years he was twice elected mayor of the town by a citizenry who had built the town known for its abolitionist and Free-state convictions. As a banker, he was, like his father, probably more interested in building the region economically than in destroying it. Fisher, on the other hand, was a man known for dishonesty and must have gotten mileage out of speculating about why his house was burned and Lykins' wasn't.[81]

Order No. 11 as a Response to Quantrill's Raid

The carnage and destruction at Lawrence threw the Borderland into an uproar. Jim Lane, Kansas Senator and a hated raider in Missouri, barely escaped death during Quantrill's raid by dodging into a cornfield in his nightshirt.[82] He began to mobilize Kansans to gather at the Kansas-Missouri River and cross into Missouri to wreak destruction and murder civilians.[83] Daniel Anthony and Senator Jim Lane held a rally in Leavenworth, Kansas, and planned to go to Paola on September 8 with arms and supplies for a fifteen-day campaign into Missouri; their purported goal was to find Kansans' stolen property and avenge the raids on Kansas. The meeting in Paola had to be conducted in the rain and was ill-attended. U.S. Army officers and soldiers attended the meeting with the intention of keeping order. According to Gilmore, "The meeting was a complete fiasco and led to nothing."[84]

In response to threats of escalating the Borderland conflicts by men such as Jim Lane, General Ewing, a politically "prominent Kansas Republican" in charge of keeping peace in the Borderland, resolved to issue a military order to de-populate the Missouri counties where guerrilla fighters seemed to have their greatest support.[85] Ewing may have been motivated by both political and military factors. As the former Chief Justice of Kansas, he was well aware of the political clout of Senator Jim Lane and wanted to curry favor with powerful Kansans in preparation for a run for the U.S. Senate.[86] In addition, he may have seen the threat of an all-out war emerging in Kansas and Missouri from the anger and fear generated by the on-going raids and violence.

In the months preceding the raid on Lawrence, Ewing and other military officials were frustrated by their lack of success in suppressing guerrilla activities. Ewing wrote to his departmental commander, General Schofield, saying that over two-thirds of the families in Western Missouri were related to the guerrillas and engaged in supporting them through providing food, clothing and other sustenance. He proposed that the families of the "worst guerrillas" be rounded up and moved to Arkansas. Ewing got approval for this plan and, consequently, issued General Orders No. 10, outlining this policy, three days before Quantrill's attack on Lawrence.[87]

Following the attack on Lawrence, Ewing issued Order No. 11 to satisfy Missouri and Kansas Unionist demands that the bushwhackers be stopped and to forestall criticism from Washington, D.C. (Jim Lane had influence with Abraham Lincoln.).[88] This order instituting martial law stated:

> 1. All persons living in Jackson, Cass, and Bates Counties, Missouri, and in that part of Vernon included in this district, except those living within 1 mile of the limits of Independence, Hickman Mills, Pleasant Hill, and Harrisonville, And except those in that part of Kaw Township, Jackson County, North of Brush Creek and west of the Big Blue, are hereby ordered to remove from their present places of residence within fifteen days from the date hereof...Officers commanding companies and detachments serving in the counties named will see that this paragraph is promptly obeyed.[89]

Historically, the idea of forcibly removing citizens who support the enemy was a common practice of military forces trying to suppress rebellion and guerrilla warfare. "General William Halleck, general in chief of the U.S. Army, assured Ewing that the measure fell 'within the recognized laws of war.'"[90] Halleck, however, did not agree with Ewing's method of implementing the order. Ewing assigned Kansas soldiers, full of anger and bent on revenge, to enforce the order. Ewing may have made this assignment in deference to Jim Lane.[91]

Castel, writing 100 years after the implementation of Order No. 11, described it as "the most drastic and repressive military measure directed against civilians by the Union Army during the Civil War. In fact, with the exception of the hysteria-motivated herding of Japanese-Americans into concentration camps during World War II, it stands as the harshest treatment ever imposed on United States citizens under the plea of military necessity in our nation's history."[92]

A leading critic of the order was a prominent political figure and painter, George Caleb Bingham, whose Unionist credentials were impeccable. Bingham twice traveled to Ewing's headquarters to demand that Order No. 11 be rescinded. When Ewing refused, Bingham promised the general that he would use his artistic work to show the nation how despicable he believed Ewing to be; his rage and the fulfillment of his promise to aid in destroying Ewing's reputation lasted until the end of his life. Bingham's painting, "Martial Law," also known as, "Order No. 11," was his weapon of choice in publicizing the horrors of the military action.

The painting shows Ewing, cold and detached, supervising troops in the process of removing a Missouri family from its home. Castel describes the scene of the painting: "A Kansas Red Leg has just shot down a young man, and another is about to shoot the elderly head of the family, oblivious to the pleas of a beautiful young woman kneeling at his feet. The house is being pillaged by Union soldiers, one of whom bears a likeness to the noted jayhawker, Colonel Charles Jennison. In the background columns of smoke rise from burning fields and a long funereal line of refugees wends its way along the road."[93]

Martial Law, or *Order No. 11*, by George Caleb Bingham

One of the victims of the Order was Martin Rice, a Unionist farmer in Jackson County, Missouri, who wrote an 1865 account of his experience. His account is remarkably measured, given the amount of suffering he endured: "It [Order No. 11] is often spoken of and referred to, and has been much condemned by some and strenuously defended by others; and while I shall not attempt to do one or the other, I will, as plainly, concisely and impartially as I can, describe what I saw, witnessed and felt of its incidents, consequences, and results, without pretending to say or to know whether the consequences would have been better or worse if that order had never been made and enforced."[94] Rice obtained his certificate of loyalty, but the next day was arrested by soldiers of the Kansas 9th Regiment along with his son, son-in-law, and five neighbor men ranging in age from 17-75. After being marched to an encampment about three quarters of a mile away, a Kansas military officer appeared and took down the names of the eight men, retired a short distance away with some of his men, and allowed the prisoners to sit down by a fence. Soon the officer reappeared and directed Rice to take his son and leave immediately; the others were not allowed to go. Rice wrote,

> *We immediately left as commanded, leaving our friends and neighbors behind, never to see them in life again: for in a very short time after reaching home, the report of several guns, in quick succession, alarmed us still more....Miss Jane Cave heroically repaired to the spot and found the company gone, and the six prisoners all dead, some of them pierced with many balls....Of neighbors left in the county, there were none that I knew of, except the families of the men who had just been killed.*
>
> *Nobody left to bury them but me and my son, and my old neighbor Mr. Hunter....My aged friend and neighbor, at the age of three score and Fifteen, helping me with his own hands to lay his two sons, his only sons, his grandson, and son-in-law, with two other relatives (one of whom was my son-in-law), in the rude and shallow grave that our own hands had dug for them.*
>
> *It may, perhaps, be asked why or for what cause this bloody tragedy was enacted; why it was that these men were killed, and that I was spared. They were all quiet, peaceable citizens, none of them had borne arms against the government, except David Hunter, a few days at the very first, at Camp Holloway, and he had afterward done duty in the enrolled militia (Union forces). True, they were all Southern men, and Southern sympathizers; and some of them had sons in the Southern army. I thought then, and still think, the principal cause was that Quantrill and his raiders, on their way to Lawrence, stopped and ate supper on the Potter farm, and that some of these men visited them while they were getting that supper.*[95]

The citizens in the western Missouri counties fled the area however they could, crowding onto steamboats, walking, and riding oxen (most horses had been confiscated). Among those forced to evacuate were President Harry S Truman's maternal grandparents. For them, it was the crowning indignation. In her reparations claim of 1902, Harriet Louisa Young, Truman's grandmother, stated that the Young farm had been pillaged five times by Union forces, beginning with those of Jim Lane in 1861.[96] The total damage claimed by Harriet was around $21,442, more than a half million dollars in today's monetary equivalent.[97] Although Harry Truman's grandfather had signed a loyalty oath more than a year earlier, the family complied with Order No. 11 and left the farm, permitted to take a wagonload of possessions. Truman's mother, Martha Ellen, was among those "trudging northward on a hot, dusty road behind the swaying wagon, headed for 'bitter exile' in Kansas City."[98]

Mattie's Expulsion from Kansas City

And where *was* the intrepid Mattie Lykins in all this? Why, right in the middle of it, of course. Mattie was one of those residents of Kansas City who was forced to leave the area because of her outspoken support of the South and, possibly, because of the accusations which had been made against her regarding the Lawrence raid. If General Ewing or his staff connected her to her insurgent brother who was active in the eastern part of the state in 1861, that would only have heightened their suspicion of her. *The Columbia Herald* published a list of persons banished from the martial law district by order of the Headquarters District of the Border, Kansas City, Missouri, August 29, 1863: "the following is a list of the disloyal persons recently banished from the District of the Border, by order of Gen. Ewing. The order for their banishment forbids them to live in the counties of Platte, Clay, Ray or Carroll, or to return to their home during the rebellion:...Mrs. Dr. Lykins, Kansas City...."[99] As she stood on the deck of a steamboat leaving the city, her husband and, possibly, George Caleb Bingham, watched her depart. A Kansas citizen, Daniel Geary, was an eyewitness:

> *Mrs. Lykins, a talented and accomplished woman for those days and a writer of short stories, was banished during the war by the military authorities for disloyalty to the government.*
>
> *I remember the incident well, as when the ferry boat upon which she took passage to the distant shores of Clay County where she was to abide, was leaving the wharf, she was calling to the doctor where he would find his underwear, and "To be sure they were quite dry" before he put them on, etc. She bore her exile philosophically. And immediate, upon the close of the war, began collecting funds to build a home for Confederate orphans.*[100]

When Ewing's successor permitted "loyal" citizens to return to Kansas City in January, 1864, Mattie returned. When she was greeted by her friend, Col. Kersey Coates, she said with her usual spark, "Here I am, Colonel, twice as big as life and twice as natural."[101]

Martha A. "Mattie" (Livingston) Lykins, wife of Johnston Lykins. She later married George Caleb Bingham

What Mattie and the other returnees found was unparalleled devastation. In Cass County, there were only 600 people of a population of 10,000 who were still there as of September 9, 1863.[102] In Bates County, the population loss was so great that there was no infrastructure left for conducting business transactions or legal procedures until after the war. "All across the border counties stood solitary, blackened chimneys surrounded by burnt timbers, the remnants of homes and plantation houses–an entire way of life destroyed. Untended cattle, hogs, and sheep ran confusedly through the woods. Wildfires ran unchecked. The western counties became known as the 'Burnt District.'"[103] Did the policy work? Castel concluded:

> It might be argued that Order No. 11 was successful since there were no more guerrilla raids into Kansas from Missouri following its issuance. But it is extremely doubtful that the order as such was more than a minor and indirect factor in achieving this result. Of greater importance were the strengthened border defenses of Kansas following the Lawrence Massacre, an improved home guard system in that state, and above all the fact that the bushwhackers in the summer of 1864 concentrated their operation in Northern and Central Missouri so as to prepare the way for Sterling Price's invasion that fall.[104]

Complicated Relationships during the War Years in Kansas City

Later in life, Mattie described the war conditions surrounding her and her family in Kansas City:

But we should forever bear in remembrance the time when our fields were ruined and our homes desolated. The anguish of broken hearts, the cries of the widow and fatherless, the pain and suffering of the crippled and maimed on both sides as an indelible warning on the pages of memory never again to resort to the sword and torch as the arbitrators of our sectional disputes. Often during the war it seemed to me that Kansas City got more than her share of the bitterness of the strife. The daily tread of thousands of soldiers in our streets, the alarming reports of the invasion of our state by the Confederate army, the harrowing telegraphic dispatches of the dreadful slaughter of the contending armies, the harassing and daily warfare carried on in our country between the Kansas Jayhawkers and the Missouri Bushwhackers kept us in a state of alarm and excitement for four years without a day's intermission.[105]

The people of Kansas City, whether Northern or Southern in sympathies, found that they were in the middle of the turmoil together. Nellie McCoy Harris wrote:

I merely will tell how, in the main, we dwelt together in those stirring times.

In the beginning we were so appalled by the "dreadful note of preparations" that we were in a manner crazed or stunned, and we discussed conditions freely with neighbors regardless of political predilections, but when our fathers, husbands or brothers buckled on their armor and tore themselves from home and loved ones, to join the army of their choice, fierce resentment against "the other side" supplanted for the moment the grief that had wrung our hearts. We sought solace in the hope and belief that our side would make short work of the war....

The Northern element in our neighborhood asserted and firmly believed that Southern men, unaccustomed to physical effort, having slaves to perform the necessary labor, were lacking in stamina and too unaccustomed to hardships long to endure a soldier's life. The Southerners considered their loyal neighbors lacking in enthusiasm or profound sentiment, and as practical and dominated by the spirit of commercialism, to be willing long

to continue a conflict that would necessarily play havoc with the nation's prosperity....
Time proved how egregiously wrong were both.
Sometimes neighbors, fearing criticism or censures from bitter partisans on their side, felt they must perform neighborly ministrations toward their foe friends secretly–but they did not fail to confer favors when needed, all the same.[106]

The death of Nellie's brother, Spencer Case McCoy, was an event which spoke to the complexities of the relationships among the citizens of Kansas City and of the ability for human decency to transcend the bitterness and division of the time. Eighteen-year-old Spencer left Kansas City to join the Confederacy and in a few months he was killed at the second battle of Springfield.[107] His father, hearing that the retreating Confederates were unable to bury their dead, drove a team and wagon 200 miles to the battlefield where he expected to find his son. Of the fifteen young men who had been buried in a mass grave by Union men, only Spencer was interred in a metallic coffin. When he inquired of the Union officer in charge there, the man said that his wife and children had been without heat the winter before and when Spencer's father, who lived across the street from the family, heard of their situation from his children, he drove into the country and returned with a load of wood for them and a supply of provisions. In gratitude, this officer purchased a coffin and arranged a separate burial for the young man, marking the spot with a wooden cross bearing his name.[108]

When John McCoy brought Spencer back for burial in Union Cemetery, his daughter wrote, the cortege that followed the coffin to the cemetery was "the most notable that had even been seen in Kansas City. All bitterness was buried, political differences forgotten. Loyal and disloyal mingled their tears on this occasion."[109] The community united to embrace their pioneer neighbor and friend.

Mattie Lykins worked beside Mrs. Coates, her close Unionist Quaker friend, to care for the wounded brought to McGee's Hotel during the Battle of Westport. Their friendship, which had begun in 1855, endured throughout their lives.[110]

The city's economy was severely disrupted during the war; at times military operations and bushwhacking had stopped all trade. The city suffered from its pro-slavery image. Many moved away from Kansas City as businesses floundered and went under. Westport struggled in poverty, having many refugees from the outlying countryside and Union dependents on its hands. The divided citizenry's only hope for the future lay in the development of a railroad center in Kansas City and the prospect of providing trade goods to the burgeoning population in the new state of Kansas.[111] Johnston was in the inner circle of a small group instrumental in winning the building of the railroad through Kansas City rather than Leavenworth or St. Joseph.

Out of these economic stresses came the birth of a "radical policy" among business leaders in Kansas City which demanded that only the people and businesses who were unquestionably loyal to the Union should be supported. In November, 1864, the editor of the *Daily Journal of Commerce* articulated the position of the city's business community:

> This is a matter of life or death to the State. Under 'conservative' misrule, we are fast drifting into anarchy, Rebel sympathy is working for the ruin of every interest. Public improvements will cease–our railroads will stop where they are and fall to ruin–our fields and farms all to desolation, unless we can inaugurate a different state of things in the State...There is but one hope of salvation for us, and that is to put the State in the hands of radically loyal men."[112]

Johnston Lykins had to walk a difficult line. He was an important businessman and stout Unionist who, at the same time, had a strong Southern-sympathizing wife, slaves,[113] and his own Southern roots. He had to walk carefully through this desperately tough economic minefield: his wife–an outspoken secessionist-- was a victim of it.

One of Johnston's sons-in-law had an honorable military career: Theodore Case enlisted as a private in the Union Army, but soon rose to the rank of colonel and finished his Civil War career as the quartermaster of the Kansas City army post.[114] Although Case was born in Georgia, his allegiance was with westward facing Kansas City.[115]

Friends and Relatives in Kansas City Who Enlisted

Name	Relation	Unit	Notes
Egbert Russell	(Johnston Lykins' son-in-law)	77th Missouri Militia (EMM)	Served 2 months
Theodore Case	(Johnston Lykins' son-in-law)	25th Missouri Infantry	Quartermaster
Spencer McCoy	(Johnston Lykins' nephew by marriage)	2nd Missouri Cavalry, CSA	Killed in action
Addison Madeira	(future son-in-law of Wm. Heiskell)	5th Reg. Iowa Infantry	Secy. to Gen. Grant / chaplain
George C. Bingham	(friend of Johnston & Mattie Lykins)	Van Horn's Battalion	Home guard
Wm. J. Livingston	(Mattie's brother)	Missouri State Guard, CSA	Captain / Hanged for treason
Judson Owen	(Mattie Lykins' nephew)	1st Kentucky Battery	Asst. Surgeon

Johnston's impetuous friend, George Caleb Bingham, enlisted in the Union Army at the age of 50. Because of his age, friends saw to it, however, that he was elected captain of the Home Guard, a reserve unit so that he did not fight directly in the battle lines.[116] Bingham, too, had been raised a Southerner, but vehemently opposed secession.[117]

1864: The Final Year of the War in the Borderland

Emeline and William Heiskell suffered a double blow when they lost their third and fourth daughters, Nellie and Blanche, in August and September, 1864.[118] Among the soldiers of the Colorado 2nd Cavalry Regiment engaged in operations against Price's army and guerrillas that October was Claiborne's son, David A. Lykins. At the Battle of Westport, cousins David and James were fighting on the battlefield while Aunt Mattie tended the wounded from that battle. In Cass County, their regiment fought within fifteen miles of his cousin Emeline and James' parents; at Marais des Cygnes the regiment was fewer than 10 miles from Paola.[119] During this drive to remove Price and his forces from Northern Missouri that October, David was killed at the Battle of Newtonia.

In 1864, too, Emeline's Uncle Claiborne was imprisoned in St. Joseph and subsequently lived apart from his long-time family and friends for the remainder of his life. Two of Johnston Lykins' little grand-daughters died a few months later; one of them was Mattie's namesake, Martha "Mattie" Lykins Case, who accompanied Mattie on the trip to Lawrence on the eve of Quantrill's raid.[120]

Mattie's brother, William J. Livingston, got his wish for his case to be resolved in 1864. Col. J. P. Sanderson, Provost Marshall General, directed the superintendent at Gratiot Prison to hang the 45-year old prisoner "by the neck until dead" on August 19, 1864 in the city of St. Louis.[121]

The war finally straggled to a miserable end, leaving behind it broken families, broken men, and a devastated Borderland. For the

Lykins and Heiskells and many other families who lived in that horrific time in the Borderland, no one was a winner. Their families were destroyed or dispersed, their neighbors and friends gone or alienated, and many of their homelands lay in ruins. William Heiskell's son Edmund stayed with the Confederacy until the final stages of the war, having refused to surrender at Vicksburg.[122] It does not appear that either he or his brother Charles ever lived in the Borderland after the war–they died or moved away. The devastation wrought by Order No. 11 was all too clear for Mattie and Cass County relatives who chose to return to the western Missouri counties.

Union or Confederate, the soldiers and their families suffered. Soldiers who survived were often plagued with the effects of wounds and disease for the remainder of their lives. In Kansas, where there were only 30,000 men of military age, 20,000 served in the Union army; of those 8,500 were casualties.[123] Within the state of Missouri, there were 1,200 distinct battles and skirmishes, a number exceeded only by the states of Tennessee and Virginia. During the war, approximately 27,000 Missourians—combatants and civilians—were killed.[124] The people of the war-exhausted Borderland turned to recovering personally, economically, and culturally, a process that continued both within the region and across the nation for decades.

One Kansas City man was uniquely suited to the task of providing comfort and hope for reconciliation to city residents, Addison Madeira, a man who became an influential minister in Kansas City. Madeira lived in the decidedly Unionist state of Iowa at the outbreak of the war. He enlisted as a chaplain in the Union Army and later became Ulysses S. Grant's personal secretary;[125] it was Madeira who confronted Grant about excessive drinking after the Shiloh campaign.[126]

On a personal level, Madeira must have had a sorrowful crisis of conscience during the war. Six of his brothers served with the Confederacy.[127] His intimate knowledge of the painful schisms which often took place between family members and friends during the war uniquely qualified him to console the war's struggling survivors. After the war, Madeira ministered to both Union and Confederate sympathizers. In 1865, when he had returned to his ministerial duties he spent a night in jail because of the occupation army officers' fear that he would support a fellow Missouri minister, Samuel Brown McPheeters, in an act of civil disobedience. A small minority of Reverend McPheeters' parishioners, had demanded that he reveal his views regarding "The Rebellion." Adhering to his belief that he serve all his parishioners regardless of affiliation, McPheeters declined to reveal his stance and was exiled from Missouri by the occupation forces' leaders. Madeira was jailed overnight so that he could not vote in the church's Presbytery meeting to support McPheeter's position.[128]

Madeira was so highly regarded by Civil War veterans that he was asked to preside over 400 or more veterans' funerals, Confederate and Union, in the years following the war.[129] This man, six years after the war's end, married William Heiskell's daughter, Price.[130] Madeira's life embodied the complexities of the war: contrary to stereotypical descriptions of "Yankees" and "Southerners," people were not monolithic in their values and beliefs. In the Borderland, these conflicting values and alliances played out dramatically among friends and family.

---

1. Thomas Goodrich, *Black Flag: Guerrilla Warfare on the Western Border, 1861-1865* (Bloomington: Indiana University Press, 1995), 45.
2. C. B. Likins, Pvt., Capt. Johnson's Company, Horse Artillery Brigade, Missouri State Militia, Company Muster-in Roll; Compiled Military Service File, Civil War; Records of the adjutant General's Office, 1780s-1917, Record Group 94; National Archives, Washington, D.C.
3. Missouri State Archives, Record of Service Card, Civil War, 1861-1865, "Soldiers' Records: War of 1812-World War I," *Missouri Digital Heritage* (http://www.sos.mo.gov/archives/soldiers/ : accessed 21 July 2008), box 38, reel s836, entry for Charles G. Heiskell, Pvt., Company E, 2nd Battalion Cavalry, Missouri State Militia.
4. Missouri State Archives, Record of Service Card, Civil War, 1861-1865, "Soldiers' Records: War of 1812-World War I," *Missouri Digital Heritage* (http://www.sos.mo.gov/archives/soldiers/ : accessed 21 July 2008), box 38, reel

s908, and box 103, reel 732, entry for Edward C. Heiskell, Pvt., Jackson's 3rd Missouri Battery, Light Artillery, CSA.

5. Missouri State Archives, Record of Service Card, Civil War, 1861-1865, "Soldiers' Records: War of 1812-World War I," *Missouri Digital Heritage* (http://www.sos.mo.gov/archives/soldiers/ : accessed 21 July 2008), box 72, reel s811, entry for E. F. Russell, Pvt. Company C, 77th Enrolled Missouri Militia.

6. Jeremy Neely, *The Border Between Them: Violence and Reconciliation on the Kansas-Missouri Line* (Columbia, Missouri: University of Missouri Press, 2007), 114-115.

7. 1870 US Census, Jackson County, Missouri, Household 1022, Family 1063, p. 371, William Keller household.

8. "Civil War Pension Index: General Index to Pension Files, 1861-1934," database, *Ancestry.com* (http://www.ancestry.com : accessed 10 Dec 2009); Judson R. Owens [sic] (Medical Department U.S. Volunteers) index card; imaged from *General Index to Pension Files, 1861-1934*, T288 (Washington, D.C.: National Archives [n.d.], no roll number cited.

9. Ira M. Rutkow, "Introduction," in John Wesley Wells, compiler, *An alphabetical list of the battles of the War of the Rebellion compiled from the official records of the office of the Adjutant-General and the Surgeon-General, U.S.A. and a roster of all the regimental surgeons and assistant surgeons in the late war and hospital service* (1883; reprint, San Francisco: Norman Publishing 1990), v.

10. Ira M. Rutkow, *American surgery: an Illustrated History* (Philadelphia: Lippincott-Raven, 1998), 125.

11. Alfred J. Bollet, *Civil War Medicine, Challenges and Triumphs* (Tucson, Arizona: Galen Press, 2002), 27.

12. Peter J. D'Onofrio, President of the Society of Civil War Surgeons, Reynoldsburg, Ohio, to Rose Ann Findlen, email, 19 Jan 2010; Civil War Contract Surgeons, Martha Livingston File

13. Bollet, *Civil War Medicine*, 30-31.

14 *The Medical and Surgical History of the War of the Rebellion (1861-1865)* (Washington, D.C.: Government Printing Office, 1876), vol. 2, pt. 3, p. 247.

15. Bollet, *Civil War Medicine*, 161-162.

16. Andrew C. Lykins, Pvt., Company B, 12th Regiment, Missouri Cavalry, Muster and Descriptive Roll; Compiled Military Service File, Civil War; Records of the Adjutant General's Office, 1780s-1917, Record Group 94; National Archives, Washington, D.C.

17. *Colorado Territory Civil War volunteer records: a comprehensive index to the twelve volumes of military clothing books found in the Colorado State Archives, containing the historical background of the volunteers of Colorado Territory during the Civil War period, 1861-1865* (Littleton, Colorado: Columbine Genealogical and Historical Society, 1994), 217.

18. Claiborne B. Lykins, Company L, 1st Missouri State Militia Cavalry Volunteers, Company Muster Roll, May & June 1862, Certificate of Disability for Discharge, 5 Aug 1863; Compiled Military Service File, Civil War; Records of the Adjutant General's Office, 1780s-1917, Record Group 94; National Archives, Washington, D.C.
19. Howard V. Canan, "The Missouri Paw Paw Militia of 1863-1864," *Missouri Historical Review* 62 (July 1968): 433.
20. Canan, "The Missouri Paw Paw Militia of 1863-1864," 441.
21. Canan, "The Missouri Paw Paw Militia of 1863-1864," 440.
22. "Horse Stealing," *The [Saint Joseph, Missouri] Morning Herald*, 21 Jan 1864, 2.
23. James M. McPherson, *Battle Cry of Freedom: the Civil War Era* (New York: Oxford University Press), 13.
24. "Honor Among Thieves," *The [Saint Joseph, Missouri] Morning Herald*, 24 Jan 1864, 3.
25. Canan, "The Missouri Paw Paw Militia of 1863-1864," 438-440.
26. Order to send prisoner, C. B. Lykins, under guard to judge advocate for examination, Saint Joseph, Missouri, 9 June 1864; file of papers relating to individual citizens, Missouri's Union Provost Marshal Papers, 1861-1866; Missouri State Archives, Jefferson City, Missouri.
27. Eugene Ferguson to [unnamed] niece, letter, nd, typed transcript, Lykins file; Union Cemetery Historical Society, Kansas City, Missouri.
28. 1870 US Census, Osage Township, Labette County, Kansas, p. 2, family 19, household of Solomon Adamson household. 1875 Kansas State Census, Osage Township, Labette County, p. 21, dwelling 169, William Johns household; Kansas State Historical Society, Topeka, Kansas. 1870 U.S. Census, Washington Township, Buchanan County, Missouri, p. 72, dwelling 473, Nancy Lykens household.
29. Christian Ludwig Rutt, *History of Buchanan County and the City of St. Joseph and Representative Citizens, 1826 to 1904* (Chicago: Biographical Publishing, 1904), 382. *The History of Buchanan County* (Saint Joseph, Missouri: Union Historical Company, 1881), 817.
30. Andrew C. Lykins, Pvt., Company B, 12th Regiment, Missouri Cavalry, diagnosis and treatment card, Post Hospital, Fort Leavenworth, Kansas; Compiled Military Service File, Civil War; Records of the Adjutant General's Office, 1780s-1917, Record Group 94; National Archives, Washington, D.C.
31. Frederick H. Dyer, *A Compendium of the War of the Rebellion Compiled and Arranged from Official Records of the Federal and Confederate Armies, Reports of the Adjutant Generals of the Several States, the Army Registers, and Other Reliable Documents and Sources* (Des Moines, Iowa: Dyer Publishing, 1908), 3: 1310-1311.
32. F. M. Betteys, Affidavit to Origin of Disability, 16 Feb 1878, Andrew C. Lykins (Pvt., Company B, 12th Regiment, Missouri Cavalry), invalid pension application 249,241, Civil War and Later Pension Files; Department of Veterans Affairs, Record Group 15, National Archives, Washington, D.C.

33. William J. King, General Affidavit, 22 June 1895, Andrew C. Lykins invalid pension application 249,241; Pension Application Files based upon Service in the Civil War and Spanish-American War, Records of the Department of Veterans Affairs, 1773-1985, Record Group 15, National Archives, Washington, D.C.
34. F. M. Betteys, Affidavit to Origin of Disability, 16 Feb 1878, Andrew C. Lykins, invalid pension application 249,241; Pension Application Files based upon Service in the Civil War and Spanish-American War, Records of the Department of Veterans Affairs, 1773-1985, Record Group 15, National Archives, Washington, D.C.
35. [Surgeon name illegible], Examining Surgeon's Certificate, 20 June 1878, and Brief for Reopening, 6 Mar 1903, Andrew C. Lykins invalid pension application 249,241; Pension Application Files based upon Service in the Civil War and Spanish-American War, Records of the Department of Veterans Affairs, 1773-1985, Record Group 15, National Archives, Washington, D.C.
36. J. O. Sauks affidavit, 27 Nov 1885, and cover jacket, petition to reopen application, Andrew C. Lykins invalid pension application 249,241; Pension Application Files based upon Service in the Civil War and Spanish-American War, Records of the Department of Veterans Affairs, 1773-1985, Record Group 15, National Archives, Washington, D.C.
37. Columbine Genealogical and Historical Society, *Colorado Territory Civil War volunteer records*, 217.
38. Frederick H. Dyer, compiler, *A Compendium of the War of the Rebellion* (Des Moines, Iowa: Dyer Publishing, 1908), 3: 1304. Missouri State Archives, Record of Service Card, Civil War, 1861-1865, "Soldiers' Records: War of 1812-World War I," *Missouri Digital Heritage* (http://www.sos.mo.gov/archives/soldiers/ : accessed 21 July 2008), box 38, reel s836, entry for Charles G. Heiskell, Pvt., Company E, 2nd Battalion Cavalry, Missouri State Militia.
39. Dyer, *Compendium of the War of the Rebellion*, 3: 1304.
40. Goodrich, *Black Flag*, 46.
41. Missouri State Archives, Record of Service Card, Civil War, 1861-1865, "Soldiers' Records: War of 1812-World War I," *Missouri Digital Heritage* (http://www.sos.mo.gov/archives/soldiers/ : accessed 21 July 2008), box 38, reel s908, and box 103, reel 732, entry for E. C. Heiskell, Pvt., Jackson's 3rd Missouri Battery, Light Artillery, CSA.
42. Albert Castel, "Foreword," *The South's Finest: The First Missouri Confederate Brigade from Pea Ridge to Vicksburg* by Phillip Thomas Tucker (Shippensburg, PA: White Mane Publishing Company, 1993), viii.
43. Castel, "Foreword," *The South's Finest*, viii.
44. Phil Gottschalk, *In Deadly Earnest: the History of the First Missouri Brigade, CSA* (Columbia, Missouri: Missouri River Press, 1991), 314.
45. Report of Col. Francis M. Cockrell, Second Missouri Infantry, commanding First Brigade, 1 Aug 1863, United States War Department, *The War of the Rebellion: A*

Compilation of the Official Records of the Union and Confederate Armies (Washington, D.C.: Government Printing Office, 1889), vol. 24, pt. 2, p. 417.
46. Ephraim McDowell Anderson, *Memoirs, historical and personal: including the campaigns of the First Missouri Confederate Brigade*, 2d ed., editor, Edwin C. Bearss (Dayton, Ohio: The Press of Morningside Bookshop, [1972]), 360.
47. Phillip Thomas Tucker, *The South's Finest: The First Missouri Confederate Brigade from Pea Ridge to Vicksburg* (Shippensburg, Pennsylvania: White Mane Publishing, 1993), 206.
48. Missouri State Archives, Record of Service Card, Civil War, 1861-1865, "Soldiers' Records: War of 1812-World War I," *Missouri Digital Heritage* (http://www.sos.mo.gov/archives/soldiers/ : accessed 21 July 2008), box 103, reel 732, entry for E[dward] C. Heiskell, Pvt., Jackson's 3rd Missouri Battery, Light Artillery, CSA.
49. *History of Marion County, Missouri : written and compiled from the most authentic official and private sources : including a history of its townships, towns, and villages, together with a condensed history of Missouri, the city of St. Louis, a reliable and detailed history of Marion County, its pioneer record, war history, resources, biographical sketches and portraits of prominent citizens : general and local statistics of great value, and a large amount of legal and miscellaneous matter, incidents and reminiscences, grave, tragic and humorous*. 1884 reprint. (La Crosse, Wis.: Brookhaven Press, 2000), 365.
50. *History of Marion County, Missouri*, 397.
51. *History of Marion County, Missouri*, 642.
52. *History of Marion County, Missouri*, 397.
53. Testimony of William Carmon, 19 Apr 1862, William Jackson Livingston case, Papers Relating to Individual Citizens, microcopy 345, Missouri Union Provost Marshal Papers, 1861-1866, Missouri State Archives, Jefferson City, Missouri.
54. Roll of Prisoners of War at Military Prison, Alton, Illinois, William Jackson case, Papers Relating to Individual Citizens, microcopy 345, Missouri Union Provost Marshal Papers, 1861-1866, Missouri State Archives, Jefferson City, Missouri.
55. United States War Department, *General Orders of the War Department, embracing the Years 1861, 1862 & 1863* (New York: Derby and Miller, 1864), General Order no. 151, (vol. 2, p. 171-172).
56. United States War Department, General Orders, Head Quarters, Department of the Missouri (Saint Louis: H. H. Hine, 1865), General Order no. 135 (pp. 7-8).
57. William J. Livingston to Col. C. W. Marsh, 19 Jan 1864, William Jackson Livingston case, Papers Relating to Individual Citizens, microcopy 345, Missouri Union Provost Marshal Papers, 1861-1866, Missouri State Archives, Jefferson City, Missouri.
58. "Execution of a Spy," *Lowell Daily Citizen and News*, 26 Aug 1864, 2:e.
59. Paul C. Nagel, *George Caleb Bingham: Missouri's Famed Painter and Forgotten Politician* (Columbia, Missouri: University of Missouri Press, 2005), 144.

60. "Once a Proud Home,"*The Kansas City Times*, 4 Aug 1989, E:1.
61. *Kansas City Star*, 30 Dec 1987.
62. Martha Livingston Lykins Bingham, Mattie Lykins'Scrapbook, Dr. Johnston Lykins (1800-1876) and Martha Lykins Bingham (1824-1890) Collection, KC-0294; Native Sons Archives, Western Historical Manuscript Collection, University of Missouri-Kansas City University Archives, Kansas City, Missouri.
63. Johnston Lykins, "Letter to the People," *Kansas City Daily Journal of Commerce*, 31 Jan 1861, np, cited by Theodore Brown, *Frontier Community: Kansas City to 1870* (Columbia, Missouri: University of Missouri Press, 1963), 162.
64. Brown, *Frontier Community*, 162-163.
65. C.C. Spalding, *Annals of the City of Kansas: Embracing Full Details of the Trade and Commerce of the Great Western Plains* . . . (Kansas City, Kansas: Van Horn & Abeel, 1858), 46.
66. Gilmore, *Civil War on the Missouri-Kansas Border*, 228.
67. Gilmore, *Civil War on the Missouri-Kansas Border*, 184.
68. Gilmore, *Civil War on the Missouri-Kansas Border*, 229.
69. Martha A. (Livingston) Lykins Bingham, "Recollections of Old Times in Kansas City," 67-page, handwritten manuscript, ca 1883 - 1890. Jackson County Historical Society Archives, Independence, Missouri, Gift of Robert Dewit Owen, in memory of his grandmother, Mrs. Dewit Livingston (Ada Campbell) Owen, Document ID 110F7. Adrienne Tinker Christopher transcribed a portion of this manuscript in *The Kansas City Genealogist* 25 (Winter & Spring, 1985): 116.
70. "Recollections of Old Times in Kansas City," *Kansas City Genealogist*, 112.
71. Gilmore, *Civil War on the Missouri-Kansas Border*, 233.
72. Gilmore, *Civil War on the Missouri-Kansas Border*, 246-247.
73. Burton Williams, "Quantrill's Raid on Lawrence: A Question of Complicity," *Kansas Historical Quarterly* 34 (Summer, 1968): 145-146.
74. Rev. Hugh D. Fisher, "The Lawrence Massacre," manuscript; Kansas Room, University of Kansas Library, Lawrence, Kansas; quoted in Williams, "Quantrill's Raid," 146-147.
75. Williams, "Quantrill's Raid," 147.
76. Williams, "Quantrill's Raid," 149.
77. "Recollections of Old Times in Kansas City," *Kansas City Genealogist*, 113-114.
78. *The Commonwealth of Missouri: A Centenniel Record* , C. R. Barns, editor (Saint Louis: Bryan, Brand and Company, 1877), 770.
79. C. E. Lewis to "Dear Bro.," letter, 27 Aug 1864; Kansas Methodist Historical Librry, Baker University, Baldwin City, Kansas, quoted in Williams, "Quantrill's Raid," 5.
80. Eugene Ferguson to "Dear Niece," letter, no date, no recipient name, typescript, Lykins file; Union Cemetery Historical Society, Kansas City, Missouri.
81. Williams, "Quantrill's Raid," 148-149.

82. Ted P. Yeatman, *Frank and Jesse James* (Nashville, Tennessee: Cumberland House Publishing, 2003), 44.
83. Albert Castel, "Order No. 11 and the Civil War on the Border," *Missouri Historical Review* 57 (July 1963): 359.
84. Gilmore, *Civil War on the Missouri-Kansas Border*, 254.
85. Castel, "Order No. 11," 359.
86. Castel, "Order No. 11," 359.
87. Castel, "Order No. 11," 360.
88. Gilmore, *Civil War on the Missouri-Kansas Border*, 251.
89. Gilmore, *Civil War on the Missouri-Kansas Border*, 252-253.
90. Gilmore, *Civil War on the Missouri-Kansas Border*, 253.
91. Gilmore, *Civil War on the Missouri-Kansas Border*, 255.
92. Castel, "Order No. 11," 2.
93. Castel, "Order No. 11," 5.
94. Martin Rice, "What I Saw of Order No. 11," manuscript, 10 June 1865, Howard N. Monnett, transcriber, *The Westport Historical Quarterly* 2 (Feb 1967): 6-13.
95. Rice, "What I Saw of Order No. 11," *The Westport Historical Quarterly*, 11-12.
96. David McCullough, *Truman (*New York: Simon and Schuster, 1992), 30.
97. McCullough, *Truman*, 1.
98. McCullough, *Truman*, 2.
99. [Verna Gail Johnson], "Those Banished by Order No. 11 August 1863," *The Pioneer Wagon* 12 (Oct 1992): 89-90.
100. Daniel Geary, "Looking Backward," *Annals of Kansas City* 1 (Dec 1922): 227.
101. "Mystery in an Opened Corner Stone," undated clipping from unidentified newspaper, Kansas History Clippings, 6:314; Kansas State Historical Society Library, Topeka, Kansas.
102. Richard S. Brownlee, *Gray Ghosts of the Confederacy* (Baton Rouge: Louisiana State University Press, 1958), 126.
103. Gilmore, *Civil War on the Missouri-Kansas Border*, 257.
104. Castel, "Order No. 11," 9-10.
105. "Recollections of Old Times in Kansas City," *The Kansas City Genealogist*, 115.
106. Nellie McCoy Harris, "Where a War was Not a War," *Kansas City Star*, 2 Apr 1911, 15:c,d.
107. *Liberty Weekly Tribune*, 6 Feb 1863. Liberty, Missouri, np., transcription; Clay-Ray-Platte County, Missouri, Archives News: Battle of Springfield, 6 Feb 1863 (http://files.usgwarchives.org/mo/clay/newspapers/battleof27gnw.txt; accessed on 18 Nov 2008).
108. Delilah Tyler, "Social Conditions During the War," *Under Both Flags: a Panorama of the Great Civil War*, editor, George Morley Vickers (San Francisco: J. Dewing, [1896]), 315-316.
109. Harris, "Where a War was Not a War," *Kansas City Star*, 15:c,d.

110. "Mystery in an Opened Corner Stone," 314.
111. Joe Klassen, "The Civil War in Kansas City," *The Bulletin–Missouri Historical Society* 16 (Jan 1960):148-149.
112. Klassen, "The Civil War in Kansas City," 148.
113. 1860 U.S. Census, Kansas City, Jackson County, Missouri, slave schedule, p. 1, Johnston Lykins, owner.
114. "Theodore S. Case, M.D.," *The United States Biographical Dictionary and Portrait Gallery of Eminent and Self-made Men. Missouri Volume* (New York: United States Biographical Publishing, 1878), 51.
115. "Theodore S. Case, M.D.," *The United States Biographical Dictionary*, 51.
116. Nagel, *George Caleb Bingham*, 108.
117. Nagel, *George Caleb Bingham*, 104.
118. Annie Lynch, "Peery Families of Virginia," *Utah Genealogical and Historical Magazine* 3 (July 1917): 125.
119. Frederick H. Dyer, *A compendium of the War of the Rebellion*), 3: 1005.
120. Sarah Lykins Russell, "The Little Ones That Are Gone: Lines to the Memory of Mattie and Belle," and M.A.L. (Martha Ann Lykins), "Died," *Daily Journal,* City of Kansas, 25 Jan 1865, np, clippings; Martha Livingston Lykins Bingham, Mattie Lykins'Scrapbook, np, Dr. Johnston Lykins (1800-1876) and Martha Lykins Bingham (1824-1890) Collection, KC-0294; Native Sons Archives, Western Historical Manuscript Collection, University of Missouri-Kansas City University Archives, Kansas City, Missouri.
121. J. P. Sanderson, Provost-Marshal-General, Special Order No. 202, 5 Aug 1864, William Jackson Livingston case, Papers Relating to Individual Citizens, microcopy 345, Missouri Union Provost Marshal Papers, 1861-1866, Missouri State Archives, Jefferson City, Missouri.
122. Missouri State Archives, Record of Service Card, Civil War, 1861-1865, "Soldiers' Records: War of 1812-World War I," *Missouri Digital Heritage* (http://www.sos.mo.gov/archives/soldiers/ : accessed 21 July 2008), box 38, reel s908, and box 103, reel 732, entry for E[dward] C. Heiskell, Pvt., Jackson's 3rd Missouri Battery, Light Artillery, CSA.
123. Debbie Wassemiller, "Kansas and the Centennial of the Civil War," *Kansas Historical Quarterly* 31 (Spring 1965): 62.
124. Military Order of the Loyal Legion of the United States, "Civil War in Missouri Facts" (http://home.usmo/~momullus/MOFACTS.HTM accessed on 18 Nov 2009).
125. "Rev. Addison Dashiel Madeira," *Soldiers of Various Wars Interred at Union Cemetery, a List* (Kansas City, Missouri: Union Cemetery Historical Society, 1989), 5: 16.
126. Harold Wells, "Rev. Addison Dashiel Maderia, an Unsung Hero Buried in Union Cemetery," *The* [Union Cemetery Historical Association] *Epitaph* 16 (Jan-Feb 1997), 5-8.
127. Harold Wells, "Rev. Addison Dashiel Maderia, 5-8.

128. Donald Rau, "Three Cheers for Father Cummings," *Yearbook, Supreme Court Historical Society* (1977): 22.
129. Wells, "Rev. Addison Dashiel Madeira," 5-8.
130. Wells, "Rev. Addison Dashiel Madeira," 5-8.

CHAPTER 6

A Decade of Continuing Losses

The decade following the Civil War was a time of personal upheaval and transition in the lives of the Lykins and Heiskell families of the Borderland. The pioneering Lykins uncles were aging, the Borderland was reeling from the devastation suffered during the war, and unbridled health conditions were exacting their toll among the families.

In the 1870s, a significant number of Emeline and Mattie's extended family members lost their livelihoods, their homelands and their lives.

The Vanquished and their Children

The soldiers of the Confederacy and their families struggled against the loss of their health and livelihoods. When they returned to civilian life in Missouri, there were no safety nets for them, and members of the now dominant Unionist society could not easily forget the pain and loss suffered within their own ranks. Mattie Lykins saw the war's aftermath of deprivation and suffering around her and advocated for the many voiceless men, women and children left destitute and vulnerable. She wrote to President Andrew Johnson in 1866 imploring him to grant clemency to a man jailed in Lawrence for allegedly participating in the raid three years earlier.[1]

That year, she and several women friends in Kansas City began a campaign to establish a home for widows and orphans of Confederate soldiers. In a letter to the Editor of *The Republican*, July 11, 1866, Mattie explained their purpose:

Permit me through your columns to announce to the suffering widows and orphans of Southern soldiers from Missouri who perished in the late war, that the ladies of Kansas City and Jackson county are organizing a society for the maintenance and education of the widows and orphans of the persons alluded to. The design is to establish a parent society in Kansas City, and to invite the formation and co-operation of auxiliary societies in all of the counties of the State, in order to raise a fund for the founding of an orphan asylum and home for the destitute of our own bereaved and helpless sufferers, to be located in this city.[2]

In this time, emotions were still raw from the trauma of the past five years, so in taking on the humanitarian effort, Mattie, always controversial, was criticized. Beneath the headline, "A Disgraceful Letter," a detractor wrote:

The following disgraceful letter appeared in the St. Louis Republican of yesterday. Being written by a lady, we have no comment to make. It will, however, be pardonable to also state that we think the writer ought to be largely reorganized, fully reconstructed and let the Confederate dead, who have been properly killed and decently interred, alone. The writer of the letter was banished from this city, as a secessionist; has always been a consistent, outspoken rebel and is the sister of a man who was executed by the U.S. authorities, as a spy, during the war.[3]

Indeed Mattie had first-hand knowledge of the suffering of the wives and children of Confederate dead, not only from her first-hand observation of the bereft families in Kansas City, but also, quite possibly, from knowing of the plight of her dead brother's family. In 1863, he had written from Gratiot Prison to the Provost Marshall to ask for the money taken from him at the time of his arrest: "General I would like very much to have the money for my family dependent on me for a support and are now suffering. For something to live. And are very destitute of cloth. If I had the money it would be a great relief to me and my family."[4] Livingston's family moved near his brother, Stephen J. Livingston, right after the war both, undoubtedly, to escape the notoriety of their dead father's hanging and to seek financial support.[5]

A writer in a subsequent letter defended Mattie and the committee's work, saying "This is commendable, for however great may have been the error of these deluded and mistaken men Christianity teaches us to care for the widow and the orphan irrespective of the causes which produced their unhappy condition. There is a moral beauty and heroism in such efforts, which when the passions of the hour shall have passed away, will be recognized and appreciated by every being possessed of a human heart."[6]

In one of her appeals, Mattie pointed out that individuals and organizations had gone around the state to seek support for the education and maintenance of Southern orphans, "but, thus far, not one dollar has been set aside for the relief and education of the suffering ones of Missouri." She described the desperate situation of women and children:

> *And now, the clash of arms is heard no more, their cry for bread comes from every desolate and waste place throughout our State–Again and again we hear of mothers toiling in the fields; others with less health and strength, but burdened with the care of children are occupying a servant place in strangers' kitchens. Not only this, but from their ragged tents and pallets of straw, they plead in piteous accents for a shelter from the coming winter.*[7]

Transitions: Moves, Marriages, Deaths-1870s

Lykins Family

Juliana Betteys

Joseph & Merb Lykins

Claiborne Lykins
    son-Wm. C. Lykins
    son-Samuel Lykins

David Lykins'
    son-Wayland Lykins
    son-Edward W. W. Lykins

Johnston Lykins
    son - Wm. H.R. Lykins
    daughter-Sarah Russell
    granddaughter-Effie Russell
    grandson-William Lykins Russell
    daughter-Juliana Case

Heiskell Family

William Heiskell
    daughter-Price Madeira
    daughter-Fannie Heiskell
    Emeline & William's daughter-Sue Heiskell=W.F. Wallace
        Sue & W.F. Wallace's son-Leslie Wallace

Baptiste Peoria

daughter-Elizabeth Baptiste=David Lykins Peery
    Elizabeth & David's daughter-Clara Peery=Patrick McNaughton

Livingston Family

Mattie's sister-Elizabeth Owen
    Elizabeth's son-Judson Owen

Area newspapers carried numerous reports of fund-raising events such as a grand ball: "the Ex-Confederates, their friends and sympathizers, contemplate giving a free dinner in this city on the 27th of October....General Beauregard is expected. Ten thousand people or more will be present. Grand ball at night, the net proceeds of which will be donated to the Widows' and Orphans' Home of Kansas City, Mo. Admission to ball–Two dollars."[8]

The women tried various approaches to raising funds for the home, and responded to critics that their work was a humanitarian rather than partisan effort. In making an appeal for funds, Mattie writes,

We believe that even the veriest enemies of the South would not take the responsibility of opposing so noble an enterprise. Their animosity does not reach beyond the grave, nor to the widow and orphan of the brave dead. They will bid us Godspeed in this benevolent undertaking; and many will give of their abundance to this "Home" for the widow and fatherless. They will see in it no political or individual distinction; no desire to renew the strife and bitterness of feeling which has filled our land, but simply a desire to do good–to save from ruin the truly friendless, and a "desire to offend neither heaven nor earth."[9]

The committee succeeded in raising the funds to build the home at 32nd and Locust in Kansas City and elected Mattie President, a position she held until 1874 when the home became the state-owned Industrial Home for the Orphans and Indigent Children of Missouri, its clientele no longer Civil War orphans.[10]

In 1874, Mattie and her friend, Mrs. George Caleb Bingham, cosponsored a proposal to the state legislature to give the land to the state for the establishment of this home. The legislature passed a large appropriations bill to give annual funds to the home. The passage of "Mrs. Lykins' Bill" was celebrated by the Kansas City community and the women savored the success of their tireless campaign. By the next year, however, the political mood had changed and the appropriations for the home were withdrawn–a bitter disappointment for Mattie and the committee.[11] Private investors in the home could not sustain the financial burden and, in time, the orphanage went into the hands of the Little Sisters of the Poor.[12]

More Endings and Beginnings

Many who stayed in the Borderland after the war turned their eyes westward and to the future. Johnston Lykins continued his work in the inner circle of Kansas City businessmen maneuvering to establish Kansas City as a major railway center opening wider the gates to western settlement. He and other supporters saw the railroad in the borderland as their ticket to the future; critic of the railroad expansion complained of higher taxes, unfair rates charged to western farmers and corruption. The sides people took in this struggle, however, were not defined by the sectarian and political struggles of the past. Instead, border residents chose sides based on their ideological and economic interests. The war-exhausted citizens were trying to determine how they would move forward now that the war was over. Emeline and William's neighbor, John Rice of *The Miami County Republican* wrote, "Our political hope for the future is in the restoration of the old fraternal feelings which ought to grow year by year stronger since the cause of estrangement is removed. The political fomentation of the past ten years have resulted in nothing but loss to them [Missouri Confederates] and to us, and any future attempts in this direction should be resisted as inimical to the best interests of the whole people."[13]

Emeline and William were fairly well positioned to succeed in postwar Kansas. Emeline had grown up on frontier farms in Indiana and Illinois and had cultural affinities with the new free-soil settlers who came predominantly from the farmlands north of the

Ohio River. In 1860, more than 80% of the settlers in southeastern Kansas had been born in states west of the Appalachians, and families on both sides of the Kansas-Missouri borderland had similar economic skills and experience. "Familiar with the rigorous demands of migration and settlement, the people who settled the border counties had staked their futures to that of the new West, and they maintained a shared interest in the conditions, such as the availability of good land and access to market opportunities, that they saw as necessary to its growth."[14] Though he was a Virginian by birth, William had long demonstrated an interest in mercantile enterprises and real estate. Since 1855, he had seen the potential of platting the town of Paola and preparing for settlement. In the Federal Census of 1870, William Heiskell said his business was "real estate."

The End of the Indian Territory in Kansas

It is likely that his occupation was intimately linked to the removal of the Native American tribal members who did not choose to become U.S. citizens. William had been Baptiste Peoria's business manager for many years and probably continued in that capacity as the tribal members began to sell their lands.

On February 1, 1868, *The Miami Republican* reported that those who wished to retain their tribal identities were re-located in a new "Indian Territory, Oklahoma. "The Indians are preparing to leave the county and B. Peoria and Co. is selling their lands which are the finest in the county. There is much immigration and real estate is much in demand."[15] Even as the Native Americans prepared for yet one more removal (Baptiste Peoria's fourth experience of it), one positive beginning for Emeline occurred that year when she gave birth to her fifth daughter, Minnie, and Sue finally had a sister who would live into adulthood.[16]

In December, 1868, *The Miami Republican* informed its readers that "The last payment which will probably be made in this county to the confederated tribes of Peoria, Piankishaw, Kaskaskia and Wea Indians, in their tribal capacity, was made this week. By early spring, the remainder of these once great and powerful tribes will have departed from here."[17] Emeline's brother, David Peery, an adopted tribal member, elected to move with his family and his former father-in-law/employer to Oklahoma. Land records from 1868-1873 show transactions related to Peery's sale of his holdings in Kansas. He sold lots at the corner of Piankeshaw and Agate Streets to Emeline where she lived while Sue and Minnie were growing up.[18]

Because David Lykins' sons, Wayland and Edward, had been adopted into native tribes, they were able to claim land in the new Indian Territory in Oklahoma. According to Edward's son Willis:

David Peery

When Father was seventeen, David Perry [sic] sent him to the Indian Territory to fence and to help prepare his location here for the coming of his family and that winter Father made or rather split a thousand rails and later it was discovered that he had placed them on the wrong headright. At eighteen, he joined the 19th Kansas Volunteers to help put the Indians on the Reservation at Fort Sill....Father again returned to the home of Mr. Perry and later came with him and his family when the Peorias removed to this country, making his home with that family near Peoria.[19]

Edmund's brother, Wayland, named Ash-Pun-Ge-Ah, joined him in the Oklahoma territory a few years later.[20] In Oklahoma, Edward's son Willis befriended the famed warrior, Chief Joseph, of the Nez Perce. He commented that as the two fished together, Chief Joseph spoke in bewilderment of he and his people's exile there, unable to grasp why the Nez Perce had to suffer so greatly for only trying to defend what was theirs. His people were lost, demoralized and without purpose in an alien environment.[21]

Not all tribal members left for Oklahoma, but their lives and the town of Paola were forever changed. *The Miami Republic* noted the dissolution of one of the tribes, the Wea, in 1870:

> Read more about Chief Joseph in, "*Chief Joseph's Story*," in the Related Stories and Poems section at the end of the book.

> Alas for the Wea's! This once large and prosperous tribe of "Ye noble red man" shall be known no more forever. The remnant of the tribe who remained in Kansas after the Passage of the treaty by which they were to sell their lands and leave the State, received their last "wampum" on Thursday last in this city, dissolved their tribal relations and became citizens of the United States. These numbered 55 men, women and children. The remaining members of The old tribe, some 165 are in the Quapaw Nation, assuming the name of the latter tribe. The amount paid to those who assumed citizenship was $75,000 which after paying some debts owing by them as a nation, left about $1375 apiece. This wipes out the Weas who once roamed the prairies, hunted in the woods and fished in the streams of our own beautiful county long before a pale face had dared to enter this territory.[22]

A piece of Emeline's way of life and that of the state of Kansas ended. Johnston and Delilah Lykins and Isaac McCoy brought the Wea, Piankeshaw, and Peoria tribes to the newly declared Kansas Territory roughly 30-40 years earlier. Several Lykins brothers had worked in the early missions: Johnston, David, Joseph, Jonas; now some Lykins descendants maintained their family ties and intertwined destinies with the Native Americans they had come to know and love and moved with them to the new territory. For Emeline, the re-location of her brother and his family, Baptiste Peoria (one of the first people she met at the Wea Mission 16 years earlier), her cousin Edward W. W Lykins (the toddler she had come to Kansas to tend), and many other friends marked an enormous change in the life she had known in Paola. The voices in the town square were those of the many white businessmen and farmers flooding into Kansas from the East–not the voices of transplanted Missourians, traders or Indian neighbors racing horses on the town commons.

> For more information about Baptiste Peoria and David Peery's daughter, Clara McNaughton, see *Tales of Lost Spanish Gold,*" in the Related Stories and Poems section at the end of the book.

The end of the war, Statehood, and the departure of the tribes transformed Emeline's home town from a Southern stronghold and an outpost on the western frontier to an emerging Midwestern farm community. The demographic make-up of towns and farmlands in the border counties of both Missouri and Kansas changed dramatically in the five years following the war, bringing with it the emergence of a new regional identity. In the late 1860s, immigrants flocked to the area, and additional settlers, many of them Union Army veterans, came primarily from Illinois, Indiana and Ohio. Although Border counties in Missouri had more profound demographic changes than the Kansas counterparts, the result was greater homogeneity of the two states' borderland populations.

The reasons behind the shifting sources of immigration lay with the disparate impacts of the Civil War on the South and the North. Like Missouri, many Southern states had been ravaged by a long war fought largely on their own soil. In addition to the extensive damage to the region's infrastructure and economy, the high casualty rate sustained by the Confederate army had claimed a significant proportion of the South's adult male population, further compounding the difficult plight of many southern families. Given the widespread destruction, poverty, and personal losses they faced, southerners may have been less likely to emigrate than their northern counterparts.[23]

The new demographic mix of the area, dramatically changed in western Missouri and incrementally changed in Kansas, resulted in the region's central identity becoming Midwestern more than it was Southern or Northern.

Also, with the war behind the residents, the excitement of new residents, growth and development invigorated the Borderland. In Paola, *The Miami Republican*, one of the town's major newspapers, carried report after report of new buildings, new residents, the establishment of community groups and civic organizations beginning in the latter half of the 1860s and the early 1870s. The editor wrote of seeing heavy travel through the town: "80 wagons loaded with goods and agricultural implements passed through in one day, to say nothing of immigration wagons."[24] In 1869, the *Miami Republican* reported that "There have been 200 buildings erected here during the past season and in a jaunt around town we counted 30 more in the process of erection."[25]

Paola Park and Town Square, 1870

Paola's Silver Cornet Band, complete with uniforms and plans to have a specially decorated band wagon, competed with bands of nearby towns. A baseball team had been formed which traveled to nearby towns to play. Sue Heiskell likely attended a new school complete with desks that held two scholars each. A fancy new oyster salon for diners, a new calaboose, new sidewalks, five churches, winter balls, and a furniture store complete with a stock of coffins were a few of the town additions the editor celebrated. The train tracks now ran from Kansas City to Fort Scott, a distance of 160 miles, the train having displaced the stage coach line.[26] Before the railroad came to Paola, David Peery and cousin Andrew Willis Lykins, engaged in carrying freight.[27] The new town residents were proud, seeing Paola thrive. It was no longer the community on the edge of the wilderness to which Emeline originally came.

The Death of William Heiskell

When her husband became ill and died in August, 1870, Emeline's life took on a new shape which can be inferred from newspaper accounts about William's death, details gleaned from land records, and the ages of their two daughters in that year's census. A little over two months after the census-taker enumerated William A. Heiskell's household, he died at age 63. According to the obituary, Heiskell "had been sick for several weeks, during which time he suffered severely from the effects of a cancer." The death notices emphasized his ethical character and kindness. *The Paola Advertiser* commented that "he managed Major Baptiste's business for a number of years, always acting towards the Major as he would have done had he been doing business for himself. He was a true Christian in every sense of the word, always doing as he wished to be done by."[28] On the same date, *The Miami Republican* commented that "he was a man honored and respected by all who knew him. He was a kind and affectionate husband and father, a true friend, and leaves a large family and a large circle of friends and acquaintants to mourn his death."[29]

It is not known whether the children of his first marriage attended the funeral. His two daughters resided in the Kansas City area at the time of his death: Price with her aunt, Emeline Price,[30] and Fannie with cousins Charles and Florence Keller, and the William Austin family.[31] The whereabouts of Heiskell's two sons from that marriage have not been identified.

William was buried beneath an oak near his three baby daughters. Today, one of the earliest pioneer citizens of Paola's slate marker lies on the ground, broken off near the base by vandals.

Not far from William and Emeline, a marker memorializes his brother-in-law, David Lykins, and his first wife. Abigail Webster Lykins. Born in Maryland or Hampshire County, Virginia, (the boundary lines between those states varying across time) and raised in the mountains of Hampshire County, Virginia, William died far,

far away from the West Virginia plantation he left with his first family in 1849 to settle in the Borderland.[32]

Emeline watched her husband suffer through his last painful weeks and was left alone at forty with their two surviving daughters, one thirteen and the other two. William's fraternity brothers at the local Odd Fellows lodge watched over the young widow and her family, stepping in to buy the homestead when the sheriff had to sell it for nonpayment of taxes and transferring the deed to her.[33] It is not clear how Emeline provided for her daughters in the 1870s. Her bright young daughter Sue excelled in school and was teaching by 1874: "Miss Sue Heiskell has quite a large school for primary pupils at her residence, and is meeting with gratifying success."[34] An advertisement in a local newspaper in 1877 recommended Mrs. Heiskell's boarding house.[35] The Hoovers and the Lykins family members who remained in Paola possibly helped the family.

Continued Loss and Death

Deaths of important people in Emeline's life continued. Joseph Lykins' wife, Merb, died in Paola six months after William.[36] Eight months later, her cousin, Juliana Lykins Case, age 33, died of an unidentified disease of the stomach in the Fall, 1872.[37] In a memorial to Juliana written by her stepmother, Mattie Lykins, the writer alluded to a special burden shared by Juliana and a cousin who was probably Emeline. Each had lost three little daughters in the 1860s: "To the loss of her dear little ones, she had become reconciled, and often spoke with great joy of meeting them in heaven. To a cousin who had suffered a like bereavement, she wrote, "Do you reflect that we are the mothers of angels in heaven?"[38]

> Be sure to check out, "*Memories of the Dead*," by Sarah Lykins Russell, in the Related Stories and Poems section at the end of the book.

Emeline's aunt, Juliann Betteys, died in 1872,[39] and her cousin, James F. Lykins, one of the earliest residents in Paola, died of typhoid-pneumonia at 40 in 1873.[40] A poem published by Sarah Lykins Russell mourns the loss of her sister and a daughter in 1872 and her only son William at the beginning of 1874.[41]

Three years after William Heiskell's death, his long-time friend and employer, Baptiste Peoria, was buried in the tribal cemetery in Oklahoma.[42] He was remembered as "a man of large stature, possessed of great strength, activity and courage and was like Keokuk, the great chief of the Sac and Fox Indians, a fearless and expert horseman."[43] He was characterized as "a man of large and enlightened views, and was distinguished for the virtues which spring from a kindly heart and generous spirit."[44] Emeline had told her nephew Wayland that she first saw him as a tall, courtly gentleman offering greetings to her on his first morning in the Kansas Territory.[45] Remembering him from that morning, she must have realized that his death and William's marked the end of an important part of her life and an uncertain beginning to the next.

Baptiste Peoria

One of the stresses on her and her family was an inundation of locusts of Biblical proportions in Paola and its surrounding area:

The panic of 1873, the ensuing depression, and a period of drought had already made life miserable for a great many settlers but economic difficulties and a lack of rain were things which most people had coped with and could understand. Nobody was ready to battle this strange phenomenon-this plague of locusts that descended on the land from the Dakotas to Texas in mid-summer.[46]

Although the settlers planted their crops a second time that season, following the total devastation of their first planting, and actually had a good return that year, many farmers did not survive. *The Miami Republican* listed 12 sheriff's sales in a single issue of the newspaper.[47] Farmers who survived the panic of 1873 and the locust infestation of 1874 had more to come. As the locusts departed in 1874, they left behind millions of eggs. Farmers tried to prevent the eggs from hatching by covering the soil where the eggs lay buried just under the surface with straw and setting the straw on fire. The locusts won. They hatched in the Spring of 1875, creating a "cruel meteorological event.... Locusts covered the entire ground like a blanket of damp snow. The insects that took flight formed a hazy cloud, dimming the afternoon sun and giving the western sky a 'strange and wildly weird appearance.'" Sue and Minnie would have heard grasshoppers pelting their roof like hail and, during the seven weeks that the insects ravaged the borderland, they would have seen the leaves stripped from the trees and bare dirt where grass had been devoured by the masses of grasshoppers. At this point, more settlers found the hardship and financial loss unbearable and left the borderland.[48]

Economic Loss and Death in Kansas City

General William Heiskell's daughter Price married Reverend A.D. Madeira in 1872. During Rev. Madeira's ministry in Kansas City, Price suddenly died in 1878, leaving two children.[49] The newspaper announcement did not name her cause of death or provide details of her life, but focused on the shock and devastation of the family she left behind, another human life for whom the person is defined and noted only by negative space outlined by the family's grief.

Mattie Lykins' family suffered an unexpected loss in 1870. Her nephew, Judson, home from the war and working as a physician to support his wife and three children, died suddenly.[50] In July 1870, a census taker at Pine Tavern, Kentucky, listed Judson as the head of household along with his wife, Albin, their two young children, and an infant.[51] By October 1871, Albin filed a widow's pension application.[52] She may not have known that Acting Assistant Surgeons were contract surgeons and, as such, did not qualify for a pension.

In the late 1860s and early 1870s, tumultuous economic conditions dominated the lives of businessmen and farmers in the region. Both Johnston Lykins and his son William were caught up in economic difficulties. Speculation abounded in the post-war environment, particularly in railroads. "Industry and trade had flourished beyond precedent during the first years after the war.... In 1873 railroad mileage had doubled itself since 1860, and this was a prolific cause of rash speculation. While business was expanding the currency was contracting. Paper money had depreciated and the conditions forbode a crash."[53]

An article in *The Leavenworth Daily Commercial* noted that William Lykins' mental health was causing great concern: "We learn from *The Kansas Journal* that Mr. W.H.R. Lykins, a prominent Banker of Lawrence, and, last year Mayor of that city, is deranged, and while laboring under a fit of insanity, attempted self-destruction. Misfortune in business has led to this distressing event, and his friends are said to entertain great fears for him in the future."[54] The Banking House of W.H.R. Lykins failed in 1868 and William left Lawrence to live in Kansas City. His business failure resulted in his working as a clerk. This less high-powered work allowed him to pursue his true passion: scholarship. He became a widely published scientific and geological writer, sending archaeological reports to the Smithsonian. One of his obituaries reads: "Mr. Lykins was naturally a student. He was a well-read man particularly on biology, geology and mineralogy. When he lived at Lawrence he had the finest library in Kansas. He was greatly interested in the mound builders and he assisted in opening and examining several Indian mounds of the vicinity.... He was an entertaining and interesting conversationalist and was much sought after by students and writers generally who respected his literary views and scientific theories."[55]

The effects of the speculative, over-heated economy were felt in both Paola and Kansas City during the next decade. In 1873, a severe financial depression swept through the country following the failure of Jay Cooke and Co., a banking firm financing the Northern Pacific Railroad. Speculators abounded in the post-war environment until an October day ushered in the "Panic of 1873;" one of those speculators was Johnston Lykins, president and founder of the Mechanic's Bank of Kansas City and a prominent realtor/developer in the city. He had been instrumental in bringing the railroad to Kansas City before the Civil War, and both he and William were heavily involved in railroads and banking. Paul C. Nagel, a George Caleb Bingham biographer, wrote that Bingham's friend Johnston "lost his wealth" in the economic downturn of the 1870s and died in bankruptcy.[56]

As is the case in all economic downturns, philanthropic contributions declined. Consequently, the Orphans' Home was in financial trouble at the same time as Johnston lost his money. In one of Mattie's appeals for funds for the Confederate Women and Children's Home, she alluded to the panic squeezing the funds of Kansas City's donors.[57] Her effective management was instrumental in the survival of the Confederate Women's and Children's Home as a privately funded institution for seven years.[58] She had to run public relations and fund raising campaigns to overcome the negative views some had of her because of her stances during the war and, in addition, struggle through the economic depression gripping the country from 1873-1878.[59]

The Generational Exodus

Two of Emeline's uncles who had been among the first white settlers in the Kansas Territory died within a year of each other; by the end of the decade, only one of the five pioneer Lykins brothers remained alive. In 1876, Johnston died in financial ruin, but his legacy continues in Kansas City today. Johnston was an extraordinary human being, an articulate man of vision, intellect, and energy. R. A. Campbell described him as a man who worked with Native American populations for over 30 years as a teacher, missionary, negotiator, physician and editor.[60] Johnston worked in the Carey Mission in Michigan in 1822, and escorted several tribes to the newly formed Indian Territory in Kansas, where he and his brothers established missions as the first Anglo settlers in the territory.

The string of "firsts" attached to Johnston's name attests to his pioneering frame of mind. He was one of the first to translate hymns and parts of the Bible into Indian languages. The first newspaper printed in Kansas, *Siwinowe Kesibwi*, (The Shawnee Sun), was printed under his leadership at the Shawnee Baptist Indian Mission beginning in 1835.[61]

Johnston Lykins was a founder of Westport and Kansas City:

After locating permanently in Kansas City in 1851, Johnston [p]ursued his profession, and has been identified with nearly every project for the welfare and advancement of Kansas City, and was its first mayor. He was active in the establishment of the *Kansas City Enterprise*-now the *Journal of Commerce*. He called together the first railroad meeting and presided over it; was the first president of the Mechanic's Bank and was in the organization of the first Baptist church;

was one of the founders of the chamber of commerce and at various times its president.⁶²

He exerted leadership for remaining in the Union during the time when Missouri debated whether to secede, and, at the same time, stood beside his equally courageous and articulate wife as she faced harsh criticism for her stances on secession, civil liberties and the conditions of women and children. In the *Gazetteer of Missouri*, he was acknowledged as "a thoroughly public-spirited citizen, a useful man in all positions of life, strong in energy, morality, and intellect."⁶³ In 1872, *The Kansas City Times* wrote of him as:

> A man who has been identified with Kansas City from the time of her first habitation unto the present, a man great in energy, morality, intellect who saw far into the future, who had the faith of reason and sound mental philosophy, and who lived up to what he believed and practiced what he preached....Not tall of stature, the eagle eye is yet undimmed; the head erect like a flame upon a torch; the gait firm and elastic; the hair just a little gray, where the relentless years as a fire passed . . . the form sturdy as an oak . . . .
> And his life has been an eventful one. Boating in the rapids of the Yellowstone; fighting small-pox as an epidemic, and holding off death as it were by the threat; dancing war dances with Indian tribes, and lying far out on the mysterious margin of the midnight, to surprise the stealthy savages on the war path; "red hand in foray, sage counsel in chamber; frank and real to friend and companion; fighting the battle of life ever in the front rank; truthful above all things; generous to enemies; strong in the indomitable hardihood of his nature, Dr. Lykins is a man who has left his mark on the age in which he lives.⁶⁴

The legacy left behind by Johnston's youngest brother, Claiborne, is not so clear; rather, it is surrounded by scandal and sorrow. Following the Civil War, Claiborne moved to the newly opened lands which had belonged to the Native American tribes who fought with the Confederacy. There he lived alone as a boarder: in 1870, he lived in the household of a young family in Labette County, in the newly settled, remote corner of Southeast Kansas.[65] In the 1875 Kansas census, Claiborne was recorded as living as a boarder on the farm of William Johns and several unrelated people.[66]

Johnston Lykins. Portrait by George Caleb Bingham. Courtesy of Bingham-Waggoner Historical Society, 313 W Pacific Avenue, Independence, Missouri.

A history of Labette County tells us that Osage Township was established in the Fall of 1866; in naming its first settlers, the author noted, "Dr. Lakins [sic] was the first in the township to offer his services as an aid to those desiring relief from physical ailments. He died a number of years ago, but his faithful mule, 'Joab,' it is said, still survives him [as of 1893].[67]

When Claiborne died in 1877, he was buried in Griffith Cemetery, a small, rural cemetery near the tiny village of Mound

Valley.⁶⁸ His wife Nancy and several grown children continued to live in the St. Joseph area. Curiously, his son William Lykins told the writer of his own biographical sketch that his father was a "a staunch Union man all through the Rebellion;"⁶⁹ in the entry related to Nancy, the writer made a point of what a responsible farmer her husband had been, having cleared 160 acres of good land which his widow had tried to hold together since his death (though Claiborne had been gone from it for a dozen years.)⁷⁰

The family clearly wanted to cast Claiborne and their own families in a favorable light as they continued to live in the St. Joseph area among those who remembered the reasons for his sudden departure from the community. He embodied the divided sympathies that continued to roil beneath the surface for decades after the war. In Ravenwood, a small town 50 miles from St. Joseph, Civil War veterans of both sides dressed up in their army uniforms each Memorial Day, their passions stirred anew each year as late as 1910. One old Confederate warrior used to get drunk and drive his horse and buggy down Main Street, whipping to horses to a gallop as he yelled, "Hurrah for Jeff Davis and the Confederacy!" as the team passed the cursing, muttering Union veterans standing in front of the street's stores.⁷¹ The pain, the loss, and the need to affirm that the fractured lives of people after the Civil War had been for justifiable, even elevated, moral purposes shaped the memory and loyalties of those who lived through those times for decades.⁷² At the community level, rituals (both formal and, like the one described above, informal), parades and ceremonies emerged to keep the memories of the warriors and their much romanticized battle exploits fresh. However, for Claiborne's family there appeared to be an attempt to restore Claiborne's reputation as a pioneer settler and to draw a veil over his clandestine activities during the war years in the hotly divided Borderland.

Of the Lykins brothers, only Joseph remained alive by the end of the decade. He remained on his farm near Paola and walked daily to take meals with the Hoovers, until he no longer had the strength to do so. Then he moved in with them until the end of his life in 1882.[73] Joseph—pioneer, missionary, teacher, pharmacist and farmer—was the last of the original Lykins family cluster of pioneers and missionaries in Kansas.

The Departure of Borderland Relatives

In addition to deaths of family members, a number of Emeline's cousins and her brother moved to Southeastern Kansas and the Oklahoma Indian Territory. Four Lykins men and David Peery lived within a fifty mile radius of Mound Valley, Kansas. David Lykins' younger son, Edward, and David Peery lived just across the Kansas border in the Oklahoma Indian Territory, about 50 miles from the Kansas border. About thirty-five miles from where Claiborne died, David's older son, Wayland, put down his roots in Southeastern Kansas. He entered the retail business and married his boss's daughter, Anna Middaugh. The Middaugh Company business, Wayland and Anna moved to Columbus, Kansas, where they remained several years. There he gained respect as a civic leader, serving as mayor, owning a hall that would house 600 people, having mining interests in the area and belonging to both the Odd Fellows and Masonic Lodges. He made important contributions to building the region when he relocated to the nearby Oklahoma Territory where he was instrumental in founding the town of Miami.[74] Wayland and Edward's childhood home near Paola was still on their minds. The brothers attempted to regain title to the land on which Wea Mission sat. They pushed a lawsuit all the way to the U.S. Supreme Court claiming that they had inherited the land from their father and that it had been improperly sold before their father's death. They did not prevail and their beloved homestead remained beyond their reach.[75]

Before returning to Paola, James F. Lykins lived in the area for several years. Following the removal of the Osage Tribe from their tribal lands in Southeastern Kansas, settlers had flocked to the area. These Lykins men may have gone to that area because of the new land and opportunities opening up there and, possibly, because of proximity to each other and the new Indian Territory where there were other family members.

William C. Lykins and Doc Middleton

Two of Claiborne's sons, Samuel and William, headed west to the Wyoming territory. William lived in the Cheyenne, Wyoming, area for about 20 years.[76] For part of that time he worked for the Wyoming Detective Association, a job that brought him face to face with the notorious outlaw, Doc Middleton. (Both William and, later, his son engaged in catching thieves, an ironic situation considering Claiborne Lykins' arrest for stealing horses.) In 1878, Doc Middleton and his gang stole forty horses; after learning of a reward for Middleton offered by Wyoming and Nebraska stockmen and the Union Pacific Railroad, "Billy" Lykins and a posse went after the gang and overtook them.[77] Writing about the event in 1910, Edgar Beecher Bronson described Lykins:

> Billy Lykins was one of the most efficient inspectors of the Wyoming Stock Growers Association, a short man of heavy muscular physique and a round, cherubic, pink and white face, in which a pair of steel-blue glittering eyes looked strangely out of place. A second glance, however, showed behind the smiling mouth a set of the jaw that did not belie the fighting eyes. So far as I can now recall, Billy never failed to get what he went after while he remained in our employ.[78]

Doc Middleton and Lykins encountered each other twice over the next few weeks. In the first incident, Lykins pursued Middleton "so close that Doc raced to the crest of a low conical hill, jumped off his mount, dropped flat on the ground and covered Lykins with a Springfield rifle, meantime yelling to him, 'Duck, you little Dutch fool; I don't want to kill you;' for they knew each other well, and in a way were friends."[79] Billy, however, "never knew when to stop." He spurred his horse on to where Doc lay, his Springfield ready to fire. Doc's gun misfired and before he could fire again, Lykins jumped on him.

After languishing in jail for a couple of weeks, Doc was released and immediately assembled a gang. Lykins found out where the gang was, took along two posse members and the three lay in wait for an opportunity to capture Middleton. Lykins' two companions posed as campers and, riding along with the gang, led them past where Lykins lay in wait. "When the band were come within twenty yards of him, he drew a careful bead on Doc's head and pulled the trigger. By strange coincidence his Sharps missed fire, precisely as had Doc's Springfield a few weeks before." Doc heard the gun hammer strike and turned to escape when Billy jumped from his hiding place, pistol blazing, and wounded Doc in the thigh. As Doc fell from his saddle, he shot one of Lykins' men; then Lykins and his remaining partner dispatched two of Middleton's men before the remaining gang members escaped and Doc was arrested.[80]

Middleton was taken to Sidney, Nebraska, to wait in jail until the necessary paperwork to take him back across the Wyoming state line into Cheyenne for trial was completed. Some of his friends sent word to Lykins that he should not attempt to take Middleton from the state. When the time came to transport the prisoner, two very heavily armed and alert men carried Middleton a quarter of a mile to the train station on a stretcher. Lykins walked in front of them armed with two colt 45s and a double-barreled shotgun, having informed Middleton's gang members that he would kill their leader should there be any attempt to rescue him.[81]

At his trial in Cheyenne, Doc Middleton was sentenced to five years in prison; William stayed in Wyoming a few more years, returning to his boyhood home in Missouri to become a highly successful apple-grower and community member in St. Joseph in the

1880s.[82] As a second irony, William's only son was killed by a thief after the family returned to St. Joseph. As his father had done years before, William, a deputy of his neighborhood's protection association, engaged in a pursuit of thieves who had been stealing from the farmers in the vicinity. When he came close to the thieves, he raised his shotgun and called for the them to stop. One turned and fired, hitting the 23-year-old newlywed right below the heart.[83] Unlike his grandfather, the young man did not survive his midnight escapade.

Mattie Lykins and George Caleb Bingham

While Emeline's young cousins were continuing the family's pioneering legacy in Southwestern Kansas, Oklahoma and Wyoming, Mattie Lykins constructed a new life following the bankruptcy and death of her husband. She sold the beautiful mansion she and Johnston had built (probably because she had to) and returned to the education work she had done before her marriage by establishing the Lykins Institute, an academy for young women, in Kansas City. She and George Caleb Bingham, both having recently lost their spouses, began to spend time together. Her friendship with the renowned painter and Missouri politician deepened into a serious romantic relationship and Mattie found herself again at the center of controversy. She gradually influenced George to affiliate with Unitarianism, which would have been considered a radical departure from conventional faith. But what caused Kansas City tongues to wag the most was that Bingham moved in with Mattie.[84]

A further cause for scandal was that one of her avowed enemies, a Mr. Piper, was the brother-in-law of Bingham's deceased wife. Piper had earlier opposed Mattie's plan for establishing the orphanage; in a public exchange, Mattie had thoroughly outdone him and he was determined to get revenge. When Mattie and Bingham began to live together, he saw an opportunity. He and his wife turned Bingham's sixteen-year old son against Mattie, filling the boy's imagination with visions of Mattie robbing him of his father's wealth and legacy. Bingham's best friend, James Rollins, stepped in and told the boy he was in danger of having his father cut off his allowance, a move which abruptly quieted the teenager who had been trumpeting his displeasure with Mattie throughout the city.[85]

Soon afterward, Mattie and Bingham were married at the Institute on June 18, 1878.[86] A guest at the wedding described the festive decorations for the event:

From the centre of the back parlor...was a magnificent wedding bell...constructed of the sombre bloom of the smoke tree, festooned with heliotrope and honeysuckle....The pair stood there, he the successful artist whose well-known paintbrush has painted pictures that shall live forever, and she, an acknowledged equal in taste, aesthetic culture and expressive sensibility, the scene was not joyous but impressive. The congratulations were prompt and hearty, all the guests but one being younger than the newly married couple....A most bountiful breakfast was partaken by the guests–a royal feast–its real and true description impossible.[87]

Bingham's health improved for a short time, and he was very happy with Mattie, telling his friend James Rollins "that he hoped he hoped to live long enough so 'that I may be able in some measure, to compensate her for the unselfish love which exhibits itself in her every act relating to myself.'"[88]

Their marital happiness was short-lived. In a little over a year, Bingham died in July 1879. Mattie arranged for his burial in the plot next to Johnston Lykins and had a large monument erected for Bingham on which she had inscribed, "Eminently gifted, almost unaided he won such distinction in his profession that he is known as the Missouri artist."[89]

Mrs. Martha A. "Mattie" (Livingston) Lykins Bingham, in her later years.

When Mattie died eleven years later, she again caused comment by having arranged to be buried between the two eminent husbands with a small stone marking her grave. A more conventional practice was to bury spouses of a first marriage together; Mattie chose to rest beside both husbands with the monument she placed for Bingham dwarfing both hers and Johnston's. Mattie's unconventional choices, outspoken ways, and controversial stances did not obscure the substance of her character. In a newspaper article written years after her death:

> The contemporaries of Mrs. Lykins pronounced her the biggest-hearted and broadest-minded of all the pioneer women of Kansas City. She was one of the most remarkable characters that ever lived in this community. With a strong mind, strengthened by a broad and liberal education, a commanding presence, manners of the most cultivated society, a powerful intellect and a tenacious will, she devoted her life to the welfare and happiness of the helpless and destitute. She was the foremost woman in every charitable and public work of early Kansas City. With success she was never satisfied and in defeat, she never surrendered.[90]

She was an articulate, bright and compassionate woman who would not be constrained by the roles and opinions commonly held in her time. As George Bingham said of her, "I think I can safely say in the highest sense of the term, she is no ordinary woman."[91] Mattie did not know–or care to know–how to walk a conventional path: it would never have occurred to her.

By the end of the decade many members of the Lykins/Peery/Heiskell extended families had died or moved. The major issues of the 1850s and 1860s which dominated their lives had been resolved, whether or not forgotten, and the identities of the remaining family members evolved within the context of a burgeoning Kansas City, the dynamic little town of Paola, and the firmly established small farms of Kansas and Missouri.

---

1. *Case files of applications from former Confederates for Presidential pardons (Amnesty papers) 1865-1867*, Microfilm publication M1003, roll 36 (Washington, D.C.: National Archives and Records Service, 1977), roll 36, Mattie Lykins to President Andrew Johnson, letter, 11 June 1866, as transcribed by Carolyn M. Bartels, compiler, *Amnesty in Missouri* (Shawnee Mission, Kansas: C. M. Bartels, 1990), np, and reprinted in *Kansas City Genealogist*, 35 (Fall 1994): 86-87.
2. "A Disgraceful Letter," undated clipping from unidentified newspaper, Martha Livingston Lykins Bingham, Mattie Lykins' Scrapbook, Dr. Johnston Lykins (1800-1876) and Martha Lykins Bingham (1824-1890) Collection, KC-0294, p. 60; Native Sons Archives, Western Historical Manuscript Collection, University of Missouri-Kansas City University Archives, Kansas City, Missouri.
3. "A Disgraceful Letter," Mattie Lykins' Scrapbook, p. 60; Western Historical Manuscript Collection.
4. William Jackson Livingston to [Lt.] Col. J[ames]. O. Broadhead, 16 Sept 1863, William Jackson Livingston case, Papers Relating to Individual Citizens, microcopy 345, Missouri Union Provost Marshal Papers, 1861-1866, Missouri State Archives, Jefferson City, Missouri.
5. 1870 U.S. Census, Monmouth, Shawnee, Kansas, p. 17, dwelling 116, family 117.
6. "Commendable," undated clipping from unidentified newspaper, Mattie Lykins' Scrapbook, p. 59; Western Historical Manuscript Collection.
7. Mrs. J. Lykins, "An Appeal in Behalf of the Widows and Orphans of Deceased Confederate Soldiers of Missouri,"Undated clipping from unidentified newspaper, Mattie Lykins' Scrapbook, p. 58; Western Historical Manuscript Collection.
8. "Grand Re-Union,"Undated clipping from unidentified newspaper, Mattie Lykins' Scrapbook, p. 60; Western Historical Manuscript Collection.

9. Mrs. J. Lykins, "An Appeal in Behalf of the Widows and Orphans of Deceased Confederate Soldiers of Missouri," p. 58; Western Historical Manuscript Collection.
10. "Mrs. Martha A. Lykins nee Livingston," C. R. Barns, editor, *The Commonwealth of Missouri; A Centennial Record* (Saint Louis: Bryan, Brand & Company, Publishers, 1877), 770.
11. "Dr. Johnston Lykins," *The Kansas City Genealogist* 25 (Winter-Spring 1985): 118.
12. "The Orphan's Home,"*Early History of Greater Kansas City, Missouri and Kansas: The Prophetic City at the Mouth of the Kaw, Diamond Jubilee Edition, 1928* (Kansas City, Missouri: Charles P. Detherage, 1927), 496.
13. Jeremy Neely, *The Border Between Them: Violence and Reconciliation on the Kansas-Missouri Line* (Columbia, Missouri: University of Missouri Press, 2007), 200-201.
14. Neely, *The Border Between Them*, 82.
15. *Miami Republican*, 1 Feb 1868, np, cited in *Paola, Kansas, A 150 Year Timeline: One Hundred and Fifty Years of History Events that Made Paola What it is Today* (Paola, Kansas: Miami County Historical Society, 2006), 42.
16. 1870 U.S. Census, East Ward, Paola City, Miami County, Kansas, p. 4, dwelling and family 46, Wm. A. Heiskell household.
17. *Miami Republican*, 5 Dec 1868, np, cited in *Paola Kansas, a 150-Year Timeline*, 43.
18. Miami County, Kansas, Register of Deeds, Deed Book P: 345, D. L. Peery to E. J. Heiskell, warrantee deed, 6 Feb 1869; Register of Deeds, Miami County Administration Building, Paola, Kansas.
19. Willis Lykins, interview by Nannie Lee Burns, 28 Oct 1937; Indian Pioneer Collection, vol. 56, Interview 12029; Manuscript Division, Western History Collections, University of Oklahoma Library, Norman, Oklahoma.
20. "Ancestors of Harry C. Lykins, Generation No. 2," unauthored genealogical print-out, Lykins file; Miami County Historical and Genealogical Society, Paola, Kansas.
21. Willis Lykins, interview, 28 Oct 1937.
22. *Miami Republican*, 15 Oct 1870, np, quoted in "Miami Republican Excerpts, 1870," *Miami County Genealogy Society Newsletter* 10 (Winter, 1995): 7.
23. Neely, *The Border Between Them*, 148.
24. *Miami Republican*, 1868, np, quoted in *Paola Kansas, a 150-Year Timeline*, 42.
25. *Miami Republican*, 4 Dec 1869, np, cited in *Paola Kansas, a 150-Year Timeline*, 48.
26. Selected extracts from *Miami Republican*, 1868-1869, np, cited in *Paola Kansas, a 150-Year Timeline*, 42-48.
27. Anonymous, handwritten note, Lykins file; Miami County Genealogical and Historical Society, Paola, Kansas.

28. "Death of W.A. Heiskell," *Paola Advertiser*, 20 Aug 1870, np, as reprinted in the Romney, West Virginia, *South Branch Intelligencer*, 2 Sept 1870, np, clipping, Heiskell vertical file; Romney Public Library, Romney, West Virginia.
29. *Miami Republican*, 20 Aug 1870, 3:4.
30. 1870 U.S. Census, Westport, Jackson County, Missouri, p. 2, dwelling and family 8, Emeline A. Price household.
31. 1870 U.S. Census, Kansas City, Jackson County, Missouri, p. 375, dwelling 1085 and family 1127, William Austin household.
32. "Heiskell Family", W.W. Glass Papers, Box 3, File 78, p. 7; Stewart Bell Jr. Archives, Handley Regional Library, Winchester, Virginia. William L. Kerns, *Historical Records of Old Frederick and Hampshire Counties, Virginia* (Bowie, Maryland: Heritage Books, 1992), 194.
33. Miami County, Kansas, Register of Deeds, Deed Book 29: 133-134, County Clerk to Trustees, Paola I. O. O. F. Lodge 11, tax deed, 9 Dec 1875; Register of Deeds, Miami County Administration Building, Paola, Kansas.
34. *Miami Republican*, 28 Feb 1874, 3:c.
35. *Western Spirit*, 19 Jan 1877, 3:d.
36. *Cemeteries of Miami County, Kansas* (Paola, Kansas: Miami County Genealogy Society, 1997), 3:445.
37. "In Memoriam," Juliana Lykins Case obituary, undated clipping from unidentified newspaper; Mattie Lykins' Scrapbook, np; Western Historical Manuscript Collection.
38. "In Memoriam," Juliana Lykins Case obituary; Mattie Lykins' Scrapbook, np.
39. Eva Dow Nance, Lykins Genealogy Notes, about 1931; Lykins Vertical File, Vigo Public Library, Terre Haute, Indiana.
40. "Lykins," *Miami Republican*, 3 Jan 1874.
41. Sarah Lykins Russell, "Memories of the Dead," Apr 1873, clipping from unidentified newspaper, Mattie Lykins' scrapbook, np; Western Historical Manuscript Collection.
42. *The Tulsa Sunday World*, 22 Oct 1967, *Paola Kansas, a 150-Year Timeline*, 63.
43. Cutler, *History of the State of Kansas*, 876.
44. Cutler, *History of the State of Kansas*, 876.
45. "Notes"; Lykins file; Miami County Historical and Genealogical Society, Paola, Kansas.
46. Robert W. Richmond, Kansas State Archivist, nd, quoted in *Paola Kansas, a 150-Year Timeline*, 63.
47. Nettie Murray, research paper prepared for the Pleasant Hour Club, 1936, and undated clipping from unidentified newspaper, Newspaper Clipping Collection of Ethel J. Hunt, both cited in *Paola Kansas, a 150-Year Timeline*, 63-64.
48. Neely, *The Border Between Them*, 203-205.
49. Ancestry.com, "Missouri Marriages, 1851-1900," database (http://www.ancestry.com : accessed 10 Mar 2008), Heiskell - Madeira entry. "At

Rest: Funeral Services Yesterday over the Remains of Mrs. Dr. Madeira," *Kansas City Times*, 7 Nov 1878, 4:5.
50. Robert D. Owen to Rose Ann Findlen, email, 12 Feb 2010. Robert Owen recalls his grandmother, Ada Armintha (Campbell) Owen, Judson Owen's daughter-in-law, telling him this information when Robert was a boy.
51. 1870 U.S. Census, Pine Tavern District, Bullitt County, Kentucky, pp. 27-28, dwelling and family 190, J. B. [sic] Owen.
52. "Civil War Pension Index: General Index to Pension Files, 1861-1934," database, *Ancestry.com* (http://www.ancestry.com : accessed 10 Dec 2009); Judson R. Owens [sic] (Medical Department U.S. Volunteers) index card; imaged from *General Index to Pension Files, 1861-1934*, T288 (Washington, D.C.: National Archives [n.d.], no roll number cited.
53. Charles Morris, "Reconstruction and Progress," *The Great Republic by the Master Historians,* editor, Charles Morris (New York: Great Republic Publishing Company, 1913), 3: 352.
54. *Leavenworth Daily Commercial*, 23 Nov 1867, 4:2.
55. "The Death of a Pioneer," *Kansas City Star,* 16 June 1893, 4.
56. Paul C. Nagel, *George Caleb Bingham: Missouri's Famed Painter and Forgotten Politician*, (Columbia, Missouri: University of Missouri Press, 2005), 144.
57. "A Short Sermon," [Jefferson City] *Daily State Journal*, Mattie Lykins' Scrapbook, p. 16; Western Historical Manuscript Collection.
58. Frances S. Bush, "Helping Hand for Civil War Vanquished," *Kansas City Times*, 15 Aug 1975, np; clipping, Lykins: Johnston and Mattie vertical file; Midcontinent Public Library, Independence, Missouri.
59. Frances S. Bush, "Helping Hand for Civil War Vanquished," *Kansas City Times*, 15 Aug 1975, np.
60. Robert Allen Campbell, *Campbell's Gazetteer of Missouri* (Saint Louis: R. A. Campbell, 1875), 272k.
61. Esther Clark Hill, "Some Background of Early Baptist Missions of Kansas, *Kansas Historical Quarterly* 2 (Feb 1932): 90.
62. *Campbell's Gazetteer of Missouri*, 272k.
63. *Campbell's Gazetteer of Missouri*, 272k.
64. "Our Real Estate Men -- No. 2: Dr. Johnston Lykins," Mumford and Fancher, *The Real Estate Index*, no volume, date, or page; re-published in *The Kansas City Times*, 7 July 1872, np; clipping, Mattie Lykins' Scrapbook. np; Western Historical Manuscript Collection.
65. 1870 US Census, Osage, Labette County, Kansas, p. 2, household 18, Solomon Adamson household..
66. 1875 Kansas State Census, Osage, Labette County, Kansas, p. 21, household 169, William Johns household.
67 . Nelson Case. *History of Labette County, Kansas, From the First Settlement to the Close of 1892* (Topeka, Kansas: Crane and Company, 1893), 110.

68. Tina Rice, "Griffith Cemetery," *Tombstone Inscriptions: Labette County Kansas,* (np: Tina Rice, 1981), 1: 460.
69. Christian Ludwig Rutt, *History of Buchanan County and the City of St. Joseph and Representative Citizens, 1826 to 1904* (Chicago: Biographical Publishing, 1904), 382.
70. *The History of Buchanan County, Missouri* (Saint Joseph, Missouri: Union Historical Company, 1881), 817.
71. Personal knowledge of Pearl West Gard as told to her daughter, Rose Ann Findlen. Pearl West was eight years old in 1910. Her grandfather who was still alive had fought on the Union side. The village had a population of about 341 in that year, and the annual event was widely discussed in local homes.
72. Drew Gilpin Faust, *This Republic of Suffering: Death and the American Civil War* (New York: Vintage Books, 2008), 193.
73. Joseph Lykins obituary, undated clipping from unidentified newspaper, Lykins file; Miami County Historical and Genealogical Society, Paola, Kansas.
74. D. C. Gideon, "Wayland C. Lykins," *Indian Territory. Descriptive, Biographical, and Genealogical . . . with a General History of the Territory* (New York: Lewis Publishing, 1901), 444-446.
75. *Lykins v McGrath*, 184 US 169 (1902).
76. Christian Ludwig Rutt, *History of Buchanan County*, 382.
77. "Doc Middleton Was Infamous Road Agent and Bandit," Cheyenne *Tribune-Eagle*, 23 July 1972, p. C-6; clipping, Crime and Criminals -- Early Outlaws file, Western History Collection; Wyoming Room, Sheridan County Fulmer Public Library, Sheridan, Wyoming.
78. Edgar Beecher Bronson, *The Red-Blooded Heroes of the Frontier* (London: A.C. McClurg, 1910), 39.
79. Bronson, *Red-Blooded Heroes*, 40.
80. Bronson, *Red-Blooded Heroes*, 41.
81. "Doc Middleton, Road Agent & Bandit."
82. Rutt, *History of Buchanan County*, 382.
83. *Saint Joseph News-Press*, 18 Jan 1912, 1:a.
84. Nagel, *George Caleb Bingham: Missouri's Famed Painter and Forgotten Politician*, 145.
85. Nagel, *George Caleb Bingham*, 145-146.
86. Nagel, *George Caleb Bingham*, 146.
87. *Kansas City Times*, June 1878; quoted in Alberta Wilson Constant, *Paintbox on the Frontier: The Life and Times of George Caleb Bingham* (New York: Crowell, 1974), 174.
88. Nagel, *George Caleb Bingham*, 146.
89. Nagel, *George Caleb Bingham*, 150.

90. "Mystery in an Opened Corner Stone," undated clipping from unidentified newspaper; Kansas History Clippings, v. 6, p. 314; Kansas State Historical Society, Topeka, Kansas.
91. Constant, *Paintbox on the Frontier*, 175.

CHAPTER 7

Along Came William F. Wallace

Sue Heiskell-William F. Wallace Connections

William Heiskell=Emeline Peery		William True Wallace=Lydia Waterman	
David = Minnie Heenan Heiskell	Sue Heiskell (1) =	William F. Wallace =	(2) Addie Gilman
		-Leslie Wallace	
		-Elyse = Wallace	Rolf Osterman
		-Josie Wallace	
		-Alice = Wallace	Philip Kimball

    Emeline's daughter Sue benefitted from the rapid expansion of education in the Borderland as its citizenry built schools between 1865-1870. Before the Civil War, Kansas and Missouri boys attended school in larger numbers than girls, but their primary school in the 1860s was the battlefield rather than the classroom. By 1870, the number of girls and boys enrolled in school was roughly equal.[1] An excellent student, Sue began to teach from the Heiskell home before she was 16 and, soon thereafter, started teaching in a country school. Within the pioneer communities, a bright young woman of 16 was considered ready to begin teaching, and it was probably also well known to the community that Emeline and her daughter had few financial resources. *The Miami Republican* noted in February 1874, that, "Miss Sue Heiskell has quite a large school for primary pupils at her residence and is meeting with gratifying success." In the months to follow, the newspaper routinely reported on school events, noting that Sue delivered "The Recitation" at the Miami County Teachers' Association at the brand new school in Paola.[2]

The editor of the *Miami Republican* and the community were smitten with young Sue's talent and sparkle. In her obituary many years later, she was described as having been "a charming girl, hair jet black and hung to her waist and her eyes a brilliant black that spoke at every glance. Classical features and queenly grace distinguished her wherever she went. Nor did the attention paid her lead to vanity, for she was self-balanced, modest and gentle."[3]

School room in Paola, Kansas

Her energy and imagination as a teacher led her to institute public spelling bees at her school for the entertainment of the community:

"On last Wednesday evening Miss Sue Heiskell, the accomplished young teacher of District 47, three miles northeast of this city, conducted a spelling exercise at her school house. The children and the old folks gathered in full force; and the presence of a large number of ladies and gentlemen from this city and its suburbs added much to the interest and pleasures of the occasion. Miss Heiskell announces another spelling for Friday evening of next week." By December of that year, the spelling bees had become "exceedingly popular in our school districts and considerable rivalry exists between a number of neighboring schools. Miss Heiskell, on Friday evening of last week, had a full house at her spelling school and that of I.M. Boothe of District 49 on Thursday evening last had an unusually full attendance."

Sue's popularity with the *Miami Republican* editor and other community members continued; on an April evening in 1875, the editor enthusiastically reviewed her performance at a public reading: "A very entertaining feature of the evening was the reading of one of Will Carlton's [sic.] poems entitled 'The Editor's Sanctum, [sic.] by Miss Sue Heiskell. Miss Heiskell entered fully into the spirit of 'Carleton' and read with rare pathos and splendid articulation, which was highly appreciated by the audience, *the editors and printers in particular.*" [5]

Will Carleton was a popular poet in nineteenth century America known for his ability to charm the American public with his poetic treatments of ordinary daily events. The poem Sue read was published in one of his books, *Farm Ballads*, in 1875.[6]

The *Miami Republican* editor's sly phrasing was undoubtedly an allusion to the attentiveness of one journalist in particular, William F. Wallace, co-editor of the *Rice County Herald* in Peace, Kansas. Sue's interest in editors and

> Refer to *"The Editor's Guests,"* in the Related Stories and Poems section at the end of the book.

their sanctums centered on the twenty-six-year-old New Englander who stood five foot eight inches tall and had a fair complexion, blue eyes, and brown hair.[7]

W. F. Wallace had lived in Paola in 1872-73 and studied law with Benjamin F. Simpson, the former state attorney general and Republican state legislator. After he was admitted to the bar in June 1873, he relocated in Rice County. At that time, the *Miami Republican* editor, Basil Simpson, seemed to hold him in high regard: "W.F. Wallace of Rice County, late a resident of this city, is in town on business, whose exact nature is not known. He speaks encouragingly of his own prospects and those of Rice County, and we hope that he may to the fullest extent realize his expectations."[8]

By the spring of 1875, however, Basil Simpson's opinion appears to have changed. Around the time W.F. and Sue were becoming romantically involved, W.F. became the topic of heated, insulting letters to the editor in March because of remarks he made about Benjamin F. Simpson, his mentor and teacher. The writer expressed his anger without restraint, apparently not concerned that W.F. would charge him with libel:

**William F. Wallace.
Courtesy of Wallace Kimball family.**

"INGRATITUDE–The editor of the Rice County Herald speaking of Hon. Ben Simpson being employed to prosecute "a poor devil," as he calls him, in Bourbon County, says, "the County Commissioners of Bourbon go on the principle that it takes a thief to catch a thief." The editor of the Herald is named W.F. Wallace, and out of kindness Ben Simpson took him into his office, where he had the use of Simpson's books, and received instruction for more than a year, without fee or reward. When he left, Maj. Simpson gave him some forty dollars worth of books, and he has been depending on Simpson for brains ever Since, in the form of briefs in the few cases he does have. Go, you d____d dog! You are too mean to live and too mean to die. Hide your diminishing head in some place, if you can find one, where gentlemen are unknown."[9]

The journalistic fury continued into the next week:

"INTERROGATORY–Mr. Editor: Is the Mr. Wallace mentioned in last week's issue of the paper the same creature who was *dead beating* it round Paola in 1872? If so, it would be but natural for Him to slander and malign any one who had befriended him. This exterior covering of a Bologna sausage [pig intestine, in other words] Was a Grant man in the last Presidential campaign, but was low enough to enter a Liberal Republic or Greeley caucus and vote for delegates to attend their State Convention. He did think that, however, as a favor to 'Sugg Fort,' Bob Mitchell, perhaps. If Wallace is editor of a Rice County paper, as reported, who in thunder reads and corrects the proof–for such orthography as he is author of would be a discredit to Nasby. -Paola. Note (from editor)–Yes sir, the same w.f. wallace, that figured as you state, read law with Ben Simpson and now returns his kindness with lies. A miserable ingrate that would blacken the character of the mother that bore him, for the sake of notoriety.–(Ed.)"[10]

Besides insulting Simpson, Wallace had apparently gotten himself into a thicket of Kansas politics and a continuing virulent battle between the editors of *The Miami Republican* and *The Western Spirit*, edited by a relative newcomer to the city, William Perry. In the social news (some would say "gossip columns") of *The Western Spirit*, Perry consistently reported news of W.F. Wallace's comings and goings in a neutral manner–they may have been friends or newspaper colleagues. For example, *The Western Spirit* alludes to W.F. Wallace having dropped by its office in December, 1873, noted that Wallace planned to "spend the holidays with his old friends in this county." During that holiday season, *The Miami Republican* warmly wished him success "in his profession as a lawyer, in his labor as an editor, and in his visits to Paola as a suitor."[11]

Perhaps pretty Sue Heiskell should have paid more attention to the unflattering views of Wallace later expressed in *The Miami Republican*.

William and Sue decided to marry, and on June 27, 1875, "a joyful wedding followed" at the bride's home. The editor of *The Western Spirit*, ever the punster, published a verse in honor of their marriage:

> Not all who trust their claims to law
> Can *Sue* with such success,
> Or find at one great master stroke
> Both *Peace* and happiness.[12]

William had recently shut down his newspaper in Peace, and the couple set off for their life together in Hutchinson, Kansas, where William established a newspaper, *The Reno Independent*.[13]

Neither the newspaper nor the marriage lasted long. Nine months after the wedding, Sue, now three months' pregnant, returned to Paola.[14] *The Western Spirit* reported the following month that William, "late of Peace and Hutchinson, arrived in Paola on Monday. He has sold out his newspaper in Hutchinson and will seek a new location."[15] What the newspaper editor may not have known is that he had likely seen the last of W.F. Wallace.

When Sue petitioned the court for a divorce in July, 1877, she identified May 2, 1876, as the date her husband abandoned her. Stating that William had sent no money to provide for her during her pregnancy or to feed and clothe the baby, Sue asked for custody of their son, Leslie Earle, and was granted both the divorce and the custody. In the text of the petition for divorce, a phrase indicating that William was possibly in New Hampshire was crossed out.[16] It turns out that he had indeed returned to New Hampshire. In William's application for disability pension related to his service in the Civil War, two residents of Epsom County, New Hampshire, said that William lived continuously in the Epsom County vicinity from 1877-1883.[17]

The reason for the failure of the Heiskell-Wallace marriage is lost, although a look at William's life to the time of his marriage gives some indication of his disjointed journey into adulthood and the impact that might have had. William's father, William T. Wallace, was a carpenter in Concord, New Hampshire, at the time he married William's mother, Lydia Waterman.[18] William had lost his wife, Mary Ann Dana, three years earlier.[19] William and Mary Ann's child, Nathaniel Dana Wallace, lived in the home of his aunt, Rachel Babb Sanders, in Epsom, while his father boarded on a farm and worked as a bricklayer thirteen miles away in Hooksett.[20] (In the 1840s and 1850s, William Senior's brother was leading a life very different from that of his carpenter brother. George Benjamin Wallace, one of the founders of Salt Lake City, had converted to Mormonism in 1842. By 1845, he moved to Nauvoo, Illinois, to a Mormon settlement without his wife, who does not appear to have converted to the Mormon faith or to have embraced polygamy. Within the next seven years, however, he had married four other wives (three of them sisters married to him on the same day) moved across the country to remote Utah, and become a highly valued leader of that community.)[21]

William's father re-married after his first wife's death. Ten months after Lydia Waterman and William married, William F. was born. A year later, his father William lived at a boarding house in Concord, New Hampshire, while Lydia and baby William lived with Eliza Marcy in Hillsborough, New Hampshire.[22] William's death certificate gave his mother's name as "Lydia Marcy," not "Lydia Waterman," so there is a strong possibility that Lydia was much more closely connected to the Marcy family than to the Waterman family in W.F.'s mind. It was Joshua Marcy, listed next to Eliza and Lydia in the 1850 census, who married Lydia and William T. Wallace.[23]

By 1860, Lydia and William T. were still not living under the same roof. William and his son Dana lived in a boarding house in Concord where they worked as carpenters; William F. was listed as "a laborer," age eleven, in the household of William T.'s sister, Rachel Babb Sanders in Epsom County. W.F.'s mother Lydia was not listed at either location.[24]

The advent of the Civil War brought even more upheaval. William's father and 18-year-old half-brother enlisted in Company B, Second Regiment of the New Hampshire Infantry in 1861.[25] They were immediately thrust into the bloody conflict: the defeat at the First Battle of Bull Run and the siege of Yorktown. The First Battle of Bull Run was the Second New Hampshire's first battle, the regiment having been formed in April of 1861.[26] The two Wallace's Company B was a rifle unit which came under heavy fire in its first combat. *The National Republican* in Washington reported:

> During the late engagement the Second New Hampshire regiment behaved with the utmost gallantry. Arriving on the field the second regiment, they were instantly called upon to support the right of the Rhode Island Battery; and with the

coolness of veterans, although swept by the fire of the rebels, formed line of battle and remained in this trying position for more than an hour. When ordered to charge, they rushed forward with great impetuosity, driving the enemy from their position to the woods, and sweeping everything before them. At one time, when a retreat was sounded, Companies B and I remained in their position half an hour after every other company had retreated, and poured in a destructive fire on the rebels, who were advancing to outflank them, only retiring when capture or annihilation became inevitable.[27]

The Union lost the battle; however, the Second New Hampshire went on to fight many other battles. Less than a year after he had enlisted, Dana was wounded at Williamsburg, Virginia. In that battle, Company B was ordered to skirmish over fallen logs placed in defense of the first of 13 heavily fortified redoubts at Fort Magruder.[28]

Two months later Dana was captured at Gettysburg, at the infamous Peach Orchard where the New Hampshire Second "received and withstood that shower of shot and shell which put *hors de combat* three-fifths of all the men of our command who answered to the roll-call that fateful morning."[29] At the dedication of the Second New Hampshire memorial at Gettysburg in 1886, Martin A. Haynes recalled,

> *The Second had made its record at Gettysburg. The plain figures chiseled upon that block of granite are the eloquent record of the deed. One hundred and ninety-three men, stricken, not from a division, not from a brigade, but from one little skeleton regiment, numbering but three hundred and fifty-five officers and men. Do those who have never stood in the battle line understand what such figures mean? Why, battles have been fought which were pivotal events in history and are quoted as monuments of valor, with less aggregate loss than that of the*

Second New Hampshire upon this spot. . . . It was a veteran regiment that fought here, and it can be safely assumed that none but a veteran regiment could have stood such a test and done such work.[30]

Dana's father was not with him at Gettysburg. His Civil War Service Record does not list it among the battles he fought. Likely William T. was already ill with the condition that was going to result in his mustering out six weeks later. Shortly after his son's capture, William had been given a medical discharge in August 1862, suffering from phthisis (an older term for tuberculosis).[31]

On November 13, 1863, Dana died in a Confederate prison in Richmond, Virginia.[32]

William T. signed up again in 1864, this time with Troop G of the 1st New Hampshire Cavalry, where he was promoted to Commissary Sergeant and stationed in the greater greater Washington, D.C. area. For the last four months of his service, he was transferred to Unassigned Detachment 1, of the Veterans' Reserve Corps.[33]

Young William F. moved into his third line of work in 1865, when he signed up as a musician in the 18th New Hampshire Infantry, Company I. His first work was as a laborer on his aunt's farm when he was 11. When he enlisted at age 16, he was a carpenter, as both his father and Nathaniel had been.[34] As part of the Army of the Potomac, W.F.'s Regiment participated in the assault on and the fall of Petersburg, Virginia. By the end of April 1865, the regiment moved to the Washington, D.C. area, camping at Alexandria and performing "Provost duty" at Georgetown until July. This regiment performed guard duty in Washington during the trial of Abraham Lincoln's assassins.[35] Though the young man was in the army for only four months, he did not come away from the war unscathed. He acquired malarial poisoning, rheumatism and a weakened heart which affected his health throughout his life.[36]

When W. F.'s father returned to New Hampshire after the war, he filed for divorce, citing "willful absence" as the grounds for his petition.[37] Three years later, William F.'s father died in San Felipe, California.[38] While the cause of William T.'s untimely death is unknown, he likely died from the effects of his progressive illness. In 1870,[39] William's mother, meanwhile, lived near her father, Amasa Waterman, in Manchester, New Hampshire.

Around the time William was studying law in Paola, his mother married a locomotive engineer and moved to Michigan where she remained until she died.[40] It is not known where young William F. was between 1865 and 1872, when he showed up in Paola, but he appears to have been restless and lost, and in many ways, not a good candidate for marriage.

Following the divorce, Sue stayed in Paola. About a year and a half later, she met Hiram L. Phillips of nearby Louisburg. "High" Phillips was three years older than Sue's mother, having been born in Kentucky in 1827.[41] Before coming to Kansas, High had lived in Missouri and Illinois, raising a family there. When he arrived as a widower in Louisburg in 1877, he engaged in the lumber business and soon found himself immersed in politics. His background as a practicing attorney and District Attorney in Missouri and his service as a school teacher and superintendent there no doubt sharpened his awareness of the importance of good government. According to Cutler, "Mr. Phillips has always been a great reader and thinker and entertains advanced ideas in regard to the theories and practice of good government under our system. His conclusions arrayed him against the dominant party and for fourteen years he has labored by voice and pen in the interest of good government and in opposition to monopolies and rings."[42]

In the months prior to marrying Sue, progressive anti-monopolists nominated him to run for State Senator for the 21st District of Kansas.[43] The editor of *The Western Spirit* of Paola commented, "Honorable H.L. Phillips, of Louisburg, and Greenback candidate for State Senator, gave us a friendly call yesterday. He is a pleasant gentleman and is now engaged in making a canvass of the county in behalf of his ticket. He went to Stanton last evening and was at Antioch the night before. If Mr. Phillips was only a Democrat, we would be pleased to lend him a helping hand."[44]

When Phillips concluded his canvassing in December, *The Western Spirit* again praised him: "Honorable H.L. Phillips of Louisburg, was in town Tuesday, looking hale and hearty after his recent political canvass. He is a gentleman of fine ability and we hope to see him representing this county in a position where his talents can be displayed."[45] Phillips' "defeat was a foregone conclusion from the relative strength of the parties, but he made a creditable run, receiving about 600 votes." The Greenbacks nominated Phillips for Lieutenant Governor in 1880 and for Congressman at large in 1882, but Phillips and the small party were not able to win against the powerful majority parties.[46]

He did, however, succeed in winning Sue's hand. When Sue and High were married in February, 1879, at Emeline's home, the editor of *The Western Spirit* again wrote a verse, inserting a waggish allusion to the groom's age: "The thanks of *The Spirit* are tendered to Mr. and Mrs. Phillips for their kind remembrance in the shape of a bountiful supply of cake.

> May heaven smile on your sweet grace
> And strew your path with virtue and peace,
> And fill your cup with earthly joys,
> And the old man's arms with little____and etc, and etc.[47]

The couple lost no time fulfilling the editor's wish for them. Their first daughter was born the following December.[48]

Sue and High had at least some awareness of W.F.'s whereabouts at that time. In the 1880 census, the person reporting (probably High) said that baby Earl (Leslie Earle)'s father was born in Ohio. Although W.F. was born in New Hampshire, he was, in fact, living in Ohio in 1880 with a physician and his family. That year he was graduated from Columbus Medical College in that state.[49]

As Sue Heiskell Phillips and William F.'s lives went in their respective directions, Emeline's life also took a satisfying new direction when she was appointed head of the Paola Free Library in 1880, serving in that capacity until 1897.[50] While Emeline worked at the library, her younger daughter, sixteen-year-old Minnie, helped support the family by working as a bookkeeper in 1880.[51] As librarian Emeline became an institution, amazing and delighting townspeople with her knowledge of the library collection.

Her grandson Leslie recalled her energy and dedication to the library:

> *Through storm and calm, through winter's cold and summer's heat, she was always at her post, day and night, at an age when most persons have retired from any sort of active service. She had an unusually keen mind, and was widely read, and her knowledge of books and current events of the thousands of*

volumes which comprised the Paola library was almost unbelievable. No new book came to the library which she did not read, even when she was far past sixty. A patron coming to the library had merely to give her the faintest inkling of the content of some book of which he did not know the name, and she could tell him instantly the title and the author of the book. In the dark she could find any book on the shelf.[52]

Emeline's devotion to the library as well as the financial support of a local sponsor are credited with the survival of the little fledgling library which began with "but few books, a little stove, some rude shelves, a few chairs and some benches. The library was her store, her home, her all, except her children and her God. Many and many a man visited the library, as much to talk with the librarian, as to look after a volume."[53]

Interior of the Paola Free Library

The Death of Emeline Peery Heiskell

When Emeline died in 1916, she had out-lived almost everyone in her generation. She was one of the last Kansas pioneers still alive on the eve of World War I. Her life in the Kansas Territory began in an Indian mission at the height of the missionaries' importance to the settlement of the region. For better or worse, her extended family figured prominently in the Borderland disputes leading up to the Civil War. As personal tragedies occurred and family fortunes fell throughout the 1860s and 1870s, she endured, and, in spirit, triumphed. In her last years, she lived with daughter Sue in Louisburg, but made visits by train to visit her grandson Leslie in Kansas City. She made these trips with the agility of a forty-year old and enjoyed going to the historical society to remind herself of the life and times of her Uncle Johnston and other friends and family members of the city.[54] Family and "a large assemblage of old settlers" in the Paola community turned out to honor her when her body was brought from Louisburg to Paola for burial. She was remembered as the spark who kept the Paola Free Library alive and energetically led community readers to find knowledge and entertainment in books. When people wanted to dwell on the difficulties of the past, she vigorously affirmed that challenge was also an important, exciting part of the experience.

The editor of the "Western Spirit" reported, "Then the dust of Emelin Peery Heiskell was given back to earth and rests in peace in the family burial ground. Under a large oak tree, the casket was opened and a number of people looked for the last time upon the face of the beloved woman, whose life deeds were threaded with the history of Miami county. In her 87th year she went back to earth, like a ripe apple falls to the ground."[55] Emeline's body lies in an unmarked grave, the ultimate symbol of having been identified or demarcated primarily in the negative space around the lives of others.

If Emeline could speak for herself, she would probably say that it is more meaningful to have her portrait hanging in the Paola Free Library not far from shelves of books and children seated at tables absorbed in their reading than it is to have a fallen-over grave marker. She might also point proudly to her influence on her grandson Leslie, who grew up to be one of the state's most revered journalists. Though she continues in history to exist in the negative space forming the background for others, in life she lived for them positively and affirmatively, a woman of courage and joy.

The Lives of Sue and William F. in the 1880s

In the years Sue and High had together, Sue gave birth to three other daughters, Nellie, Lenora, and Jessie, and High continued running for political office on the Greenback and Prohibition ticket: for Congress in 1882 and for Governor in 1884. He took a business trip in Spring, 1885, and returned from it with pneumonia; when he died two weeks later, hundreds attended his funeral to honor him and his wife.[56] The Kansas State Census for 1885 listed Sue as head of household and gave her youngest daughter's age as 8 months. At 27, Sue was raising Leslie, two young daughters, and the infant Jessie. Sue supported the family by teaching school. The same census listed Leslie Earle (then nine years old) as living with his grandmother in Paola.[57] Emeline was probably helping Sue cope with her husband's death and her struggle to support the family.

In October 1889, Sue married a third time to a twice-widowed man who was many years her senior, Philip F. Latimer.[58] Philip had emigrated from Ireland during the famine years. After learning his early trade as a wagonwright's apprentice, he moved with his brothers to Westport, Missouri in 1851 and on to Wea Township to farm in 1864.[59] At the time of his marriage to Sue, he was 59 and lived in Louisburg, where he was a merchant.[60] In about

1895, Sue's sister Minnie married another Irish immigrant, David Heenan, who settled in Wichita, Kansas.⁶¹

Sue's third husband "touched the lives of many Miami County residents. He was a school superintendent, trustee of Wea Township, commissioner, member Home Guard, police judge and councilman of Louisburg, Kansas, estate administrator, etc. Starting small, his farm acreage was increased to 704 acres."⁶² By marrying Sue, he also acquired a second young family to help raise. In the 1900 census, he and Sue had in their household Sue's three daughters and their son, Philip H. Latimer, age eight. In both the 1900 and 1910 censuses, Sue identifies her occupation as "milliner" in a Louisburg store.⁶³

Sue Heiskell (Wallace) Phillips Latimer

Sue's widowed mother Emeline lived with them at least part of the time after she retired from the library. The 1910 census lists Emeline as residing with Philip and Sue.

William F. remarried in 1883 surrounded once again by controversy because he assisted his future wife, Addie Mary Gilman French, in running away from her first husband. Descendants of Addie and William remember the story Addie told about leaving her first husband. She described Merwin French as a crass, dirty man who was so indifferent to cleanliness and manners that he openly relieved himself in her kitchen! This behavior was the final blow to their unhappy marriage. She made arrangements to leave the marriage: her doctor, William F. Wallace, drove up to the front of the house in a buggy and took her away. In March of that year, her husband obtained a divorce from Addie and was awarded custody of the three children of that marriage, John, Willie and Mabel.[64] A month later, Addie and William were married by a justice of the peace in Dover, New Hampshire.[65] In time, Mabel came to live with her mother and William.[66]

William practiced medicine in three New Hampshire locations: Milton, Bradford and Plaistow until his heart condition forced him to retire.[67] During his time in Bradford, he saw patients at his home, with his advertisement in the *Kearsarge Independent* reading, "Physician and Surgeon, Special attention given to diseases of women and children. Office Hours: 7 to 10 AM and 7 to 9 PM." In addition to practicing medicine, William was a certified pharmacist and operated the Central Drug Store out of his house in the 1890s.[68]

W. F. Wallace and family in New Hampshire.

He began applying for a pension as early as 1890, when he was 41. In his application, his examining physician described his condition: "suffers from acid dyspepsia all the time and is gradually losing flesh. Suffers from pain in region of heart from palpitation and slight-exercise, suffers from general rheumatism nearly all the time, and from sick headache about twice a week."[69]

Addie and William met at a revival. His religious fervor may have stemmed from his time in the army. Civil War historian Drew Gilpin Faust wrote that the horrors of the war caused many soldiers to embrace religion as they struggled to make sense of the nightmarish existence in which they found themselves. Many soldiers converted to evangelical Christianity during the war as "revivals swept armies of both North and South."[70] Family members told stories of his holding religious services in his back yard, frequently standing up to excoriate the female gender as wicked and manipulative, leading good men into sin. He did not spare his own wife and daughters in his diatribes. His daughters grew up resentful and rebellious; when he wrote a letter of apology to them late in his life, his words of regret could not heal the wounds he had earlier inflicted.[71]

In Rochester his health continued to decline and he confided to friends that he was deeply concerned about leaving his wife and two daughters penniless. The two friends provided an affidavit in support of Addie's application for a Widow's Pension, one stating: "so far as I have been able to learn Mrs. Wallace has no property or income from any source except what she earns by her labor as a housekeeper. Just before William F. Wallace died he sent for me and said, 'I have but a short time to live and I have got to go and leave them without any mean of support,' and asked me as a friend to give such advice to Mrs. Wallace and her children as would be helpful to them."[72]

At age 56, William died of heart disease, which appears to have developed from the illnesses he contracted during his brief stint as a musician in the Union Army. According to his obituary, "He had been in ill health for a long time. Wednesday morning he arose at 6 o'clock, ate his breakfast, and later, not feeling well, lay down on the bed in his room. At about 9 o'clock he was found dead by a member of the family."[73] He was buried in Bradford beside his little daughter Josie who died when she was six.[74]

His concern that his wife and two daughters would be destitute was well founded. Census data in subsequent years hint at their struggle. In the 1910 census, Addie was no longer living at the family home on Leonard Street, but with her employer, Frank Preston and his children.[75] Ten years later, Addie, her daughter Elsye and her husband, Rolf Osterman, and her 27-year-old daughter Alice lived with a supply man, William Wingate, his wife, Mabel French Wingate, and their children. (Mabel was Addie's daughter from her first marriage.)

Alice was a singer and dancer who performed in the U.S. and Canada and was a well-known church soloist in New Hampshire. In later life, she taught her kindergarten-age granddaughter songs from the 1920s. "She would sing and play them on the piano, teaching me to play them and sing harmony."[76] In 1920, Alice married Dr. Philip Albert Kimball at Elyse's tea shop, Ye Ragged Robin Tea Shop.

In the 1920 census, a Swedish immigrant, Rolf, and Elsye gave acting as their occupations.[77] Rolf was "a stand-up comedian and a vaudeville song and dance man;" Elyse was a " lead singer, dancer and actress in a vaudeville troupe. She was a graduate of the Boston Conservatory of Music and a voice teacher at Buena Vista College in Iowa.[78] Rolf and Elsye's marriage did not last. The Milton, New Hampshire, City Directory for 1927 listed Elsye W. Osterman as the owner of the Ragged Robbin Tea Room.[79] In the 1930 census, Rolf identified himself as a divorced manager of a "theatrical house" in Milton, New Hampshire, and by 1935, he worked as a doorman at the Colonial Theater.[80] Barbara Kimball, Elsye's niece by marriage, remembers the Ragged Robin as the "first tea room between Rochester and the mountains. With its handmade rustic furniture, it was a favorite place for vacationers to stop.[81]

At 81, Addie lived with Alice and her husband, Philip Kimball, in Bristol, New Hampshire.[82] She appeared not to have lived in a home of her own from the time William died until her own death in 1933, 27 years later. Neither William F. Wallace's son nor his grandchildren from either of his marriages would ever have known him. It is not surprising that his son's tombstone says that his elusive father was "A Scot" and his mother was "Sue Huskell."[83] Their paths since their brief marriage took widely disparate and circuitous routes in the following decades, with genealogists and family members wandering through the brambles, far off their trails. East did not very well meet West in the lives of William F. Wallace and Sue Heiskell, but both would have been proud of the widely respected, well-known product of their marriage, their son Leslie.[84]

---

1. Jeremy Neely, *The Border Between Them: Violence and Reconciliation on the Kansas-Missouri Line* (Columbia, Missouri: University of Missouri Press, 2007), 155-156.
2. (Paola, Kansas) *Miami Republican*, 28 Feb 1874, 3:c, and 7 Mar 1874, 3:f.
3. Sue Latimer obituary, undated clipping from unidentified newspaper, Obituary Collection, Hunt-Russell Genealogical Research Library, Miami County Historical and Genealogical Society, Paola, Kansas.
4. *Miami Republican*, 28 Nov 1874, 3:b, and 17 Dec 1874, 3:a.
5. *Miami Republican*, 24 Apr 1875, 3:b.
6. "Carleton, Will," Stanley J. Kunitz and Howard Haycraft, eds., *American Authors, 1600-1900* (New York: H. W. Wilson, 1938), 133-134. Will Carleton, *Farm Ballads* (New York: Harper and Brothers, 1875), 82-86.
7. For Wallace's ownership of the *Rice County Herald*, see *The* (Paola, Kansas) *Western Spirit*, 26 Dec 1873, 3:I; and, Cutler, *History of the State of Kansas*, 755. For Wallace's physical description, see abstract of Company Muster and Descriptive Roll, 22 Mar 1865, William F. Wallace (Musician, Co. I, 18th N.H. Vol. Inf., Civil War) pension no. Inv. 749,743, Case Files of Approved Pension Applications, 1861-1934; Civil War and Later Pension Files; Department of Veterans Affairs, Record Group 15; National Archives, Washington, D.C.
8. For Wallace's law teacher and mentor, see "Hon. Benjamin F[ranklin] Simpson" in Cutler, *History of the State of Kansas*, 885. For Wallace's admission to the bar and relocation to Rice County, see *Miami Republican*, 7 June 1873, 3:d. For Basil Simpson's views of Wallace, see *Miami Republican*, 26 July 1873 (no page on clipping).
9. *Miami Republican*, 6 Mar 1875, 3:c.
10. *Miami Republican*, 13 Mar 1875, 3:b.

11. *Western Spirit*, 26 Dec 1873, 3:1; *Miami Republican*, 27 Dec 1873 (no page on clipping).
12. For the reference to the joyful wedding, see Sue Latimer obituary, Obituary Collection, Hunt-Russell Genealogical Research Library, Miami County Historical and Genealogical Society, Paola, Kansas. For the editor's send-off see *Western Spirit*, 2 July 1875, 3:b.
13. Cutler, *History of the State of Kansas*, 755.
14. *Miami Republican*, 31 Mar 1876, 3:b.
15. *Western Spirit*, 28 Apr 1876, 3:e.
16. Sue A. Wallace, Divorce Petition, 23 July 1877, Case 1704, Divorce Case Files (1857-1879); Kansas State Historical Society Archives and Library, Topeka, Kansas, microfilm AR4240.
17. Josiah C. Sear and Clara A. Cotterell, General Affidavit, 1 June 1908, widow's pension application 856,919, certificate 664,937; service of William F. Wallace (Musician, Co. I, 18th N.H. Vol. Inf., Civil War); Case Files of Approved Pension Applications, 1861-1934; Civil War and Later Pension Files; Department of Veterans Affairs, Record Group 15; National Archives, Washington, D.C.
18. Wallace-Waterman marriage record, Bride's Index, 1640-1900, New Hampshire Division of Vital Statistics; Family History Library, film 975,693.
19. Mary Ann Langdon Dana entry, Epsom History (http://wc.rootsweb.ancestry.com/ : accessed 19 Apr 2008).
20. Nathan Sanders household, 1850 US Census, Epsom, Merrimack County, New Hampshire, p. 217-B, dwelling 7434, family 749. Samuel Prescott household, 1850 US Census, Hooksett, Merrimack County, New Hampshire, p. 252, dwelling 91, family 92.
21. George Benjamin Wallace biography, Early Epsom Settlers (http://www.usgennet.org/usa/nh/town/epsom/history/wallace.htm : accessed 25 Apr 2008).
22. Eliza A. Marcy household, 1850 US Census, Hillsborough, Hillsborough County, New Hampshire, p. 18 [stamped], dwelling 138, family 148.
23. William F. Wallace death record, Rochester, Strafford County, New Hampshire; New Hampshire Division of Vital Records Administration, Concord, New Hampshire. Joshua Marcy household, 1850 US Census, Hillsborough, Hillsborough County, New Hampshire, p. 18 [stamped], dwelling 137, family 147. William Wallace – Lydia M. Waterman marriage record, Hillsboro [sic.], New Hampshire, 27 Sept 1848; Bride's Index, 1640-1900, New Hampshire Division of Vital Records; Family History Library film 975,694.
24. Albert Foster household, 1860 US Census, Concord, Merrimack County, New Hampshire, p. 213, dwelling 1653, family 1702. William Sanders household, 1860 US Census, Epsom, Merrimack County, New Hampshire, p. 95, dwelling 800, family 763.

25. Martin A. Haynes, *A History of the Second Regiment, New Hampshire Volunteer Infantry, in the War of the Rebellion* (Lakeport, New Hampshire: np, 1896), 117.
26. Martin A. Haynes, *A History of the Second Regiment*, 19-41.
27. Haynes, *A History of the Second Regiment*, 40.
28. Haynes, *A History of the Second Regiment*, 65.
29. J.N. Patterson, Frank Wasley, and Thomas B. Little, Circular, "Ho! Second New Hampshire for Gettysburg," 8 June 1886, in Haynes, *A History of the Second Regiment*, 305-306.
30. Haynes, *A History of the Second Regiment*, 310.
31. Casualty Sheet, William F. Wallace (Musician, Co. I, 18th N.H. Vol. Inf., Civil War) pension no. Inv. 749,743, Case Files of Approved Pension Applications, 1861-1934; Civil War and Later Pension Files; Department of Veterans Affairs, Record Group 15; National Archives, Washington, D.C.
32. Haynes, *A History of the Second Regiment*, 117.
33. Adjutant General's Office, New Hampshire, "First Regiment, New Hampshire Volunteer Cavalry," *Revised Register of the Soldiers and Sailors of New Hampshire in the War of the Rebellion, 1861-1865* (Concord, New Hampshire: I. C. Evans, Public Printer, 1895), 886.
34. Albert Foster household, 1860 US Census, Concord, Merrimack County, New Hampshire, p. 213, dwelling 1653, family 1702. William Sanders household, 1860 US Census, Epsom, Merrimack County, New Hampshire, p. 95, dwelling 800, family 763. Volunteer Enlistment, 6 Mar 1865, William F. Wallace (Musician, Co. I, 18th N.H. Vol. Inf., Civil War) pension no. Inv. 749,743, Case Files of Approved Pension Applications, 1861-1934; Civil War and Later Pension Files; Department of Veterans Affairs, Record Group 15; National Archives, Washington, D.C.
35. Thomas L. Livermore, *History of the Eighteenth New Hampshire Volunteers, 1864-5* (Boston: Fort Hill Press, 1904), 73.
36. Surgeon's Certificate, 25 Mar 1891, and Approvals, Invalid Pension, 30 Mar 1892, William F. Wallace (Musician, Co. I, 18th N.H. Vol. Inf., Civil War) pension no. Inv. 749,743, Case Files of Approved Pension Applications, 1861-1934; Civil War and Later Pension Files; Department of Veterans Affairs, Record Group 15; National Archives, Washington, D.C.
37. Wallace-Waterman, Record of Divorce, Merrimack [County] Superior Court, 6 Dec 1865; New Hampshire Registrar of Vital Statistics, Index to Divorces and Annulments Prior to 1938; Family History Library film 1,001,330. In New Hampshire, "willful absence" was a legal term equivalent to the more common term, "abandonment." See *The General Laws of the State of New Hampshire* (Manchester: John B. Clarke, 1878), Ch. 182, Divorces, Sect. 3, Para. XII (p. 432).
38. Haynes, *A History of the Second Regiment*, 117.
39. *The Manchester Directory for 1871* (Boston: Sampson and Davenport, 1871), 184.
40. Lydia Grant obituary, *The* [Lansing, Michigan,] *State Journal*, 18 Sept 1912, 7:3.

41. Cutler, *History of the State of Kansas*, 893
42. Cutler, *History of the State of Kansas*, 893.
43. Cutler, *History of the State of Kansas, 893*.
44. *Western Spirit*, 11 Oct 1878, 3:c.
45. *Western Spirit*, 5 Dec 1878, 3:d.
46. Cutler, *History of the State of Kansas*, 893.
47. *Western Spirit*, 21 Feb 1879, 3:d.
48. 1880 US Census, Louisburg, Wea Township, Miami County, Kansas (ED 167, p. 28), household 253, family 258. The Census taker listed baby May as 5 months old when he came by on 22 June 1880.
49. 1880 US Census, Louisburg, Wea Township, Miami County, Kansas (ED 167, p. 28). 1880 US Census, Fairfield, Madison County, Ohio (ED 67, p. 27), household 216, family 219. Necrology, *Journal of the American Medical Association* 47 (Sept 1906): 2.
50. Inscription, portrait of Mrs. E. J. Heiskell, ca. 1890, Paola Free Library, Paola, Kansas.
51. E. J. Haskell [sic.] household, 1885 Kansas State Census, Paola, Miami County, p. 66, household 3, family 3.
52. "Miami-Co's Oldest Citizen Dead," Emeline Heiskell obituary, undated clipping from unidentified newspaper; Obituary File, Hunt-Russell Research Library, Miami County Swan River Museum and Genealogy Society, Paola, Kansas.
53. Tribute to Emeline Heiskell, undated clipping from unidentified newspaper, Obituary File, Hunt-Russell Research Library, Miami County Swan River Museum and Genealogy Society, Paola, Kansas.
54. "The Death of Mrs. Heiskell," undated clipping from *"The Western Spirit,"* Obituary File, Obituary File, Hunt-Russell Research Library, Miami County Swan River Museum and Genealogy Society, Paola, Kansas.
55. "The Death of Mrs. Heiskell."
56. Hiram Phillips obituary, *Western Spirit*, 10 Apr 1885, 3:h.
57. Sue A. Phillips household, 1885 Kansas State Census, Louisburg, Wea Township, [Miami County], p. 20, dwelling and family 7. E. J. Haskell [sic.] household, 1885 Kansas State Census, [Paola, Paola Township, Miami County], p. 66, dwelling and family 3.
58. Latimer-Phillips marriage record, Miami County Marriages, Births, Deaths, 1885-1892, License No. 221, p. 52; Kansas State Historical Society Library, Topeka, Kansas, microfilm AR3987.
59. John E. Hysom, *Latimer: Wickline, Hysom, Gaither, Beck, Heiskell, Wallace, Phillips* ([Tucker, Georgia]: J. E. Hysom, 1994), Preface, np.
60. Latimer-Phillips marriage record, Miami County Marriages, Births, Deaths, 1885-1892, License No. 221, p. 52; Kansas State Historical Society Library, Topeka, Kansas, microfilm AR3987.

61. David Heenan obituary, undated clipping from unidentified newspaper, Obituary File, Hunt-Russell Genealogical Research Library, Swan River Museum and Genealogy Society, Paola, Kansas.
62. P. F. Latimer biographical sketch, Cutler, *History of the State of Kansas*, 893.
63 1900 US Census, Louisburg, Miami County, Kansas (ED 138, sheet 3-A), household 51, family 52. 1910 US Census, Louisburg, Miami County, Kansas (ED 143, sheet 15-B), household & family 260.
64. Divorce Decree, Supreme Court, Laconia, Belknap County, New Hampshire, 27 Mar 1883; copy made 16 Oct 1906; widow's pension application 856,919, certificate 664,937; service of William F. Wallace (Musician, Co. I, 18th N.H. Vol. Inf., Civil War); Case Files of Approved Pension Applications, 1861-1934; Civil War and Later Pension Files; Department of Veterans Affairs, Record Group 15; National Archives, Washington, D.C. See also Addie M. Wallace, General Affidavit, 21 Feb 1908, in the same pension file.
65. William T. [Sic.] and Addie M. French Marriage Record, Groom's Index, 1640-1900, New Hampshire Division of Vital Statistics, Concord, New Hampshire; Index to Marriages, Early to 1900; Family History Library, Salt Lake City, UT, film 1,001,314.
66. Barbara Hammond Kimball, daughter-in-law of William F. Wallace's daughter Alice (Agawam, Massachusetts), interview by George Findlen, 15 Apr 2009; notes held by Rose Ann Findlen, Madison, Wisconsin.
67. Dr. William F. Wallace obituary, *Rochester* [New Hampshire] *Courier*, 7 Sept 1906, n.p., col. d.
68. Bradford, New Hampshire, History Committee and Bicentennial Committee, *Two Hundred Plus: Bradford, New Hampshire in Retrospect* (Canaan, New Hampsire: Phoenix Publishing, 1976), 82, 140.
69. Surgeon's Certificate, 25 Mar 1891, pension claim number 840,468, William F. Wallace (Musician, Co. I, 18th N.H. Vol. Inf., Civil War); Case Files of Approved Pension Applications, 1861-1934; Civil War and Later Pension Files; Department of Veterans Affairs, Record Group 15; National Archives, Washington, D.C.
70. Drew Gilpin Faust, *This Republic of Suffering: Death and the American Civil War* (New York: Vintage Civil War Library), 176.
71. Barbara Hammond Kimball, interview, 15 Apr 2009.
72. Frank Preston and Charles Masury, General Affidavit, 8 Feb 1908; widow's pension application 856,919, certificate 664,937; service of William F. Wallace (Musician, Co. I, 18th N.H. Vol. Inf., Civil War); Case Files of Approved Pension Applications, 1861-1934; Civil War and Later Pension Files; Department of Veterans Affairs, Record Group 15; National Archives, Washington, D.C.
73. Dr. William F. Wallace obituary, *Rochester Courier*.
74. Francis Lane Childs, *Gravestone Inscriptions from Bradford, New Hampshire* (Salem, Massachusetts: Higginson Book Co, 1997), 46.

75. 1910 US Census, Rochester, Strafford County, New Hampshire (ED 294, sheet 2-A), household 175, family 34. "Wallace, Addie M . . . house keeper private family."
76. Email, Karen Kimball Hull, Agwam, Massachusetts, to George Findlen, 9 May 2009.
77. 1920 US Census, Rochester, Strafford County, New Hampshire (ED 181, sheet 8-B), household 170, family 203.
78. E-mail, Karen Kimball Hull, Agawam, Massachusetts, to George L. Findlen, 9 May 2009.
79. Elyse W. Osterman entry, Milton; Brookfield, Milton, Wakefield, Lebanon, New Hampshire Directory, 1927, p. 44; New Hampshire City Directories, on-line database, Ancestry.com (Provo, UT: The Generations Network, 2005).
80. 1930 US Census for Milton, Strafford County, New Hampshire (ED 9-18, sheet 11-B), household 47, family 50. Osterman entry, *Directory for Rockingham-Strafford Counties, New Hampshire* (Detroit, Michigan: R. L. Polk, 1935), 503.
81. Barbara Hammond Kimball, interview, 20 Dec 2008.
82. 1930 US Census, Bristol, Grafton County, New Hampshire (ED 5-7, sheet 12-B), household 319, family 358.
83. Leslie Wallace grave marker, Larned Cemetery, Larned, Pawnee County, Kansas.
84. At the time of this publication, a Kansas City Fire Department station is on the site at the southeast corner of East Missouri Avenue and Oak Street. Frazier, Harriet C. *Death Sentences in Missouri, 1803-2005*. (Jefferson, North Carolina: McFarland & Co., Inc., Publishers, 2006), 102.

CHAPTER 8

Leslie Earle Wallace: a Kansan for All Seasons

Lineage of Leslie Wallace

Hannah Lykins = William Peery
|
Emeline Peery = William Heiskell
|
Sue A. Heiskell = William F. Wallace
(Step-fathers: Hiram Phillips-Philip F. Latimer)
|
Leslie Wallace = Sara LeMaistre Johnson
(Second wife: Bobbie Lee Victor)
|
Children of Leslie and Sara Johnson Wallace:
Eunice Wallace Shore Rhea
Ralph Wallace

Leslie was raised by intellectually lively people, Emeline, Sue, Hiram Phillips, and Philip Latimer, who molded him into the witty, engaging man he became. In addition, his extended family of writers, missionaries, educators, political activists and community leaders had been instrumental in the development of the Borderland since 1828, when Johnston Lykins first came to the Kansas Indian Territory as a missionary. As a descendant of pioneer families in the

Kansas-Missouri Borderland, Leslie had deep awareness of himself as part of the evolution of the State of Kansas; this sense of place and regional loyalty deeply informed his work as public relations advisor to state political officials, writer and newspaper editor; Kansas was integral to his public and professional identity.

"Earle," as he was known as a child, was an imaginative boy. He may have known that his father had been a newspaper editor. He published his own newspaper, *The Bucyrus Chief*, at fourteen.[1] Leslie later described his first job in journalism for the "Who's Who in Kansas" column about him: "I learned the printer's trade as a boy on the old Paola *Times*," he reminisced, "spending the summer with my grandmother [Emeline Heiskell]; building fires in the office of mornings, sprinkling the ready prints the night before press day, and carrying the papers in a big clothes basket through the park to the post office on Thursday afternoons."[2]

Both Emeline and Sue were local institutions, Emeline as a reader and Sue as a teacher. Emeline rode a horse alone across Indian Territory to Harrisonville, Missouri, in her pioneer days in Kansas to learn to read. As librarian, she was known to have read voraciously every title in the building and to have a very complete recall of each book's contents. When library patrons went to the Paola Free Library in search of something a neighbor had read, she nimbly crossed the library floor to put her hands instantly on precisely the fact, passage or book her patrons requested.[3]

Emeline was a vivid storyteller and loved recalling the early days of the Borderland; this storytelling captured the imagination of her grandson.[4] When he assumed the editorship of the Sunday Edition of the *The Kansas City Star* in the early 1900s, his columns always had room for feature stories and interviews about the history and ways of life in those times. One winter while Emeline was visiting Leslie and his family in Kansas City, she was interviewed for *The Kansas City Star's Sunday Edition* on her life as one of the first women in the Kansas Territory. Her interview contained such arresting details on her pioneer life that it was reprinted in *The New*

York Sun.⁵ The woman who interviewed her, Nelly McCoy Harris, was related to the family by marriage and was the "first white child born in Westport." Her father was Isaac McCoy's son, John. He and Johnston Lykins were important leaders in the founding of Westport and Kansas City. Nelly and Emeline's recollections of the early days and their first-hand knowledge of how the Borderland had evolved must have given Leslie ample ideas for his Sunday Editions.

Emeline's pioneer daughter Sue had a way with words as well. From her beginning days as a teacher to the end of her life, Leslie's mother was characterized as a gifted teacher and an avid student. Sue was the bright-eyed girl at the head of her class and, as a teenager, the lively teacher and organizer of spelling bees; in her twenties, she returned to the classroom as a widow and taught students throughout the Louisburg area. Her interest in dramatic reading and her service as the Secretary of the Louisburg Council, no. 3, of the Royal Templar of Temperance, a temperance insurance organization known almost universally throughout the U.S. and Canada as R.T of T., would have created a home in which language facility was a valued tool.⁶ She was in the classroom when women who married had to resign from their teaching positions, but because of her popularity as a teacher and her early widowhood she had returned to the classroom by the time Leslie was eight.⁷ His mother and grandmother's emphasis on reading and language must have spurred his interest in language.

Hiram's involvement in government and Sue's facility in writing established her in Louisburg's political circles. In the listing of town officials of Louisburg, she is the only woman there. She was an old stock, pioneer Kansan. There is scarcely an account of her that does not include a statement that she was the first white child born in Paola. Leslie grew up well aware of the power of language and of social and political connections.

Leslie's two stepfathers were influential citizens in Louisburg. In each of their biographies, Cutler described them as avid readers and engaged members in their community.⁸ Hiram's progressive political philosophy, his love of reading, and his community involvement are reflected in Leslie's own career. Leslie lived under his roof for six years until he was about nine. Philip Latimer, his second stepfather, was also characterized as an avid reader who engaged in public affairs, serving as school superintendent, city council member and county commissioner. Latimer married Sue four years after Hiram's death and Leslie spent the remainder of his childhood in Latimer's household.

Leslie's early careers suggest the stepfathers' influences as involved citizens. In a 1940 tribute to Leslie, a writer for the *Topeka Journal* commented: "Wallace accepted political activity as a matter of good citizenship, but his heart was in his newspaper and publishing business."⁹ Like Hiram, Leslie identified with a short-lived progressive political party: in Hiram's case, the Greenback Party; in Leslie's, the Bull Moose Movement.¹⁰ The 1912 founder of the Bull Moose Movement's Progressive Party, Theodore Roosevelt, was Leslie's idol; however, when Roosevelt returned to the Republican Party, Leslie instead became a staunch Democrat.¹¹ Both the Greenback and Progressive Parties advocated women's suffrage, anti-big business regulation, revised currency policies and pro-agriculture positions.

Even his absent father, William F., may have been a shaping influence on Leslie's aspirations if he knew or remembered that his father had been a newspaper editor at the time of his marriage to Sue. In Sue's obituary, he writes of him as "a college-bred New Englander," which is an interesting interpretation of the facts.¹² His father described himself as a carpenter in his Civil War enlistment record, and there is no evidence that he went to a college between 1865 and his marriage to Sue.¹³ Leslie's description probably referred to William's medical training in Ohio after he left Sue and returned East; Leslie may have learned that his father was a physician about two months before his mother's obituary was written in August, 1918. In the preceding Spring, Leslie had written to the Office of

Pensions asking for information about his father's Civil War service and seemed to have little concrete information about him:

April 29, 1918
The Honorable
The Commissioner of Pensions,
Washington, D.C.

Dear Sir:

I am trying to ascertain the company, regiment, etc., to which my father belonged in the Civil War. I think he was receiving a pension at the time of his death, and at the time of his death was living in either Plaistow or Milton, N.H. His name was Wm. F. Wallace. I have no further information, but would be glad if from this you can give me the facts desired.

Yours truly,
Leslie E. Wallace[14]

Like fatherless boys (and men) everywhere, Leslie no doubt longed for a connection or a positive identification with him and was shaped by him in that way.

Leslie's parents, grandmother and stepfathers all died before 1920. Although Leslie had not yet accomplished his greatest achievements, his family would have recognized that he was on his way to becoming the versatile, skilled, compassionate man who brought so much to Kansas later in his life. Emeline, who died in 1916, visited him and his family in Kansas City and had the opportunity to know his talented wife and his two bright young children.[15] Sue and Philip Latimer, who died in 1918 and 1913, respectively, lived long enough to see their son's journalistic success at *The Kansas City Star*.[16] They missed seeing him in his maturity as a well-respected leader, a journalist, a man of letters, and a statesman.

Leslie's Time Back East

Throughout his life, Leslie loved the written word. His first reporting job began in 1898 with *The Topeka Daily Capital* under the editorship of Arthur Capper. After two years there, Leslie had an opportunity to live in Washington, D.C. as private secretary to Representative Charles Scott. In addition, Leslie was a correspondent for the *Topeka State Journal* and *The Leavenworth Times*, during his time in Washington.[17] In the 1900 census, Leslie was a boarder in the home of a government clerk and smack in the middle of the byzantine circle of Washington politics, a crucible for learning the high arts of political strategy and public relations.[18]

Leslie was on hand in New York City during the election of 1900, when Tammany boss Richard Croker was handed a defeat as Teddy Roosevelt, his arch-enemy, won the Presidential election. He wrote an account of the election for the *Kansas Weekly Capitol*:

Despite the heady political environment of Washington, D.C., it was writing and Kansas that held his heart. He left the Washington scene to return to Kansas and newspaper work.

> **For more information, refer to, "A Roaring Mob," in the Related Stories and Poems section at the end of the book.**

While secretary to Representative Charles Scott, he had also managed *The Iola Daily Register* for Scott, who was in Washington. He moved back to the Borderland with his Maryland bride to take up the editing of the Iola paper full time.

Adjusting to Iola, Kansas, must have been quite an undertaking for his wife, Sara, a graduate of Goucher College in Baltimore and a descendant of an old Quaker family.[19] Sixty miles south of Paola, Iola was a town of 1500 in 1895, but a discovery of a large supply of natural gas caused the town to boom to a population of 11,000 over the next fifteen years.[20] When Leslie and Sara arrived, Iola was in the middle of this dramatic expansion; the town itself was young, having been established 47 years earlier, and first generation settlers were still among its inhabitants. Sara adapted, at least outwardly, to the situation. Writing about Sara in 1927, a writer for the "Kansas City Star" said,

> Not every woman who comes to Kansas from the Eastern States takes kindly to the transplanting, even if she honestly wants to. Sara Wallace, born in Wilmington, Del., considers herself on a footing with any of the native daughters of the Sunflower state. Her affections and her interests are here. Every year of her married life has been spent in Kansas or the Missouri Valley. She has entered into all of her husband's newspaper ventures with an ardor equal to his own, and her keen and quick gasp of things political has given them much more in common than their own personal affairs.[21]

Their first child, Eunice, was born there.[22] After a brief time with *"The Iola Daily Register,"* from 1906-1908, Leslie took a reporting job with "The Kansas City Times," the most widely read newspaper in the Borderland.[23] The year 1908 was a year of big life changes: a new city, a new job and a second child, Ralph Leslie Wallace.[24] Leslie fit in well at "The Star," forming lifelong friendships. In a memorial article, the newspaper reported:

Sara LeMaistre Johnson, as she appeared in her college yearbook

His associates in those days on The Star retained their friendship for "Les" Wallace" through the years. They observed his successes in newspaper work, in politics, and in literature with gratification....

A quiet, thoughtful man, Mr. Wallace did not show the aptitude for politics while on the staff of The Star that was evidenced when he went to Larned and began to impress his personality on the community and state. Associates remember that he was witty, given to dry humor which he could make biting. He wore a hat all the time he was at work at The Star. It was a sailor in summer and a felt hat in winter, but he never took it off. While he was handling the Sunday section of The Star he wrote many of the articles.

He had a forelock which was a forerunner of the Will Rogers look and he had a way of sitting and listening to things, retaining facts in his head, and he had the ability to put those ideas and facts down on paper in a delightful, authentic manner. He was a facile writer, given to turning good phrases. His verse was well known to readers of The Star and to the readers of his own newspaper.[25]

Soon he was promoted to an editorial position. His deep knowledge of and appreciation for the region made him a wonderful choice for the Editor of the Sunday section of the paper, which focused on the history and people of the area; his love of a good story and his many connections to people in and around Kansas City assisted him in finding appealing feature articles.

Leslie, Sara and their children lived in Kansas City for five years, but Leslie took the opportunity to operate his own newspaper in 1914, when he became a partner in *The Tiller and Toiler* of Larned, Kansas. The family moved to Larned and established themselves: Leslie became the sole proprietor of the newspaper in 1916, the children grew up there, and Sara began to take a much more active role in the newspaper world, writing columns and reviews for *The Tiller and Toiler* and other Kansas newspapers. "Known to readers of *The Tiller and Toiler* as Sara Wallace (she) was an able and voluminous contributor to the columns of that newspaper. Besides natural ability in the production of news and editorial matter, she was a writer of fine literary taste and broad experience. Her column of book reviews, a regular feature of the paper, compared favorably with similar features in the metropolitan press."[26]

Leslie assumed an additional role with his editorship: that of "An Accomplished Worrier." In her 1927 interview with Leslie, Esther Clark Hill remarked on this role,

> And having settled in the wheat belt, Mr. Wallace proceeded to take it to his heart and become its leading prophet. "Since that hour," he continued, expanding on his subject, "I have spent most of my time worrying about the wheat crop. I doubt if I achieved any tangible results, but it is the custom in Western Kansas and it disclosed that I was standardized. When I came out here, Jay House wrote a paragraph about me in which he said it would now be unnecessary for anyone in this section to do any further worrying, as I would attend to it. I've done that, but I have not become pre-eminent nor been elected to congress on that outstanding qualification. But I still contend that I am the best worrier west of Newton.[27]

Eight years earlier, Leslie had published the "Wheat Edition" of *The Tiller and Toiler*. Unique in its day, it was a promotional piece about the Larned area designed to attract new residents.

> The purpose of the wheat edition is to show vividly the resources of Pawnee county, with particular reference to agriculture....Now the magic of electricity is to lift the living rivers of water which have passed under its soil for centuries,

and bring them to the surface...Irrigation is to become an everyday thing, placing thousands and thousands of acres under the pump....And it (the editorial) believes that opportunities will be created for thousands of persons and that the county is on the eve of a vast increase in the number of its inhabitants through more intensive cultivation.[28]

This bold publication represented revolutionary thinking in public relations and the role of the newspaper in economic development. The edition included photographs of new, modern farm equipment and homes; it described local attractions and displayed local store advertisements. It even featured poems expressing affection for Kansas. Among them was "Kansas Day," by the nationally renowned editor of *The Emporia Gazette,* William Allen White. Leslie and White were colleagues. Both worked at *The Kansas City Star* earlier in their careers, became editors of well-respected small-town newspapers, and supported, in 1912, the populist agenda and candidates of the Progressive Party.[29]

When Leslie put together The Wheat Edition, he could not have foreseen the Great Depression and the Dust Bowl in the coming years. Certainly he would not have predicted the present agricultural environment in which corporate farming, big box stores and the global economy ravage the small rural towns and family owned farms for which he advocated. While Pawnee County remains a sparsely populated area, the Wheat Edition stands as a model piece of journalism for the time. Copies of it are preserved in rare book repositories in libraries.

For more information view, "*The Glory of Pawnee County,*" in the Related Stories and Poems section at the end of the book.

Sara developed an ear for her Kansas community as well, and by the end of the 1920s, both Leslie and Sara Wallace were identified as the publishers of *The Tiller and Toiler.*

In a tribute to Sara, Cora G. Lewis wrote that:

> She was a writer of distinction, weaving into her work the story of life of her own community. With a heart tender toward humanity she saw values in the daily lives of those about her, worth writing into literature. A series of stories about women of her own town published in The Tiller and Toiler as part of the day's work is a rare chapter in the literature of Kansas. Everything in the community which promised to add to happiness or enrich culture commanded her gifted pen.[30]

The couple invested their energies in community development in other ways. Sara was an officer in the local historical society and worked to get a community building for Larned. She was featured as a speaker at women's clubs, at a Convocation at the Agricultural college (now known as Kansas State University in Manhattan), and at the Kansas Editorial Association.[31] News clippings announced meetings scheduled at the Leslie E. Wallace Lodge on the grounds of the Country Club, a building named in honor of his community leadership. Sara was "the leader among the Business and professional women, loved by all of them."[32] They hosted an annual meeting of the Southern Kansas Editorial Association for newspaper editors and their families throughout the region. Leslie led the local tour and was Toastmaster at the banquet; he and Sara hosted the luncheon at their "home on the hill."[33] One of their guests remarked:

> "The House on the Hill," their large, gracious home at 323 State Street, had its doors always open for friends, and on its altar the light of fine conversation always burned. Delightful people were to be found there, from many places, and things worth while were talked about around the hospitable table so often filled with friends. 'The House on

the Hill' looked out into tree tops, and far across the wide valley to the hills beyond, its windows open to sunrise, sunset, and starlight, and there the hearts of family and friends found rest, and peace.³⁴

The House on the Hill as it appeared in 2008

By 1924, Leslie needed a vacation and a chance to explore the world outside Kansas. He first went to the Pacific Coast and then telegraphed his wife to say he wanted to travel to Asia. While he was away, Sara assumed all responsibility for *The Tiller*. When Leslie returned after four months, he found her "still at the helm and things running as smoothly as if they'd been greased." Sara began to work, in addition, as a feature writer and correspondent to metropolitan dailies.³⁵ Leslie wrote a series of travel features for *The Kansas City Star*, and several poems during his sabbatical from the daily work of *The Tiller*.

They built a new office for *The Tiller and Toiler*, which the visiting editors toured during the Southwest Kansas Editorial Association's spring meeting.[36] It was a Spanish adobe building meant to evoke the memory of Larned as a stop on the Santa Fe Trail.[37] Designed by Sara, "It is a low Spanish type with wide windows, entered through a gate leading into a patio on the east where vines and flowers grow. It is the loveliest bit of architecture in the city and a delightful place for the home of the newspaper."[38]

***Tiller and Toiler* office, Larned, Kansas, as it appeared in 2008**

Because of their efforts, *The Tiller and Toiler* thrived. After the Southwest Kansas Editorial Association meeting in 1930, the editor of the *Hoisington Dispatch* commented, "Larned is a good town–a splendid town and is growing all the time. The city boasts of having one of the best weekly newspapers in the United States, if not the best."[39] In the 1927 *Kansas City Star* column, "Who's Who in Kansas," *The Tiller and Toiler* was described as "one of the best weekly papers in the middle West."[40] A *Kansas City Times* tribute to Leslie characterized his editorial style as honest and loyal to the public good:

> As publisher of his fine newspaper he became the apostle of the wheat country, an able editor who conceived that he owed special obligation to the public he served. He did not hesitate to criticize officials of the state or the nation when they were wrong–even if they belonged to his own party to which he gave a lifetime of loyal devotion.
>
> His was a trenchant pen and tongue when he chose to use them to castigate what he conceived to be contrary to the public weal, but he was by nature gentle and his dry humor rarely stung.[41]

A Family of Writers

A candid portrait of Leslie Wallace, courtesy of the Leslie Zygmund family

The couple's writing range expanded, with writing becoming a family affair between 1925-1930. Leslie published *The Harp*, a national poetry journal.[42] As he and Sarah experienced the "empty nest" period of their lives when their two children had gone to the University of Kansas, Leslie wrote a poem, "Children." The poem won the Sarah Bixby Smith prize for "the best poem published in the *Lyric West*," a journal edited by the chairman of the English Language and Literature Department at the University of Southern California.[43]

Children

They shall go out in mist,
Through years, my dears–
Whither the four winds list,
My dears, through tears;
Whither the east winds rise,
And the west wind dies.

They shall pass out and in
As sunlight does,
Where singing leaves have been
And the soft wind was;
And we, at last, shall wait
By a shut gate.

Their daughter Eunice, according to her classmate and future husband, Chester Shore, was active in university life. He surmised that if she had stayed at the university any longer she would have caused the yearbook to be two pages longer in order to list her activities.[44] She was a serious poet. In 1925, she was "recognized by literary critics as one of the most promising free verse writers in the country."[45]

Her younger brother Ralph, in his freshman year at the university, was awarded the first William Herbert Carruth Poetry Award for his sonnet sequence, "Sung to Youth."[46] Leslie, Eunice and Ralph all have poems included in the 1927 anthology, *Contemporary Kansas Poetry*.[47]

Neither Ralph nor Eunice stayed at the University, but both chose writing for their life's work. When their mother died in 1930, both were working with their parents at *The Tiller and Toiler*.[48] The 1930 census listed Eunice as a newspaper reporter living with her parents.[49] That fall, Sara died of a paralytic stroke after fighting high blood pressure for many years.[50] May Williams Ward wrote of Sara:

Sara Wallace had everything—exceptional beauty of person, keen perception with powers to express what she perceived, and a spiritual insight into the minds and motives of others that brought out their best. Her reviews and comment sparkled in the family newspaper. She read deeply in biography, philosophy and poetry, and it was she who saved The Harp for Kansas....

And she added beauty to everything, as she loved it in everything. Merely to see her walk down the street in her favorite blue, was a joy.[51]

Sara Wallace
from *The Harp*, **July 1931**

Sara's legacy contains contradictions. The tributes to her character, her work, and her devotion to her family and to civic affairs in Kansas have a certain fairy tale quality. Even her associates' notice of her striking beauty accentuated by her frequent wearing of delphinium blue carries with it a mythical dimension.[52] The family story as told by her descendants has indicated that the interior life of the family was not as sanguine as the public face put on it. Family members spoke of her hatred of Kansas, her driving of her children to succeed, her emotional abuse.

Both parts probably hold some truth: in public, she was the model wife, mother, writer and patroness of the arts; in private, she may have been plagued by the effects of high blood pressure, cultural dissonance, and, some suggest, heavy drinking. It is possible, too, to embrace the contradiction that the Kansas landscape–the slant of sun on the wheat, the enormous sky–could have become a part of her psyche and that her roots could have taken hold there through family and community events regardless of whether that was her preference, and regardless of her frustration with living outside the main currents of the social life, arts and culture more easily accessed in the East. Sara had probably become a Kansan at the same time that a part of her never became a Kansan at all.

Throughout the thirties, Sara's children went about the business of their writing careers. Eunice and her husband Chester, editor of *The Augusta Gazette*, took over the editing and publishing of *The Harp*, dedicating Volume VII, nos. 3 and 4 to Sara. Writers who knew Sara, including her two children, wrote poems of tribute. The young couple continued *The Harp* until the financial hardships of the Great Depression forced them to stop its publication.[53] Eunice continued to write poetry, improving her skill and expanding her publishing record in regional journals.

Ralph built his career around public relations and feature writing. After a period of reporting for *The Tiller and Toiler*, *The Pittsburg (Kansas) Headlight*, and *The Baltimore Sun*, he switched to feature writing. In 1938, his brother-in-law's newspaper, *The Augusta Gazette*, published an article which summarizes his work in the 1930s:

With Crowell Publications

>Ralph L. Wallace, son of Leslie E. Wallace of Larned, has accepted a position as staff writer for the Crowell Publications in New York City . . . . He also will serve as Associate Editor of the *Country Home* magazine published

monthly by the Crowell Publications. He will continue to make his home in New York. Until last April, Mr. Wallace was associated with the publicity department of Warner Brothers Pictures, but since that time has been with Business Organization, Inc., a public relations firm.[54]

Several of his articles appeared as reprints in the *Reader's Digest* and *The New York Herald Tribune*.[55] In the 1950s, both Eunice and Ralph edited the *Tiller and Toiler* periodically.

Although Leslie continued to publish *The Tiller and Toiler* after his wife's death, his life began to have another focus. He stopped writing verse,[56] he married Bob Lee Victor, a native of Pawnee County, in 1931,[57] and he began to spend each February in Mexico.[58] He became more heavily involved in the political affairs of the state.

Statesman Behind the Scenes

Leslie Wallace

While serving as Scott's private secretary early in life, Leslie acquired the savvy and diplomacy to fill that role for two Kansas state governors in the 1930s.[59] His public relations ability and his intimate knowledge of Kansas and its people, had grown during his years in the newspaper business. The role of "Private Secretary" in Kansas state politics was prominent: "The office of private secretary is regarded as one of the most important state offices; the secretary is the personal representative of the governor, and in some instances shares honors with him."[60]

In its eulogy to Leslie, *The Topeka Capital* expressed high regard for his political skill:

> Two Democratic Governors, Harry Woodring and Walter Huxman, each selected him as his private secretary and they showed excellent judgment in so doing. The most important business of a Governor's private secretary is to keep his chief out of trouble and smooth over the rough places in the road the Governor, regardless of his politics, has to travel. In performing that sometimes delicate task, Leslie was an artist. If he ever made a bad break we never heard of it and his polite and diplomatic manner of handling his office we know helped his superior officer in numberless instances. Political quarrels in state politics are frequent, sometimes bitter, but while Leslie was always called on usually by both sides we never knew him to be either the starter or prolonger of a row. We have seen him when there seemed to be reason for him getting somewhat excited but never saw him when his serenity was disturbed. We once heard a prominent and hardboiled Republican say that Leslie Wallace had more good hard sense and better political judgment that any other Democrat in Kansas, and then added that the Republican Party members would be better off if some of its active members had as much sense as Leslie.[61]

Leslie was publicity director of the Democratic state committee in the campaigns of 1932 and 1936[62] and was credited for his resourcefulness and ability in bringing Democratic victories to his party.[63] Had he lived long enough, he was to be a delegate to the Democratic Convention in 1940.[64] In commenting on Governor Huxman's choice of Wallace for his secretary, the late B.J. Sheridan, editor of the *Miami Republican* newspaper, made the following observation: "He has gratitude in his makeup. He doesn't lie and doesn't forget; therefore his word is dependable. He has a genuine sympathy for the underdog and is never out of the spirit that prompts charitable work. Of course, he has a few enemies here and there, but this newspaper can say of him, as General Bragg said of Grover Cleveland… 'We love him for the enemies he has made.'"[65]

When he resigned from his position as Governor Woodring's private secretary in 1931, Leslie remarked that he was resigning because he couldn't bear "to be away from his newspaper" any longer.[66] Woodring and Leslie parted on good terms: soon after Leslie's resignation, the governor appointed him to the Kansas Board of Regents.[67]

Leslie was asked to run for governor a number of times, but always refused.[68] According to *The Kansas City Star*, "Mr. Wallace's name frequently had been mentioned as a candidate for governor. He had never encouraged this, however, preferring to remain in the background, advising and coordinating, free to manage his Tiller and Toiler….As to the governorship, 'Les' waved it away, remarking that 'an editor makes a poor candidate.'"[69]

When he returned to Larned, Leslie probably put his editorial role as "worrier" to good use. The nation's economy was depressed and the numbers of homeless people and repossessed farms mounted. The economic situation was exacerbated in the Great Plains by severe droughts resulting in the creation of the Dust Bowl. In the "dirty thirties," the soil dried and turned to dust. Enormous clouds of black dust blew to the east and south, blowing precious top soil as far as Washington D.C. and into the Atlantic Ocean. The Dust Bowl was caused by the lack of rain, decades of over-farming the prairie lands without crop rotation, the deep plowing of virgin prairie soil which killed the native grasses.[70] Larned was at the far eastern edge of the Dust Bowl, but close enough. The Black Sunday dust storms of April 14, 1935 pounded 20 regions of the Great Plains from Ontario to Mexico; one of the locations hit was Dodge City, Kansas, a mere 60 miles from Larned.[71] *The Tiller and Toiler* reported that "The storm arose suddenly about two o'clock and a huge black cloud of dust settled on the city [Larned] in such short notice that darkness came like an eclipse of the sun."[72] The severe three-year drought finally ended in 1936. About that time, Leslie wrote a relieved, grateful editorial about the rains that had finally begun.

By 1939, Leslie, then in his sixties, savored travel and his grandchildren. Commercial air travel, a glamorous, frightening activity, fascinated him. The Midcontinent Airport in Kansas City offered intercontinental flights with sleeping compartments to passengers and stewardesses were on board to ensure their safety and comfort. In 1936, the Douglas Skysleeper Transport with 14 sleeper berths flew between Los Angeles and New York with stops at Albuquerque, Kansas City, and Chicago.[73] Midcontinent Airport offered services between Los Angeles and New York, and sometime during the winter of 1939 or 1940, Leslie's son Ralph and his grandson Jerome flew from Kansas City to New York in one of those amazing harbingers of modern American life: cross-country commercial air travel. Leslie wrote about the event in the editorial section of *The Tiller and Toiler*:

An Airplane Comes Close

The miracle of flight was brought home to us the other night when our son [Ralph Wallace] with his small son [Jerry] flew from Kansas City to New York. It requires an experience like that to appreciate fully the wonder of this manmade metal eagle that soars off into the darkness with a fierce staccato whirr of wings down a lighted runway and in a moment is a mere speck of red light high up in the enveloping gloom of the night sky. To fully appreciate the emotional angles of the miracle, someone who is near you must be making the flight.

You leave the hotel in a taxicab and cross a long bridge, and thread your way through a labyrinth of railroad yards. In the hotel room, of course, you have been talking of many things but thinking of only one. Even though a year has gone by and not a passenger has been lost along the commercial airlines of the United States, the peril of such a journey grips your heart, and you are tense with apprehension.

At the airport there is no atmosphere of distrust or dread. There is the usual crowd of people reminiscent of a big railway station, the usual hum of conversation, people are moving about the waiting room, buying plane tickets, excess baggage is being weighed, the arrival and departure of planes is being called, children are at play, many are in the restaurant, and some are at the bar taking a farewell drink, for liquor is not served on planes. A stewardess and two pilots are taking a *soft* drink at a table in the restaurant–an unerringly efficient picker of chic and personable girls is the personnel officer of an airline–or maybe it's the uniform. Occasionally a big throbbing plane comes in and the lights on the runway are flashed on, occasionally one departs and they are flashed off.

And finally a big sleeper plane drums in from Los Angeles. This is *the* plane. Immediately a small army of airport attaches swarms around the plane, climbs onto the wings, tests this and that, measures the gasoline supply, check, check, check; a big gasoline transport backs up to the plane and fills the tanks in the wings. No smoking, please! You are relieved to hear somebody say that it is the custom now for the big passenger planes to carry 2 ½ times as much gasoline as is needed to reach its first destination, as for example if a plane is flying from Washington to Detroit sufficient gasoline is carried to fly to Detroit, back to Washington and half way to Detroit again. This is just one of the precautions against failure to land at some airport where conditions may make a landing impossible.

The big shining envelope looks enormously heavy and cold and metallic and inhospitable as the landing steps are rolled up to the door and the passengers go aboard. One passenger who is a little late (although the plane itself is nearly an hour behind) arrives after the door has been slammed shut and locked, but he gets aboard and the door is slammed shut and locked again.

And that is all. In a breath-taking moment the big plane taxies down the field, turns around and whirls past with tremendous commotion, a violent blast of wind from the propellers almost upsets you, and down the field a few hundred feet the great bulk of a plane, weighing many tons, rises lightly as on a bird's wings. Before you can glance at the plane a second time it is gone, only a faint drum from her exhaust drifts down from the night sky. It is ten o'clock.

Back at the hotel you sleep if you can. It's unfortunate that in the morning you glance out of the window of your eighteenth floor room and realize with some dismay that a blizzard is raging and that snow is swirling about in a high wind. But the plane has been

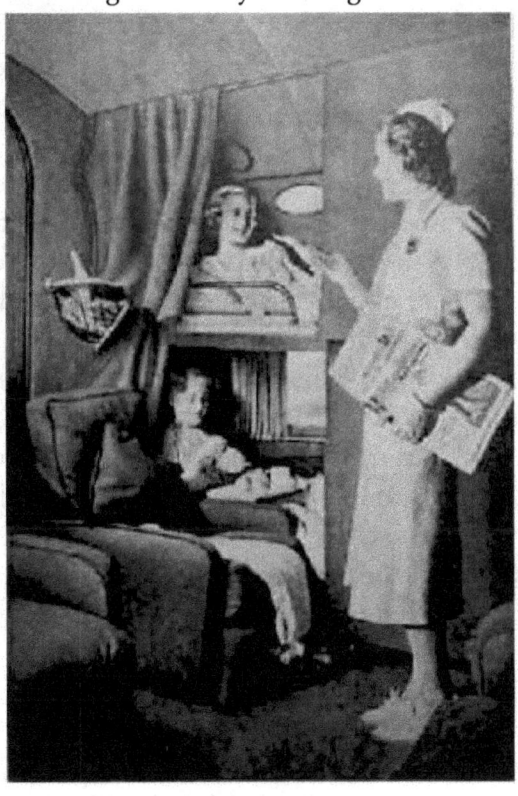

The Douglas Skysleeper Transport Plane

gone for hours. At daylight it landed at LaGuardia field, and before you get out of bed the bellboy brings a reassuring telegram from Forest Hills, filed at 6:55, Eastern standard time.

Plane travel seems much safer now–much safer indeed![74]

Along with national air travel, the coming decade promised to bring changes to the American way of life at an amazing rate. Leslie, as always an astute observer of his life and times would have had plenty to write about in his beloved Tiller and Toiler. He did not, however, live to see the events of the 1940s unfold.

Kansan for All Seasons

When Leslie died unexpectedly of a heart attack in 1940, hundreds of associates and friends were bereft of an accomplished, highly respected professional and an insightful, kind companion. His colleagues in the newspaper world wrote eloquently of his integrity, competence and loyalty, and there is probably no one on earth whose respect and affection would have meant more to him than these fellow journalists. A writer for the *Tiller and Toiler* commented, "It is trite to say that the Kansas newspaper and political will never be the same without him. But something fine and strong and true–something of its innate and irreplaceable virtue has gone from it. Great Heart is no more. And so, star dust to star dust–and glorious memories of a charming and gallant spirit!"[75]

The editor of *The Hays Daily News* wrote: "Leslie Wallace was exceptionally well read and well-informed. A delightful companion and enlivening conversationalist, it was a rare privilege to enjoy his company.... His death brings deep sorrow to the heart of everyone who knew him well for his friendship was one of those treasures of life which are sacrificed only when death steps in to intervene."[76] From *The Emporia Gazette* (and likely the pen of William Allen White), came this: "He was a man among a thousand, modest, kindly, even gentle in his personal approach, but always true and loyal and high minded. Kansas will miss him for he occupied places of honor and trust and never betrayed his state or his ideals or his good and loyal friends. There was a man."[77]

His deep devotion to Kansas and to the world of writing shaped his life. The editor of *The Great Bend Tribune* noted, "He was admired and respected for doing extremely well whatever he attempted.... Kansas newspaper and political tradition is infinitely richer for his having lived and worked here. The state will miss him so long as the memory of the man and his unusual accomplishments survives."[78]

It is fitting that the story of this Kansas journey of the Lykins, the Heiskells, and the Wallaces end here. Leslie died at the end of a little over a century of the families' presence in Kansas. In their time, they were part of the state's development, products of the foment and potential inherent in its settlement. Leslie died just before the country's engagement in World War II, an event which marked a major transition in the ways of being of Americans and of their place in the world. Following the war, political and technological developments gave rise to national and global identities eclipsing those of statehood and regional identity. The inter-state highway system, national television networks, post-war occupation of countries in Western Europe and Japan, the globalization of the economy, and the development of enormous farm machines and corporations have radically changed the farms, towns and villages the Lykins, Heiskell and Wallace families knew.

In the words Leslie Wallace's contemporaries wrote about him in 1940, however, the family would have recognized Leslie's character traits as their own. Leslie embodied a character trait which defined the Lykins-Heiskell families in Missouri and Kansas during the first hundred years of the two states' inter-twined histories. They were people of conviction: they had beliefs and they acted on them. Many of them wrote about their beliefs and opinions, expressing them in poems, newspaper editorials and features, letters, speeches and scholarly articles. Their beliefs and the choices they made, popular or unpopular, were highly visible. Many were leaders and opinion-makers who left traces of themselves in the broader paintings of Kansas and Missouri history, even though today, from the perspective of the twenty-first century, the lives of Emeline and her families are dim, barely discernible, brushstrokes concealed in the negative spaces of history.

---

1. "Leslie Wallace," Kansas Newspaper Hall of Fame, (www.kspress.com/img/HOF/members/wallace.html : accessed 5 May 2005).
2. Esther Clark Hill, "Who's Who in Kansas: Wallace, Leslie," *Kansas City Star*, 12 June 1927, unpaginated clipping, Biography file; Kansas State Historical Society, Topeka, Kansas.
3. "The Death of Mrs. Heiskell," *(Paola) Western Spirit*, 11 Aug 1916, p. 3.
4. Leslie Earle Wallace, "Miami Co's Oldest Citizen Dead," undated clipping, ca. Aug 1916, from unidentified newspaper; Heiskell file, Miami County Historical and Genealogical Society, Paola, Kansas.
5. Nellie McCoy Harris, "The Make Shifts of the Pioneers: An Interview, " *Kansas City Star*, 12 Dec 1911, *Reminiscences of Pioneer Days*, n.p., typescript;; Missouri Valley Collection, Kansas City Public Library, Kansas City, Missouri.
6. Cutler, *History of the state of Kansas*, 891.
7. 1885 Kansas State Census, Louisburg, Wea Township, Miami County, p. 20, Sue A. Phillips household; Kansas State Historical Society, Topeka, Kansas, microfilm KS1885-87.
8. Cutler, *History of the State of Kansas*, 893.
9. "[Tribute to Leslie E. Wallace] From *Topeka State Journal*," 10 May 1940, clipping, reprinted in *The Tiller and Toiler,* 13 May 1940, n.p., Biography file; Kansas State Historical Society, Topeka, Kansas.
10. "Western Spirit," Oct. 11, 1878, p. 3, col c.
11. [Tribute to Leslie E. Wallace] From *Topeka State Journal*," 10 May 1940.
12. "Mrs. Sue A. Latimer Dead," Obituary Collection, Hunt-Russell Genealogical Research Library, Miami County Historical and Genealogical Society, Paola, Kansas.
13. Volunteer Enlistment, 6 Mar 1865, William F. Wallace (Musician, Co. I, 18th N.H. Vol. Inf., Civil War) pension no. Inv. 749,743, Case Files of Approved Pension Applications, 1861-1934; Civil War and Later Pension Files; Department of Veterans Affairs, Record Group 15; National Archives, Washington, D.C.
14. Leslie E. Wallace, letter to The Commissioner of Pensions, U.S. Pension Office, 29 Apr 1918, William F. Wallace (Musician, Co. I, 18th N.H. Vol. Inf., Civil War) pension no. Inv. 749,743, Case Files of Approved Pension Applications, 1861-1934;

Civil War and Later Pension Files; Department of Veterans Affairs, Record Group 15; National Archives, Washington, D.C.
15. "The Death of Mrs. Heiskell," (Paola, Kansas) *Western Spirit*, 11 Aug 1916, 3.
16. "Mrs. Sue A. Latimer Dead," and "P.J. Latimer Dead," Obituary Collection, Hunt-Russell Genealogical Research Library, Miami County Historical and Genealogical Society, Paola, Kansas.
17. "Who's Who in Kansas: Wallace, Leslie," *Kansas City Star*, 12 June 1927, n.p.
18. 1900 US Census, Washington, D.C. (ED 140, sheet 8-A), dwelling 126, family 144, household of William Keiser.
19. "The Prize that Leslie Wallace Won for Kansas," *Kansas City Star*, 27 Feb 1927, n.p., clipping, Biography file: Wallace, Sara (Mrs. Leslie); Kansas State Historical Society, Topeka, Kansas.
20. Iola, Kansas, "History" (http://www.cityofiola.com/history.html : accessed on 15 Sept 2008).
21. "The Prize that Leslie Wallace Won for Kansas,"*Kansas City Star*, 27 Feb 1927, n.p.
22. "Wallace, Eunice," *Who Was Who Among North American Authors, 1921-1939*, editor, Alberta Lawrence (Detroit, Michigan: Gale Research, 1976), 2:1369.
23. "Who's Who in Kansas: Wallace Leslie," *Kansas City Star*, 12 June 1927, n.p.
24. "Wallace, Ralph," *Who's Who Among North American Authors*, editor, Alberta Lawrence (Los Angeles: Golden Syndicate Publishing Company, [1925]), 4: 1300.
25."Leslie E. Wallace Dies," *Kansas City Star*, 9 May 1940, n.p. clipping, Biography file: Wallace, Leslie; Kansas State Historical Society, Topeka, Kansas.
26. "Mrs. Leslie Wallace Dies", *Topeka Journal*, Oct. 25, 1930, n.p., clipping; Biography file: Wallace, Sara (Mrs. Leslie); Kansas State Historical Society, Topeka, Kansas.
27. "Who's Who in Kansas: Wallace, Leslie," *Kansas City Star*, 12 June 1927, n.p.
28. [Leslie Wallace], "Editorial," The Wheat Edition, *The Tiller and Toiler, 1919*; Rare Books Archive, Memorial Library, University of Wisconsin, Madison, Wisconsin.
29. William Allen White School of Journalism and Mass Communications, "White Biographies" (http://www.journalism.ku.edu/school/waw/bio/biographies.html : accessed on 29 Oct 2008).
30. Cora G. Lewis, "A Tribute," *Tiller and Toiler*, 30 Oct 1930, 1:b.
31. "The Prize that Leslie Wallace Won for Kansas") 27 Feb 1927, n.p.
32. Cora G. Lewis, "A Tribute," *Tiller and Toiler*, 30 Oct 1930, 1:b.
33. *Tiller and Toiler,* 19 June 1930, 8.
34. Cora G. Lewis, "A Tribute," *Tiller and Toiler*, 30 Oct 1930, 1:b. "Wallace, Leslie E.," *Who's Who Among North American Authors*, editor, Alberta Lawrence (Detroit, Michigan: Gale Research, 1967), 2:1470.
35. "The Prize that Leslie Wallace Won for Kansas,"*Kansas City Star*, 27 Feb 1927, n.p.

36. *Tiller and Toiler*, 18 June 1930, 8.
37. "Leslie E. Wallace," in "Kansas Personalities" *Topeka Journal*, 8 Nov 1935, n.p. clipping in the Biography file: Wallace, Leslie; Kansas State Historical Society Library, Topeka, Kansas.
38. Cora G. Lewis, "A Tribute," *Tiller and Toiler*, 30 Oct 1930, 1:b. "Wallace, Leslie E.," *Who's Who Among North American Writers*), 2: 1470.
39. *Tiller and Toiler,* Thursday, 19 June 1930, p. 8.
40. Esther Clark Hill, "Who's Who in Kansas" *Kansas City Star*, 12 June 1927, n.p.
41. "Tributes to Mr. Wallace: From the Emporia Gazette," T*he Daily Tiller and Toiler*, 10 May 1940, n.p., clipping, Wallace, Leslie, Biography file; Kansas State Historical Society, Topeka, Kansas.
42. "Tributes to Mr. Wallace: From the Emporia Gazette," *The Daily Tiller and Toiler, Larned,* no. 172, 10 May 1940. Clipping., n.p.
43. *Kansas City Star*, 28 Mar 1927, clipping. Biography file: Wallace, Leslie; Kansas State Historical Society, Topeka, Kansas.
44. "Chet Describes Wedding," *Tiller and Toiler*, 17 Sept 1931, n.p.
45. "Kansas Co-ed Wins Fame," *Topeka Capital*, 30 Nov 1925, n.p., clipping, Mrs. Eunice (Wallace) Shore, Biography file; Kansas State Historical Society, Topeka, Kansas.
46. *Who's Who Among North American Authors, 1929-1930*, editor, Alberta Chamberlain Lawrence, (Los Angeles: Golden Syndicate Publishing, 1929), 1300.
47. *Contemporary Kansas Poetry*, editor, Helen Rhoda Hoopes (Lawrence, Kansas: Franklin Watts–the Book Nook, 1927), 112-118.
48. "Mrs. Leslie Wallace Dies," *Topeka Journal*, 25 Oct 1930, clipping, n.p.
49. 1930 U.S. Census, Larned, Pawnee County, Kansas, (ED 73-10, sheet 8-B), dwelling 176, family of Leslie E. Wallace.
50. *Tiller and Toiler*, 30 Oct 1930, 1:a-g.
51. *Tiller and Toiler*, 30 Oct 1930, 1.
52. May Williams Ward, "M. W. W. To E. W.," Victoria Unruh Harvey, "Delphinium: to Sara Wallace," *The Harp* 7 (Sept-Oct and Nov-Dec 1931): 2-3.
53. Editorial note on Chester Shore, "A Bucking Hobby," *The Kansas Magazine*, 1945, p. 11.
54. "With Crowell Publications*," Augusta Gazette*, 16 June 1938, n.p., clipping; Biography file: Wallace, Ralph Leslie, Kansas State Historical Society, Topeka, Kansas.
55. "Makes Reader's Digest," *Augusta Gazette*, 30 Nov 1938, and "Has Article in Digest, " *Augusta Gazette,* 7 Sept 1942, unpaginated clippings; Biography file: Wallace, Ralph Leslie, Kansas State Historical Society, Topeka, Kansas.
56. "Leslie E. Wallace," in "Kansas Personalities" *Topeka Journal*, 8 Nov 1935, n.p.
57. "Marriage Licenses Issued*, 'Tiller and Toiler*, 17 Sept 1931, 1:e.
58. "Leslie E. Wallace," in "Kansas Personalities" *Topeka Journal*, 8 Nov 1935, n.p.
59. "Leslie E. Wallace," *The Topeka Capital*, 10 May 1940, clipping, n.p.

60. "Resigns State Job: Wallace Resigns as Woodring's Secretary,"*Topeka Capital*, 25 June 1931, n.p., clipping; Biography file: Wallace, Leslie E.; Kansas State Historical Society, Topeka, Kansas.
61. "Leslie E. Wallace," *The Topeka Capital*, 10 May 1940, n.p., clipping.
62. "Larned Editor Dies Suddenly Yesterday," *Western Spirit*, 10 May 1940, n.p., clipping; Biography file: Wallace, Leslie E.; Kansas State Historical Society, Topeka, Kansas.
63. "Leslie E. Wallace," *The Topeka Capital*, 10 May 1940, clipping, n.p.
64. "Leslie E. Wallace Dies Thursday," *Miami Republican*,.nd, clipping; Biography file: Wallace, Leslie E.; Kansas State Historical Society, Topeka, Kansas.
65. "Tributes to Mr. Wallace: From *The Miami Republican*,".*The Daily Tiller and Toiler*, 10 May 1940, n.p., clipping; Biography file: Wallace, Leslie E.; Kansas State Historical Society, Topeka, Kansas.
66. "Resigns State Job: Wallace Resigns as Woodring's Secretary," *Topeka Capital*, 25 June 1931, n.p.
67. "To Board of Regents: Leslie Wallace Succeeds Charles W. Spencer of Sedan," *Topeka Capital*, July 18, 1931, n.p., n.p., clipping; Biography file: Wallace, Leslie E.; Kansas State Historical Society, Topeka, Kansas.
68. "Leslie E. Wallace Dies, "*Kansas City Star*, 9 May 1940, n.p., clipping; Biography file: Wallace, Leslie E.; Kansas State Historical Society, Topeka, Kansas.
69. "Leslie E. Wallace Dies, "*Kansas City Star*, 9 May 1940, n.p., clipping.
70 R. Douglas Hurt, *The Dust Bowl: an Agricultural and Social History* (Chicago: Nelson-Hall, 1981), 17-32.
71. "Sunday, April 14, 1935, Dust Clouds Rolling Over the Prairies;" Stovall Studio, Dodge City, Kansas; Soul of a People: Writing America's Story, Special Collections and University Archives, Wichita State University Libraries, Wichita, Kansas.
72. "And Still It's Dusty," *The Daily Tiller and Toiler, 18* Apr 1935, 1:e.
73. "TWA 1937 Trans-Continental Routes," DC-3 Airways Virtual Airline (http://www.dc3airways.com/flights/routes/twa_route_notes.htm: accessed 18 Nov 2009). "DC-3 Commercial Transport," History, Boeing (http://www.boeing.com/history/mdc/dc-3.htm : accessed 18 Nov 2009).
74. Editorial Page of *The Tiller and Toiler*, Larned, Kansas, reprinted in *Kansas Magazine*, 1941.
75. "Leslie E. Wallace, Leading Publisher, Passes Yesterday," *The Daily Tiller and Toiler*, 10 May 1940, n.p., clipping; Biography file: Wallace, Leslie E.; Kansas State Historical Society, Topeka, Kansas.
76. "Tributes to Mr. Wallace: From the *Hays Daily News,"The Daily Tiller and Toiler*, 13 May 1940, n.p., clipping, Wallace, Leslie, Biography file; Kansas State Historical Society, Topeka, Kansas, n.p.
77. "Tributes to Mr. Wallace: From *The Emporia Gazette,"*.*The Daily Tiller and Toiler, Larned*, 13 May 1940, n.p., clipping; Biography file: Wallace, Leslie E.; Kansas State Historical Society, Topeka, Kansas.

78. "Tributes to Mr. Wallace: From *The Great Bend* Tribune," *The Daily Tiller and Toiler*, 13 May 1940, n.p., clipping; Biography file: Wallace, Leslie E.; Kansas State Historical Society, Topeka, Kansas.

CHAPTER 9

Family Genealogical Charts

The genealogies in this chapter are provided to aid the reader in following the families that are at the heart of this book. They are not developed as fully as they would for a stand-alone genealogy.

While the author believes the information contained in these genealogies is accurate, many names, dates, places, and relationships have only secondary sources. Readers wanting to develop these genealogies will want to do research to locate primary sources to confirm or correct the sources provided here.

Descendants of David L. Lykins and Jemima Willis

Generation No. 1

1. **David L. Lykins** was born May 10, 1773, in Franklin County, Virginia,[1] and died March 11, 1835, in Prairie Creek Township, Vigo County, Indiana.[2] He married **Jemima Willis** December 26, 1797, in Franklin County, Virginia,[3] daughter of Isaiah Willis and Hannah Johnston. She was born September 21, 1780, in Virginia,[4] and died February 04, 1833, in Prairie Creek Township, Vigo County, Indiana.[5]

Children of David Lykins and Jemima Willis are:

+ 2   i. Jared Lykins, born September 16, 1798, in Franklin County, Virginia; died March 22, 1835.
+ 3   ii. Johnston Lykins, born April 15, 1800, in Franklin County, Virginia; died August 15, 1876, in Kansas City, Jackson County, Missouri.
+ 4   iii. Joseph Willis Lykins, born March 01, 1802, in Franklin County, Virginia; died October 31, 1882, in Paola, Miami County, Kansas.
+ 5   iv. Hannah Lykins, born July 30, 1804, in Franklin County, Virginia; died August 10, 1840, in Prairie Creek Township, Vigo County, Indiana.
+ 6   v. Cynthia Lykins, born October 30, 1806, in Franklin County, Virginia.
+ 7   vi. Jonas Philip Lykins, born March 17, 1809, in Cumberland County, Kentucky; died 1859, in Mission Township, Shawnee County, Kansas.
+ 8   vii. Juliann Lykins, born February 14, 1811, in Cumberland County, Kentucky; died 1872, in Prairie Hill, Dallas County, Iowa.
+ 9   viii. Claiborne Bloomfield Lykins, born February 03, 1813, in Cumberland County, Kentucky; died July 05, 1877, in Mound Valley, Labette County, Kansas.
   10   ix. Ruth Lykins, born December 26, 1814, in Cumberland County, Kentucky;[6] died August 06, 1818, in Cumberland County, Kentucky.[7]

+	11	x.	Eliza Ritchie Lykins, born January 20, 1817, in Knox County, Indiana; died March 14, 1889, in Fremont, Dodge County, Nebraska.
+	12	xi.	David Lykins, born May 08, 1821, in Vigo County, Indiana; died August 13, 1861, in Denver, Denver County, Colorado.
	13	xii.	Jemima Lykins, born July 22, 1823, in Vigo County, Indiana;[8] died October 14, 1824.[9]

Generation No. 2

2. **Jared Lykins** (David) was born September 16, 1798, in Franklin County, Virginia,[10] and died March 22, 1835.[11] He married **Cynthia Peery** November 29, 1827,[12] daughter of Samuel Peery and Elizabeth Ashmore. She was born August 04, 1806.[13]

Child of Jared Lykins and Cynthia Peery is:
  14   i. Sophronia Lykins.[14]

3. **Johnston Lykins** was born April 15, 1800, in Franklin County, Virginia,[15] and died August 15, 1876, in Kansas City, Jackson County, Missouri.[16] He married **(1) Delilah McCoy** February 27, 1828, in Michigan,[17] daughter of Isaac McCoy and Christiana Polk. She was born November 24, 1809, in North Carolina,[18] and died September 23, 1844, in Potawatomi Station, Kansas-Nebraska Territory.[19] He married **(2) Martha A. "Mattie" Livingston** October 12, 1851, in Lexington, Lafayette County, Missouri,[20] daughter of Stephen Livingston and Martha Jackson. She was born January 1824, in Shelbyville, Shelby County, Kentucky,[21] and died September 20, 1890, in Kansas City, Jackson County, Missouri. Mattie Lykins subsequently married George Caleb Bingham, June 18, 1878, in Kansas City, Jackson County, Missouri.[22]

Children of Johnston Lykins and Delilah McCoy are:
+ 15   i. William Hall Richardson Lykins, born November 29, 1828, in Lexington, Fayette County, Kentucky; died June 15, 1893, in Kansas City, Jackson County, Missouri.
  16   ii. Charles Rice McCoy Lykins, born 1832, in Louisville, Jefferson County, Kentucky; died May 14, 1841, in Westport, Jackson County, Missouri.
+ 17 iii. Sarah J. Lykins, born December 16, 1834, in Westport, Jackson County, Missouri; died December 14, 1901, in Kansas City, Jackson County, Missouri.

+ 18 iv. Julia McCoy Lykins, born November 14, 1839, in Louisville, Jefferson County, Kentucky; died September 14, 1872, in Kansas City, Jackson County, Missouri.

4. **Joseph Willis Lykins** was born March 01, 1802, in Franklin County, Virginia,[23] and died October 31, 1882, in Paola, Miami County, Kansas.[24] He married **(1) Margaret Nixon** June 5, 1831.[25] He married **(2) Mariah Brown-Williams** Aft. 1843. She was born December 31, 1815, in Ohio, and died January 02, 1871, in Paola, Miami County, Kansas.[26]

Children of Joseph Lykins and Margaret Nixon are:
  19 i. James F. Lykins, born November 05, 1834;[27] died December 27, 1873, in Paola, Miami County, Kansas.[28]
+ 20 ii. Mary Elizabeth Lykins, born August 13, 1837, in LaPorte, Indiana; died May 19, 1909, in Paola, Miami County, Kansas.
  21 iii. Marion Lykins, born Abt. 1843.[29]
  22 iv. Andrew Willis Lykins, born April 26, 1842, in Laporte, Indiana; died April 26, 1902, in Paola, Miami County, Kansas.[30]

5. **Hannah Lykins** was born July 30, 1804, in Franklin County, Virginia,[31] and died August 10, 1840, in Prairie Creek Township, Vigo County, Indiana.[32] She married **William Peery** November 09, 1826, in Middle Town, Vigo County, Indiana,[33] son of Samuel Peery and Elizabeth Ashmore. He was born January 07, 1789, in Knoxville, Knox County, Tennessee,[34] and died December 03, 1848, in Prairie Creek Township, Vigo County, Indiana.[35]

Children of Hannah Lykins and William Peery are:
  23 i. Albert J. Peery, born August 25, 1828, in Prairie Creek Township, Vigo County, Indiana;[36] died October 05, 1850, enroute to California.[37]
+ 24 ii. Emeline Jamima Peery, born August 28, 1830, in Prairie Creek Township, Vigo County, Indiana; died August 03, 1916, in Louisburg, Miami County, Kansas.
+ 25 iii. David Lykins Peery, born May 31, 1834, in Prairie Creek Township, Vigo County, Indiana; died July 01, 1896.

6. **Cynthia Lykins** was born October 30, 1806, in Franklin County, Virginia.[38] She married **Lewis Earnest** November 04, 1824.[39] He was born May 16, 1800,[40] and died Abt. 1839.[41]

Children of Cynthia Lykins and Lewis Earnest are:
- 26   i.   Delilah Earnest.
- + 27   ii.   Mary Ann Earnest, born August 08, 1832, in Vigo County, Indiana.
- 28   iii.   Jane Earnest.
- + 29   iv.   Willis Earnest, born Abt. 1833, in Sullivan County, Indiana; died January 03, 1862, in Camp Calhoun, Kentucky.
- 30   v.   Eliza Earnest.
- 31   vi.   Andrew Earnest.
- 32   vii.   Caroline Earnest.
- 33   viii.   Emma Earnest.

7. **Jonas Philip Lykins** was born March 17, 1809, in Cumberland County, Kentucky,[42] and died 1859, in Mission Township, Shawnee County, Kansas.[43] He married **(1) Sarah Kelso** January 03, 1833.[44] She was born 1813, and died 1840.[45] He married **(2) Prudence —?—** 1846, in Ossawatomie, Kansas.[46]

Children of Jonas Lykins and Sarah Kelso are:
- 34   i.   Jane Lykins, born November 20, 1833.
- 35   ii.   Eliza Lykins, born 1835.
- 36   iii.   Amanda Lykins, born 1838.
- 37   iv.   W. Leopold Lykins, born 1840.

8. **Juliann Lykins** was born February 14, 1811, in Cumberland County, Kentucky,[47] and died 1872, in Prairie Hill, Dallas County, Iowa.[48] She married **Alonzo Betteys** August 26, 1833, in Prairie Creek Township, Vigo County, Indiana,[49] son of Eli Betteys and Martha Rich.

Children of Juliann Lykins and Alonzo Betteys are:
- + 38   i.   Wealthy Ann Betteys, born Abt. 1836, in Indiana.
- 39   ii.   Eliza M. Betteys, born Abt. 1837.
- 40   iii.   Margaret Betteys, born Abt. 1841.
- + 41   iv.   Franklyn M. Betteys, born Abt. 1844, in Indiana.
- 42   v.   Sarah J. Betteys, born Abt. 1846.
- 43   vi.   William Betteys, born Abt. 1849.

9. **Claiborne Bloomfield Lykins** was born February 03, 1813, in Cumberland County, Kentucky,[50] and died July 05, 1877, in Mound Valley, Labette County, Kansas. He married **Nancy Johnson** June 01, 1837,[51] daughter of Samuel Johnson and Sally Travis. She was born March

28, 1820 in Cooper County, Missouri,[52] and died August 03, 1886, in Saint Joseph, Buchanan County, Missouri.

Children of Claiborne Lykins and Nancy Johnson are:
+ 44   i.   Andrew C. Lykins, born Abt. 1839; died June 06, 1884, in Dallas County, Iowa.
    45   ii.   Mary V. Lykins, born Abt. 1841. She married Marcus Hustad December 03, 1865, in Buchanan County.[53]
    46   iii.   Julia A. Lykins, born Abt. 1842. She married William J. King.
    47   iv.   David A. Lykins, born Abt. 1844; died October 1864, in Newtonia, Missouri.
    48   v.   John Johnson Lykins, born March 15, 1845, in Andrew County, Missouri; died January 05, 1926, in Buchanan County, Missouri.[54] He married Paulina E. Dyerley; born January 16, 1860 in Missouri; died June 12, 1947, in St. Joseph, Buchanan County, Missouri.[55]
+ 49   vi.   William C. Lykins, born February 28, 1847; died August 30, 1920 in Washington, Franklin County, Missouri.
    50   vii.   Cynthia Ann Lykins, born Abt. 1851.
    51   viii.   Emma V. Lykins, born Abt. 1853. She married Charles L. Simmons April 15, 1873.[56]
    52   ix.   James Samuel Lykins, born Abt. 1856, in St. Joseph, Buchanan County, Missouri; died Bef. 1930 in Hale, Garland, Arkansas.
    53   x.   Charles R. Lykins, born September 08, 1858, in Andrew County, Missouri; died June 02, 1936, in Buchanan County, Missouri.[57] He married Sarah Brosi September 12, 1888, in St. Joseph, Missouri;[58] born February 02, 1872, in Andrew County, Missouri; died October 01, 1932, in St. Joseph, Buchanan County, Missouri.[59]
    54   xi.   Sarah E. Lykins.
    55   xii.   unnamed infant Lykins.

11. **Eliza Ritchie Lykins** was born January 20, 1817, in Knox County, Indiana,[60] and died March 14, 1889, in Fremont, Dodge County, Nebraska.[61] She married **Athol Ferguson** January 01, 1830 in Vigo County, Indiana.[62] He was born Abt. 1815, in Ohio,[63] and died Abt. 1851, in San Francisco, San Francisco County, California.[64]

Children of Eliza Lykins and Athol Ferguson are:
    56   i.   Thomas Ferguson, born Abt. 1835;[65] died in Waterloo, Iowa.[66]
    57   ii.   David Ferguson, born Abt. 1839, in Taylor, Ogle County,

58	iii.	Illinois;[67] died November 13, 1861, in Camp Nevin, Kentucky.[68] John Ferguson, born Abt. 1842.
59	iv.	Albert Lee Ferguson, born Abt. 1844.
+ 60	v.	Eugene C. Ferguson, born Abt. 1849; died Aft. 1931.

12. **David Lykins** was born May 08, 1821, in Vigo County, Indiana,[69] and died August 13, 1861, in Denver, Denver County, Colorado.[70] He married **(1) Abigail Ann Webster** January 07, 1843, in Westport, Jackson County, Missouri.[71] She was born 1815, in Concord, Merrimack County, New Hampshire,[72] and died January 15, 1852, in Wea Baptist Mission Station, Paola, Miami County, Kansas.[73] He married **(2) Sarah D. Tull** March 20, 1853, in Wea Mission, Paola, Miami County, Kansas.[74] She died Bef. 1860. He married **(3) Grace Tull** December 04, 1860 in Paola, Lykins County, Kansas Territory.[75]

Children of David Lykins and Abigail Webster are:
61	i.	Charles C. S. Lykins, born Abt. December 16, 1845, in Wea Baptist Mission Station, Paola, Miami County, Kansas[76]; died January 17, 1852, in Wea Baptist Mission Station, Paola, Miami County, Kansas.[77]
+ 62	ii.	Wayland Carey Lykins, born November 12, 1847, in Wea Baptist Indian Mission, Kansas Territory; died March 11, 1937, in Commerce, Ottawa County, Oklahoma.
+ 63	iii.	Edward W. W. Lykins, born March 05, 1850 in Wea Baptist Mission Station, Paola, Miami County, Kansas; died March 11, 1937, in Commerce, Oklahoma.

Generation No. 3

15. **William Hall Richardson Lykins** was born November 29, 1828, in Lexington, Fayette County, Kentucky,[78] and died June 15, 1893, in Kansas City, Jackson County, Missouri.[79] He married **Cornelia Victoria Smith** December 10, 1857,[80] daughter of James Smith and Susan Cole. She was born January 16, 1837, in Charleston, Charleston County, South Carolina, and died April 29, 1914, in Kansas City, Jackson County, Missouri.

Children of William Hall Richardson Lykins and Cornelia Victoria Smith are:
64	i.	Johnston Franklin Lykins, born October 16, 1858;[81] died February 03, 1889, in Kansas City, Jackson County, Missouri.[82]
65	ii.	Susan Elizabeth Lykins, born November 09, 1860;[83] died

May 21, 1892.[84] She married William Whitehead Thatcher in Kansas City, Jackson County, Missouri.[85]

66 iii. Delilah McCoy Lykins, born June 24, 1863, in Lawrence, Douglas, Kansas;[86] died May 01, 1944, in Kansas City, Jackson County, Missouri.[87] She married Henry C. Schwitgebel March 09, 1918, in Jackson County, Missouri;[88] born January 04, 1857, in Missouri;[89] died 1937.[90]

17. **Sarah J. Lykins** was born December 16, 1834, in Westport, Jackson County, Missouri,[91] and died December 14, 1901, in Kansas City, Jackson County, Missouri.[92] She married **Egbert Freeland Russell** March 25, 1850 in Lafayette County, Missouri.[93] He was born August 1828,[94] and died October 21, 1871.[95]

Children of Sarah J. Lykins and Egbert Freeland Russell are:
+ 67 i. Zaenett Russell, born Abt. 1852; died Abt. 1886.
  68 ii. Mattie Russell, born 1853.
  69 iii. William Lykins Russell, born 1855; died 1874.
+ 70 iv. Julia Russell, born 1858, in Westport, Jackson County, Missouri; died October 30, 1935, in Glendale, Los Angeles County, California.
  71 v. Effie Russell, born 1859; died Abt. 1871.
+ 72 vi. Theodora Case Russell, born 1865, in Westport, Jackson County, Missouri; died October 1933.
+ 73 vii. Cornelia Victoria Russell, born May 09, 1868; died January 17, 1953, in Independence, Jackson County, Missouri.

18. **Julia McCoy Lykins** was born November 14, 1839, in Louisville, Jefferson County, Kentucky,[96] and died September 14, 1872, in Kansas City, Jackson County, Missouri. She married **Theodore Spencer Case** October 12, 1858, in Kansas City, Jackson County, Missouri,[97] son of Ermine Case and Mary Bowen. He was born January 26, 1832, in Jackson, Butts County, Georgia, and died February 16, 1900 in Kansas City, Jackson County, Missouri.[98]

Children of Julia Lykins and Theodore Case are:
74 i. Emily Arabella Case, born September 15, 1961; died March 8, 1865.
75 ii. Mattie Lykins Case, born July, 1860; died January 20, 1865.
76 iii. Olive Spencer Case, born September 3, 1865; died February 9, 1869.

+	77	iv.	Delilah McCoy Case, born August 25, 1867, in Kansas City, Jackson County, Missouri; died October 04, 1939, in Kansas City, Jackson County, Missouri.
	78	v.	Johnston Lykins Case, born February 15, 1870 in Kansas City, Jackson County, Missouri; died June 13, 1951, in Kansas City, Missouri.
+	79	vi.	Ermine Cowles Case, born 1872, in Kansas City, Jackson County, Missouri; died 1953, in Milwaukee, Wisconsin.

20. **Mary Elizabeth Lykins** was born August 13, 1837, in LaPorte County, Indiana, and died May 19, 1909, in Paola, Miami County, Kansas.[99] She married **Woodson D. Hoover**. He was born July 05, 1834, in Jessamine County, Kentucky, and died May 21, 1899, in Paola, Miami County, Kansas.[100]

Children of Mary Lykins and Woodson Hoover are:
80	i.	Clatta Hoover. She married Charles S. Flanders 1894.
81	ii.	Archie B. Hoover, born August 03, 1875, in Paola, Miami County, Kansas; died August 24, 1949, in Paola, Miami County, Kansas.
82	iii.	Julia Hoover. She married J. C. Hersperger.
83	iv.	Samuel Hoover.

24. **Emeline Jamima Peery** was born August 28, 1830 in Prairie Creek Township, Vigo County, Indiana,[101] and died August 03, 1916, in Louisburg, Miami County, Kansas.[102] She married **William Alexander Heiskell** March 20, 1853, in Wea Mission, Paola, Miami County, Kansas,[103] son of Christopher Heiskell. He was born November 16, 1807, in Hampshire County, West Virginia,[104] and died August 19, 1870 in Paola, Miami County, Kansas.[105]

Children of Emeline Peery and William Heiskell are:
+	84	i.	Sue Austin Heiskell, born May 31, 1857, in Paola, Miami County, Kansas; died July 16, 1918, in Louisburg, Miami County, Kansas.
	85	ii.	Alberta Heiskell, born August 16, 1860 in Paola, Miami County, Kansas; died April 20, 1861, in Paola, Miami County, Kansas.
	86	iii.	Nellie V. Heiskell, born February 15, 1862, in Paola, Miami County, Kansas; died August 13, 1864, in Paola, Miami County, Kansas.

| | 87 | iv. | Blanche Heiskell, born August 17, 1864, in Paola, Miami County, Kansas; died September 16, 1864, in Paola, Miami County, Kansas. |
| + | 88 | v. | Minnie M. Heiskell, born November 08, 1868, in Paola, Miami County, Kansas; died Aft. 1930. |

25. David Lykins Peery was born May 31, 1834, in Prairie Creek Township, Vigo County, Indiana,[106] and died July 01, 1896.[107] He married **(1) Elizabeth Peoria** September 23, 1860 in Miami County, Kansas,[108] daughter of Baptiste Peoria and Mau-me-way. She died May 04, 1870.[109] He married **(2) Sarah Caroline Harris** October 08, 1872, in Miami County, Kansas.[110] She was born Abt. 1838, in Kansas, and died December 26, 1887.[111]

Children of David Lykins Peery and Elizabeth Peoria are:
+ 89   i.   Albert J. Peery, born June 30, 1861.
+ 90   ii. Clara E. Peery, born October 01, 1863, in Paola, Miami County, Kansas; died April 10, 1935, in Miami, Ottawa County, Oklahoma.
+ 91   iii. William Baptiste Peery, born January 05, 1866; died July 19, 1932, in Claremore, Oklahoma.
  92   iv. Samuel L. Peery, born May 03, 1868.

Children of David Lykins Peery and Sarah Caroline Harris are:
+ 93   i.   Maud Mabel Peery, born April 04, 1874, in Oak Hill Farm, Miami County, Kansas; died February 03, 1955, in California.
  94   ii. Nellie Lucile Peery, born February 29, 1876, in Peery Farm, Peoria Reserve, Indian Territory, Oklahoma; died February 26, 1895, in Sister's School, Muskogee, Indian Territory, Oklahoma.
  95   iii. Eva May Peery, born September 11, 1877.
+ 96   iv. Elsie Ethel Peery, born July 05, 1882.
+ 97   v.   Frank Cleveland Peery, born September 28, 1884.

27. Mary Ann Earnest was born August 08, 1832, in Vigo County, Indiana.[112] She married **Thomas Galloway Finley**, son of Jonas Finley and Sally McNair. He was born February 04, 1828, in Sullivan County, Indiana,[113] and died June 25, 1870 in Indiana.

Child of Mary Earnest and Thomas Finley is:
+ 98   i.   Mary E. Finley, born 1852; died July 1930.

29. **Willis Earnest** was born Abt. 1833, in Sullivan County, Indiana, and died January 03, 1862, in Camp Calhoun, Kentucky.[114] He married **Rhoda Starkey** January 08, 1857, in Sullivan County, Indiana. She was born Abt. 1838, in Sullivan County, Indiana, and died Abt. 1880.

Children of Willis Earnest and Rhoda Starkey are:
- 99   i.   Sarah E. Earnest, born October 18, 1858. She married Ed Stevens.
- 100   ii.   Mary T. Earnest, born November 23, 1860. She married --?-- Cusick.

38. **Wealthy Ann Betteys** was born Abt. 1836, in Indiana. She married (1) **Augustus Storrs Dow** February 14, 1857, in Boone County, Iowa,[115] son of Agrippa Dow. He was born October 14, 1827, in Hanover, Grafton County, New Hampshire, and died June 1860 in Shorter County, Nebraska.[116] She married (2) **James Shepherd** January 13, 1872, in Boone County, Iowa.[117]

Children of Wealthy Betteys and Augustus Dow are:
- 101   i.   Della S. Dow, born Abt. 1857.
- + 102   ii.   Eva E. Dow, born December 1859, in Iowa.
- 103   iii.   Margaret Dow, born Abt. 1860.

41. **Franklyn M. Betteys** was born Abt. 1844, in Indiana. He married **Virginia J. Wade** January 01, 1874, in Boone County, Iowa.[118] She was born Abt. 1855, in Illinois.

Children of Franklyn Betteys and Virginia Wade are:
- 104   i.   Eugene Betteys.
- 105   ii.   Imogene Betteys.
- 106   iii.   M. Betteys.
- 107   iv.   Edwin Betteys.
- 108   v.   Winnie Betteys.

44. **Andrew C. Lykins** was born Abt. 1839, and died June 06, 1884, in Dallas County, Iowa.[119] He married **Laveria A. Pierce**. She died July 14, 1886, in Dallas County, Iowa.[120]

Children of Andrew Lykins and Laveria Pierce are:
- 109   i.   Mary Jane Lykins, born August 12, 1870.[121] She married Amos V. Strange.[122]
- 110   ii.   John Samuel Lykins, born May 12, 1873.[123] He married Pearl Periman; born Abt. 1874.
- + 111   iii.   Sylvia A. Lykins, born July 06, 1882. She married Job R. Bernard; born Abt. 1871, in Iowa.

49. William C. Lykins was born February 28, 1847,[124] and died August 30, 1920 in Washington, Buchanan, Missouri.[125] He married **Ida B. Cloud** March 28, 1878,[126] daughter of R.W. Cloud and --?-- Mehaley. She was born Abt. 1860 in Kansas.

Children of William Lykins and Ida Cloud are:
- + 112   i.   Jessie Lykins, born August 07, 1879, in Wyoming; died December 26, 1964, in Alameda, California.
- 113   ii.   Ivy Lykins, born November 16, 1883, in Wyoming; died May 1973, in St. Joseph, Buchanan, Missouri. She married Harvey M. Rector June 20, 1904, in St. Joseph, Buchanan, Missouri; born Abt. 1874, in Kansas.
- 114   iii.   W. Ray Lykins, born October 28, 1889, in Cheyenne, Wyoming; died January 18, 1912, in St. Joseph, Buchanan, Missouri.

60. Eugene C. Ferguson was born April, 1848; died Aft. 1931. He married **Marie --?--** 1886. She was born Abt. 1864.

Children of Eugene Ferguson and Marie are:
- 115   i.   Imogene B. Ferguson, born 1888.
- 116   ii.   Claud E. Ferguson, born 1890.
- 117   iii.   Herbert B. Ferguson, born 1892.
- 118   iv.   Louise B. Ferguson, born 1894.
- 119   v.   Cecil J. Ferguson, born 1896.

62. Wayland Carey Lykins was born November 12, 1847, in Wea Baptist Indian Mission, Kansas Territory,[127] and died March 11, 1937, in Commerce, Ottawa County, Oklahoma.[128] He married **Anna Abbie Middaugh** December 15, 1871, in Columbus, Cherokee County, Kansas,[129] daughter of Charlton Middaugh and Martha Curtice. She was born December 15, 1856, in Webster, Monroe County, New York, and died January 26, 1936, in Hope, Hempstead County, Arkansas.

Children of Wayland Lykins and Anna Middaugh are:
- 120   i.   Webster M. Lykins, born November 06, 1874; died March 10, 1940 in Joplin, Missouri.
- 121   ii.   Curtis E. Lykins, born January 07, 1877, in Columbus, Kansas; died August 17, 1880.
- + 122   iii.   Fred Carey Lykins, born December 28, 1878, in Columbus, Kansas; died July 02, 1943, in San Diego, California.
- 123   iv.   Charles Gustavus Lykins, born December 07, 1881; died December 1953, in San Diego, California. He married Jennie May Nolte.
- + 124   v.   Queenie Lykins, born April 03, 1886, in Peoria Reservation, Oklahoma; died February 21, 1988, in Lamar, Colorado. She married Don Carl Wills.
- + 125   vi.   Harry C. Lykins, born September 13, 1888, in Columbus, Cherokee County, Kansas; died August 01, 1971, in Miami, Ottawa County, Oklahoma Territory.
- 126   vii.   Martha Lykins, born February 18, 1891; died March 26, 1961, in Baton Rouge, Louisiana. She married Frank Lamont Padgitt June 21, 1912, in Murray County, Minnesota.

63. Edward W. W. Lykins was born March 05, 1850 in Wea Baptist Mission Station, Paola, Miami County, Kansas,[130] and died March 11, 1937, in Commerce, Oklahoma.[131] He married **(1) Sara Whitefeather** Abt. 1872.[132] She died Abt. 1894. He married **(2) Sarah "Lena" Williams** 1896, in Miami, Oklahoma.[133] She was born in New York.

Children of Edward Lykins and Sarah Williams are:
- 127   i.   Willis Lykins. He married Hazel Trudgeon.
- 128   ii.   Elsie Lykins.
- 129   iii.   David P. Lykins, died May 04, 1915, in Kansas City, Jackson County, Missouri.
- 130   iv.   Lorene Lykins.

Generation No. 4

67. Zaenett Russell was born Abt. 1852, and died Abt. 1886.[134] She married **Harlow Johnson Boyce** 1874. He was born April 17, 1844, in Castalia, Ohio.[135]

Children of Zaenett Russell and Harlow Boyce are:
    131   i.   Charles McCoy Boyce, born November 18, 1873.
    132   ii.   Johnson Lykins Boyce, born November 18, 1877.

70. **Julia Russell** was born 1858, in Westport, Jackson County, Missouri, and died October 30, 1935, in Glendale, Los Angeles, California. She married **Samuel Seaman Barnhill**. He was born September 25, 1853, in Mattoon, Coles County, Illinois, and died April 03, 1932, in Downey, Los Angeles County, California.

Children of Julia Russell and Samuel Barnhill are:
    133   i.   William Allen Barnhill, born September 18, 1880 in Kansas City, Jackson County, Missouri.
    134   ii.   Claude Raymond Barnhill, born September 1883, in Jewel, Kansas.
    135   iii.   Darby B. Barnhill, born January 1886, in Jewel, Kansas.
    136   iv.   Bernice Cecelia Barnhill, born June 21, 1888, in Kansas City, Jackson County, Missouri.

72. **Theodora Case Russell** was born 1865, in Westport, Jackson County, Missouri,[136] and died October 1933.[137] She married **Elijah H. Bettis** 1880.[138] He was born Abt. 1856,[139] and died October 27, 1937, in Kansas City, Jackson County, Missouri.[140]

Children of Theodora Russell and Elijah Bettis are:
    137   i.   Zennette Bettis.
+ 138   ii.   Frank Allison Bettis, born April 11, 1882.
+ 139   iii.   Alexander Erwin Bettis, born December 16, 1885.

73. **Cornelia Victoria Russell** was born May 09, 1868, and died January 17, 1953, in Independence, Jackson County, Missouri. She married **Isaac Newton Browne** Abt. January 09, 1884, in Jackson County, Missouri[307].

Children of Cornelia Russell and Isaac Browne are:
    140   i.   Sarah Browne.
    141   ii.   William Browne.
    142   iii.   Theodora Browne.
    143   iv.   Lillian Browne.
    144   v.   Julia Browne.

145 vi. Helen Browne.
146 vii. Robert Browne, born December 09, 1909.

77. Delilah McCoy Case was born August 25, 1867, in Kansas City, Jackson County, Missouri, and died October 04, 1939, in Kansas City, Jackson County, Missouri.[141] She married **George Carroll Cowles** December 25, 1889, in Jackson County, Missouri.[142] He was born January 16, 1862, in Butler, Kentucky, and died November 07, 1940 in Kansas City, Jackson County, Missouri.

Children of Delilah Case and George Cowles are:
147 i. Theodore Williams Cowles, born Abt. 1890.
148 ii. Margaret Cowles.

79. Ermine Cowles Case was born September 11, 1871, in Kansas City, Jackson County, Missouri,[143] and died September 7, 1953, in Milwaukee, Wisconsin. He married **Mary Margaret Snow** June 23, 1898, in Lawrence, Kansas, daughter of F. H. Snow. She died May 21, 1923, in Cape Town, South Africa.[144]

Children of Ermine Case and Mary Snow are:
149 i. Francis H. Case, born April 4, 1899.
150 ii. Theodore Johnston Case, born March 15, 1901; died February 15, 1987, in Alameda, California.

84. Sue Austin Heiskell was born May 31, 1857, in Paola, Miami County, Kansas,[145] and died July 16, 1918, in Louisburg, Miami County, Kansas.[146] She married **(1) William F. Wallace** June 27, 1875, in Paola, Miami County, Kansas,[147] son of William True Wallace and Lydia Waterman. He was born July 11, 1849, in Concord, Merrimack County, New Hampshire,[148] and died September 05, 1906, in Rochester, Strafford County, New Hampshire.[149] She married **(2) Hiram Lafayette Phillips** February 18, 1879, in Paola, Miami County, Kansas,[150] son of Alfred Phillips and Susannah Cullom. He was born September 20, 1827, in Wayne County, Kentucky,[151] and died April 05, 1885, in Louisburg, Miami County, Kansas.[152] She married **(3) Philip Fletcher Latimer** October 08, 1889, in Louisburg Presbyterian Church, Louisburg, Miami County, Kansas,[153] son of Robert Latimer and Anna Fletcher. He was born September 10, 1830 in Ireland,[154] and died February 09, 1913, in Louisburg, Miami County, Kansas.[155]

Child of Sue Heiskell and William Wallace is:
+ 151   i. Leslie Earle Wallace, born September 15, 1876, in Paola, Miami County, Kansas; died May 09, 1940 in Larned, Pawnee County, Kansas.

Children of Sue Heiskell and Hiram Phillips are:
    152   i. Nellie Phillips, born December 1879.
+ 153   ii. Lenora Phillips, born February 1882.
+ 154   iii. Jessie Phillips, born August 1884.

Child of Sue Heiskell and Philip Latimer is:
    155   i. Philip H. Latimer, born June 07, 1891, in Louisburg, Miami County, Kansas;[156] died August 06, 1982, in Overland Park, Johnson County, Kansas.[157] He married (1) Maude Ragan.[158] She was born February 4, 1891, in Louisburg, Kansas, and died February 11, 1949, in Kansas City, Missouri.[159] He married (2) Blanche Rife Linder January 06, 1938, in Harrisonville, Cass County, Missouri;[160] born 1899; died 1983.[161]

88. Minnie M. Heiskell was born November 08, 1868, in Paola, Miami County, Kansas,[162] and died Aft. 1930. She married **David Heenan** Bet. 1894 - 1896, in Kansas,[163] son of David Heenan. He was born August 15, 1868, in Belfast, County Antrim, Northern Ireland,[164] and died March 03, 1951, in Wellington, Sumner County, Kansas.[165]

Child of Minnie Heiskell and David Heenan is:
    156   i. David Heenan, born March 24, 1898, in Sedgwick County, Kansas; died January 09, 1955, in Aberdeen, Washington.[166] He married Mary --?--; born 1898, in Ohio.

89. Albert J. Peery was born June 30, 1861.[167] He married **Alice Rocker** August 28, 1884, in D.L. Peery Home, Peoria Reservation, Quapaw Agency Indian Territory, Oklahoma,[168] daughter of John Rocker and Gemima Langston.

Children of Albert Peery and Alice Rocker are:
+ 157   i. Albert Edward Peery, born March 04, 1901; died Bet. 1984 - 1985.
    158   ii. Alice Elizabeth Peery, born October 10, 1904.

159   iii. Charles Williams Lennox Peery, born October 29, 1909.

90. **Clara E. Peery** was born October 01, 1863, in Paola, Miami County, Kansas,[169] and died April 10, 1935, in Miami, Ottawa County, Oklahoma.[170] She married **J. P. McNaughton** November 01, 1881, in Quapaw Agency, Oklahoma.[171] He was born June 13, 1853, in Winchester, Franklin County, Tennessee,[172] and died November 12, 1932, in East of Miami, Ottawa County, Oklahoma.[173]

Children of Clara Peery and J. McNaughton are:
- 160   i. Willis McNaughton, born October 23, 1882, in Mirage View Farm, Peoria Reserve, Indian Territory, Oklahoma; died July 28, 1969, in Miami, Ottawa County, Oklahoma.
- 161   ii. Clarence Earl McNaughton, born January 14, 1885, in Mirage View Farm, Peoria Reserve, Indian Territory, Oklahoma; died July 20, 1886, in Mirage View Farm, Peoria Reserve, Indian Territory, Oklahoma.
- 162   iii. Ray McNaughton, born August 07, 1886, in Mirage View Farm, Peoria Reserve, Indian Territory, Oklahoma.
- + 163   iv. Guy Peery McNaughton, born December 18, 1887, in Mirage View Farm, Peoria Reserve, Indian Territory, Oklahoma.
- 164   v. Clara Pearl McNaughton, born November 09, 1889, in Mirage View Farm, Peoria Reserve, Indian Territory, Oklahoma; died October 07, 1911, in Coal Hill, Arkansas.

91. **William Baptiste Peery** was born January 05, 1866,[174] and died July 19, 1932, in Claremore, Oklahoma.[175] He married **Lora Ellen Walker** August 12, 1888,[176] daughter of Jacob Walker and Lora.

Children of William Peery and Lora Walker are:
- 165   i. Clyde Vest Peery.
- 166   ii. Christine Elizabeth Peery. She married Lee Hopkins in Pawhuska, Oklahoma.
- 167   iii. Nell Naomi Peery.
- 168   iv. David Baptiste Peery.

93. **Maud Mabel Peery** was born April 04, 1874, in Oak Hill Farm, Miami County, Kansas,[177] and died February 03, 1955, in California. She married **(1) Paul M. Boyles**. She married **(2) Clyde E. Goodner** November 01, 1891, in D.L. Peery Home, Peoria Reservation, Quapaw Agency Indian Territory, Oklahoma.[178]

Children of Maud Peery and Clyde Goodner are:
- 169   i.   Clara Goodner.
- 170   ii. Nita Goodner.

96. Elsie Ethel Peery was born July 05, 1882.[179] She married **A. Scott Thompson** June 26, 1904, in J.P. McNaughton home, Peoria Reserve.[180]

Children of Elsie Peery and A. Thompson are:
- 171   i.   John Stewart Thompson.
- 172   ii.   Virginia Thompson.
- 173   iii. Joseph Thompson.
- 174   iv. Daniel Thompson.

97. Frank Cleveland Peery was born September 28, 1884.[181]

Children of Frank Cleveland Peery are:
- 175   i.   Frances Albert Peery.
- 176   ii. Evan David Peery, born in Phoenix, Arizona.

98. Mary E. Finley was born 1852, and died July 1930. She married **Edward C. Reyher**, son of Jacob Reyher and Mary Ella. He died Abt. March 25, 1931.

Children of Mary Finley and Edward Reyher are:
- 177   i.   Grace Reyher, born Abt. 1884. She married --?-- Frurip.
- 178   ii. Robert Edmund Reyher, born April 06, 1886, in Garrett, Indiana.

102. Eva E. Dow was born December 1859, in Iowa. She married **Sevigna Edgar Nance**. He was born January 1860 in Illinois, and died 1917.

Children of Eva Dow and Sevigna Nance are:
- 179   i.   Roy C. Nance, born June 1880.
- 180   ii.   Ross Augustus Nance, born March 1882.
- 181   iii. Bessie Nance, born June 1884.
- 182   iv. Norma Nance, born August 1888.
- 183   v.   Fern Nance, born February 1889.

111. **Sylvia A. Lykins** was born July 06, 1882.[182] She married **Job R. Bernard**,[183] son of Lon Bernard and Lidia Vernon. He was born Abt. 1881, in Iowa.

Children of Sylvia Lykins and Job Bernard are:
    184   i.   Bonnel Bernard, born 1903.
    185   ii.   John Bernard, born 1909.
    186   iii.   Glendolan Bernard, born 1911.
    187   iv.   Carmelite Bernard, born 1915.

112. **Jessie Lykins** was born August 07, 1879, in Wyoming,[184] and died December 26, 1964, in Alameda, California.[185] She married **Harvey B. Jeffers**. He was born Abt. 1871, in Missouri.

Children of Jessie Lykins and Harvey Jeffers are:
    188   i.   Floyd F. Jeffers, born 1900.
    189   ii.   Kenneth M. Jeffers, born 1910.

122. **Fred Carey Lykins** was born December 28, 1878, in Columbus, Kansas,[186] and died July 02, 1943, in San Diego, California.[187] He married **Myrtle Alta Talbot**.

Child of Fred Lykins and Myrtle Talbot is:
    190   i.   Ralph Wayland Lykins, born June 07, 1906, in Oklahoma; died November 20, 1978, in Meadow Vista, Placer County, California.

124. **Queenie Lykins** was born April 03, 1886, in Peoria Reservation, Oklahoma,[188] and died February 21, 1988, in Lamar, Colorado.[189] She married **Don Carl Wills** June 29, 1902, in Miami, Indian Territory, Oklahoma. He was born March 14, 1882 and died June 26, 1964, in Lancaster, Los Angeles County, California.[190]

Children of Queenie Lykins and Don Wills are:
    191   i.   Ruth M. Wills, born Abt. 1903. She married William Walker.
            ii.   Anna E. Wills, born Abt. 1904.
            iii.   Don L. Wills, born Abt. 1912.
            iv.   Beulah B. Wills, born Abt. 1916.

125. **Harry C. Lykins** was born September 13, 1888, in Columbus, Cherokee County, Kansas,[191] and died August 01, 1971, in Miami, Ottawa County, Oklahoma Territory.[192] He married **Flora Evelyn Hamilton**

September 28, 1907, in Miami, Indian Territory.[193]

Child of Harry Lykins and Flora Hamilton is:
+   192   i.   Alexander Wayland Lykins, born December 29, 1908, in Miami, Oklahoma; died October 25, 1994, in Joplin, Missouri.

Generation No. 5

138. **Frank Allison Bettis** was born April 11, 1882.[194] He married **Vera Daisy Barwick** December 18, 1909.[195]

Children of Frank Bettis and Vera Barwick are:
   193   i.   Frank A. Bettis.
   194   ii.   Gordon Bettis.
+ 195   iii. Maurice E. Bettis.

139. **Alexander Erwin Bettis** was born December 16, 1885.[196] He married **Mabel Pickett** October 30, 1907.[197]

Child of Alexander Bettis and Mabel Pickett is:
+   196   i.   Russell Harrington Bettis, born Abt. 1908, in Kansas City, Jackson County, Missouri; died November 1978, in Kansas City, Jackson County, Missouri.

151. **Leslie Earle Wallace** was born September 15, 1876, in Paola, Miami County, Kansas,[198] and died May 09, 1940 in Larned, Pawnee County, Kansas.[199] He married **(1) Sara Le Maître Johnson** May 24, 1905, in Baltimore, Maryland,[200] daughter of Albert Johnson and Cora Harlan. She was born September 22, 1881, in Wilmington, New Castle County, Delaware,[201] and died October 25, 1930 in Larned, Pawnee County, Kansas.[202] He married **(2) Bob Lee Victor** September 15, 1931, in Larned, Pawnee County, Kansas,[203] daughter of Robert Victor and Mary Garrett. She was born November 01, 1883,[204] and died September 19, 1979.[205]

Children of Leslie Wallace and Sara Johnson are:
+   197   i.   Eunice Cora Wallace, born February 09, 1907, in Iola, Allen County, Kansas; died March 09, 1953, in Larned, Pawnee County, Kansas.

+ 198 ii. Ralph Leslie Wallace, born October 14, 1908, in Kansas City, Jackson County, Missouri; died September 16, 1959, in Manhattan, New York City, New York County, New York.

153. **Lenora Phillips** was born February 1882. She married **Daniel W.Thomas**. He was born Abt. 1880 in Kentucky.

Child of Lenora Phillips and Daniel W.Thomas is:
199 i. Jessie May Thomas, born Abt. 1911.

154. **Jessie Phillips** was born August 1884. She married **John T. Venable** July 21, 1915, in Marion County, Indiana.[206] He was born October 03, 1882, in Illinois, and died February 1966, in Eaton, Delaware County, Indiana.[207]

Children of Jessie Phillips and John Venable are:
200 i. Wilma Venable, born 1919.
201 ii. Margaret Venable, born 1921.
202 iii. John Venable, born 1928.

155. **Philip H. Latimer** was born June 07, 1891, in Louisburg, Miami County, Kansas;[208] died August 06, 1982, in Overland Park, Johnson County, Kansas.[209] He married (1) Maude Ragan.[210] She was born February 4, 1891, in Louisburg, Kansas, and died February 11, 1949, in Kansas City, Missouri.[211] He married (2) Blanche Rife Linder January 06, 1938, in Harrisonville, Cass County, Missouri;[212] born 1899; died 1983.[213]

Children of Philip Latimer and Maude Ragan are:
26 i. Ellis James Latimer, born December 11, 1914, in Louisburg, Montgomery County, Kansas;[214] died December 11, 1999, in Grand Junction, Mesa County, Colorado[215].
27 ii. Philip Latimer, born Abt. 1917; died February 28, 1942.[216]
28 iii. Cloyd Latimer, born September 03, 1917, in Louisburg, Montgomery, Kansas;[217] died February 1971.[218]

157. **Albert Edward Peery** was born March 04, 1901,[219] and died Bet. 1984 - 1985.[220] He married **Elphie Dorothy Johnson** June 29, 1930 in Johnson home, Tulare County, California,[221] daughter of A.H. Johnson and Anna --?--. She died 1975.[222]

Children of Albert Peery and Elphie Johnson are:
- 203   i.   David L. Peery.
- 204   ii.   John Philip Peery, born December 15, 1936, in Los Angeles, California.

163. Guy Peery McNaughton was born December 18, 1887, in Mirage View Farm, Peoria Reserve, Indian Territory, Oklahoma.[223] He married **Bernice May Dodson**.

Children of Guy McNaughton and Bernice Dodson are:
- \+ 205   i.   John Lewis McNaughton, born June 25, 1914; died in Pace, Florida.
- 206   ii.   Clara Bernice McNaughton, born May 25, 1916.

192. Alexander Wayland Lykins was born December 29, 1908, in Miami, Oklahoma,[224] and died October 25, 1994, in Joplin, Missouri.[225] He married **Ruth Gordon** March 25, 1934.[226] She was born October 27, 1915, in Ottawa County, Oklahoma.

Children of Alexander Lykins and Ruth Gordon are:
- 207   i.   Orville Lee Lykins, born June 14, 1935, in Miami, Oklahoma. He married Verna Fay Cowan January 03, 1954, in Rock Creek Baptist Church, Auburn, California; born April 19, 1934.
- 208   ii.   Fred Gordon Lykins, born June 30, 1936, in Miami, Oklahoma. He married Loveda Faye Cowan September 30, 1954, in Rock Creek Baptist Church, Auburn, California; born June 30, 1935.

Generation No. 6

195. Maurice E. Bettis

Children of Maurice E. Bettis are:
- 209   i.   Maurine Bettis, born 1941.
- 210   ii.   Nanette Bettis.

196. Russell Harrington Bettis was born Abt. 1908, in Kansas City, Jackson County, Missouri,[227] and died November 1978, in Kansas City, Jackson County, Missouri.[228] He married **(1) Lucile Reynolds**. She was born November 19, 1907, in Paradise, Missouri,[229] and died February 23, 2001.[230]

Children of Russell Harrington Bettis are:
211   i.   Russell H. Bettis.
212   ii. Beverly Bettis.
213   iii. Sondra Bettis.

197. Eunice Cora Wallace was born February 09, 1907, in Iola, Allen County, Kansas,[231] and died March 09, 1953, in Larned, Pawnee County, Kansas.[232] She married **(1) Chester Klinefelter Shore** September 12, 1931, in Great Bend, Barton County, Kansas,[233] son of Benjamin Shore and Laura Kleinfelter. He was born May 25, 1900 in Castleton, Reno County, Kansas,[234] and died February 1979, in Helena, Lewis and Clark County, Montana.[235] She married **(2) William A. Rhea** Aft. 1943. He was born February 04, 1903,[236] and died January 1966, in Larned, Pawnee County, Kansas.[237]

Children of Eunice Wallace and Chester Shore are:
214   i.   Ralph Wallace Shore, born November 04, 1932, in Kansas; died March 04, 2005, in San Francisco, California.
215   ii. Earle Michael Shore, born Abt. 1936.
216   iii. John Christopher Shore, born April 30, 1937; died May 03, 1997, in Bozeman, Gallatin County, Montana.
217   iv. Sara Leslie Shore, born April 29, 1939, in Wichita, Kansas; died March 30, 2010 in Helena, Lewis and Clark County, Montana. She married Jack Zygmond, born December 27, 1929; died April 28, 1986.
218   v.   David Anthony Shore, born Abt. 1942.

198. Ralph Leslie Wallace was born October 14, 1908, in Kansas City, Jackson County, Missouri,[238] and died September 16, 1959, in Manhattan, New York City, New York County, New York.[239] He married **(1) Hortense Hostetter**, daughter of Sam Hostetter and Velna White. She was born November 16, 1911, in Hutchinson, Reno County, Kansas,[240] and died November 16, 1979, in Hutchinson, Reno County, Kansas.[241] He married **(2) Meck McCall** on November 30, 1946, in Eddy County, New Mexico.[242]

Children of Ralph Wallace and Hortense Hostetter are:
219   i.   Jerome Bruce Wallace, born March 10, 1938, in New York. He married Rose Ann Gard September 21, 1965, in Courthouse, Bloomington, McLean County, Illinois; born March 06, 1942, in Maryville, Nodaway County, Missouri.

220   ii.   Suzanne Wallace, born April 1941.

Children of Ralph Wallace and Meck McCall are:
221   i.   Elizabeth Wallace, Aft. 1946.
222   ii.   Virginia Wallace, Aft. 1946.

205. John Lewis McNaughton was born June 25, 1914,[243] and died in Pace, Florida.[244] He married **Anna Frances Carter** July 12, 1944. She was born June 12, 1919, in Birmingham, Alabama,[245] and died July 13, 1995, in Crofton, Maryland.[246]

Children of John McNaughton and Anna Carter are:
223   i.   John Carter McNaughton, born June 27, 1947, in Birmingham, Alabama.
224   ii.   Ann McNaughton, born August 23, 1952, in Birmingham, Alabama. She married James Riccard Walkinshaw March 20, 1976, in Birmingham, Alabama; born March 15, 1953, in Norfolk, Virginia.[247]

---

1. For date, see Lykins Family Bible, Missouri Valley Special Collections, Kansas City Public Library, Kansas City, Missouri. For place, see Fred Lee, "Genealogical Background of Dr. Johnston Lykins," *Kansas City Genealogist* 36 (Winter, Spring, 1985): 125.
2. For date, see Lykins Family Bible. For place, see Lee, "Genealogical Background of Dr. Johnston Lykins," 125.
3. For date, see Lykins Family Bible. For place, see Dorothy J. Clark, "Before the Snow Flies", [Terre Haute, Indiana] *Tribune-Star*, 13Oct 1963, np, clipping, Lykins Family file; Special Collections, Vigo County Public Library, Terre Haute, Indiana.
4. For date, see Lykins Family Bible. For place, see Lee, "Genealogical Background of Dr. Johnston Lykins," 125.
5. For date, see Lykins Family Bible. For place, see Lee, "Genealogical Background of Dr. Johnston Lykins," 125.
6. For date, see Lykins Family Bible. For place, see Lee, "Genealogical Background of Dr. Johnston Lykins," 126.
7. Lykins Family Bible.
8. For date, see Lykins Family Bible. For place, see Lee, "Genealogical Background of Dr. Johnston Lykins," 126.
9. For date, see Lykins Family Bible. For place see Lee, "Genealogical Background of Dr. Johnston Lykins," 126.
10. For date, see Lykins Family Bible. For place, see Lee, "Genealogical Background of Dr. Johnston Lykins," 125.
11. For date, see Lykins Family Bible. For place, see Lee, "Genealogical Background of Dr. Johnston Lykins," 125.
12. For date, see Lykins Family Bible. For place, see Lee, "Genealogical Background of Dr. Johnston Lykins," 125.
13. Lynch, "Peery Families of Virginia," 25.

14. Edith Brown, list of Lykins descendants, Lykins Family File; Special Collections, Vigo County Public Library, Terre Haute, Indiana.
15. For date, see Lykins Family Bible. For place, see "Johnston Lykins and Delilah McCoy Family Group Sheet," Johnston Lykins and Martha Lykins Bingham Papers; Native Sons Archives, Western Historical Manuscript Collection, University of Missouri at Kansas City, Kansas City, Missouri.
16. Union Cemetery Historical Society, *Tombstone Inscriptions* (Kansas City: Union Cemetery Historical Society, 1986), 53.
17. For date, see Lykins Family Bible. For place, see "Johnston Lykins and Delilah McCoy Family Group Sheet," Johnston Lykins and Martha Lykins Bingham Papers; Native Sons Archives, Western Historical Manuscript Collection, University of Missouri at Kansas City, Kansas City, Missouri.
18. "Johnston Lykins and Delilah McCoy Family Group Sheet," Johnston Lykins and Martha Lykins Bingham Papers; Native Sons Archives, Western Historical Manuscript Collection, University of Missouri at Kansas City, Kansas City, Missouri.
19. "Johnston Lykins and Delilah McCoy Family Group Sheet," Johnston Lykins and Martha Lykins Bingham Papers; Native Sons Archives, Western Historical Manuscript Collection, University of Missouri at Kansas City, Kansas City, Missouri.
20. C. R. Barnes, editor, *The Commonwealth of Missouri: A Centennial Record* (Saint Louis: Bryan, Brand & Company, 1877), 770.
21 C. R. Barnes, *The Commonwealth of Missouri: A Centennial Record*, 770.
22. Alberta Wilson Constant. *Paintbox on the Frontier: The Life and Times of George Caleb Bingham* (New York: Crowell, 1974), 174.
23. For date, see Lykins Family Bible. For place, see Lee, "Genealogical Background of Dr. Johnston Lykins," 125.
24. *Cemeteries of Miami County, Kansas* (Paola, Kansas: Miami County Genealogy Society, 1985), 3: 445.
25. "Indiana Marriage Collection, 1800-1941, database, *Ancestry.com* (http://www.ancestry.com : accessed 10 Dec 2009), Joseph Lykins and Margaret Nixon marriage; information taken from Clerk of the Circuit Court, St. Joseph County, Indiana, Marriage Record, v. 1-3, 1830-1854; Family History Library, microfilm 1503384, item 3.
26. Death Notice, (Paola, Kansas) *Miami Republican*, 7 Jan 1871, np; Obituary Collection, Hunt-Russell Genealogical Research Library, Swan River Museum, Miami County Genealogy and Historical Societies, Paola, Kansas.
27. *Cemeteries of Miami County, Kansas*, 3: 445.
28. *Cemeteries of Miami County, Kansas*, 3: 445.
29. 1860 U.S. Census, Paola, Lykins County, Kansas Territory, p. 24, dwelling 172, family 159, household of Joseph W. Lykins.
30. *Cemeteries of Miami County, Kansas*, 3: 445.
31. For date, see Lykins Family Bible. For place, see Lynch, *Peery Families of Virginia*, 125.
32. For date, see Lykins Family Bible. For place, see Lynch, *Peery Families of Virginia*, 125.
33. For date, see Lykins Family Bible. For place, see Grace Reyher Frurip to A. R. Markle, letter, nd., postmarked 10 Dec 1930, Lykins Family File; Special Collections, Vigo County Public Library, Terre Haute, Indiana.
34. Lynch, *Peery Families of Virginia*, 25, 125. The birth date supplied on p. 25 does not agree with the one on p. 125.
35. Lynch, *Peery Families of Virginia*, 125.

36. Lynch, Peery Families of Virginia, 125.
37. Lynch, *Peery Families of Virginia*, 125.
38. Lykins Family Bible.
39. Lykins Family Bible.
40. Grace Reyher Frurip to Bonnie Farrell, letter, 9 Oct 1930, Lykins Family File; Special Collections, Vigo County Public Library, Terre Haute, Indiana.
41. Grace Reyher Frurip to A. R. Markle, 17 Nov 1930.
42. For date, see Lykins Family Bible. For place, see Lee, "Genealogical Background of Dr. Johnston Lykins," 126.
43. Robert Lykins, Will E. Lykins and Mrs. Ruth Walker, Personal Genealogy Chart, Lykins file; Hunt-Russell Genealogical Research Library, Swan River Museum, Miami County Genealogy and Historical Societies, Paola, Kansas.
44. Lykins Family Bible.
45. Robert Lykins, Will E. Lykins and Mrs. Ruth Walker, Personal Genealogy Chart, Lykins file; Hunt-Russell Genealogical Research Library, Swan River Museum, Miami County Genealogy and Historical Societies, Paola, Kansas.
46. Frye Williams Giles, *Historical Sketch of Shawnee County Kansas* (Topeka, Kansas: Commonwealth Steam Book and Job House, 1876), 9.
47. Lykins Family Bible.
48. Brown, list of Lykins descendants, Lykins Family File.
49. For date, see Lykins Family Bible. For place, see Brown, list of Lykins descendants, Lykins Family File.
50. Lykins Family Bible.
51. *The History of Buchanan County, Missouri,* (Saint Joseph, Missouri: Union Historical Company, 1881), 817.
52. *History of Buchanan County, Missouri*, 817.
53. Buchanan County, Missouri, "Marriages: Buchanan County, Missouri, 1839-1905," bk. C. p. 93, Hustad – Lykins; Northwest Missouri Genealogical Society, St. Joseph, Missouri.
54. Missouri State Archives, "Missouri Death Certificates, 1910-1958," digital images, Missouri Digital Heritage (http://www.sos.mo.gov/archives/resources/birthdeath/ : accessed 5 Nov 2007), John Johnson Lykins, Buchanan County; Bureau of Vital Records, Missouri Department of Health and Human Services, Jefferson City, Missouri.
55. Missouri State Archives, "Missouri Death Certificates, 1910-1958," digital images, Missouri Digital Heritage (http://www.sos.mo.gov/archives/resources/birthdeath/ : accessed 5 Nov 2007), Paulina E. Lykins, Buchanan County; Bureau of Vital Records, Missouri Department of Health and Human Services, Jefferson City, Missouri
56. Buchanan County, Missouri, "Marriages: Buchanan County, Missouri, 1839-1905," bk. C, p. 429, Simmons – Lykins; Northwest Missouri Genealogical Society, Saint Joseph, Missouri.
57. Missouri State Archives, "Missouri Death Certificates, 1910-1958," digital images, Missouri Digital Heritage (http://www.sos.mo.gov/archives/resources/birthdeath/ : accessed 5 Nov 2007), Charles R. Lykins, Buchanan County; Bureau of Vital Records, Missouri Department of Health and Human Services, Jefferson City, Missouri.
58. Buchanan County, Missouri, "Marriages: Buchanan County, Missouri, 1839-1905," bk. H, p. 66, Lykins – Brosi; Northwest Missouri Genealogy Society, Saint Joseph, Missouri.
59. Missouri State Archives, "Missouri Death Certificates, 1910-1958," digital images, Missouri Digital Heritage (http://www.sos.mo.gov/archives/resources/birthdeath/ : accessed 5 Nov 2007), Sarah [Brosi] Lykins, Buchanan County; Bureau of Vital Records, Missouri

Department of Health and Human Services, Jefferson City, Missouri.
60. For date, see Lykins Family Bible. For place, see Lee, "Genealogical Background of Dr. Johnston Lykins," 125-126.
61. Eugene C. Ferguson to A.R. Markle, letter, 13 Feb 1931, Lykins Family File; Special Collections, Vigo County Public Library, Terre Haute, Indiana.
62. Lykins Family Bible. .
63. 1850 U.S. Census, Lafayette Township, Ogle County, Illinois, p. 132, dwelling and family 3, household of Athol Ferguson.
64. Eugene C. Ferguson to A.R. Markle, 13 Feb 1931, Lykins Family File.
65. U.S. Census, Lafayette Townshiop, Ogle County, Illinois, p. 132, dwelling and family 3, household of Athol Ferguson.
66. Eugene C. Ferguson to A.R. Markle, 16 Feb 1931, Lykins Family File.
67. Fred Delap and Illinois State Archives, "Illinois Civil War Muster and Descriptive Rolls Database," CyberDriveIllinois (http://www.ilsos.gov/genealogy/ : accessed 21 Dec 2009), entry for David Ferguson.
68. Fred Delap and llinois State Archives, "Illinois Civil War Muster and Descriptive Rolls Database," CyberDriveIllinois (http://www.ilsos.gov/genealogy/ : accessed 21 Dec 2009), entry for David Ferguson.
69. Lykins Family Bible.
70. David Lykins Memorial Stone, Paola Cemetery, Paola, Kansas. See also Lykins vs. McGrath, 184 U.S. 169 (1902). The two sources disagree by one day.
71. Recorder of Deeds, Jackson County, Missouri, "Marriage Records," (http://www.records.jacksongov.org/ : accessed 7 Nov 2007), Lykins – Webster; Office of the Recorder of Deeds, Jackson County Courthouse, Kansas City, Missouri.
72. David Lykins Memorial Stone, Paola Cemetery.
73. David Lykins Memorial Stone, Paola Cemetery.
74. Mrs. Howard W. Woodruff, *Marriage Records: Cass (Van Buren) County, Missouri, Books A & B, 1836-1865* (Independence, Missouri: Howard W. Woodruff, 1969), 28.
75. Lykins – Tull marriage certificate, photocopy, Lykins file; Hunt-Russell Genealogical Research Library, Swan River Museum, Miami County Genealogy and Historical Societies, Paola, Kansas.
76. David Lykins Memorial Stone, Paola Cemetery.
77. David Lykins *Memorial Stone, Paola Cemetery.*
78. "Johnston Lykins and Delilah McCoy Family Group Sheet," Johnston Lykins and Martha Lykins Bingham Papers; Native Sons Archives, Western Historical Manuscript Collection, University of Missouri at Kansas City, Kansas City, Missouri.
79. "Johnston Lykins and Delilah McCoy Family Group Sheet," Johnston Lykins and Martha Lykins Bingham Papers; Native Sons Archives, Western Historical Manuscript Collection, University of Missouri at Kansas City, Kansas City, Missouri.
80. "Johnston Lykins and Delilah McCoy Family Group Sheet," Johnston Lykins and Martha Lykins Bingham Papers; Native Sons Archives, Western Historical Manuscript Collection, University of Missouri at Kansas City, Kansas City, Missouri.
81. Lee, "Gone But Not Forgotten: William Hall Richardson Lykins," 157.
82. Lee, "Gone But Not Forgotten: William Hall Richardson Lykins," 156.
83. Lee "Gone But Not Forgotten: William Hall Richardson Lykins," 156.
84. Lee "Gone But Not Forgotten: William Hall Richardson Lykins," 157.
85. Lee "Gone But Not Forgotten: William Hall Richardson Lykins," 156.

86. Lee, "Gone But Not Forgotten: William Hall Richardson Lykins," 157.
87. Lee "Gone But Not Forgotten: William Hall Richardson Lykins," 157.
88. "Missouri Marriage Records, 1805-2002," database, Ancestry.com (http://ancestry.com : accessed 16 Mar 2007) Schwitzgebel – Lykins, 1918.
89. "US Passport Applications, 1795-1925," database, Ancestry.com (http://ancestry.com : accessed 5 Jan 2007), Henry C. Schwitzgebel, 1922; citing NARA micropublication M1490.
90. Lee, "Gone But Not Forgotten: William Hall Richardson Lykins," 157.
91. "Johnston Lykins and Delilah McCoy Family Group Sheet," Johnston Lykins and Martha Lykins Bingham Papers; Native Sons Archives, Western Historical Manuscript Collection, University of Missouri at Kansas City, Kansas City, Missouri.
92. "Johnston Lykins and Delilah McCoy Family Group Sheet," Johnston Lykins and Martha Lykins Bingham Papers; Native Sons Archives, Western Historical Manuscript Collection, University of Missouri at Kansas City, Kansas City, Missouri.
93. "Johnston Lykins and Delilah McCoy Family Group Sheet," Johnston Lykins and Martha Lykins Bingham Papers; Native Sons Archives, Western Historical Manuscript Collection, University of Missouri at Kansas City, Kansas City, Missouri.
94. [Theodore S. Case], Kansas City, Missouri, Statistical facts regarding its appearance in May 1857, and its subsequent growth, Johnston Lykins and Martha Lykins Bingham Papers; Native Sons Archives, Western Historical Manuscript Collection, University of Missouri at Kansas City, Kansas City, Missouri.
95. Daughters of the American Revolution, *Vital Historical Records of Jackson County, Missouri, 1826-1876* (Kansas City, Missouri: Kansas City Chapter, Daughters of the American Revolution, 1934), 317.
96. "Johnston Lykins and Delilah McCoy Family Group Sheet," Johnston Lykins and Martha Lykins Bingham Papers; Native Sons Archives, Western Historical Manuscript Collection, University of Missouri at Kansas City, Kansas City, Missouri.
97. "Johnston Lykins and Delilah McCoy Family Group Sheet," Johnston Lykins and Martha Lykins Bingham Papers; Native Sons Archives, Western Historical Manuscript Collection, University of Missouri at Kansas City, Kansas City, Missouri.
98. Missouri State Archives, "Missouri Birth and Death Database, pre-1910," database, Missouri Digital Heritage (http://www.sos.mo.gov/archives/resources/birthdeath/ : accessed 5 Nov 2007), Theodore S. Case, Jackson County; Missouri State Archives, Jefferson City, Missouri.
99. Paola Cemetery (Paola, Miami County, Kansas), Mary Elizabeth Lykins Hoover marker, transcription by Mrs. William Walker, nd., Lykins file; Hunt-Russell Genealogical Research Library, Swan River Museum, Miami County Genealogy and Historical Societies, Paola, Kansas.
100. Death Notice, *Miami Republican*, 16 May 1949, np., typescript, "Fifty Years Ago," *Miami County Genealogy Society Quarterly*, v. 13, p. 23.
101. David Heenan obituary, undated clipping from unidentified newspaper, Obituary Collection, Hunt-Russell Genealogical Research Library, Swan River Museum, Miami County Genealogy and Historical Societies, Paola, Kansas.
102. David Heenan obituary.
103. Woodruff, *Marriage Records: Cass (Van Buren) County, Missouri*, 211.
104. Wilmer L. Kerns, *Historical Records of Old Frederick and Hampshire Counties, Virginia* (Cullman, Alabama: Gregath Company, 1988), 63.
105. Death Notice, *Miami Republican*, 20 Aug 1870, 3:4.

106. Lynch, *Peery Families of Virginia*, 71.
107. Lynch, *Peery Families of Virginia*, 71.
108. "Kin of Baptiste Peoria is a Visitor," (Paola, Kansas) *Western Spirit*, 20 June 1966, np., typescript copy, Wayland Lykins file; Hunt-Russell Genealogical Research Library, Swan River Museum, Miami County Genealogy and Historical Societies, Paola, Kansas.
109. Lynch, *Peery Families of Virginia*, 71.
110. Lynch, *Peery Families of Virginia*, 71.
111. David C. Gideon, *Indian Territory: Descriptive, Biographical and Genealogical, Including the landed Estates, County Seats, Etc., with a General History of the Territory* (New York: Lewis Publishing, 1901), 319-320.
112. Grace Reyher Frurip to A. R. Markle, 17 Nov 1930, Lykins Family File.
113. Jonas Finley and Sally McNair Family Group Sheet, Lykins Family File; Special Collections, Vigo County Public Library, Terre Haute, Indiana.
114. [W. H. H. Terrell], *Report of the Adjutant General of the State of Indiana* (Indianapolis: Samuel M. Douglas, 1866), 5: 42. For place of burial, see United States Department of Veterans Affairs, "gravesite locator" (http://gravelocator.cem.va.gov/ : accessed 12 Dec 2008), Willis M. Earnest, 1862.
115. "Iowa Marriages, 1851-1900," database, Ancestry.com (http://ancestry.com : accessed 17 Mar 2007) Augustus S. Dow – Wealthy A. Betteys, 1857.
116. 1860 U.S. Census, Shorter County, Nebraska Territory, mortality schedule, p. 1, line 3, entry for A. S. Dow.
117. "Iowa Marriages, 1851-1900," database, Ancestry.com (http://ancestry.com : accessed 17 Mar 2007) James Shepherd – Wealthy A. [Betteys] Dow, 1872.
118. "Iowa Marriages, 1851-1900," database, Ancestry.com (http://ancestry.com : accessed 17 Mar 2007) Franklyn M. Betteys – Virginia J. Wade, 1874.
119. J[ohn] J. Lykins, "General Affidavit -- March 11, 1895," minor children's pension application no. 600297, certificate no. 421398; service of Andrew C. Lykins (Pvt., Co. B, 22 Regt. Missouri Cavalry, Civil War); Case Files of Approved Pension Applications, 1861-1934; Civil War and Later Pension Files; Department of Veterans Affairs, Record Group 15; National Archives, Washington, D.C.
120. J[ohn] J. Lykins, "General Affidavit -- March 11, 1895," Andrew C. Lykins pension no. 421398, RG 15, NA—Washington.
121. Mary J. Strange & John S. Lykins, "Claim for Completion of Claim of Andrew C. Lykins, dec'd No. 249241," Jan 30, 1897, minor children's pension application no. 600297, certificate no. 421398; service of Andrew C. Lykins (Pvt., Co. B, 22nd Regt. Missouri Cavalry, Civil War); Case Files of Approved Pension Applications, 1861-1934; Civil War and Later Pension Files; Department of Veterans Affairs, Record Group 15; National Archives, Washington, D.C.
122. Mary Jane [Lykins] Strange and Sylvia A. Lykins Bernard, "General Affidavit -- October 1901," minor children's pension application no. 600297, certificate no. 421398; service of Andrew C. Lykins (Pvt., Co. B, 22 Regt. Missouri Cav., Civil War); Case Files of Approved Pension Applications, 1861-1934; Civil War and Later Pension Files; Department of Veterans Affairs, Record Group 15; National Archives, Washington, D.C.
123. Mary J. Strange & John S. Lykins, "Claim for Completion of Claim of Andrew C. Lykins, dec'd No. 249241," Jan 30, 1897, Andrew C. Lykins pension no. 421398, RG 15, NA—Washington.
124. Christian L. Rutt, *History of Buchanan County and the City of St. Joseph and*

Representative Citizens (Chicago: Biographical Publishing Company, 1904), 382.
125. Missouri State Archives, "Missouri Death Certificates, 1910-1958," digital images, Missouri Digital Heritage (http://www.sos.mo.gov/archives/resources/birthdeath/ : accessed 5 Nov 2007), William C. Lykins, Buchanan County; Bureau of Vital Records, Missouri Department of Health and Human Services, Jefferson City, Missouri
126. Christian L. Rutt, *History of Buchanan County and the City of St. Joseph and Representative Citizens* (Chicago: Biographical Publishing Company, 1904), 382.
127. Gideon, *History of Indian Territory*, 444-446.
128. David Heenan obituary.
129. Cutler, *History of the State of Kansas*, 1158.
130. Paola [Kansas] Chamber of Commerce, Application for Historical Site Status, 2006.
131. Ethyl Hunt to Mrs. Albert E. Peery, letter, [Aug] 1966, Wayland C. Lykins file; Hunt-Russell Genealogical Research Library, Swan River Museum, Miami County Genealogy and Historical Societies, Paola, Kansas.
132. Ethyl Hunt to Mrs. Albert E. Peery, [Aug] 1966.
133. Willis Lykins, interview by Nannie Lee Burns, 28 Oct 1937; Indian Pioneer Collection, vol. 56, Interview 12029; Manuscript Division, Western History Collections, University of Oklahoma Library, Norman, Oklahoma.
134. Russell H. Bettis, miscellaneous Bettis genealogy notes, Bettis file, Union Cemetery Historical Society, Kansas City, Missouri.
135. Russell H. Bettis, miscellaneous Bettis genealogy notes, Bettis file.
136. "A Pioneer Family Death," undated clipping from unidentified newspaper, scrapbook, Theodore Spencer Case Collection (KC0295); Native Sons Archives, Western Historical Manuscript Collection, University of Missouri at Kansas City, Kansas City, Missouri.
137. "A Pioneer Family Death," Theodore Spencer Case Collection.
138. "A Pioneer Family Death," Theodore Spencer Case Collection.
139. "E.H. Bettis is Dead," clipping, hand-dated Oct. 27, 1937, Bettis file; Westport Historical Society, Kansas City, Kansas.
140. "E.H. Bettis is Dead," Oct. 27, 1937.
141. Delilah McCoy Cowles obituary, clipping from unidentified newspaper, hand dated 4 Oct 1939, scrapbook, Theodore Spencer Case Collection (KC0295); Native Sons Archives, Western Historical Manuscript Collection, University of Missouri at Kansas City, Kansas City, Missouri.
142. "Missouri Marriage Records, 1805-2002," database, Ancestry.com (http://ancestry.com : accessed 16 Mar 2007) Cowles – Case, 1889.
143. "Mystery in an Opened Corner Stone," undated clipping from unidentified newspaper, Martha Lykins Bingham vertical file; Kansas State Historical Society Library, Topeka, Kansas.
144. Mrs. Ermine C. Case obituary, clipping from unidentified newspaper, hand dated 1923, scrapbook, Theodore Spencer Case Collection (KC0295); Native Sons Archives, Western Historical Manuscript Collection, University of Missouri at Kansas City, Kansas City, Missouri.
145. Cutler, *History of the State of Kansas*, 893.
146. "Mrs. Sue A. Latimer Dead," Obituary Collection, Hunt-Russell Genealogical Research Library, Swan River Museum, Miami County Genealogy and Historical Societies, Paola, Kansas.
147. Marriage announcement, (Paola, Kansas) *Western Spirit*, 2 July 1875, 3:B.

148. 1900 US Census, Plaistow, Rockingham County, New Hampshire, ED 205, Sheet 2A, dwelling 35, family 39, household of William F. Wallace.
149. Registrar of Vital Records, New Hampshire Department of State, Death Certificate, William F. Wallace, 5 Sept 1906 (Doc. 1028504); Division of Vital Records Administration, Concord, New Hampshire.
150. Cutler, *History of the State of Kansas*, 893
151. Hiram Phillips obituary, (Paola, Kansas) *Western Spirit*, 10 Apr 1885; 3:h.
152. Hiram Phillips obituary.
153. Miami County Clerk, Miami County Marriages, Births, Deaths, 1885-1892, 52, marriage 221; Kansas State Historical Society Library, Topeka, Kansas, microfilm AR 3987.
154. Cutler, *History of the State of Kansas*, 893. See also John E. Hysom, *Latimer [with] Wickline - Hysom - Gaither - Beck - Heiskell - Wallace - Phillips*, (np: np, 1994), np.
155. "P. F. Latimer Dead," undated clipping from unidentified newspaper, Obituary Collection, Hunt-Russell Genealogical Research Library, Swan River Museum, Miami County Genealogy and Historical Societies, Paola, Kansas.
156. "P. F. Latimer Dead," Hunt-Russell Genealogical Research Library.
157. "P. F. Latimer Dead," Hunt-Russell Genealogical Research Library.
158. Clay County, Missouri, [Application for License to Marry], Philip Heiskell and Maude E. Ragan, 23 Apr 1910; "Missouri Marriage Records, 1805-2002," digital images, *Ancestry.com* (http://www.Ancestry.com ; accessed 1 Oct 2007).
159. Missouri State Archives, "Missouri Death Certificates, 1910-1958," digital images, Missouri Digital Heritage (http://www.sos.mo.gov/archives/resources/birthdeath/ : accessed 5 Nov 2007), Maude Whitney, Jackson County; Bureau of Vital Records, Missouri Department of Health and Human Services, Jefferson City, Missouri.
160. "P. H. Latimer Dead." See also Cass County, Missouri, [Application for License to Marry], Philip Heiskell and Blanche M. Linder, 9 Feb 1938; "Missouri Marriage Records, 1805-2002," digital images, *Ancestry.com* (http://www.Ancestry.com ; accessed 1 Oct 2007).
161. *Cemeteries of Miami County, Kansas*, 2: 14.
162. Lynch, *Peery Families of Virginia*, 125.
163. David Heenan obituary.
164. David Heenan obituary.
165. David Heenan obituary.
166. Washington Secretary of State, "Washington State Death Certificate Index, 1907-1960," Washington State Digital Archives (http://www.digitalarchives.wa.gov/ : accessed 10 Jan 2009), entry for David Heenan, 1955.
167. Lynch, *Peery Families of Virginia*, 71.
168. Lynch, *Peery Families of Virginia*, 71.
169. Lynch, *Peery Families of Virginia*, 71.
170. Ann M. Walkinshaw to Ms. Vera Dakin or Ms. Helen Gilliland, letter, 9 Aug 1996; David Peery file, Hunt-Russell Genealogical Research Library, Swan River Museum, Miami County Genealogy and Historical Societies, Paola, Kansas.
171. Lynch, *Peery Families of Virginia*, 71.
172. Ann M. Walkinshaw to Ms. Vera Dakin or Ms. Helen Gilliland, 9 Aug 1996.
173. Ann M. Walkinshaw to Ms. Vera Dakin or Ms. Helen Gilliland, 9 Aug 1996.
174. Lynch, *Peery Families of Virginia*, 71.
175. Ethyl Hunt to Mrs. Albert E. Peery, [Aug] 1966, Wayland C. Lykins file.
176. Lynch, *Peery Families of Virginia*, 71.

177. Lynch, *Peery Families of Virginia*, 71.
178. Lynch, *Peery Families of Virginia*, 71. See also Ethyl Hunt to Mrs. Albert E. Peery, [Aug] 1966, Wayland C. Lykins file.
179. Lynch, *Peery Families of Virginia*, 71.
180. Ethyl Hunt to Mrs. Albert E. Peery, [Aug] 1966, Wayland C. Lykins file.
181. Lynch, *Peery Families of Virginia*, 71.
182. Mary J. Strange & John S. Lykins, "Claim for Completion of Claim of Andrew C. Lykins, dec'd No. 249241," 30 Jan 1897, Andrew C. Lykins pension no. 421398, RG 15, NA—Washington.
183. Mary Jane [Lykins] Strange and Sylvia A. Lykins Bernard, "General Affidavit -- October 1901," Andrew C. Lykins pension no. 421398, RG 15, NA—Washington.
184. 1880 U.S. Census, Larimer County, Colorado, ED 71, p. 1, dwelling and family 2, household of R. W. Cloud.
185. "California Death Index, 1940-1997," database, *Ancestry.com* (http://ancestry.com ; accessed 1 Feb 2008), Jessie B. Jeffers, 1964, Alameda County.
186. Gideon, *History of Indian Territory*, 444-446.
187. "California Death Index, 1940-1997," database, *Ancestry.com* (http://ancestry.com ; accessed 1 Feb 2008), Fred Carey Lykins, 1943, San Diego County.
188. Gideon, *History of Indian Territory*, 444-446.
189. Notes, Wayland C. Lykins file; Hunt-Russell Genealogical Research Library, Swan River Museum, Miami County Genealogy and Historical Society, Paola, Kansas.
190. "California Death Index, 1940-1997," database, Ancestry.com (http://www.ancestry.com : accessed 21 Sept 2010), entry for Don Carl Wills, 1964, SS no. 570-22-5931.
191. Ancestors of Harry C. Lykins, Wayland Lykins file; Hunt-Russell Genealogical Research Library, Swan River Museum, Miami County Genealogy and Historical Societies, Paola, Kansas.
192. Ancestors of Harry C. Lykins, Hunt-Russell Genealogical Research Library.
193. Ancestors of Harry C. Lykins, Hunt-Russell Genealogical Research Library.
194. Russell H. Bettis, miscellaneous Bettis genealogy notes, Bettis file.
195. Russell H. Bettis, miscellaneous Bettis genealogy notes, Bettis file.
196. Russell H. Bettis, miscellaneous Bettis genealogy notes, Bettis file.
197. Russell H. Bettis, miscellaneous Bettis genealogy notes, Bettis file.
198. "Leslie E. Wallace Dies," *Kansas City Star*," 9 May 1940, np., clipping; Leslie E. Wallace Vertical File, Kansas State Historical Society Library, Topeka, Kansas
199. Margaret Buzzard Corbet, *Larned Cemetery, Pawnee County, Kansas: Where is Everybody?* (Larned, Kansas: M. B. Corbet, 1990), np.
200. Mrs. Leslie Wallace obituary, *The Tiller and Toiler*, 30 Oct 1930, p. 1.
201. Mrs. Leslie Wallace obituary, The Tiller and Toiler, 30 Oct 1930, p. 1.
202. Mrs. Leslie Wallace obituary, *The Tiller and Toiler*, 30 Oct 1930, p. 1.
203. "Wallace – Victor," *Tiller and Toiler*, 17 Sept 1931, 3:c.
204. Corbet, *Larned Cemetery, Pawnee County, Kansas: Where is Everybody?*, np.
205. Corbet, *Larned Cemetery, Pawnee County, Kansas: Where is Everybody?*, np.
206. Ancestry.com, "Indiana Marriage Collection, 1800-1941," database (http://www.ancestry.org : accessed 15 Aug 2007), John T. Venable and Jessie C. Phillips, 21 July 1915, Marion County, Book 81, p. 695.

207. Social Security Administration, "U.S. Social Security Death Index," database, *Rootsweb* (http://ssdi.rootsweb.ancestry.com : accessed 3 Dec 2007), entry for John Venable, 1966, SS no. 308-40-7203.
208. "P. F. Latimer Dead," Hunt-Russell Genealogical Research Library.
209. "P. F. Latimer Dead," Hunt-Russell Genealogical Research Library.
210. Clay County, Missouri, [Application for License to Marry], Philip Heiskell and Maude E. Ragan, 23 Apr 1910; "Missouri Marriage Records, 1805-2002," digital images, *Ancestry.com* (http://www.Ancestry.com : accessed 1 Oct 2007).
211. Missouri State Archives, "Missouri Death Certificates, 1910-1958," digital images, Missouri Digital Heritage (http://www.sos.mo.gov/archives/resources/birthdeath/ : accessed 5 Nov 2007), Maude Whitney, Jackson County; Bureau of Vital Records, Missouri Department of Health and Human Services, Jefferson City, Missouri.
212. "P. H. Latimer Dead." See also Cass County, Missouri, [Application for License to Marry], Philip Heiskell and Blanche M. Linder, 9 Feb 1938; "Missouri Marriage Records, 1805-2002," digital images, *Ancestry.com* (http://www.Ancestry.com ; accessed 1 Oct 2007).
213. *Cemeteries of Miami County, Kansas*, 2: 14.
214. Social Security Administration, "U.S. Social Security Death Index," database, *Rootsweb* (http://ssdi.rootsweb.ancestry.com : accessed 12 Nov 2007), entry for Ellis Latimer, 1999, SS no.720-14-9480.
215. Social Security Administration, "U.S. Social Security Death Index," database, *Rootsweb* (http://ssdi.rootsweb.ancestry.com : accessed 12 Nov 2007), entry for Ellis Latimer, 1999, SS no. 720-14-9480.
216. Defense Prisoner of War / Missing Personnel Office, Department of Defense, "Service Personnel Not Recovered Following World War II," database (http://www.dtic.mil/dpmo/wwii/reports/MAV_M_L.HTM : accessed 20 Dec 2009, entry for Latimer, Philip E., Navy, serial number 4109909.
217. Social Security Administration, "U.S. Social Security Death Index," database, *Rootsweb* (http://ssdi.rootsweb.ancestry.com : accessed 12 Nov 2007), entry for Cloyd Latimer, 1971, SS no. 514-05-7684.
218. Social Security Administration, "U.S. Social Security Death Index," database, *Rootsweb* (http://ssdi.rootsweb.ancestry.com : accessed 12 Nov 2007), entry for Cloyd Latimer, 1971, SS no. 514-05-7684.
219. Notes, Wayland C. Lykins file, Hunt-Russell Genealogical Research Library.
220. Notes, Wayland C. Lykins file, Hunt-Russell Genealogical Research Library.
221. Notes, Wayland C. Lykins file, Hunt-Russell Genealogical Research Library.
222. Handwritten note, Lykins file, Miami County Historical Society, Paola, Kansas.
223. Ann M. Walkinshaw to Ms. Vera Dakin or Ms. Helen Gilliland, 9 Aug 1996.
224. Notes, Wayland C. Lykins file, Hunt-Russell Genealogical Research Library.
225. Notes, Wayland C. Lykins file, Hunt-Russell Genealogical Research Library.
226. Notes, Wayland C. Lykins file, Hunt-Russell Genealogical Research Library.
227. "Russell H. Bettis," clipping from unidentified newspaper, hand-dated 8 Nov 1978, Bettis file, Westport Historical Society, Kansas City, Missouri.
228. "E.H. Bettis is Dead," clipping from unidentified newspaper, hand-dated 27 Oct 1937, Bettis file, Westport Historical Society, Kansas City, Missouri.
229. Lucile Reynolds Bettis obituary, undated clipping from unidentified newspaper, Bettis file; Westport Historical Society, Kansas City, Missouri.
230. Lucile Reynolds Bettis obituary, Bettis file.

231. Jessie Perry Stratford, *Butler County's eighty years, 1855-1935: a History of Butler County, Biographical Sketches and Portraits* (El Dorado, Kansas: Butler County News, 1934), 345.
232. Mrs. Eunice Rhea obituary, *The Tiller and Toiler*, 12 Mar 1953, 1.
233. *Augusta Gazette*, 12 Sept 1931, photo of Eunice Wallace Shore with caption, unpaginated clipping, Eunice Wallace vertical file; Kansas State Historical Society Library, Topeka, Kansas.
234. Stratford, *Butler County's Eighty Years*, p. 345.
235. Social Security Administration, "U.S. Social Security Death Index," database, *Rootsweb* (http://ssdi.rootsweb.ancestry.com : accessed 12 Nov 2007), entry for Chester Shore, 1979, SS no. 515-03-0712.
236. Social Security Administration, "U.S. Social Security Death Index," database, *Rootsweb* (http://ssdi.rootsweb.ancestry.com : accessed 12 Nov 2007), entry for William Rhea, 1966, SS no. 509-05-8452.
237. Social Security Administration, "U.S. Social Security Death Index," database, *Rootsweb* (http://ssdi.rootsweb.ancestry.com : accessed 12 Nov 2007), entry for William Rhea, 1966, SS no. 509-05-8452.
238. Corbet, *Larned Cemetery, Pawnee County, Kansas: Where is Everybody?*, np.
239. Corbet, *Larned Cemetery, Pawnee County, Kansas: Where is Everybody?*, np.
240. Social Security Administration, "U.S. Social Security Death Index," database, *Rootsweb* (http://ssdi.rootsweb.ancestry.com : accessed 17 Nov 2007), entry for Hortense Wallace, 1979, SS no. 513-48-3693.
241. Social Security Administration, "U.S. Social Security Death Index," database, *Rootsweb* (http://ssdi.rootsweb.ancestry.com : accessed 17 Nov 2007), entry for Hortense Wallace, 1979, SS no. 513-48-3693.
242. Marriage Records 1890-1940, Eddy County, New Mexico, Lord-McPherson. Submitted by Richard Wilkinson. http://eddy.nmgenweb us/bridesLord-McPherson.text. Accessed 21 Sept 2010.
243. Ann M. Walkinshaw to Ms. Vera Dakin or Ms. Helen Gilliland, letter, 9 Aug 1996.
244. Ann M. Walkinshaw to Ms. Vera Dakin or Ms. Helen Gilliland, letter, 9 Aug 1996.
245. Ann M. Walkinshaw to Ms. Vera Dakin or Ms. Helen Gilliland, letter, 9 Aug 1996.
246. Ann M. Walkinshaw to Ms. Vera Dakin or Ms. Helen Gilliland, letter, 9 Aug 1996.
247. "Prisoners Must Be Vaccinated," *Kansas City* (Mo.) *Star*, 17 Nov 1921, 1.

Descendants of William Alexander Heiskell-Evalina Price-Emeline Peery

Generation No. 1

1. **William Alexander Heiskell** was born November 16, 1807, in Hampshire County, West Virginia,[1] and died August 19, 1870 in Paola, Miami County, Kansas.[2] He married **(1) Evalina Price** March 05, 1831, in Hampshire County, West Virginia, daughter of Silas Price.[3] He married **(2) Emeline Jamima Peery** March 20, 1853, in Wea Mission, Paola, Miami County, Kansas,[4] daughter of William Peery and Hannah Lykins. She was born August 28, 1830 in Prairie Creek Township, Vigo County, Indiana,[5] and died August 03, 1916, in Louisburg, Miami County, Kansas.[6]

Children of William Heiskell and Evalina Price are:

- 2   i. Edmund C. Heiskell, born Abt. 1834, in Hampshire County, West Virginia.
- + 3   ii. Elisabeth Price Heiskell, born Abt. 1842; died Abt. November 04, 1878, in Kansas City, Jackson County, Missouri.[7]
- 4   iii. Fanny Heiskell, born Abt. 1844.
- 5   iv. Charles S. Heiskell, born Abt. 1845, in Virginia.
- 6   v. Frederick Heiskell, born Abt. 1846.

Children of William Heiskell and Emeline Peery are:

- + 7   i. Sue Austin Heiskell, born May 31, 1857, in Paola, Miami County, Kansas; died July 16, 1918, in Louisburg, Miami County, Kansas.
- 8   ii. Alberta Heiskell, born August 16, 1860 in Paola, Miami County, Kansas;[8] died April 20, 1861, in Paola, Miami County, Kansas.[9]
- 9   iii. Nellie V. Heiskell, born February 15, 1862, in Paola, Miami County, Kansas;[10] died August 13, 1864, in Paola, Miami County, Kansas.[11]
- 10   iv. Blanche Heiskell, born August 17, 1864, in Paola, Miami County, Kansas;[12] died September 16, 1864, in Paola, Miami County, Kansas.[13]

+ 11   v. Minnie M. Heiskell, born November 08, 1868, in Paola, Miami County, Kansas;[14] died Abt. 1938, in Kansas City, Missouri.[15]

Generation No. 2

3. **Elisabeth Price** was born Abt. 1842, and died Abt. November 04, 1878, in Kansas City, Jackson County, Missouri.[16] She married **Addison Dashiell Madeira** October 15, 1872, in Westport, Jackson County, Missouri,[17] son of Jacob Madeira and Mary Dashiell. He was born April 21, 1828, in Cincinnati, Hamilton County, Ohio,[18] and died June 23, 1915, in Kansas City, Jackson County, Missouri.[19]

Children of Elisabeth Heiskell and Addison Madeira are:
12   i. Romaine Madeira, born 1875;[20] died January 20, 1897, in Independence, Jackson County, Missouri.[21]
13   ii. May Madeira, born March 17, 1878, in Kansas City, Jackson County, Missouri;[22] died August 20, 1948, in Kansas City, Jackson County, Missouri.[23] She married E. Trice Bryant April 1913, in Jackson County, Missouri;[24] died Aft. 1948.

7. **Sue Austin Heiskell** was born May 31, 1857, in Paola, Miami County, Kansas,[25] and died July 16, 1918, in Louisburg, Miami County, Kansas.[26] She married **(1) William F. Wallace** June 27, 1875, in Paola, Miami County, Kansas,[27] son of William Wallace and Lydia Waterman. He was born July 11, 1849, in Concord, Merrimack County, New Hampshire,[28] and died September 05, 1906, in Rochester, Strafford County, New Hampshire.[29] She married **(2) Hiram Lafayette Phillips** February 18, 1879, in Paola, Miami County, Kansas,[30] son of Alfred Phillips and Susannah Cullom. He was born September 20, 1827, in Wayne County, Kentucky, and died April 05, 1885, in Louisburg, Miami County, Kansas.[31] She married **(3) Philip Fletcher Latimer** October 08, 1889, in Louisburg Presbyterian Church, Louisburg, Miami County, Kansas,[32] son of Robert Latimer and Anna Fletcher. He was born September 10, 1830 in Ireland[33] and died February 09, 1913, in Louisburg, Miami County, Kansas.[34]

Child of Sue Heiskell and William Wallace is:
+ 14   i. Leslie Earle Wallace, born September 15, 1876, in Paola, Miami County, Kansas; died May 09, 1940 in Larned, Pawnee County, Kansas.

Children of Sue Heiskell and Hiram Phillips are:
- 15   i. Nellie Phillips, born December 1879.
- + 16   ii. Lenora Phillips, born February 1882.
- + 17   iii. Jessie Phillips, born August 1884.

Child of Sue Heiskell and Philip Latimer is:
- + 18   i. Philip Heiskell Latimer, born June 07, 1891, in Louisburg, Miami County, Kansas; died August 06, 1982, in Overland Park, Johnson County, Kansas.

11. **Minnie M. Heiskell** was born November 08, 1868, in Paola, Miami County, Kansas,[35] and died Abt. 1938, in Kansas City, Missouri. She married **David Heenan** Bet. 1894 - 1896, in Kansas,[36] son of David Heenan. He was born August 15, 1868, in Belfast, County Antrim, Northern Ireland, and died March 03, 1951, in Wellington, Sumner County, Kansas.[37]

Child of Minnie Heiskell and David Heenan is:
- 19   i. David Heenan, born March 24, 1898, in Sedgwick County, Kansas;[38] died January 09, 1955, in Aberdeen, Washington.[39] He married Mary L.; born 1898, in Ohio.[40]

Generation No. 3

14. **Leslie Earle Wallace** was born September 15, 1876, in Paola, Miami County, Kansas,[41] and died May 09, 1940 in Larned, Pawnee County, Kansas.[42] He married **(1) Sara Le Maître Johnson** May 24, 1905, in Baltimore, Maryland,[43] daughter of Albert Johnson and Cora Harlan. She was born September 22, 1881, in Wilmington, New Castle County, Delaware,[44] and died October 25, 1930 in Larned, Pawnee County, Kansas.[45] He married **(2) Bob Lee Victor** September 15, 1931, in Hutchinson, Kansas,[46] daughter of Robert Victor and Mary Garrett. She was born November 01, 1883,[47] and died September 19, 1979.[48]

Children of Leslie Wallace and Sara Johnson are:
- 20   i. Eunice Cora Wallace, born February 09, 1907, in Iola, Allen County, Kansas;[49] died March 09, 1953, in Larned, Pawnee County, Kansas.[50] She married (1) Chester Klinefelter Shore September 12, 1931, in Great Bend, Barton County, Kansas;[51] born May 25, 1900 in Castleton, Reno County, Kansas;[52] died

February 1979, in Helena, Lewis and Clark County, Montana.[53] She married (2) William A. Rhea Aft. 1943; born February 04, 1903;[54] died January 1966, in Larned, Pawnee County, Kansas.[55]

21   ii.   Ralph Leslie Wallace, born October 14, 1908, in Kansas City, Jackson County, Missouri;[56] died September 16, 1959, in Manhattan, New York City, New York County, New York.[57] He married (1) Hortense Hostetter; born November 16, 1911, in Hutchinson, Reno County, Kansas;[58] died November 16, 1979, in Hutchinson, Reno County, Kansas.[59] He married (2) Meck McCall, November 30, 1946.[60]

16. **Lenora Phillips** was born February 1882.[61] She married **Daniel W. Thomas**. He was born Abt. 1880 in Kentucky.

Child of Lenora Phillips and Daniel W. Thomas is:
22   i.   Jessie May Thomas, born Abt. 1911.

17. **Jessie Phillips** was born August 1884. She married **John T. Venable** July 21, 1915, in Marion County, Indiana.[62] He was born October 03, 1882, in Illinois,[63] and died February 1966, in Eaton, Delaware County, Indiana.[64]

Children of Jessie Phillips and John Venable are:
23   i.   Wilma Venable, born 1919.
24   ii.   Margaret Venable, born 1921.
25   iii.   John Venable, born 1928

18. **Philip Heiskell Latimer** was born June 07, 1891, in Louisburg, Miami County, Kansas,[65] and died August 06, 1982, in Overland Park, Johnson County, Kansas.[66] He married (1) **Maude Ragan**.[67] She was born February 4, 1891 and died February 11, 1949.[68] She was born February 4, 1891, in Louisburg, Kansas and died February 11, 1949, in Kansas City, Missouri.[69] He married (2) **Blanche M. Linder** January 06, 1938, in Harrisonville, Cass County, Missouri.[70] She was born 1899[71] and died 1983.[72]

Children of Philip Latimer and Maude Ragan are:
26   i.   Ellis James Latimer, born December 11, 1914, in Louisburg, Montgomery, Kansas;[73] died December 11, 1999, in Grand Junction, Mesa, Colorado[74]

27   ii.   Philip E. Latimer, born Abt. 1917; died February 28, 1942.[75]
28   iii. Cloyd Latimer, born September 03, 1917, in Louisburg, Montgomery, Kansas;[76] died February 1971.[77]

---

1. Wilmer L. Kerns, *Historical Records of Old Frederick and Hampshire Counties, Virginia*, (Cullman, Alabama: Gregath Company, 1988), 63.
2. William A. Heiskell obituary, *Miami (Ohio) Republican*, 20 Aug 1870, 3:4.
3. Ira D. Hyskell, *Early Heiskells and Hyskells, with a Genealogical Table of the First Seven Generations in America*, (New York: n.p., 1958), 42.
4. Mrs. Howard W. Woodruff, compiler, *Marriage Records: Cass (Van Buren) County, Missouri, Books "A" &" B," 1836-1865* (Independence, Missouri: Mrs. Howard W. Woodruff, 1969), 28.
5. Annie Lynch, compiler, "Peery Families of Virginia," Utah Genealogical and Historical Magazine 8 (July 1917): 125.
6. "The Death of Mr. Heiskell," (Paola, Kansas) *Western Spirit*, 11 Aug 1916, np; Obituary Collection, Hunt-Russell Genealogical Research Library, Swan River Museum, Miami County Genealogy and Historical Societies, Paola, Kansas.
7. Union Cemetery Historical Society, *Soldiers of Various Wars Interred at Union Cemetery; Obituaries and Biographical Sketches* (Kansas City, Missouri: Union Cemetery Historical Society, 1989), 16.
8. Annie Lynch, *Peery Families of Virginia*, 125.
9. Annie Lynch, *Peery Families of Virginia*, 125.
10. Annie Lynch, *Peery Families of Virginia*, 125.
11. Annie Lynch, *Peery Families of Virginia*, 125.
12. Annie Lynch, *Peery Families of Virginia*, 125.
13. Annie Lynch, *Peery Families of Virginia*, 125.
14. Annie Lynch, *Peery Families of Virginia*, 125.
15. Annie Lynch, *Peery Families of Virginia*, 125.
16. Union Cemetery Historical Society, *Soldiers of Various Wars Interred at Union Cemetery*, 16.
17. Ancestry.com, "Missouri Marriages, 1851-1900," database (http://www.ancestry.com : accessed 15 Aug 2007), Rev. A. D. Madeira and Price E. Heiskell, 15 Oct 1872, Jackson County, Missouri.
18. Bureau of Vital Statistics, Missouri State Board of Health, Certificate of Death, file no. 19132, A. D. Madeira, 23 June 1915; digital image, Missouri Digital Heritage, Missouri Office of the Secretary of State (http://www.sos.mo.gov/mdh/ : accessed 8 Dec 2007).
19. Missouri State Board of Health, Certificate of Death, file no. 19132, Addison Dashiel Madeira, 23 June 1915; Bureau of Vital Records, Missouri Department of Health and Senior Services, Jefferson City, Missouri.
20. "Death of Romaine Madeira," *Kansas City Star*, 21 Jan 1897, 10:d.
21. "Death of Romaine Madeira," *Kansas City Star*, 21 Jan 1897, 10:d.
22. Missouri Division of Health, Standard Certificate of Death, State File No. 26172, May (Madeira) Bryant, 20 Aug 1948; Bureau of Vital Records, Missouri Department of Health and Senior Services, Jefferson City, Missouri.

23. Missouri Division of Health, Standard Certificate of Death, State File No. 26172 (1948), May (Madeira) Bryant; Bureau of Vital Records, Missouri Department of Health and Senior Services, Jefferson City, Missouri.
24. Ancestry.com, "Missouri Marriage Records, 18005-2002," database (http://www.ancestry.org : accessed 6 Aug 2007), E. Trice Bryant and May Madeira, 16 Apr 1913, Jackson County, Missouri, Application 57964.
25. Cutler, *History of the State of Kansas,* 893.
26. "Mrs. Sue A. Latimer Dead," Obituary Collection, Hunt-Russell Genealogical Research Library, Swan River Museum, Miami County Genealogy and Historical Societies, Paola, Kansas.
27. Marriage License, No. 401, MARRIAGE LICENSE / STATE OF KANSAS / Miami County.
28. 1900 US Census, Plaistow, Rockingham County, New Hampshire, ED 205, sheet 2A, dwelling 35, family 39.
29. Registrar of Vital Records, New Hampshire Department of State, Death Certificate, William F. Wallace, 5 Sept 1906; Division of Vital Records Administration, Concord, New Hampshire.
30. Cutler, *History of the State of Kansas,* 893.
31. Hiram Phillips obituary, *The* (Paola, Kansas) *Western Spirit,* 10 Apr 1885, 3:h.
32. Miami County Clerk, Miami County Marriages, Births, Deaths, 1885-1892, (Kansas Historical Library), p. 52, marriage 221.
33. John E. Hysom, compiler, *Latimer: Wickline, Hysom, Gaither, Beck, Heiskell, Wallace, Phillips,* 3rd ed. ([Tucker, Georgia: J. E. Hysom, 1994, np.
34. "P.F. Latimer Dead," undated clipping from unidentified newspaper, Obituary Collection, Hunt-Russell Genealogical Research Library, Swan River Museum, Miami County Genealogy and Historical Societies, Paola, Kansas.
35. Annie Lynch, *Peery Families of Virginia,* 125.
36. David Heenan obituary, undated clipping from unidentified newspaper, Lykins File, Hunt-Russell Genealogical Research Library, Swan River Museum, Miami County Genealogy and Historical Societies, Paola, Kansas.
37. David Heenan obituary, Lykins File, Hunt-Russell Genealogical Research Library.
38. "World War I Draft Registration Cards, 1917-1918, " digital images, *Ancestry.com* (http://www.ancestry.com : accessed 1 Oct 2007), David Heenan, serial no. 1794, order no. 1869, Local Board 14, Kansas City, Missouri.
39. Washington Secretary of State, "Washington State Death Records," database (http://www.digitalarchives.wa.gov/ : accessed 23 Nov 2008), entry for David Heenan.
40. 1930 US Census, Los Angeles, Los Angeles County, California, ED 19-621, sheet 48-A, dwelling and family 139.
41. Alberta Lawrence, editor, *Who's Who Among North American Authors* (Los Angeles: Golden Syndicate Publishing, 1930), 4: 1300.
42. "Leslie E. Wallace Dies," *Kansas City Star,*" 9 May 1940, np.; Leslie E. Wallace Vertical File, Kansas Historical Library, Topeka, Kansas.
43. Mrs. Leslie Wallace obituary, *The Tiller and Toiler,* 30 Oct 1930, p. 1.
44. Mrs. Leslie Wallace obituary, *The Tiller and Toiler,* 30 Oct 1930, p. 1.
45. Mrs. Leslie Wallace obituary, *The Tiller and Toiler,* 30 Oct 1930, p. 1.
46. "Wallace – Victor," *Tiller and Toiler,* 17 Sept 1931, 3:c.
47. Margaret Buzzard Corbet, *Larned Cemetery, Pawnee County, Kansas: Where is*

Everybody? (Larned, Kansas: M. B. Corbet, 1990), np.
48. Corbet, *Larned Cemetery*, np.
49. Stratford, *Butler County's Eighty Years, 1855-1935: A History of Butler County*, p. 345.
50. Mrs. Eunice Rhea obituary, *The Tiller and Toiler*, 12 Mar 1953, 1.
51. Photo caption of Eunice Wallace Shore, *Augusta Gazette*, 2 Sept 1931, np; Eunice Wallace Shore Vertical File, Kansas Historical Library, Topeka, Kansas.
52. Jessie Perry Stratford, *Butler County's Eighty Years, 1855-1935: A History of Butler County, Biographical Sketches and Portraits* (El Dorado, Kansas: Butler County News, 1934), 345.
53. Social Security Administration, "U.S. Social Security Death Index," database, *Rootsweb* (http://ssdi.rootsweb.ancestry.com : accessed 12 Nov 2007), entry for Chester Shore, 1979, SS no. 515-03-0712.
54. Social Security Administration, "U.S. Social Security Death Index," database, *Rootsweb* (http://ssdi.rootsweb.ancestry.com : accessed 12 Nov 2007), entry for William Rhea, 1966, SS no. 509-05-8452.
55. Social Security Administration, "U.S. Social Security Death Index," database, *Rootsweb* (http://ssdi.rootsweb.ancestry.com : accessed 12 Nov 2007), entry for William Rhea, 1966, SS no. 509-05-8452.
56. Corbet, *Larned Cemetery*, np.
57. Corbet, *Larned Cemetery*, np.
58. Social Security Administration, "U.S. Social Security Death Index," database, *Rootsweb* (http://ssdi.rootsweb.ancestry.com : accessed 12 Nov 2007), entry for Hortense Wallace, 1979, SS no. 513-48-3693.
59. Social Security Administration, "U.S. Social Security Death Index," database, *Rootsweb* (http://ssdi.rootsweb.ancestry.com : accessed 12 Nov 2007), entry for Hortense Wallace, 1979, SS no. 513-48-3693.
60. Marriage Records 1890-1940, Eddy County, New Mexico, Lord-McPherson. Submitted by Richard Wilkinson. (http://eddy.nmgenweb us/bridesLord-McPherson.text. Accessed 21 Sept 2010).
61. 1900 U.S. Census, Wea Township, Miami County, Kansas, ED 138, sheet 3, dwelling 51, family 53.
62. Ancestry.com, "Indiana Marriage Collection, 1800-1941," database (http://www.ancestry.org : accessed 15 Aug 2007), John T. Venable and Jessie C. Phillips, 21 July 1915, Marion County, Book 81, p. 695.
63. Social Security Administration, "U.S. Social Security Death Index," database, *Rootsweb* (http://ssdi.rootsweb.ancestry.com : accessed 12 Nov 2007), entry for John Venable, 1966, SS no. 308-40-7203.
64. Social Security Administration, "U.S. Social Security Death Index," database, *Rootsweb* (http://ssdi.rootsweb.ancestry.com : accessed 12 Nov 2007), entry for John Venable, 1966, SS no. 308-40-7203.
65. "World War I Draft Registration Cards, 1917-1918, " digital images, *Ancestry.com* (http://www.ancestry.com : accessed 1 Oct 2007), Philip Heiskel Latimer, serial no. 992, order no. 11, Fourth Precinct, Wea, Miami County, Kansas.
66. "Latimer," Obituary Collection, Hunt-Russell Genealogical Research Library, Swan River Museum, Miami County Genealogy and Historical Societies, Paola, Kansas.

67. Clay County, Missouri, [Application for License to Marry], Philip Heiskell and Maude E. Ragan, 23 Apr 1910; "Missouri Marriage Records, 1805-2002," digital images, *Ancestry.com* (http://www.Ancestry.com ; accessed 1 Oct 2007).
68. Missouri State Archives, "Missouri Death Certificates, 1910-1958," digital images, Missouri Digital Heritage (http://www.sos.mo.gov/archives/resources/birthdeath/ : accessed 5 Nov 2007), Maude Whitney, Jackson County; Bureau of Vital Records, Missouri Department of Health and Human Services, Jefferson City, Missouri.
69. Missouri State Archives, "Missouri Death Certificates, 1910-1958," digital images, Missouri Digital Heritage (http://www.sos.mo.gov/archives/resources/birthdeath/ : accessed 5 Nov 2007), Maude Whitney, Jackson County; Bureau of Vital Records, Missouri Department of Health and Human Services, Jefferson City, Missouri.
70. Cass County, Missouri, Application for License to Marry, Philip H. Latimer and Blanche M. Linder, 9 Feb 1938; "Missouri Marriage Records, 1805-2002," digital images, *Ancestry.com* (http://www.ancestry.com : accessed 1 Oct 2007).
71. *Cemeteries of Miami County, Kansas*, (Paola, Kansas: Miami County Genealogy Society, 1985), 2: 14.
72. *Cemeteries of Miami County, Kansas*, (Paola, Kansas: Miami County Genealogy Society, 1985), 2: 14.
73. Social Security Administration, "U.S. Social Security Death Index," database, *Rootsweb* (http://ssdi.rootsweb.ancestry.com : accessed 12 Nov 2007), entry for Ellis Latimer, 1999, SS no.720-14-9480.
74. Social Security Administration, "U.S. Social Security Death Index," database, *Rootsweb* (http://ssdi.rootsweb.ancestry.com : accessed 12 Nov 2007), entry for Ellis Latimer, 1999, SS no. 720-14-9480.
75. Defense Prisoner of War / Missing Personnel Office, Department of Defense, "Service Personnel Not Recovered Following World War II," database (http://www.dtic.mil/dpmo/wwii/reports/MAV_M_L.HTM : accessed 20 Dec 2009), entry for Latimer, Philip E., Navy, serial number 4109909.
76. Social Security Administration, "U.S. Social Security Death Index," database, *Rootsweb* (http://ssdi.rootsweb.ancestry.com : accessed 12 Nov 2007), entry for Cloyd Latimer, 1971, SS no. 514-05-7684.
77. Social Security Administration, "U.S. Social Security Death Index," database, *Rootsweb* (http://ssdi.rootsweb.ancestry.com : accessed 12 Nov 2007), entry for Cloyd Latimer, 1971, SS no. 514-05-7684.

Descendants of William T. Wallace-Mary Ann Dana-Lydia M. Waterman

Generation No. 1

1. **William T. Wallace** was born April 21, 1819, in Epsom, Merrimack County, New Hampshire,[1] and died May 27, 1868, in San Felipe, California.[2] He married **(1) Mary Ann Langdon Dana** abt. 1842, daughter of Nathaniel Dana and Mary Harris. She was born May 09, 1821, in Portsmouth, Rockingham County, New Hampshire,[3] and died October 24, 1845, in Epsom, Merrimac County, New Hampshire.[4] He married **(2) Lydia M. Waterman** September 27, 1848, in Hillsborough, Hillsborough County, New Hampshire[5]. She was born in 1824, in Rhode Island,[6] and died September 17, 1912, in Lansing, Ingham County, Michigan.[7]

Child of William Wallace and Mary Dana is:
- 2   i.   Nathaniel Dana Wallace, born Abt. 1843, in Concord, Merrimack County, New Hampshire[8]; died November 13, 1863, in Richmond, Henrico County, Virginia.[9]

Children of William Wallace and Lydia Waterman are:
- + 3   i.   William F. Wallace, born July 11, 1849, in Concord, Merrimack County, New Hampshire;[10] died September 05, 1906, in Rochester, Strafford County, New Hampshire.[11]
- 4   ii.   Deceased Infant Wallace, [12] born May 14, 1856, in Epsom, Merrimack County, New Hampshire.

Generation No. 2

3. **William F. Wallace** was born July 11, 1849, in Concord, Merrimack County, New Hampshire, and died September 05, 1906, in Rochester, Strafford County, New Hampshire. He married **(1) Sue Austin Heiskell** June 27, 1875, in Paola, Miami County, Kansas,[13] daughter of William Heiskell and Emeline Peery. She was born May 31, 1857, in Paola, Miami County, Kansas,[14] and died July 16, 1918, in Louisburg, Miami County, Kansas.[15] He married **(2) Addie Mary Gilman** April 11, 1883, in Dover, Strafford, New Hampshire,[16]

daughter of John Gilman and Elizabeth Page. She was born March 12, 1849, in Gilmanton, New Hampshire,[17] and died November 16, 1933, in Union, New Hampshire.[18]

Child of William Wallace and Sue Heiskell is:
+ 5   i.   Leslie Earle Wallace, born September 15, 1876, in Paola, Miami County, Kansas;[19] died May 09, 1940 in Larned, Pawnee County, Kansas.[20]

Children of William Wallace and Addie Gilman are:
6   i.   Elsye Maude Wallace, born December 07, 1884, in Bradford, New Hampshire;[21] died 1949, in Cambridge, Massachusetts.[22] She married Rolf Alexander Osterman, born February 16, 1891, in Massachusetts;[23] died June 1969, in Rochester, Strafford, New Hampshire.[24]
7   ii. Josie L. Wallace, born Abt. November 16, 1886, in New Hampshire;[25] died November 19, 1892, in Bradford, Merrimack County, New Hampshire.[26]
+ 8   iii. Alice Josephine Wallace, born July 23, 1893, in Bradford, Merrimack County, New Hampshire;[27] died July 01, 1971, in Chicopee, Massachusetts.[28]

Generation No. 3

5. **Leslie Earle Wallace** was born September 15, 1876, in Paola, Miami County, Kansas,[29] and died May 09, 1940 in Larned, Pawnee County, Kansas.[30] He married **(1) Sara Le Maître Johnson** May 24, 1905, in Baltimore, Maryland,[31] daughter of Albert Johnson and Cora Harlan. She was born September 22, 1881, in Wilmington, New Castle County, Delaware,[32] and died October 25, 1930 in Larned, Pawnee County, Kansas.[33] He married **(2) Bob Lee Victor** September 15, 1931, in Larned, Pawnee County, Kansas,[34] daughter of Robert Victor and Mary Garrett. She was born November 01, 1883[35] and died September 19, 1979.[36]

Children of Leslie Wallace and Sara Johnson are:
9   i.   Eunice Cora Wallace, born February 09, 1907, in Iola, Allen County, Kansas;[37] died March 09, 1953, in Larned, Pawnee County, Kansas.[38] She married (1) Chester Klinefelter Shore September 12, 1931, in Great Bend, Barton County, Kansas;[39] born May 25, 1900 in Castleton, Reno County, Kansas;[40] died February 1979, in Helena, Lewis and Clark County, Montana.

        [41] She married (2) William A. Rhea Aft. 1943; born February 04, 1903;[42] died January 1966, in Larned, Pawnee County, Kansas.[43]

10   ii.   Ralph Leslie Wallace, born October 14, 1908, in Kansas City, Jackson County, Missouri;[44] died September 16, 1959, in Manhattan, New York City, New York County, New York. [45] He married (1) Hortense Hostetter; born November 16, 1911, in Hutchinson, Reno County, Kansas;[46] died November 16, 1979, in Hutchinson, Reno County, Kansas. [47] He married (2) He married **(2) Meck McCall** on November 30, 1946, in Eddy County, New Mexico .[48]

8. **Alice Josephine Wallace** was born July 23, 1893, in Bradford, Merrimack County, New Hampshire,[49] and died July 01, 1971, in Chicopee, Massachusetts.[50] She married **Philip Albert Kimball** November 03, 1920 in Ye Ragged Robin Tea Room, Plummer's Ridge, Milton County, New Hampshire. [51] He was born October 08, 1889, in Tamworth, New Hampshire,[52] and died September 02, 1944, in Northampton, Massachusetts.[53]

Child of Alice Wallace and Philip Kimball is:
11   i.   Wallace O. Kimball, born September 27, 1921, in Rochester, New Hampshire. [54] He married Barbara Griswold Hammond September 05, 1943, in Union, New Hampshire;[55] born May 22, 1919, in Putnam, Connecticut.[56]

---

1. Epsom Historical Society, "Epsom History Genealogy," database, *Epsom Early Settlers* (http://ssdi.rootsweb.ancestry.com : accessed 12 Nov 2007), entry for William T. Wallace.
2. New Hampshire Adjutant's Office, *Revised Register of the Soldiers and Sailors in the War of the Rebellion, 1861-1866* (Concord, New Hampshire: I. C. Evans, 1895), 886.
3. Epsom Historical Society, "Epsom History Genealogy," database, *Epsom Early Settlers* (http://ssdi.rootsweb.ancestry.com : accessed 12 Nov 2007), entry for Mary Ann Langdon Dana.
4. Epsom Historical Society, "Epsom History Genealogy," database, *Epsom Early Settlers* (http://ssdi.rootsweb.ancestry.com : accessed 12 Nov 2007), entry for Mary Ann Langdon Dana.
5. New Hampshire Division of Vital Statistics, "Bride's Index, 1640-1900," Wallace-Waterman marriage record; Family History Library, Salt Lake City, Utah, microfilm 975,693.
6. Mrs. Lydia M. Grant Obituary, *The* [Lansing Michigan] *State Journal*, 18 Sept 1912, 7:3.
7. Mrs. Lydia M. Grant Obituary, *The* [Lansing Michigan] *State Journal*.
8. New Hampshire Adjutant's Office, *Revised Register of the Soldiers and Sailors in the War of the Rebellion, 1861-1866*, 92.
9. New Hampshire Adjutant's Office, *Revised Register of the Soldiers and Sailors in the War of the Rebellion, 1861-1866*, 92.
10. 1900 US Census, Plaistow, Rockingham County, New Hampshire, ED 205, sheet 2A,

dwelling 35, family 39.
11. Registrar of Vital Records, New Hampshire Department of State, Death Certificate, William F. Wallace, 5 Sept 1906; Division of Vital Records Administration, Concord, New Hampshire.
12. Epsom Historical Society, "Epsom History Genealogy," database, *Epsom Early Settlers* (http://ssdi.rootsweb.ancestry.com : accessed 12 Nov 2007), entry for Lydia M. Waterman.
13. Wallace – Heiskell marriage notice, (Paola, Kansas) *Western Spirit*, 2 July 1875, 3:b.
14. "Mrs. Sue A. Latimer Dead," Obituary Collection, Hunt-Russell Genealogical Research Library, Swan River Museum, Miami County Genealogy and Historical Societies, Paola, Kansas.
15. "Mrs. Sue A. Latimer Dead," Hunt-Russell Genealogical Research Library.
16. New Hampshire Division of Vital Statistics, "Groom's Index, 1640-1900," Wallace – French marriage record; Family History Library, Salt Lake City, Utah, microfilm 1,001,314.
17. Francis Lane Childs, comp, *Gravestone Inscriptions from Bradford, New Hampshire*, (Concord, New Hampshire: New Hampshire Historical Society, ca. 1937), 45.
18. Drop Report, 19 Oct 1906, Addie M. Wallace, widow's pension application no. 749743, certificate no. 664937; service of William F. Wallace, (Musician, Co. I, 17th H.H. Vol. Inf., Civil War), certificate no. 856919; case Files of Approved Pension Applications, 1861-1934; Civil War and Later Pension Files; Department of Veterans Affairs, Record Group 15; National Archives, Washington, D.C.
19. Alberta Lawrence, editor, *Who's Who Among North American Authors*, (Los Angeles: Golden Syndicate Publishing, 1930), 4: 1300.
20. *"Leslie E. Wallace Dies,"* Kansas City Star, 9 May 1940, np, clipping; Biography file: Wallace, Leslie E.; Kansas State Historical Society, Topeka, Kansas.
21. Questionnaire, 15 Jan 1898, Addie M. [Gilman] Wallace, widow's pension application no. 664937, certificate no. 856919; service of William F. Wallace (Musician, Co. I, 18th N.H. Vol. Inf., Civil War); Case files of Approved Pension Applications, 1861-1864; Civil War and Later Pension Files; Department of Veterans Affairs, Record Group 15; National Archives, Washington, D.C.
22. Karen Hull, Agawam, Massachusetts, to Rose Ann Findlen, email, 9 May 2009, author's personal files.
23. Social Security Administration, "U.S. Social Security Death Index," database, *Rootsweb* (http://ssdi.rootsweb.ancestry.com : accessed 12 Nov 2007), entry for Rolf Osterman, 1969, SS no. 001-07-6865.
24. Social Security Administration, "U.S. Social Security Death Index," database, *Rootsweb* (http://ssdi.rootsweb.ancestry.com : accessed 12 Nov 2007), entry for Rolf Osterman, 1969, SS no. 001-07-6865.
25. Questionnaire, 15 Jan 1898, Addie M. [Gilman] Wallace, widow's pension application no. 664937, certificate no. 856919; service of William F. Wallace (Musician, Co. I, 18th N.H. Vol. Inf., Civil War); Case files of Approved Pension Applications, 1861-1864; Civil War and Later Pension Files; Department of Veterans Affairs, Record Group 15; National Archives, Washington, D.C.
26. Childs, compiler, *Gravestone Information from Bradford, New Hampshire*, 45.
27. Questionnaire, 15 Jan 1898, Addie M. [Gilman] Wallace, widow's pension application no. 664937, certificate no. 856919; service of William F. Wallace (Musician, Co. I, 18th N.H. Vol. Inf., Civil War); Case files of Approved Pension Applications, 1861-1864; Civil War and

Later Pension Files; Department of Veterans Affairs, Record Group 15; National Archives, Washington, D.C.
28. Karen Hull, Agawam, Massachusetts, to Rose Ann Findlen, email, 9 May 2009, author's personal files.
29. "Leslie E. Wallace Dies," *Kansas City Star*, 9 May 1940, np, clipping; Biography file: Wallace, Leslie E.; Kansas State Historical Society, Topeka, Kansas.
30. "Leslie E. Wallace Dies," *Kansas City Star*, 9 May 1940, np, clipping; Biography file: Wallace, Leslie E.; Kansas State Historical Society, Topeka, Kansas.
31. "Mrs. Leslie E. Wallace," [Larned, Kansas] Tiller and Toiler, 30 Oct 1930, 1:a.
32. "Mrs. Leslie E. Wallace," [Larned, Kansas] Tiller and Toiler, 30 Oct 1930, 1:a.
33. "Mrs. Leslie Wallace Dies," *Topeka Journal*, 25 Oct 1930, np, clipping, Wallace, Leslie, Biography file; Kansas State Historical Society, Topeka, Kansas.
34. Wallace – Victor wedding announcement, [Larned, Kansas] *Tiller and Toiler*, 17 Sept 1931, 3:a.
35. Corbet, Margaret Buzzard, *Larned Cemetery, Pawnee County, Kansas: Where is Everybody?* (Larned, Kansas: M. B. Corbet, 1990), np.
36. Corbet, *Larned Cemetery, Pawnee County, Kansas: Where is Everybody?*, np.
37. Mrs. Eunice Rhea obituary, *The Tiller and Toiler*, 12 Mar 1953, p. 1.
38. "In Memory," *The* [University of Kansas] *Alumni Magazine*, 51 (May 1953), 40.
39. *Augusta* [Kansas] *Gazette*, 12 Sept 1931, np; clipping, Eunice Wallace Shore Vertical File, Kansas Historical Library, Topeka, Kansas.
40. Jessie Perry Stratford, *Butler County's Eighty Years, 1855-1935: A History of Butler County, Biographical Sketches and Portraits* (El Dorado, Kansas: Butler County News, 1934), 345.
41. Social Security Administration, "U.S. Social Security Death Index," database, *Rootsweb* (http://ssdi.rootsweb.ancestry.com : accessed 12 Nov 2007), entry for Chester Shore, 1979, SS no. 515-03-0712.
42. Social Security Administration, "U.S. Social Security Death Index," database, *Rootsweb* (http://ssdi.rootsweb.ancestry.com : accessed 12 Nov 2007), entry for William Rhea, 1966, SS no. 509-05-8452.
43. Social Security Administration, "U.S. Social Security Death Index," database, *Rootsweb* (http://ssdi.rootsweb.ancestry.com : accessed 12 Nov 2007), entry for William Rhea, 1966, SS no. 509-05-8452.
44. Corbet, *Larned Cemetery, Pawnee County, Kansas: Where is Everybody?*, np.
45. Corbet, *Larned Cemetery, Pawnee County, Kansas: Where is Everybody?*, np.
46. Social Security Administration, "U.S. Social Security Death Index," database, *Rootsweb* (http://ssdi.rootsweb.ancestry.com : accessed 12 Nov 2007), entry for Hortense Wallace, 1979, SS no. 513-48-3693.
47. Social Security Administration, "U.S. Social Security Death Index," database, *Rootsweb* (http://ssdi.rootsweb.ancestry.com : accessed 12 Nov 2007), entry for Hortense Wallace, 1979, SS no. 513-48-3693.
48. Marriage Records 1890-1940, Eddy County, New Mexico, Lord-McPherson. Submitted by Richard Wilkinson. (http://eddy.nmgenweb us/bridesLord-McPherson.text. Accessed 21 Sept 2010).
49. Questionnaire, 15 Jan 1898, Addie M. [Gilman] Wallace, widow's pension application no. 664937, certificate no. 856919; service of William F. Wallace (Musician, Co. I, 18th N.H. Vol. Inf., Civil War); Case files of Approved Pension Applications, 1861-1864; Civil War and

Later Pension Files; Department of Veterans Affairs, Record Group 15; National Archives, Washington, D.C.

50. Social Security Administration, "U.S. Social Security Death Index," database, *Rootsweb* (http://ssdi.rootsweb.ancestry.com : accessed 12 Nov 2007), entry for Alice Kimball, 1971, SS no. 034-22-9804.

51. Karen Hull, Agawam, Massachusetts, to Rose Ann Findlen, email, 9 May 2009, author's personal files

52. Karen Hull, Agawam, Massachusetts, to Rose Ann Findlen, email, 9 May 2009, author's personal files

53. Karen Hull, Agawam, Massachusetts, to Rose Ann Findlen, email, 9 May 2009, author's personal files.

54. Karen Hull, Agawam, Massachusetts, to Rose Ann Findlen, email, 9 May 2009, author's personal files

54. Karen Hull, Agawam, Massachusetts, to Rose Ann Findlen, email, 9 May 2009, author's personal files

55. Karen Hull, Agawam, Massachusetts, to Rose Ann Findlen, email, 9 May 2009, author's personal files

56. Karen Hull, Agawam, Massachusetts, to Rose Ann Findlen, email, 9 May 2009, author's personal files

RELATED STORIES AND POEMS

Tecumseh's Tomahawk

Tecumseh's tomahawk (or perhaps his brother's) made a long journey from the Northwest Territory to the Kansas Territory. Along its way, it served as war weapon, booty of war, burglar's tool, curio paperweight, and historical artifact. Its journey likely began in Ohio.

"Tecumseh, a young Shawnee chief, was born about 1770 on the banks of the Scioto River in the Northwest Territory, land once claimed by Virginia, and which is now the states of Ohio, Indiana and Illinois.... In an attempt to halt the encroachments upon the territory which his people rightly thought was theirs, Tecumseh formed a confederation of Indian tribes, among them Wyandots, Ottawas, Pottawatomies, Miamis, and others, and aligned the confederation with the British during the War of 1812.

General William Henry Harrison attacked British General Henry A. Proctor near Chatham, Ontario, about seventeen miles up the Thames River on October 5, 1813. The British and their Indian allies were decisively defeated, and Tecumseh was killed by Colonel Richard Johnson, who was, himself, badly wounded.

The great chief's

tomahawk was seized by an Indian who was immediately shot by William Henry Russell, a member of the Kentucky Mounted Volunteers. Russell's son, Colonel William H. Russell, immigrated to Missouri in 1831 and took part in the Black Hawk War. During the war he met Tenskwatawa, the Prophet, who identified the tomahawk as having belonged to his brother, Tecumseh. Colonel Russell gave his own side arms in exchange for it. Later, Colonel Russell spent some time in California and the tomahawk lay on his desk while he assisted in framing the constitution of that state. When the task was completed, President Abraham Lincoln appointed him as consul to Trinidad, and he took the relic with him.

It was handed down in the family from generation to generation and thus came into the possession of the grandmother of Russell Bettis (Sarah Lykins Russell)....

Just before the turn of the twentieth century there was a large gathering of Indian tribes in Kansas City: A dyed-in-the-wool pow-wow. All the tribes in this locality were represented and from many different places. [This could have been the pow-wow which was held on Okay Creek, near the site of the Kansas City Union Station.]

Blue Jacket, a very old Shawnee Chief, was brought to the pow-wow from the Indian Territory in Oklahoma. Mrs. Bettis's mother, Mrs. Sarah Lykins Russell, took the old tomahawk to the camp. When Blue Jacket caught sight of the old weapon he became very excited. In savage glee he seized it and raised a war-whoop. With keen delight he showed Mrs. Russell his prowess by skillfully implanting it in a distant tree just above a nearby human head. The old Shawnee was a survivor of the Battle of Tippecanoe, and the memory which age had deadened to all appeals was aroused by the sight of the ancient weapon. The tomahawk was lost to Mrs. Russell.

The tomahawk seems uneasy in the white man's keeping. As menacingly as if imbued with the spirit of its old owner, and longing for action, the tomahawk only recently went on a rampage.... [In 1908] it was resting quietly in the window of an Independence,

Missouri, jeweler's shop when something about its appearance caused a couple of burglars to use it in breaking into several residences in the peaceful town. Windows were raised and doors were broken open with its trenchant blade and when the plunder had been secured, the old war hatchet was cast ignominiously into a patch of weeds.

Its loss was keenly felt by Mrs. Russell [another account says Mrs. Bettis], and her generous offers of reward inspired some small boys of the neighborhood to institute a thorough search by which it was recovered.

At the death of Sarah Lykins Russell in 1901, the tomahawk was passed on to her grandson, Alexander E. Bettis. Alexander gave the tomahawk to his brother, Frank A. Bettis, Senior, who kept it in his desk at 1307 East 81st Terrace, Kansas City, Mo. Frank A. Bettis, Jr. of the home realized its historical value so kept it safe until his death. His cousin's wife, Mrs. Russell Harrington Bettis, held the tomahawk in her keeping until she gave it to the Westport Historical Society, where it now resides."

[This narrative originated from the Westport Historical Society's Summary and Transcription from "Tecumseh's Tomahawk in Possession of Bettis Family," *The Westport Historical Quarterly*, Vol.V, No.4 (March 1970): 13-15; and, other papers at the Westport Historical Society.]

[Note: In a letter to the editor of *The Kansas City Star*, 10 Sept 1908, Fred Koehler, owner of the Independence jewelry store from which the tomahawk was stolen, wrote that Colonel Russell obtained the tomahawk in a weapons exchange with Tenskwatawa (The Prophet) and was used by him—not Tecumseh—at the Battle of Tippecanoe in 1811.]

Related newspaper accounts:

1. "Tecumseh's Tomahawk, Weapon of the Great Chief Owned in a Kansas City Home," *The Kansas City Star*, 13 Aug 1899.

2. "Tecumseh's Tomahawk Stolen," *The Kansas City Star*, 2 Sept 1908.

3. "Tecumseh's Tomahawk Found," *The Kansas City Star*, 4 Sept 1908.

4. "Was Tecumseh's Brother's Tomahawk," *The Kansas City Star*, 10 Sept 1908.

THE MARE WAS DRUGGED

WHY JIM CHARLEY SHOT SULLY, PRAIRIE FLOWER'S TRAINER.

A Stump Out in Kansas That Serves as a Dishonest Man's Tombstone–How the Peorias Repaid the "Feller" Who Fixed Their Favorite to Lose.

"There's a feller buried by that stump. He got killed, I reckon."

The reckoning, should the wayfarer pursue the subject, will be found to be correct.

The finest horses in the Indian Territory six years ago were owned by Dave Peery. He has taken less interest in horses since then, however. Peery was a white man who was adopted by the Peorias when he was a boy. He subsequently married the daughter of Baptiste Peoria, the chief of the tribe, and became a man of importance among the Indians. He had a love of fine horses, and as his wealth increased he spared neither pains nor money in obtaining first class blue grass horses from Kentucky. Although it is likely that his best would have had but small chance at Sheepshead Bay or Monmouth, yet here they were wonders.

The flower of the lot was a bay mare called Prairie Flower. At 4 years of age she was the pride and delight of every Indian at the Quapau agency, and not a buck among them but would wager his last poney and the hat on his head that she could distance anything west of the Mississippi in a mile dash, or in to miles, for that matter.

The Bait Was Taken

The fame of Prairie Flower spread until it reached Kansas City and came to the ears of the men who are called sports, and who straightway determined to see what could be done in the way of skinning the backers of Prairie Flower. A trusted jockey was sent down to look at her, and when he got back he made the hearts of the sports glad by saying that the mare could do everything that was said of her–that she could outrun anything owned in Kansas City, at least–she nevertheless was groomed by a white man, one Alfred Sully, who, for a reasonable share of the stakes, would fix the mare to lose.

Thereupon the sports sat down and waited until a day had been set for what the Indians call a payment. A lot of money was due from the Great Father at Washington, and on a certain day the agent would count it out to them. It was easy for the sports to arrange a race for Prairie Flower and an unknown from Kansas City for the day after the payment, the stakes being $500 a side.

That was a great day for the Indians. It was also a great day for the sports. The Indians, in their finest apparel, and with the money received the day before stuffed in their pockets, gathered to see the sport. Old Peery, confident of victory, backed his mare for $1,000 above the stakes. Jim Charley, Jr., who had a short time before got a big lump of money for some land he had owned in Kansas City, backed her for $2,000. Strung along below these were wagers of hundreds, and so on down to tens and ones and jack knives and brass rings. Over $10,000 of good money was put up on Prairie Flower.

Then the horses were brought out amid the hi-yas and cheers of a throng of men, women, and children, numbering, it is said, upward of 3000 people. The excitement was intense. Peery's own son, a lad of light weight and great skill, rode the mare. The unknown, to the disgust of the Peorias, was bestrode by a "nigger."

Finally, on the first try, the racers got off, with Prairie Flower slightly in the lead. For over a furlong she drew steadily away. The Indians, who were spurring their ponies in a mad gallop along, parallel with the track, in the hope of seeing every jump in the race, began to go wild. As the mare's head showed clear they yelled. Then her neck, then her shoulders showed, and when, just short of the quarter post, she was seen to be an entire length in the lead, they threw off hats and coats and acted like witches with a saint in the corral.

The Something That Happened

Then something happened. The Indians had been having all the fun. It was the white man's turn now. But the white man, especially if from Kansas City, was keeping still. The unknown began to hold its own, and at the half was lapping a neck, but there wasn't any more cheering. At the three-quarter post Prairie Flower had not only lost her pace, she was plainly in distress. The unknown finished by six good lengths ahead. Had Prairie Flower been owned in any other country than the Indian territory, and had any other people than Indians been backing her, there would have been trouble right away on that race track. The swindle was barefaced. The mare had been drugged. But the Indians had been so often swindled by white men that they allowed the sports to ride away without even making a protest. They were afraid to say anything.

But, although they lost their money, they were not wholly without revenge. There arose very soon after the race an inquiry for Sully. Sully had not been seen about the track since he had turned to mare over to her jockey, young Peery. Runners started in every direction to search for him. Among them was Jim Charley, Jr., with a party of a dozen. They went down past Charley's house, and began a search up and down the West River bank. They were joined by others. All night long they prowled through the timber without success. At daylight they crossed over. Within fifteen minutes they found a trail where Sully, who had entered and left the water without betraying himself, had returned during the night for a drink. Instead of flying under cover of darkness for the Missouri line he had hoped to hide in the brush till the search was over.

His thirst had betrayed him. Once on the trail, Jim Charley and his band followed straight to a thicket near the brown of a cliff on the north side of Warren creek. There they flushed their game. Sully was seen flying through a thicket. A bullet from Jim Charley's rifle struck him in the back as he started down the precipitous bank, away he went headlong, plunging and tumbling from rock to rock and ledge to ledge, until his body lodged against the old stump which is pointed out to the wayfarer bound along the trail there to the old Spanish mines.

He was dead before his body reached the stump. The Indians dug a grave beside the old stump, just out of the trail, tumbled the body into it and piled on the dirt. Where the dead man came from, or whether he had any relatives or friends elsewhere nobody knows, and, except for such passing interest as the wayfarer may feel, nobody cares.–*Chicago Herald.*

From "The Haverhill Bulletin," 22 Mar 1889.

Dr. Lykins Home
Kansas City's First Mansion

At the southwest corner of Twelfth and Washington streets stands the home of Dr. Johnston Lykins, the first postmaster, the first qualified mayor and a member of the first city council of Kansas City. Now it is a hotel.

The brick walls laid in cement and then painted red, the heavy wooden columns which support the double-decked porch, are as good today as they were when the Cincinnati builders turned the house over to Dr. Lykins, fifty-three years ago.

The house was built at a cost of $20,000 and was in its day the handsomest west of St. Louis. The big orchard which formed a part of the old homestead, with its red Ben Davis apples, its Winesaps and Missouri Pippins, was the favorite resort of the small boys of the surrounding country. These same small boys who appropriated the good doctor's apples were so well acquainted with his kind disposition that they were brave enough to make the old orchard their playground. Hide-and-seek, tag and Blackman, they played hidden behind the trunks of the trees and among the branches, concealed by the green leaves.

Kansas City was at that time a village of perhaps 3,000 to 4,000 inhabitants and it extended no farther south than to Fifth Street. Between the city limits and the Lykins home were cornfields not only patches of sweet corn raised for roasting ears, but fields of maize cultivated to feed the horses and cattle of the farmers.

In 1855, together with J.C. McCoy, Dr. Lykins purchased at an administration sale, seventy acres of land extending south from the corn fields between Broadway and Washington streets. Dr. Lykins took the north half and Mr. McCoy the south half, the line being where Fourteenth heads west from Broadway. Dr. Lykins conceived the idea of converting his entire property into one homestead, purposing to erect in the center a residence which he believed would be suburban for many years. Mr. McCoy sold the south half to the Rev. Robert Thomas, pastor of the First Baptist Church, who platted it and placed it on the market.

When Dr. Lykins, in the fall of 1856, had decided in a general way on the plans for his homestead, his idea was so pretentious that no architect could be found in Missouri who would attempt to build it. Through friends in Cincinnati, the Alexander Brothers, one of whom was an architect and the other a carpenter, were engaged and they came from Cincinnati, bringing with them carpenters, brick burners and steel workers. It took eighteen months to build the house.

Materials Came by Boat

None of the materials except the clay for the brick could be had any nearer than Cincinnati. The clay for the brick was dug from the banks of the Missouri River and burned in the kilns erected by the workmen. The steel beams and castings were bought in Pittsburg [sic.], Pa., and were floated down the Ohio River into the Mississippi and then up that stream and the Missouri to Kansas City. There were no railroads in the West then and the contractors were delayed weeks at a time by the movement of the steamboats.

To show how slow was the building at that time it only is necessary to mention that the window shutters were made by one man. The wood was brought from the sawmills of Ohio and the joints were sawed out and fitted together by this man, who did nothing besides. Fourteen months' were required to make them. A small army of men was employed in building the house. All the men boarded at the Lykins home. There were no banks in Kansas City then and the men were paid every Saturday night by Mrs. Lykins, afterward Mrs. George C. Bingham, wife of the noted artist.

When completed the house was regarded with some amazement by the settlers living in and around Kansas City. It was two stories high with an attic and contained fourteen large rooms. Eight of them were twenty feet square and the others were 16 by 18 feet. The main halls, which ran the entire distance through the building, upstairs and down, were fifteen feet wide. There were ten large fire places and each room, except the parlor, was abundantly supplied with closets; large closets they were, too.

The bricks of which the walls were made were laid in cement, and even the cross walls and partitions were of brick—not a plank being used in the walls of the house. It is not at all remarkable that a house so constructed should last. Today there are no cracks in the walls nor any holes in the plaster on the walls. Even the parlor ornaments, which were made by a Mr. Craford of Cincinnati, are still intact. Blooming flowers, drooping lilies and flying birds were molded from plaster of Paris especially for Dr. Lykins.

This magnificent place, with its beautiful home in the center, was the delight of the early pioneers. On state occasions there would gather there the representative residents of the community for miles around to discuss the political and civil issues of the day. When the older heads were not in conference with the doctor there, the young blood of the city and the country, too, was dancing to the lively time of the old Virginia reels or were playing pinochle or backgammon near the blaze of the chunks in the huge fireplaces. Doctor Lykins and Mrs. Lykins were distinctly Southern and enjoyed society. With much delight, it is reported, they watched the twinkling heels of the dancers as they spun over the polished parlor floors.

Great Days in the Old Home

Doctor Lykins was one of the most progressive pioneers of the region and had an abiding faith in the future of the village at the mouth of the Kaw. The home he planned should hold its own with the growth of the city.

Mrs. Laura Coates Reed, daughter of Kersey Coates, says of the Lykins home in her book on the life of her mother:

"On the south of our home stretched the fine residence and estate of Doctor Johnston Lykins, the house to comply with the desecrating demands of progress, since moved to its present location at the southwest corner of Twelfth and Washington Streets, to be used as a private seminary. Half concealed in a grove of stately forest trees, this typical Southern home, with its spacious halls and apartments, presided over by a host and hostess of the old regime of Southern hospitality, is associated with many of the happiest hours of my childhood. It was perhaps one of the greatest pleasures of my life to be permitted to frequent its fascinating precincts. Every accessory was strangely in keeping with the liberality and the great-heartedness of its owners. Its retinue of slaves, among whom I had my own personal favorites; the brick smokehouse; the commodious, comfortable outdoor slave apartments; the venerable parrot, Florita, whose profanity both shocked and delighted me; the general air of magnificence and the stock of goodies always in readiness for my childish palate, afforded a degree of enchantment of which the most exaggerated fairy tale certainly has no prototype. It is pleasant to think that the nuptials of my younger brother should have afterwards been celebrated in this house so interwoven with happy memories."

Dr. Lykins died August 15, 1876, and later his widow married Gen. George C. Bingham, the artist. The Lykins homestead was sold in 1876 to John Mastin, who held it only a short time. Then it was sold to Major R.S. Henning, who immediately sold it to L.T. Moore of the firm of Bullene, Moore & Emery. In 1885 the property was bought by Charles D. Hasbrook, a capitalist at that time in Kansas City. The land is now owned by a stock company which operates the Washington Hotel.

Before Doctor Lykins died, however, all but five acres of the magnificent homestead had been platted and sold. The five acres remained with the house until 1889, when the Washington Hotel was planned. Then the house was sold to George W. Strope, who lives at 2301 Linwood Boulevard, and still owns the house. Later all the lots were sold except those on which the hotel stands. When Mr. Strope bought the house he moved it directly across Washington street to property which he owned on that side of the street. It was moved by William Bovard and was the first brick house in Kansas City to be moved. The journey was made without so much as cracking the plaster or even breaking a window pane.

Later Days of the House

The Washington Hotel stands now where the Lykins house stood originally and the ground which grew the Ben Davis apple trees is covered by apartment houses and paved streets.

The old house today apparently is as good as it was when the carpenters from Cincinnati nailed on the last baseboard and fitted the last lock in the doors.

Mrs. Bingham in 1887 opened the old house as a boarding school for girls. The girls whose fathers were rich enough attended the school and were taught the common branches such as arithmetic, reading, writing, grammar and spelling, but Mrs. Bingham did not attempt to teach any higher courses. Mrs. Bingham's school lasted only a little more than a year. Many different families occupied the home until 1889 when it was moved. In 1889 Mrs. L.R. Upton opened in the old house a private boarding school for girls. She taught both elementary and higher branches, Latin and algebra, French and German were taught by Mrs. Upton and her daughters, but only the more adventurous students attempted to master the languages. In 1891, Mrs. Upton closed her school in the old home and Misses Brann and Barstow moved their school from Broadway to the old Lykins home. Those young women were graduates of Wellesley who had come West to "grow up with the country." Their school was and is yet a preparatory school for Wellesley, Smith and Vassar. Miss Barstow's school was moved from the old home in 1898 to a new building on Westport Avenue. When Miss Barstow's school was moved, the spacious rooms were divided by partitions into two rooms. The big fireplaces were torn out and the great chandeliers, with their pendants of sparkling cut glass, were replaced with the modern brass chandeliers. Electric lights have taken the place of the old kerosene lamps.

On the north of the building has been built a small 1-story building used as a drug store. Otherwise the house would look as it did in Doctor Lykins's day, except for the fire escape, which Dr. Lykins did not deem necessary, that has since been added on the north side of the building. But to the casual observer, the old Southern idea of building still lingers within the walls.

From the *Kansas City Star*, Sunday, 26 June 1910

Chief Joseph's Story

As white settlers pushed the Nez Perce off their lands in the state of Washington, Chief Joseph sought to negotiate with the government to allow his people to remain in the Wallowa Valley; the government reneged on its agreement for them to remain and tried to force the Nez Perce on to a reservation in Idaho. After twenty young warriors rebelled against Joseph's reluctant agreement to go to Idaho and killed several white settlers, the government troops pursued them over 1400 miles before Chief Joseph finally surrendered in 1877. During the retreat the band of 700, 200 of whom were warriors, fought 2000 U.S. soldiers and Indian auxiliaries in four major battles and several skirmishes during a 3-month period. General William Tecumseh Sherman said of them, "The Indians throughout displayed a courage and skill that elicited universal praise...[they] fought with almost scientific skill, using advance and rear guards, skirmish lines, and field fortifications." (Public Broadcasting System, *New Perspectives on the West* (www.pbs.org/weta/thewest/ : accessed 2 November 2008), People: " 'Chief Joseph,' Hin-mah-too-yah-lat-kekt (1840-1904).")

When Chief Joseph finally surrendered he made the speech which has woven itself unforgettably into the fabric of the American psyche:

I am tired of fighting. Our chiefs are killed. Looking Glass is dead. The old men are all dead. It is the young men who say "Yes" or "No." He who led the young men [Olikut] is dead. It is cold and we have no blankets. The little children are freezing to death. My people, some of them, have run away to Hills, and have no blankets, no food. No one knows where they are –perhaps freezing to death. I want to have time to look for my children, and see how many of them I can find. Maybe I shall find them among the dead. Hear me, my chiefs! I am tired. My heart is sick and sad. From where the sun now stands I will fight no more forever.

Many of Chief Joseph's people died of disease while they languished, first in Eastern Kansas and then in Oklahoma. Despite his efforts to get the federal government to return the Nez Perce to the state of Washington, he was only able to return to the state in 1885. Even then, his people were split between Idaho and a location in northern Washington rather than returned to their home, the Wallowa Valley.

From *New Perspectives on the West*, "'Chief Joseph,' Hin-mah-too-yah-lat-kekt (1840-1904)."

Tales of Lost Spanish Gold: Baptiste Peoria and Patrick McNaughton

John Patrick McNaughton and family in 1910, from Steve Wilson, *Oklahoma Treasurers and Treasure Tales* (Norman, Oklahoma: University of Oklahoma Press, 1976), 250.

Steve Wilson, author of *Oklahoma Treasures and Treasure Tales* (Norman, Oklahoma: University of Oklahoma Press, 1976), collected stories from the former Indian Territory of Oklahoma related to lost mines and buried gold stashes from the Spaniards. While the stories abounded, only a few of these legendary mines have been found. One of the stories, related by Baptiste Peoria, speaks of buried treasure; the other is a true story Patrick McNaughton's discovery of one of the old mines. Patrick McNaughton married Clara Peery, daughter of David Peery and granddaughter of Baptiste Peoria.

Baptiste Peoria's Legend
by Steve Wilson

In 1868, Baptiste Peoria, chief of the Peoria Indians, moved his tribe to a location seven miles west of Miami [Oklahoma] and settled near a large grove of locust trees. In later years, when the moon was full and the campfire burned low, the old chief often delighted in telling a story about the locust grove. It was a tale he earnestly believed, and those who listened believed it, too.

A party of Mexicans were leading a caravan of burros across his land, traveling westward. Three of the little burros were loaded with heavy deerskin sacks of gold and silver. Chief Peoria had heard that the Mexicans had mined the ore in the hills nearby. He believed the rumor to be true, for many old shafts were discovered in the region in later years.

Somehow the Mexicans received word of a patrol of United States soldiers on their trail. No one knew what the soldiers were up to, but the Mexicans were taking no chances. They knew that they could not fight because they were too few in number. Instead, they would bury the ore and return for it later.

"But how can we find our treasure again?" asked one of the men. Their leader remembered that he had brought along a bag of locust seeds. These they would plant above the treasure. The seedlings would serve as a marker. The hole was dug, and the bags were taken from the burros' backs and dropped into it. After the earth was replaced and trampled, the leader planted the seeds. The locusts would serve as an obvious landmark, for only a few such trees grew in the region.

The Mexicans rode on at a faster pace, and as far as Chief Peoria knew, the soldiers lost their trail. The locust seeds sprouted and grew, and over the years they, too, shed their seeds and those grew into more trees. In time a large locust grove had grown over the treasure the Mexicans had buried. Baptiste Peoria told his people that no one had ever returned for the "yellow iron." (pp. 293-294)

The Bonanza Patrick McNaughton Found
by Steve Wilson

Perhaps the first mine to be rediscovered was the one found in 1877 by John Patrick McNaughton. When he started his quest one hundred years ago for lost Spanish mines in the Indian Nations, he had no idea that his trail would lead him not only to lost mines but to a hidden bonanza that would one day yield millions in lead and zinc. The son of Scotch-Irish parents, McNaughton was thirteen years old at the end of the Civil War. The war had not been kind to the McNaughton family; it had taken the life of an older brother, a captain in Confederate gray, and had left his father incapacitated at the Battle of Shiloh.

Young Patrick McNaughton left his home and schooling in Petersburg, Tennessee, and migrated to Fort Smith, Arkansas, where he worked as a laborer. In 1867 he took a job as a teamster hauling cotton to Springfield, Missouri. The years that followed were spent in the Indian Territory, Fort Worth, and Salt Lake City, where he worked as a bullwhacker; in Arizona, as a mule skinner, and in Sherman, Texas, as a freighter. During those years McNaughton picked up a familiarity with minerals and a smattering of Indian languages–both of which were to prove useful in years to come.

In September, 1877, McNaughton had business in Kansas City. On the trail he met an elderly Shawnee Indian who was trying to return to his people. McNaughton detected the Indian's plight and invited him along, paying his transportation to Vinita and seeing that he had food.

As the two traveled together, McNaughton had no idea that the remainder of his life would soon be changed by the story the Indian was about to tell. The Shawnee revealed a story that was to lead McNaughton to one of the greatest and richest ore beds in the Southwest. The Indian said nothing about lead or zinc. His story concerned lost Spanish mines, to which miners from the south had journeyed with caravans in many years past and from which they had led pack animals heavily laden with shiny rock.

At first McNaughton placed little confidence in the Indian's tale, for he had heard similar stories. But as he listened, something about the Shawnee's story rang true. Business in Kansas City could wait. He parted company with the Indian at Vinita and rode to Seneca, Missouri, a border settlement, where he hired a team and buckboard and bought supplies. Then he headed west for the unsettled region along Spring River–the land of the Peoria Indians in the extreme northeastern corner of the Indian Nations.

In a few hours the frontiersman halted his horses. He found the primitive mines with little difficulty. Crude shafts and tunnels were scattered over an area of at least forty acres. It appeared that extensive digging had been done there over a long period of time. McNaughton noticed literally acres of white flint chips scattered about the excavations "like the floor of a china shop." The site was indeed old.

McNaughten believed that the Spanish miners had not exhausted the lode, and he decided to prospect the country further. First he asked the Peoria Indian agent, Hiram Jones, for permission, saying nothing about having already located the mines, but Jones would not hear of it and forbade him to enter the region. McNaughton was aware of the law prohibiting prospecting in Indian country, but it did not deter from continuing his search.

He returned to Sherman, Texas, where he interested others in his undertaking and managed a grubstake from George W. Newcombe, a wealthy resident. Together they decided to take the matter directly to the Department of the Interior. Mr. McNaughton went to Washington and persuaded the Secretary of the Interior Carl Shurz to grant him a special permit to prospect for mineral on the Peorias' land–but that was all. He was still prohibited from mining or selling ore. Even so, he could now carry on his search.

In 1878, McNaughton obtained leases from the Peorias and began prospecting west of the Spanish mines near what later became the settlement of Peoria. There he found not gold but lead and zinc. For more than a decade it seemed that he would never be permitted to exploit his bonanza. The Department of the Interior held firm to its original prospecting-only restriction.

In 1889 McNaughton's dream began to come true. He hauled in mining equipment from Texas, organized the Peoria Mining Company, and sank a shaft to pay dirt. By 1891 about fifteen hundred whites were in what was later to become Ottawa County, more than half of them miners or associated with mining. Peoria soon boasted a hotel, a blacksmith shop, a post office, and a schoolhouse surrounded by an army of miners' huts and shacks. Peoria's population swelled to eight hundred, and in the middle of it all was Patrick McNaughton.

But Peoria's boom was not to last long. The longevity of any mining camp depends upon its ore reserve. One company after another moved out, and by 1896 Peoria's population had dropped to 205. Although McNaughton had rediscovered the Spanish mines and went on to find what became a bonanza in lead and zinc, he never realized the wealth that others were to wrest from the underground treasure. (pp.249-250)

Memories of the Dead
By Sarah Lykins Russell

Along the West, the sunset splendors burn,
And soft, and still the evening shadows fall;
With lonely heart, and tearful eyes I turn,
To where there hangs, upon my chamber wall,
Three pictured faces, whose unshadowed eyes,
Serene and changeless, look into mine own;
Like birds that flit, when winter storms arise,
Their souls, to Heaven's summer clime, have flown.

My little maiden, with the nut-brown hair,
And eyes like summer lakelets, calm, and blue;
In the sweet dawn of girlhood, pure, and fair,
She was the first to vanish from our view.
Through the long golden days of Summer's bloom,
Patient and meek, she faded day by day;
And when the roses shed their last perfume,
We wept above her beauteous form of clay.

A year had told its changing seasons o'er
Above our darling Effie's place of rest,
When sorrow's cup, more bitter than before,
Again unto my shrinking lips was pressed.
My gentle sister, words can never tell,
How turned my heart, in grief's dark hours to thee-
On my sad soul, like summer sunshine fell
Thy tender words of hope and sympathy.

Little my sorrow-clouded life had known
Of joys that shed o'er happier lives their light,
But for the sweet and constant radiances thrown

From thy true heart o'er disappointment's night.
Dear, faithful heart! Dear, tender, patient hands!
　So tireless in love's holy ministry;
　Oh! Sister, scarce amid the angel bands,
　Purer or dearer couldst thou seem to me.

　When the New Year, its record had begun,
　I little thought that e'er a month had fled–
Thy bright, brief life–thy young existence done–
　Willie, that thou wouldst be among the dead,
　My noble boy–my only darling son–
In youth's fair springtime, full of promise bright;
Oh! Death, couldst thou not leave mine only one–
　My star of hope–in desolation's night?

　I look upon thy pictured face, my boy;
　On thy glad, open brow, thy forehead fair;
　And midst my anguish feel a thrill of joy,
That earth's dark passions left no shadow there,
Faithful and true wert thou in thy young years,
Walking with steadfast feet truth's shining way;
　Father! I bless thee, 'mid these bitter tears,
　For the sweet memories that are mine today.

Dear household angels, other hearts may change;
　Earth's truest ones may falter or forget,
But naught hath power to shadow or estrange
　The love whereon death's sacred seal is set.
　Like hoarded jewels, memory shall keep
Each dear familiar smile, and look, and tone,
Till I shall come to share thy dreamless sleep,
　And walk no more life's weary ways alone.

From Mattie Lykins Scrapbook, Kansas City, April, 1873. Western Historical Manuscripts Archive, University of Missouri-Kansas City, Kansas City, Missouri.

The Editor's Guests
By Will Carleton

The Editor sat in his sat in his sanctum, his countenance furrowed with care.
    His mind at the bottom of business, his feet at the top of a chair,
    His chair-arm an elbow supporting, his right hand upholding his head,
    His eyes on his dusty old table, with different documents spread:
There were thirty long pages from Howler, with underlined capitals topped,
    And a short disquisition from Growler, requesting his newspaper stopped:
There were lyrics from Gusher, the poet, concerning sweet flow'rets and zephyrs,
    And a stray gem from Plodder, the farmer, describing a couple of heifers;
There were billets from beautiful maidens, and bills from a grocer or two,
    And his best leader hitched to a letter, which inquired if he wrote it, or who?
There were raptures of praises from writers of the weakly mellifluous school,
    And one of his rival's last papers, informing him he was a fool;
There were several long resolutions, with names telling whom they were by,
Canonizing some harmless old brother who had done nothing worse than to die.
There were traps on that table to catch him, and serpents to sting and to smite him;
    There were long staring "ads" from the city, and money with never a one,
Which added, "Please give this insertion, and send in your bill when you're -done-;"
There were letters from organizations–their meetings, their wants, and their laws–
Which said, "Can you print this announcement for the good of our glorious cause?"
    There were tickets inviting his presence to festivals, parties, and shows,
    Wrapped in notes with "Please give us a notice" demurely slipped in at the close;
    In short, as his eye took the table, and ran o'er its ink-spattered trash,
    There was nothing it did not encounter, excepting perhaps it was cash.

    The Editor dreamily pondered on several ponderous things.
    On different lines of action, and the pulling of different strings;
    Upon some equivocal doings, and some unequivocal duns;
    On how few of his numerous patrons were quietly prompt-paying ones;
    On friends who subscribed "just to help him," and wordy encouragement lent,
    And had given him plenty of counsel, but never had paid him a cent;
    On vinegar, kind-hearted people were feeding him every hour,
Who saw not the work they were doing, but wondered that "printers are sour."
    On several intelligent townsmen, whose kindness was so without sting
That they kept an eye out on his business, and told him just what he should print;
    On men who had rendered him favors, and never pushed forward their claims,
    So long as the paper was crowded with "locals" containing their names;
    On various other small matters, sufficient his temper to roil,

And finely contrived to be making the blood of an editor boil;
And so one may see that his feelings could hardly be said to be smooth,
And he needed some pleasant occurrence his ruffled emotions to soothe:
He had it; for lo! On the threshold, a slow and reliable tread,
And a farmer invaded the sanctum, and these are the words that he said:

"Good-morning', sir, Mr. Printer; how is your body to-day?
I'm glad you're to home; for you fellers is al'ays a runnin'away.
Your paper last week wa'n't so spicy nor sharp as the one week before:
But I s'pose when the campaign is opened, you'll be whoopin'it up to 'em more.
That feller that's printin'–The Smasher–is goin' for you perty smart;
And our folks said this morning' at breakfast, they thought he was gettin' the start.
But I hushed 'em right up in a minute, and said a good word for you;
I told'em I b'lieved you was tryin' to do just as well as you knew;
And I told'em that some one was saying" , and whoever 'twas it is so,
That you can't expect of no one man, nor blame him for what he don't know.
But layin' aside-pleasure-for business, I've brought you my little boy Jim;
And I thought I would see if you couldn't make an editor outen of him.

"My family stock is increasin', while other folks' seems to run short.
I've got a right smart of a family–it's one of the old-fashioned sort;
There's Ichabod, Isaac, and Israel, a-workin' away on the farm–
They do 'bout as much as one good boy, and make things go off like a charm.
There's Moses and Aaron are sly ones, and slip like a couple of eels;
But they're tol'able steady in one thing–they al'ays git round to their meals.
There's Peter is busy inventin' (though "what" he invents I can't see),
And Joseph is studyin' medicine–and both of 'em boardin' with me.
There's Abram and Albert is married, each workin' my farm for myself,
And Sam smashed his nose at a shootin', and so he is laid on the shelf.

The rest of the boys are all growin', 'cept this little runt, which is Jim,
And I thought that perhaps I'd be makin' an editor outen o' him.
"He ain't no great shakes for to labor, though I've labored with him a good deal,
And give him some strappin' good arguments I know he couldn't help but to feel;
But he's built out of second-growth timber, and nothin'about him is big
Exceptin' his appetite only, and there he's as good as a pig.
I keep him a-carryin'luncheons, and fillin' and bringin' the jugs,
And take him among the potatoes, and set him to pickin' the bugs;
And then there is things to be doin' a-helpin' the women indoors;
There's churnin' and washin' of dishes, and other descriptions of chores;
But he don't take to nothin' but victuals, and he'll never be much, I'm afraid,

So I thought it would be a good notion to larn him the editor's trade.
His body's too small for a farmer, his judgment is rather too slip,
But I thought we perhaps could be makin' an editor outen o' him!

It ain't much to get up a paper–it wouldn't take him long for to learn;
He could feed the machine, I'm thinkin', with a good strappin' fellow to turn.
And things that was once hard in doin', is easy enough now to do;
Just keep your eye on your machinery, and crack your arrangements right through.
I used to wonder at readin' and where it was got up, and how;
But 'tis most of it made by machinery–I can see it all plain enough now.
And poetry, too, is constructed by machines of different designs,
Each one with a gauge and a chopper to see to the length of the lines;
And I hear a New York clairvoyant is runnin' one sleeker than grease,
And "a-rentin" her heaven-born productions at a couple of dollars apiece;
An' since the whole trade has growed easy, 'twould be easy enough, I've a whim,
If you was agreed, to be makin' an editor outen of Jim!"

The Editor sat in his sanctum and looked the old man in the eye,
Then glanced at the grinning young hopeful, and mournfully made his reply:
"Is your son a small unbound edition of Moses and Solomon both?
Can he compass his spirit with meekness, and strangle a natural oath?
Can he leave all his wrongs to the future, and carry his heart in his cheek?
Can he do an hour's work in a minute, and live on a sixpence a week?
Can he courteously talk to an equal, and browbeat an impudent dunce?
Can he keep things in apple-pie order, and do half a dozen at once?
Can he press all the springs of knowledge, with quick and reliable touch,
And be sure that he knows how much "to" know, and knows how to not know too much
Does he know how to spur up his virtue, and put a check-rein on his pride?
Can he carry a gentleman's manners within a rhinoceros' hide?
Can he know all, and do all, and be all, with cheerfulness, courage and vim?
If so, we perhaps can be makin an editor 'outen of him.'"

The farmer stood curiously listening, while wonder his visage o'erspread;
And he said, "Jim, I guess we'll be goin'; he's probably out of his head."

And lo! The rickety stair-case, another reliable tread,
And entered another old farmer, and these are the words that he said:

"Good-morning, sir, Mr. Editor, how is the folks to-day?
I owe you for next year's paper; I thought I'd come in and pay.
And Jones is agoin' to take it, and this is his money here;

I shut down on lendin' it to him, and coaxed him to try it a year.
And here is a few little items that happened last week in our town:
I thought they'd look good for the paper, and so I just jotted 'em down.
And here is a basket of cherries my wife picked expressly for you;
And a small bunch of flowers from Jennie–she thought she must send somethin' too.
You're doin' the politics bully, as all of our family agree;
Just keep your old goose-quill a-floppin', and give 'em a good one for me.
And now you are chuck full of business, and I won't be takin' your time;
I've things of my own I must 'tend to–good-day, sir, I b'lieve I will climb."

The Editor sat in his sanctum and brought down his fist with a thump:
"God bless that old farmer," he muttered, "he's a regular Editor's trump."

And 'tis thus with our noble profession, and thus it will ever be, still;
There are some who appreciate its labors, and some who perhaps never will.
But in the great time that is coming, when loudly the trumpet shall sound,
And they who have labored and rested shall come from the quivering ground;
When they who have striven and suffered to teach and ennoble the race,
Shall march at the front of the column, each one in his God-given place,
As they pass through the gates of The City with proud and victorious tread,
The editor, printer, and "devil," will travel not far from the head.

From Will Carleton, *Farm Ballads*, 1875.

A Roaring Mob:
How New York Appeared on Election Night

People Good Natured

Through Din and Tumult the Individual Rarely Lost His Temper, Being Out for a Good Time

Special Correspondence of the Capital.

New York, Nov. 15.–Crossing the great North river in the ferryboat late in the evening of election day, the closes observer did not behold any unusual spectacle. Across the expanse of tossing, fretful, shimmering, oily looking water, one saw Manhattan island a-twinkle with the lights; saw the tall buildings, silent and noncommittal, rising in a great dark company (for they were mostly deserted then); saw hundreds of lesser structures in the dim light along the water front; saw the boats and barges, and all sorts and conditions of shipping craft crouching along the island line–but heard not at all any hint of the tumult in the town. Yet there was such tumult there as is seldom witnessed in that great, impatient city.

The dome of the World building, hard by Printing House square, girt with variegated electric lights, rose proudly to a dizzy height, and seemed to say: "I am in the heart of the tumult and confusion," which was literally true. Here, about Printing House square, was the storm center, embracing an area extending from spacious Central park to ancient Bowling Green.

But not until the ferryboat from Whitehall terminal had nosed her way deliberately and carefully into her slip at the foot of Liberty street and bumped into her accustomed niche; not until the clanking chains had made her fast and the gates were thrown open suddenly for your egress, could one realize that he was about to witness such an extraordinary spectacle. For there is nothing ike it elsewhere, and the sight of New York, turned out into the streets in an atmosphere of excitement and enthusiasm, is well worth anybody's while to view.

Swinging into Liberty street there is suggestion of the hubbub at hand. The turmoil is not tuneful. The cheering and shouting and huzzaing is not melodious. The tooting of horns is not akin to cadence, nor related to concord, even remotely. It is confusion and ferment and flurry. The brow of the sensitive person will contract, and he will wear a worried look. But he ought to have stayed at home. He hasn't any business down here, anyway. And this–well, this is only the overflow; the fringe of it. This you will observe presently, walking up Liberty street to Broadway; walking up Broadway to City Hall park, peering across the wilderness of heads toward the great newspaper offices, and where the activity is intense, and the intelligence bureau keyed up to the highest possible pitch. There used to be a fountain over there in the City Hall park, and a statue of Ben Franklin close by. They have both disappeared in the chaos of election: have been lost in the blur of the teeming avenues.

A few hundred thousand people can made a deal of noise without trying very hard. But when, as on an election night, individually and collectively, they take a turn at trying, the result is bewildering. Only when human endurance ceases does the uproar ebb at all–it never ends. Where thousands leave off, other thousands begin, so that there isn't any interim.

But the most remarkable thing about New York on election night is its sweet temper; the absence of ill behavior in the streets. You are not expecting this. You made allowance for a great deal when you came to town, and you had anticipated rather a rough time of it. Well, you have been disappointed, undoubtedly. New York is all smiles: all consideration; all courtesy. Under the strong glare of the electric lights are faces wreathed in smiles, growing broader and broader as the returns favorable to the President continue to arrive; as the newspapers, fresh from the press, smelling very inky, are distributed in the thoroughfares. In a brilliantly lighted café two strangers, at separate tables are bandying words and frowning fiercely. You think there will be a fight? Not at all. When you look again in their direction they are grinning good naturedly at each other. It is in the air. The people are quite happy. Croker has been treated to a Waterloo. And if New York wouldn't go wild with joy over that, what, for goodness gracious sake, would New York go wild over? Its citizens are beginning to hope. A star is rising. Tammany Hall is enshrouded in a gloom that is new to it. Whereupon the people feel a thrill at the heart. "It is the end of

Croker," they say. And they pant for the end of Croker "as the hare panteth for the water brook."

Impromptu parades are formed later in the night. On the sidewalks and in the streets and in every conceivable place the marchers may be found, singing and shouting furiously. They must give vent to their enthusiasm in some way, and this way seems harmless enough.

Midnight–1–2 o'clock. There is an increase in the volume of the uproar, and the crowds are thinning slowly. The surface cars, with their leering lights, are better able to feel their way through the more crowded districts. The elevated trains, heavily loaded, sweep hissing over their frail looking trestles, and clatter away in divers directions. The moon has shied off from the city. In shadowy corners on the various sidestreets, certain reprehensible persons, who have been very bold and very bad lie in a state of coma, waiting for the police to get around to them. The stars are about to twinkle their last twinkle. The noises are nearer normal now. Enthusiastic little wagons rattle over the paving stones–trying to beat the day to it, maybe. New York is very tired, but very happy.

Leslie Erle Wallace

From *The Kansas Weekly Capital*, 23 Nov 1900.

Note: Richard Croker was the boss of Tammany Hall in New York. In 1900 Croker made sure that New York's Democratic party delegation endorsed William Jennings Bryan for U.S. president. The Republicans nominated a major enemy of Tammany Hall as their vice-presidential nominee, Governor Theodore Roosevelt. Roosevelt campaigned vigorously, tirelessly attacking Bryan for his association with the boss of Tammany Hall and its rampant corruption. In his final days as governor, Roosevelt fired Tammany Hall puppets. The disgruntled Croker resigned from City Hall and retired to an estate in his native Ireland.

"The Glory of Pawnee County"

Leslie Wallace, Larned, Kns., Editor, Enlightens an Inquisitive Stranger

Leslie E. Wallace, once a Kansas City newspaper man, but for three years editor of the Larned, Kas., *Tiller and Toiler*, walking up a familiar street from the Union Station today enveloped in a great coat, felt a hand tugging his arm.

The man was out of breath from a short chase.

"Pardon," broke in the stranger, "but I never saw an overcoat that caught my fancy as much as the one you wear. I said to myself, I don't know that man, but I will know the coat. Stranger, where did you come by that coat?"

"Friend," answered Mr. Wallace, "this coat comes from the short grass country."

"I knew it was a distinctive coat."

"But the mark under the collar is that of a clothing manufacturer made nationally known by advertising," Mr. Wallace continued, "It is advertised in *The Kansas City Star* and the Larned *Tiller and Toiler*. I don't mind tipping you that you can buy this coat right here in Kansas City, and I am proud you can also buy it in Larned, Pawnee County, Kansas.

"Friend, if a man needed a coat and had the time to go to Larned, Pawnee County, Kansas, for it he would be repaid.

"He would find a county of only nine thousand people subscribing to $100,000 of the bonds of the second Liberty Loan with the campaign not ended. You can figure the number of bonds to a home. He would find a county that, with a crop failure, has more deposits in the bank than ever before. A complete failure in wheat, and raising a little corn, Pawnee County just turns back and draws on the last three years of plenty. The farmers–one of them subscribed for $5000 worth of bonds yesterday.

"And out in Larned you would find the weekly *Tiller and Toiler* installing a Goss 'Comet' perfecting press that will reduce its press work from sixteen hours to ninety minutes. I wish you a good day, stranger."

"Now that was a queer incident," mused Mr. Wallace as he moved away and came up with an acquaintance of his old Kansas City days. "Still, a Larned man is never unduly suspicious of strangers. He just puts his hand on his purse and talks Pawnee County. If the stranger is of good intent, it is a word well placed."

From *The Kansas City Star*, 25 Oct 1917.

SELECTED POEMS

by

Leslie Earle Wallace,
Eunice Wallace Shore Rhea,
and Ralph L. Wallace

Dream Days

By Leslie Erle Wallace

Where are the lights that lured me here,
   Out of the gold of another year?
Where are the dreams that used to rise
   And toss their glory in the skies?
Where are the pathways leading me
   Out to the open of the sea?
Where are the faces laughing through
   The years that I have struggled to?
Oh, my heart, can you tell me where
These blossoms of our Dream Days are?
   Beyond my ken the colors flew
   Like wild birds on approach of me;
But leave the tears and tenderness
And leave me faded flowers to press,
And leave me hope that some time I
Shall walk where glory cannot died,
   Apast the mists but more than this
They leave me dreams of Old World bliss;
And these dreams were the angel wings
   That lifted me to higher things.

From the *Kansas City Star*, 13 Mar 1898.

Trees on the Plains
By Leslie Earle Wallace

Trees on the plains are braver trees
Than those found otherwhere;
For like a sailor on the seas,
Or like a soldier, trees like these
Go forth to war.

They face the boisterous winds that blow;
Now East, now West, now North;
They face the onslaughts of the foe,
They face the droughts that scourge them so,
As they fare forth.

And some are leaning in the end,
Lean in the battle's wake–
The winds may bend, but do not rend;
Invincible these trees that bend,
But do not break.

Some dwarfed and some misshapen are,
Some gnarled and some combine
The twisted fantasies that mar
Those forms that hug the hills afar,
At timberline.

Trees on the plains are braver trees
Than those found otherwhere;
For like a sailor on the seas,
Or like a soldier, trees like these
Go forth to war.

From *Contemporary Kansas Poetry*, 1927.

Steel Mill

By Ralph L. Wallace, age 20

Inferno wakes each night. The roaring cars
Thunder their hatred while the scream of steel
Is never silenced; to the lonely stars
Rises the clamor as the smoke hordes wheel
Across a sky made venomous with flame
And bitter in defilement. Broken men
Carry the cross of Greed through fires of Shame
And each red night are crucified again!

Peace and the lonely shore...the night unending
Holds the great haven of the silver sea
Lovely with final peace. O God, I'll bring
My broken body there, and stretch to Thee
My ruined arms, and catch the clean, salt breath
Of swelling waves as I sweep out to death.

Published in *The Harp: a Poetry Magazine*, January-February, 1928.

Sonnet

By Ralph L. Wallace

I shall remember all the lovely things
 Better forgotten, and recurrent pain
Will stab, sans mercy, when a woman sings,
Remembering you, who will not sing again.
 I shall remember nights, star-glorious,
  And tenderness unmuted as a star–
  All the bright hours given unto us
 Will be as winds where summer roses are.

Will be as winds–will be as winds to clear
 The desolation of our unmarked track,
Lonely as death. If in that time I hear
Your voice again, the winds will lead me back.
 I shall remember, O grave and beautiful,
 How glad we were, and now, how pitiful.

Published in *The Harp: A Poetry Magazine,* January-February, 1932.

By Ralph L. Wallace

At last I think a haven comes for those
Frail-hearted creatures who have braved the night
With frenzied courage for a dream that goes
Down through the darkness and is yet alight
In memory, in loveliness, I believe
That there are meadows in the world above
For summer merriment where flame-white Eve
Walks through bright garden toward remembered love.

In the green world there is no Hellespont,
No current to drag down the lifted hand,
No breaking waves upon the heart, that gaunt
From overmuch despairing seeks the land
As birds seek islands in a storm-whipped sea,
Beating their waves against immensity.

The Tiller and Toiler; reprinted in *The Augusta Gazette,* 1 June 1935.

Nocturne

By Eunice Wallace, age 20

My cat
Lives in the moon;
His eyes are moons;
His two eyes are green moons
Like the moon in the winter dusk,
Green, pale, almost white
Filled with white fire,
Cold moons.

His eyes are harvest moons,
Filled with red fire,
Round moons,
Which blaze unflickering.

His eyes are crescent moons,
Two slender new moons. . .
I have seen them in the eclipse.

I know that this is true,
Because the other night,
He climbed into the moon,
For a moment the moon, the full moon
Rested
On my back fence;
He jumped in,
It swallowed him.

From *Contemporary Poetry*, 1927.

Loss

By Eunice Wallace

Something has happened to the night,
So long ago it was I felt its pulse
Beating up close to mine, its dreaming shadows
Fluttered across my throat, and then lay still.
Now the low moan of winds across the hill
Clutters the leaves, and yet I know it's true
There is no wind, except in my own heart.

Where is the gift of loving that I bore?
Here with the night comes the sweet trembling song
Of shimmering leaves sweeping across the sky
And turning silver the bright gold of day.
For me the silver light is only gray.
There is no wind, and Beauty's pale, slim fingers
Have lingered here, and passed, to come no more.

No radiance any more–only the dark,
So black there is no memory of day,
Nor any mark of beauty I once loved–
Sun on the heavy trees or the swift dawn–
For me and for my heart these things are gone.
The wind is blowing cold across my heart,
And all the stars have fallen into the sea.

Published in *Kansas Magazine*, 1936.

Prairie Grave

By Eunice Wallace Shore

Warm is the midnight rain that is falling above me,
And warm is the wind that will rise when the night is over,
Quiet the night and drowsy the ones who love me,
And peaceful and still it is with the earth for cover.

I loved the sun on the ivory yucca flowers,
Loved the moonlight that covered the earth with whiteness,
Marked shining slimness of castled granary towers,
But, lying here, I miss neither blooms nor brightness.

For today I have heard the song of the sun's returning,
Have known the dream of the wheat and the corn's green gladness,
Have heard the day pass over the hills' blue burning,
And marked the death of field things without dark sadness.

For tonight I know that within this earth where I'm sleeping,
Life comes dreaming today, and Death is music tomorrow,
And we who lie with the roots of Life are not weeping,
For one with the wonder of birth, we cannot feel sorrow.

The Kansas City Star; reprinted in *Kansas Magazine*, 1944.

SELECTED BIBLIOGRAPHY

Abel, Annie Heloise. *The American Indian as Participant in the Civil War.* Cleveland, Ohio: Arthur H. Clark, 1919.

Anderson, Ephraim McDowell. *Memoirs, historical and personal: including the campaigns of the First Missouri Confederate Brigade.* Second edition. Edwin C. Bearss, editor. Dayton, Ohio: Morningside Bookshop, 1972.

Barry, Louise. *The Beginning of the West: Annals of the Kansas Gateway to the American West, 1540-1854.* Topeka: Kansas State Historical Society, 1972.

Beckwith, Hiram W. *The Illinois and Indiana Indians.* Chicago: Fergus Printing, 1884.

Bingham, Martha A. "Mattie" (Livingston) Lykins. "Recollections of Old Times in Kansas City," 67-page handwritten manuscript, ca 1883 - 1890. Jackson County Historical Society Archives, Independence, Missouri, Gift of Robert Dewit Owen, in memory of his grandmother, Mrs. Dewit Livingston (Ada Campbell) Owen, Document ID 110F7.

Bonnifield, Paul. *The Dust Bowl: Men, Dirt and Depression.* Albuquerque: University of New Mexico Press, 1979.

"Brief Survey of Religious Benevolent Societies and their Operations." *The Missionary Herald* 26 (Feb 1830): 33-36.

Brown, Theodore. *Frontier Community: Kansas City to 1870.* Columbia: University of Missouri Press, 1963.

Brownlee, Richard S. *Gray Ghosts of the Confederacy.* Baton Rouge: Louisiana State University Press, 1958.

Bradford, New Hampshire, History Committee and Bicentennial Committee, and Mildred H. Gunscheon. *Two Hundred Plus: Bradford, New Hampshire, in Retrospect.* Canaan, New Hampshire: Phoenix Publishing, 1976.

Case, Nelson. *History of Labette County Kansas and its Representative Citizens.* Chicago: Biographical Publishing Company, 1901.

Castel, Albert. "Order No. 11 and the Civil War on the Border." *Missouri Historical Review*, 57 (July 1963): 357-368.

Catlin, George. *Letters and Notes on the Manners, Customs, and Conditions of North American Indians*. 2 volumes. Originally published 1841. Reprint. New York: Dover Publications, 1973.

Clark, Charles. *Kansas Bogus Legislature*. http://www.boguslegislature.org : 2008.

Cone, William W. *Historical Sketch of Shawnee County, Kansas*. Topeka: Kansas Farmer Printing House, 1877.

Connelley, William Elsey. *History of Kansas State and People: Kansas at the First Quarter Post of the Century*. 5 volumes. Chicago: American Historical Society, 1928.

Connelley, William Elsey. *Quantrill and the Border Wars*. New York: Pageant Book Company, 1956.

Cutler, William G. *History of the State of Kansas: Containing a Full Account of its Growth from an Uninhabited Territory to a Wealthy and Important State, of its Early Settlements, its Rapid Increase in Population and the Marvelous Development of its Great Natural Resources. Also, A Supplementary History and Description of its Counties, Cities, Towns and Villages, their Advantages, Industries, Manufactures and Commerce, to which are added Biographical Sketches and Portraits of Prominent Men and Early Settlers*. Chicago: A. T. Andreas, 1883.

Etcheson, Nicole. *Bleeding Kansas: Contested Liberty in the Civil War Era*. Lawrence: University Press of Kansas, 2004.

Faust, Drew Gilpin. *This Republic of Suffering: Death and the American Civil War*. New York: Vintage Books, 2009.

Findlen, Rose Ann. *Missouri Star: The Life and Times of Martha A. "Mattie" (Livingston) Lykins Bingham*. Independence, Missouri: Jackson County Historical Society, 2011.

Frazier, Harriet C. *Runaway and Freed Missouri Slaves and Those Who Helped Them, 1763-1865*. Jefferson, North Carolina: McFarland and Company, 2004.

Geary, Daniel. "Looking Backward." *Annals of Kansas City* 1 (Dec 1922): 224-235.

Gibson, Arrell Morgan. *The American Indian: Prehistory to the Present.* Lexington, Massachusetts: D. C. Heath, 1980.

Gideon, D.C. *Indian Territory, Descriptive, Biographical and Genealogical... with a General History of the Territory.* New York: Lewis Publishing Company, 1901.

Gihon, John H. *Geary and Kansas; Governor Geary's Administration in Kansas with complete History of the Territory until June 1857.* Philadelphia: J. H. C. Whiting, 1857.

Gilmore, Donald. *Civil War on the Missouri-Kansas Border.* Gretna, Louisiana: Pelican Publishing Company, 2006.

Goodrich, Thomas. *Black Flag: Guerrilla Warfare on the Western Border, 1861-1865: A Riveting Account of a Bloody Chapter in Civil War History.* Bloomington: Indiana University Press, 1999.

Goodrich, Thomas. *War to the Knife: Bleeding Kansas 1854-1861.* Lincoln: University of Nebraska Press, 1988.

Grove, Nettie Thompson and Walter Wayne Smith. "Notes on the Pioneer School of Kansas City, Part One." *Annals of Kansas City* 1 (Dec 1922):73-177.

Haynes, Martin A. *A History of the Second Regiment, New Hampshire Volunteer Infantry, in the War of the Rebellion.* Lakeport, New Hampshire: np, 1896.

Hill, Esther Clark. "Some Background of Early Baptist Missions of Kansas." *Kansas Historical Quarterly* 1 (Feb 1932): 89-103.

Hoopes, Helen Rhoda, editor. *Contemporary Kansas Poetry.* Lawrence, Kansas: Franklin Watts, 1927.

Hutchinson, Dennis. *31st Indiana Volunteer Infantry.* http://www.psci.net/hutch/31hist.html : 2008.

Johnson, Samuel A. "The Emigrant Aid Company in Kansas." *Kansas Historical Quarterly* 1 (Nov 1932): 429-441.

Jones, James B. "The Use and Abuse of Drugs in Nineteenth Century Tennessee History." *Historical Findings*. www.netowne.com/historical/tennessee/drugs.htm: 2008.

Kansas State Board of Agriculture. *First Biennial Report of the State Board of Agriculture to the Legislature of the State of Kansas, for the Years 1877-8*. Topeka: Kansas State Board of Agriculture, 1878.

King, James L., compiler and editor. *History of Shawnee County Kansas, and Representative Citizens*. Chicago: Richmond and Arnold, 1905.

Klassen, Joe. "The Civil War in Kansas City." *The Bulletin–Missouri Historical Society* 16 (Jan 1960):34-150.

Laurent, Louis Charles. "Reminiscences by the Son of a French Pioneer." *Collections of the Kansas State Historical Society*, 13 (1913-1914): 364-373.

Lyons, Emory J. *Isaac McCoy: His Plan of and Work for Indian Colonization*. Fort Hays Kansas State College Studies, General Series, no. 9, History Series, no. 1. Topeka, Kansas: Ferd Voiland, 1945.

McBride, Lela J. *Opothleyaholo and the Loyal Muskogee: Their Flight to Kansas in the Civil War*. Jefferson, North Carolina, McFarland and Company, 2000.

McCoy, Isaac. *History of Baptist Indian Missions: Embracing Remarks on the Former and Present Condition of the Aboriginal Tribes and their Settlement within the Indian Territory, and Their Future Prospects*. Washington: William M. Morrison; New York: H. and S. Raynor, 1840.

[McCoy, Isaac]. *Periodic Account of Baptist Missions within the Indian Territory for the Year Ending December 31, 1836*. Shawanoe Baptist Mission, Indian Territory: Isaac M'Coy [J. Meeker Printer], 1837.

McCullough, David. *Truman*. New York: Simon and Schuster, 1992.

McLachlin, H.M. *The Story of Paola, Kansas, 1857-1950*. [Paola, Kansas: Miami County Historical Society, 1950?].

McMurtrie, Douglas and Albert Allen. *Jotham Meeker: Pioneer Printer of Kansas*. Chicago: Eyncourt Press, 1930.

Malin, James C. *John Brown and the Legend of Fifty-Six*. Memoirs of the American Philosophical Society, vol. 17. Philadelphia: American Philosophical Society, 1942.

Malin, James C. "Judge Lecompte and the 'Sack of Lawrence,' May 21, 1856." *Kansas Historical Quarterly* 20 (Aug 1953): 465-494, 553-597.

Miami County Historical Society. *Paola, Kansas, a 150-Year Timeline: One Hundred and Fifty Years of History Events That Made Paola What It Is Today*. Paola, Kansas: Miami County Historical Society, 2006.

Moore, Ely, Jr. "The Story of Lecompton, an Address at an Old Settlers' Meeting, 1907." *Collections of the Kansas State Historical Society, 1909-1910*, 11 (1910): 463-480.

Morgan, Lewis Henry. *The Indian Journals, 1859-1962*. Ann Arbor: University of Michigan Press, 1959.

Morris, Charles, editor. *The Great Republic by the Master Historians*, 4 volumes. New York: The Great Republic Publishing Company, 1913.

Nagel, Paul C. *George Caleb Bingham: Missouri's Famed Painter and Forgotten Politician*. Columbia, Missouri: University of Missouri Press, 2005.

Neely, Jeremy. *The Border Between Them: Violence and Reconciliation on the Missouri-Kansas Line*. Columbia, Missouri: University of Missouri Press, 2007.

Nichols, Alice. *Bleeding Kansas*. New York: Oxford University Press, 1954.

Payne, Edwin W. *History of the Thirty-Fourth Regiment of Illinois Volunteer Infantry*. Clinton, Iowa: Allen Printing, 1903.

Porter, P.B. "Report of the Secretary of War, with a Detailed Statement of the Several tribes of Indians within the U.S. and the Extent and Location of Certain Lands to which the Indian Title has been Extinguished." 20th Congress, 2d Session, Senate Document 27. Washington, D.C.: Duff Green, 1829, 1865 serial 181.

Rau, Donald. "Three Cheers for Father Cummings." *Yearbook, Supreme Court Historical Society* (1977): 20-28.

Reynolds, David S. *John Brown, Abolitionist: The Man Who Killed Slavery, Sparked the Civil War and Seeded Civil Rights*. New York: Alfred A. Knopf, 2005.

Rice, Martin. "What I Saw of Order No. 11." *The Westport Historical Quarterly*, 2 (Feb 1967): 6-13.

Robinson, Sara T.L. *Kansas: its interior and exterior life: including a full view of its settlement, political history, social life, climate, soil, productions, scenery, etc.* Boston: Crosby, Nichols, 1856.

Roustio, Edward R. *Early Indian Missions as Reflected in the Unpublished Manuscripts of Isaac McCoy*. Springfield, Missouri: Particular Baptist Press, 2000.

Rutt, Christian Ludwig. *History of Buchanan County and the City of St. Joseph and Representative Citizens, 1826 to 1904*. Chicago: Biographical Publishing, 1904.

Sanborn, F.B. *The Life and Letters of John Brown: Liberator of Kansas, and Martyr of Virginia*. New York: Negro Universities Press, 1885.

Spalding, C. C. *Annals of the City of Kansas Embracing Full Details of the Trade and Commerce of the Great Western Plains. . . .* Kansas City, Kansas: Van Horn & Abell, 1858.

Spring, Leverett Wilson. *Kansas: The Prelude to the War for the Union*. Boston: Houghton Mifflin, 1885.

Stallings, Frank L., Jr. *Black Sunday: The Great Dust Storm of April 14, 1935*. Austin, Texas: Eakin Press, 2001.

Stampp, Kenneth M. *America in 1857: A Nation on the Brink*. New York: Oxford University Press, 1990.

Thomas, John. *A history of the Thirty-First Regiment of Indiana Volunteer Infantry in the War of the Rebellion*. Cincinnati: Western Methodist Book Concern, 1900.

Trennert, Robert A. *Indian Traders on the Middle Border: the House of Ewing, 1827-54*. Lincoln: University of Nebraska Press, 1981.

Trowbridge, M[ary] E[lizabeth] D[ay]. *History of Baptists in Michigan*. [Philadelphia]: Michigan Baptist State Convention, 1909.

Tucker, Philip Thomas. *The South's Finest: The First Missouri Confederate Brigade from Pea Ridge to Vicksburg*. Shippensburg, Pennsylvania: White Mane Publishing, 1993.

Under both flags : a panorama of the great Civil War as represented in story, anecdote, adventure and the romance of reality, written by celebrities of both sides, the men and women who created the greatest epoch of our nation's history. San Francisco: J. Dewing, [1896].

Union Cemetery Historical Society. *Soldiers buried at Union Cemetery, Kansas City, MO*. 5 volumes. Kansas City, Missouri: Union Cemetery Historical Society, 1990.

Union Historical Company. *History of Buchanan County, Missouri: Containing a History of the County, Its Cities, Towns, Etc*. Saint Joseph, Missouri: Union Historical Company, 1881.

Union Historical Society. *History of Jackson County, Missouri: Containing a History of the County, its Cities, Towns, etc., Biographical Sketches of its Citizens . . . .* Kansas City, Missouri: Union Historical Society, 1881.

United States. House of Representatives. "Report of the Special Committee Appointed to Investigate the Troubles in Kansas, with the views of the minority of said committee." 34th Congress, 1st Session, House Report 200. Washington, D. C: C. Wendell, 1856, serial 869.

United States. Office of Indian Affairs. *Annual Report of the Commissioner of Indian Affairs, Transmitted with the Message of the President at the Opening of the First Session of the Thirty-Second Congress, 1851*. Washington, D. C.: Government Publishing Office, 1851.

United States. Office of Indian Affairs. *Annual Report of the Commissioner of Indian Affairs Transmitted with the Message of the President at the Opening of the Second Session of the Thirty-Second Congress, 1852*. Washington, D. C.: Government Printing Office, 1852.

United States. Office of Indian Affairs. *Report of the Commissioner of Indian Affairs for the Year 1862*. Washington, D. C.: Government Printing Office, 1863.

United States. War Department. *The War of the Rebellion: A Compilation of the Official Records of the Union and Confederate Armies*. 70 volumes. Washington, D. C.: Government Printing Office, 1889.

Villard, Oswald Garrison. *John Brown, 1800-1859; A Biography Fifty Years After*. New York: Alfred A. Knopf, 1943.

Wallace, Berenice Boyd, compiler. *History of Paola, Kansas, 1855-1955*. Paola, Kansas: Miami County Genealogy and Historical Societies, [1955].

Watts, Dale. "How Bloody was Bleeding Kansas? Political Killings in Kansas Territory, 1854-1861." *Kansas History* 18 (Summer 1995):16-129.

Wilder, Daniel Webster. *Annals of Kansas*. Topeka, Kansas: George W. Marten, 1875.

Williams, Burton. "Quantrill's Raid on Lawrence: A Question of Complicity." *Kansas Historical Quarterly* 34 (Summer 1968):43-149.

Wyeth, Walter N. *Isaac McCoy; Early Indian Missions*. Philadelphia: American Baptist Publication Society [ca. 1895].

Yeatman, Ted P. *Frank and Jesse James*. Nashville, Tennessee: Cumberland House Publishing, 2003.

ILLUSTRATIONS

Images

Cover

Detail, "St. Louis from the River Below," by George Catlin, 1832-33, Used with permission of Smithsonian American Art Museum, Gift of Mrs. Joseph Harrison, Jr., Accession number 1985.66.311.

Foreword

v. Emeline Peery Heiskell. Courtesy Paola Free Library, Paola, Kansas.

Chapter 1

12. Oil painting of Baptiste Peoria. Courtesy of Miami County Genealogical and Historical Society, Paola, Kansas.

17. "A Pioneer Dwelling," from *History of La Porte County Indiana* (Chicago: Chas. C. Chapman and Co., 1880), p. 139.

20. Map of Indian Territory "Sketch Map Showing the Main Theatre of Border Warfare and the Location of Tribes Within the Indian Country," in Annie Heloise Abel, *The Slaveholding Indians, Volume II* (Cleveland: The Arthur H. Clark Co., 1919), p. 38.

23. "St. Louis from the River Below," by George Catlin, 1832-33, Used with permission of Smithsonian American Art Museum, Gift of Mrs. Joseph Harrison, Jr., Accession number 1985.66.311.

25. "Kee-mo-ra-nia, No English, a Dandy," by George Catlin, Used with permission of Smithsonian American Art Museum, Gift of Mrs. Joseph Harrison, Jr., Accession number 1985.66.253 [Kee-mo-ra-nia aka James Baptiste, son of Baptiste Peoria].

30. Johnston Lykins. Courtesy of the Kansas State Historical Society, Topeka, Kansas.

35. Page of newspaper, "Shawnee Sun." Courtesy of Missouri Valley Special Collections, Kansas City Public Library, Kansas City, Missouri.

45. Woodcut of the Cemetery at Wea Mission Station. Courtesy of Miami County Genealogical and Historical Society, Paola, Kansas.

Chapter 2

61. Drawing of Westport Road, Westport, Missouri (present-day Kansas City, Missouri) from the lid of a box owned by Mattie Lykins, circa 1852. Courtesy of Westport Historical Society, Kansas City, Missouri.

62. Tecumseh's Tomahawk. Courtesy of Westport Historical Society, Kansas City, Missouri.

66. Wea Mission. Courtesy of Miami County Genealogical and Historical Society, Paola, Kansas

77. Flyer, "The Lykins or Robitaille Float." Courtesy of Kansas State Historical Society, Topeka, Kansas (www.territorialkansasonline.org; accessed 28 June 2008).

81. William H. R. Lykins. Courtesy Kansas State Historical Society, *Kansas Collections*, 16.

83. William Alexander Heiskell. Courtesy of Miami County Genealogical and Historical Society, Paola, Kansas.

86. William H. R. Lykins's Cabin. Courtesy of Kansas State Historical Society, Topeka, Kansas.

92. Detail from John Steuart Curry's mural in the Kansas State Capitol, Topeka, Kansas. Photo courtesy of the author.

Chapter 3

104. "Residences of Lykins and Heiskell Families and Relatives, 1855-1859." Adapted from, "The Missouri-Kansas Border 1854-1860," by Donald L. Gilmore, as published in *Civil War on the Missouri-Kansas Border* (Gretna, Louisiana: Pelican Publishing Company, 2006), inside cover.

111. Detail from John Steuart Curry's mural in the Kansas State Capitol, Topeka, Kansas. Photo courtesy of the author.

134. Town Square of Paola circa 1860. Courtesy of Miami County Genealogical and Historical Society, Paola, Kansas.

135. Sue Heiskell. Courtesy of Miami County Genealogical and Historical Society, Paola, Kansas.

Chapter 4

154. "Opium—The Poor Child's Nurse," historical cartoon from "Harper's Weekly," 29 Jan. 1859 (http://www.harpweek.com/09Catoon.asp?Month=January&Date=29; accessed 28 June 2008).

163. "Camp Nevin, Kentucky." (http://www.sonofthesouth.net/leefoundation/civil-war/1861/december/camp-nevin.htm; accessed 28 June 2008).

Chapter 5

174. Judson Owen. Courtesy of Robert Dewit Owen, Judson's great-grandson.

187. "The [Lykins] home when it was the first mansion and accredited to be the finest dwelling west of St. Louis," *The Kansas City* (Mo.) *Star,* 18 Nov 1923.

198. George Caleb Bingham's painting, "Martial Law," or, "Order No. 11." Courtesy of the State Historical Society of Missouri, Columbia, Missouri.

201. Mrs. Martha A. "Mattie" (Livingston) Lykins Bingham. Photograph from, "Home for the Orphans of Confederate Soldiers," *The Kansas City* (Mo.) *Star,* 24 July 1927.

Chapter 6

226. David Peery. Courtesy of Miami County Genealogical and Historical Society, Paola, Kansas.

230. Paola Park and Town Square, 1870. Courtesy of Miami County Genealogical and Historical Society, Paola, Kansas.

233. Baptiste Peoria. Courtesy of Miami County Genealogical and Historical Society, Paola, Kansas.

239. Johnston Lykins. Portrait by George Caleb Bingham, and used with permission of Bingham-Waggoner Historical Society, 313 W. Pacific Avenue, Independence, Missouri. This portrait is on long-term loan to the Society by the Native Sons and Daughters of Kansas City.

246. Mrs. Martha A. "Mattie" (Livingston) Lykins Bingham. Photograph from, "Helping Hand for Civil War Vanquished," by Frances Bush, *Kansas City* (Mo.) *Times*, 15 Aug. 1975.

Chapter 7

254. School Room in Paola, Kansas. Courtesy of Miami County Genealogical and Historical Society, Paola, Kansas.

256. William F. Wallace. Courtesy of Wallace Kimball family of New Hampshire.

265. Paola Free Library. Courtesy of Miami County Genealogical and Historical Society, Paola, Kansas.

266. Interior of the Paola Free Library. Courtesy of Miami County Genealogical and Historical Society, Paola, Kansas.

269. Sue Heiskell (Wallace) Phillips Latimer. Courtesy of Miami County Genealogical and Historical Society, Paola, Kansas.

270. W. F. Wallace and Family in New Hampshire. Courtesy of Wallace Kimball family of New Hampshire.

Chapter 8

285. Sara LeMaistre Johnson yearbook photograph, circa 1905. Courtesy of Special Collections and Archives, Goucher College Library, Baltimore, Maryland.

290. Sara and Leslie Wallace house on the hill, Larned, Kansas. Photograph courtesy of the author.

291. The Office of, "The Tiller and Toiler," Larned, Kansas, 2008. Photograph courtesy of the author.

292. Leslie Wallace. Courtesy of Leslie Zygmund family.

294. Sara Wallace, from *The Harp*, July 1931. Courtesy of Kansas State Historical Society Archives, Topeka, Kansas.

296. Leslie Wallace. Courtesy of Kenneth Spencer Research Library, University of Kansas, Lawrence, Kansas.

301. "Bedtime in the Sky," *The Dakota Years 7: Sleep high*. (http://blogs.timeslive.co.za/wanderer/2009/o8/26/the-dakota-years-7-sleep-high/; accessed August 2008).

Related Stories and Poems

361. "Ten-Squat-a-way, The Open Door, Known as, 'The Prophet, Brother of Tecumseh'" by George Catlin (1830) Used with permission of Smithsonian American Art Museum, Gift of Mrs. Joseph Harrison, Jr., Accession number 1985.66.279. (Referenced in Chapter 2)

377. "John Patrick McNaughton and family in 1900," from, Steve Wilson, *Oklahoma Treasures and Treasure Tales* (Norman, Oklahoma: University of Oklahoma Press, 1976), 250. "Tales of Lost Spanish Gold": Baptiste Peoria and Patrick McNaughton. (Referenced in Chapter 6)

389. "Hunting the Octopus," cover of *Harper's Weekly: A Journal of Civilization*, (New York: 6 Oct. 1900) (http://www.harpweek.com/09Cartoon.asp?Month =January &Date=29; accessed August 2008). "A Roaring Mob: How New York Appeared on Election Night," by Leslie Wallace (Referenced in Chapter 8)

Charts

Chapter 1

38. Migrants to Kansas Indian Territory, 1830-1855

Chapter 2

75. New Family Connections/New Marriages, 1851-1854

Chapter 3

102. Border War Relationships, 1855-1860

Chapter 4

150. Emeline Heiskell's Relatives during the Civil War, 1861-1865

166. Civil War Soldiers in Emeline Heiskell's Family

Chapter 5

172. Missouri Family Members during the Civil War, 1861-1865

206. Friends and Relatives in Kansas City Who Enlisted

Chapter 6

222. Transitions: Moves, Marriages, Deaths, 1870s

Chapter 7

253. Sue Heiskell-William F. Wallace Connections

Chapter 8

279. Lineage of Leslie Wallace

INDEX

A

Aberdeen, Washington 325, 347
Abolitionists viii, 3, 69, 70, 72, 78, 79, 82, 100, 103, 106, 107, 108, 113, 115, 120, 136, 142, 144, 145, 147, 148, 182, 194
Adair, Florella 106
Adair, Samuel 106
Adams, Theodore 126
air transport (DC-3) 10, 307
Alameda, California 321, 324, 328
Allen County, Kansas 329, 332, 347, 354
Anderson, Bill 189, 190
Andrew County, Missouri 178, 315
Anthony, Daniel 195
Arbuckle, (Captain) 161
Arbuckle, (Mr.) 131
Arkansas River 154
Ashmore, Elizabeth 312, 313
Ash-Pun-Ge-Ah *See* Heiskell, Wayland
Atchison, David 84, 124, 128, 129
Atchison, Kansas 72
Auburn, California 331
Augusta Gazette (newspaper) 295
Austin, Susan Keller 136, 138
Austin, William 138, 147, 231, 249

B

Baltimore Sun (newspaper) 295
Baltimore, Maryland 329, 347, 354
Banning, (Mr.) 162
Baptiste, Elizabeth 4
Baptiste, James 25
Baptiste, Major 11
Baptiste, Sam 48
Barnes, Elizabeth 132
Barnhill, Bernice Cecelia 323
Barnhill, Claude Raymond 323
Barnhill, Darby B. 323
Barnhill, Samuel Seaman 323
Barnhill, William Allen 323
Barstow School 374
Barstow, (Miss) 374
Barton County, Kansas 332, 347, 354
Barwick, Vera Daisy 329
Bates County, Missouri 161, 196
Baton Rouge, Louisiana 322
Battle of Bull Run 260
Battle of Gettysburg 261
Battle of Marais des Cygnes 161
Battle of Mine Creek 161
Battle of Newtonia 180, 207
Battle of Pea Ridge 159, 181, 212, 213
Battle of Shiloh 208, 379
Battle of the Little Blue 161
Battle of Tippecanoe 362, 364
Battle of Vicksburg (Siege) 6, 181, 182, 208
Battle of Westport 161, 205
Beaver Creek 48
Bernard, Bonnel 328
Bernard, Carmelite 328
Bernard, Glendolan 328
Bernard, Job R. 321, 328
Bernard, John 328
Bernard, Lon 328
Betteys, Alonzo 314
Betteys, Edwin 320
Betteys, Eli 314
Betteys, Eliza M. 314
Betteys, Eugene 320
Betteys, F. M. 211, 212
Betteys, Franklyn M. 5, 179, 314, 320, 338
Betteys, Imogene 320
Betteys, Juliann 7, 233
Betteys, M. 314, 320
Betteys, Margaret 314

Betteys, Sarah J. 314
Betteys, Wealthy Ann 314, 320
Betteys, William 314
Betteys, Winnie 320
Bettis, Alexander Erwin 323, 329, 363
Bettis, Beverly 332
Bettis, Elijah H. 323
Bettis, Frank A. 329, 363
Bettis, Frank Allison 323, 329
Bettis, Gordon 329
Bettis, Maurice E. 329, 331
Bettis, Maurine 331
Bettis, Nanette 331
Bettis, Russell Harrington 329, 331, 332, 339, 341, 342, 362
Bettis, Russell Harrington (Mrs.) 363
Bettis, Sondra 332
Bettis, Zennette 323
Bettys, Juliann (Lykins) 27, 53
Big Blue River 196
Bingham, George Caleb vii, viii, 5, 8, 185, 189, 194, 197, 198, 201, 207, 213, 216, 223, 236, 244, 247, 250, 251, 312, 334, 372
Bingham, Martha A. "Mattie" (Livingston) Lykins 2, 3, 5, 6, 7, 8, 9, 55, 59, 61, 81, 84, 96, 105, 106, 122, 136, 137, 143, 173, 174, 183, 185, 186, 189, 190, 191, 192, 193, 194, 200, 201, 202, 205, 206, 207, 208, 210, 214, 216, 219, 220, 221, 223, 224, 232, 235, 236, 244, 245, 246, 247, 249, 250, 312, 370, 373, 384
Birmingham, Alabama 333
Black Hawk War 362
Black Jack Creek 113
Black Sunday (Dust Bowl) 10, 298
Black, Ed 48
Bleeding Kansas 96, 110, 113, 119, 143, 145, 146
Blue Jacket 362
Boone County, Iowa 320
Boone, Albert Gallatin 60, 93, 112, 118
Boone, Daniel 16, 60
Border Ruffians 103, 118, 135, 136
Border Times (newspaper) 112
Border Wars (Missouri-Kansas) viii, 61, 73, 99, 100, 120, 148, 151, 169
borderland (Missouri-Kansas) vii, viii, x, 4, 25, 39, 40, 47, 65, 67, 82, 85, 99, 100, 101, 105, 125, 135, 137, 139, 142, 151, 156, 160, 161, 180, 189, 192, 194, 195, 207, 208, 209, 219, 224, 225, 229, 232, 234, 240, 241, 253, 267, 279, 280, 281, 284, 285
Boston Conservatory of Music 272
Boston Traveler (newspaper) 109
Bovard, William 373
Bowen, Mary 317
Boyce, Charles McCoy 323
Boyce, Harlow Johnson 322
Boyce, Johnson Lykins 323
Boyles, Paul M. 326
Brann, (Miss) 374
Bronson, Edgar Beecher 242
Brosi, Sarah 315
Brown , John 117
Brown, Frederick 107, 118
Brown, G. W. 139, 147, 152, 167
Brown, Jason 110
Brown, John vii, viii, 3, 83, 100, 106, 107, 110, 111, 113, 114, 116, 117, 118, 120, 121, 128, 129, 136, 142, 144, 145, 146, 148, 151, 161, 408
Brown, Theodore 81, 95, 187, 214
Browne, Helen 324
Browne, Isaac Newton 323
Browne, Julia 323
Browne, Lillian 323
Browne, Robert 324
Browne, Sarah 323
Browne, Theodora 323
Browne, W. H. 131
Browne, William 323
Bryant, William Cullen 71
Buchanan County, Missouri 53, 175, 211, 251, 315, 335
Bucyrus Chief (newspaper) 280
Buena Vista College 272
Bull Moose Movement x, 282

Bull Moose Party	9
Bullene, Moore & Emery	372
Burnett Cemetery	40
Burnett, Chief Abram	40
Burnett, Mary	40
Bushwhackers	139, 151, 161, 196, 202
Butler, Kentucky	324
Butler, Missouri	138
Butts County, Georgia	317

C

California Gold Rush	13, 47, 60, 68
Camp Calhoun, Kentucky	163, 314, 320
Camp Holloway	199
Camp Jackson	178
Camp Nevin, Kentucky	163, 316
Campbell, R. A.	237
Canyon City, Colorado	154
Cape Town, South Africa	324
Carey Mission	18, 237
Carleton, Will	255
Carroll County, Missouri	200
Carter, Anna Frances	333
Case, Delilah McCoy	318, 324
Case, Emily Arabella	7, 317
Case, Ermine Cowles	317, 318, 324
Case, Francis H.	324
Case, Johnston Lykins	318
Case, Juliana Lykins	7, 232, 249
Case, Mattie Lykins	7, 207, 317
Case, Olive Spencer	7, 317
Case, Theodore Johnston	324
Case, Theodore Spencer	5, 206, 317, 339
Cass County, Missouri	4, 53, 82, 83, 84, 90, 96, 97, 101, 136, 137, 138, 139, 151, 161, 173, 196, 202, 207, 208, 325, 330, 340, 342, 348, 352
Castalia, Ohio	322
Castel, Albert	181, 212, 215
Catlin, George	viii, 1, 24, 25, 52
Cato, (Judge)	113
Cato, Sterling	128
Cave, Jane	199
Charleston County, South Carolina	316
Charley, Jim	366, 367, 368
Charley, John	48
Chatham, Ontario	62, 361
Cherokee (Native American nation)	157
Cherokee County, Kansas	321, 322, 328
Cherokee Strip	9
Chesnut, William	89
Cheyenne, Wyoming	242, 321
Chickasaw (Native American nation)	157
Chicopee, Massachusetts	354, 355
Chief Joseph	227, 375, 376
Choctaw (Native American nation)	157
Chouteau, J. M.	83
Cincinnati, Ohio	23, 80, 169, 186, 346, 369, 370, 371, 373
Citronelle, Alabama	183
Claremore, Oklahoma	319, 326
Clark, Charles	90, 96, 97
Clay County, Missouri	200
Cleveland, Grover	298
Cloud, Ida B.	321
Cloud, R. W.	321
Clover, (General)	162
Clover, Seth (Colonel)	142
Clymer, Ewing	91
Coal Hill, Arkansas	326
Coates, Kersey	105, 106, 201, 372
Coates, Sarah (Chandler)	205
Cockrell, (Colonel)	182
Coffee, (candidate for councilman)	90
Coffey, (Colonel)	113
Coffey, Asbury M.	44, 55, 157
Cole, Susan	316
Coles County, Illinois	323
Columbia Herald (newspaper)	200
Columbia, Missouri	70
Columbian (newspaper)	80
Columbus Medical College	265
Columbus, Kansas	241, 322, 328
Commerce, Oklahoma	316, 322
Confederate Widows' and Orphans' Home	7, 194, 219, 223, 236
Cooper County, Missouri	315
Cooper, Douglas	158
Council Grove, Kansas	121

County Antrim, Northern Ireland	325, 347
Cove Creek, Arkansas	181
Cowan, Loveda Faye	331
Cowan, Verna Fay	331
Cowles, George Carroll	324
Cowles, Margaret	324
Cowles, Theodore Williams	324
Craford, (Mr.)	371
Creek (Native American nation)	157
Crochett (doctor)	15
Crofton, Maryland	333
Croker, Richard	9, 284, 392
Cross Hollows, Arkansas	171
Crowell Publications	295, 306
Cullom, Susannah	324, 346
Cumberland County, Kentucky	311, 314
Curry, John Steuart	ix
Curtice, Martha	321
Custer, (General)	155

D

Dagenett, Chief Christmas	23, 24
Dagenett, Mary Ann	23
Daily Conservative (newspaper)	157, 168, 191
Daily Journal of Commerce (newspaper)	205, 214
Dallas County, Iowa	311, 314, 315, 320
Dana, Mary Ann Langdon	274, 353, 355
Dana, Nathaniel	259, 353
Davis, Jefferson	149
Dazney, Chief Christmas	*See* Dagenett, Chief Christmas
Delaware (Native American nation) (Native American nation)	12
Delaware County, Indiana	330, 348
Denver County, Colorado	312, 316
Des Plaines River	12
Devlin, Pat	137
diseases	6, 18, 24, 36, 41, 42, 49, 82, 138, 142, 143, 153, 158, 163, 164, 165, 179, 180, 208, 232, 238, 270, 271, 376
Dodge County, Nebraska	312, 315
Dodson, Bernice May	331

Dole, William	158, 160, 169
Doniphan County, Kansas	72
Dooley, W. (Private)	174
Doolittle, Debby	*See* Bingham, Martha A. "Mattie" (Livingston) Lykins
Douglas, Stephen	72
Dover, New Hampshire	270
Dow, Agrippa	320
Dow, Augustus Storrs	320
Dow, Della S.	320
Dow, Eva E.	320, 327
Dow, Margaret	320
Dust Bowl	10, 288, 298, 307
Dyerley, Paulina E.	315

E

Earnest, Andrew	314
Earnest, Caroline	314
Earnest, Cynthia (Lykins)	29
Earnest, Delilah	314
Earnest, Eliza	314
Earnest, Emma	314
Earnest, Jane	314
Earnest, Lewis	67, 313, 314
Earnest, Mary Ann	314, 319
Earnest, Mary T.	320
Earnest, Sarah E.	320
Earnest, Willis	5, 6, 163, 164, 169, 314, 320
Eddy County, New Mexico	332, 343, 351, 355, 357
Eisle, John	131
Eldridge Hotel	105, 106
Eldridge, (Colonel)	105
Emergency Military Militia	171, 173, 206
Emigrant Aid Society	*See* New England Emigrant Aid Society
Emporia Gazette (newspaper)	288, 302, 306, 307
Enterprise, The (newspaper)	74
Epsom County, Kansas	260
Evansport, Mississippi	179
Ewing, Thomas (General)	6, 189, 190, 195, 197, 200, 201

F

Faust, Drew Gilpin 271
Fayette County, Kentucky 312, 316
Ferguson, Albert Lee 316
Ferguson, Athol 51, 67, 169, 315, 336
Ferguson, Cecil J. 321
Ferguson, Claud E. 321
Ferguson, David 5, 6, 163, 169, 315, 336
Ferguson, Eliza (Lykins) 13, 28, 65
Ferguson, Eugene 93, 94, 211, 214
Ferguson, Eugene C. 51, 178, 194, 316, 321, 336
Ferguson, Herbert B. 321
Ferguson, Imogene B. 321
Ferguson, John 316
Ferguson, Louise B. 321
Ferguson, Marie 321
Ferguson, Thomas 315
Findlay, Charles 26
Findley, (doctor) 16
Finley, Jonas 319, 338
Finley, Mary E. 319, 327
Finley, Thomas Galloway 319
Finley, William H. 44
First Baptist Church 370
Fisher, Hugh D. (Reverend) 191, 214
Five Civilized Tribes 5, 157
Five Tribes viii, 13
Flanders, Charles S. 318
Fletcher, Anna 324, 346
Fort Leavenworth, Kansas 24, 40, 72, 80, 114, 115, 120, 179, 192, 211
Fort Magruder 261
Fort Riley, Kansas 74, 115
Fort Scott, Kansas 65, 101, 142, 162, 230
Fort Smith, Arkansas 379
Fort Sumter 149
Fort Towson 40
Fox (Native American nation) 25, 158
Franklin County, Missouri 315
Franklin County, Tennessee 326
Franklin County, Virginia 311, 312, 313
Franklin, Kansas 194
Free State Hotel 108
Free-soil *See* Free-staters
Free-stater 191
Free-staters 3, 70, 78, 79, 80, 84, 86, 87, 88, 100, 101, 103, 105, 106, 107, 108, 109, 110, 111, 115, 118, 120, 121, 123, 125, 126, 127, 130, 137, 140, 152, 162, 194
French, Addie Mary (Gilman) 8, 269, 353, 354
French, John 270
French, Mabel 270
French, Merwin 269
French, Willie 270
frontier 16, 17, 18, 26, 34, 63, 92, 140, 224, 228
fur traders 24

G

Gallatin County, Montana 332
Gard, Rose Ann 332
Garrett, Indiana 327
Garrett, Mary 329, 347, 354
Geary, Daniel 95, 201, 215
Geary, John W. (Governor) viii, 115, 125
General Orders No. 10 190, 196
General Orders No. 9 190
Gilliss House Hotel 105
Gilman, John 354
Gilmore, Donald x, 94, 120, 145
Goodner, Clara 327
Goodner, Clyde E. 326
Goodner, Nita 327
Goodrich, Thomas 96, 100, 107, 120, 130, 139, 143, 147, 168, 181, 209
Gordon, Ruth 331
Goucher College 284
Grafton County, New Hampshire 320
Grant, Ulysses S. 208
Gratiot Prison 207, 220
Great Bend Tribune (newspaper) 303
Great Depression x, 10, 288, 295
Greeley, Horace 70, 136
Grimes, (Mr.) 131
Grinnell, Josiah 136
guerrilla warfare 115, 125, 127, 140, 141, 151, 152, 156, 159, 160, 168, 171, 173,

175, 176, 177, 178, 181, 189, 190, 193, 194, 195, 196, 202, 207

H

Halleck, William (General)	196
Hamilton County, Ohio	346
Hamilton, Charles	152
Hamilton, Flora Evelyn	328
Hammond, Barbara Griswold	355
Hampshire County, Virginia	96, 231
Hampshire County, West Virginia	82, 84, 318, 345
Hannibal, Missouri	3, 184
Harlan, Cora	329, 347, 354
Harp, The (journal)	ix, 10, 292, 294, 295, 306, 399, 400
Harris, Mary	353
Harris, Nellie (McCoy)	65, 94, 203, 215, 304
Harris, Sarah Caroline	319
Harrison, William Henry (General)	361
Harrisonville, Missouri	63, 65, 84, 93, 116, 136, 137, 138, 196, 280, 325, 330, 348
Hasbrook, Charles D.	373
Haskell, (candidate for representative)	90
Haynes, Martin A.	261, 275
Hays Daily News (newspaper)	302, 307
Hays, (U.S. Marshal)	113
Hebrew relic	30
Hedges, Tom	131
Heenan, David	269, 277, 325, 337, 339, 340, 347, 350
Heenan, Mary L.	347
Heiskell, Alberta	4, 149, 155, 318, 345
Heiskell, Blanche	7, 207, 319, 345
Heiskell, Charles S.	4, 5, 6, 82, 134, 149, 180, 183, 345
Heiskell, Christopher	82, 318
Heiskell, Edmund C.	6, 82, 90, 101, 138, 171, 181, 183, 208, 212, 227, 345
Heiskell, Elisabeth Price	82, 345, 346
Heiskell, Emeline Jamima (Peery)	vii, viii, ix, x, 1, 2, 3, 4, 5, 7, 8, 9, 10, 11, 12, 13, 16, 17, 18, 22, 23, 25, 36, 39, 44, 45, 47, 49, 51, 57, 58, 59, 60, 63, 64, 65, 66, 67, 73, 74, 76, 79, 81, 82, 83, 84, 86, 88, 89, 90, 91, 92, 93, 94, 99, 100, 103, 106, 113, 116, 121, 129, 142, 149, 153, 155, 156, 160, 163, 164, 165, 171, 175, 180, 207, 219, 224, 225, 226, 228, 230, 231, 232, 233, 237, 241, 244, 249, 253, 254, 264, 265, 266, 267, 268, 269, 276, 279, 280, 281, 283, 304, 313, 318, 345, 353
Heiskell, Evalina (Price)	i, 2, 82, 96, 345
Heiskell, Fanny	4, 82, 138, 345
Heiskell, Florence	138
Heiskell, Frederick	82, 345
Heiskell, Minnie M.	7, 234, 265, 269, 319, 325, 346, 347
Heiskell, Nellie V.	4, 7, 156, 207, 318, 345
Heiskell, Price	209, 231, 234
Heiskell, Sue Austin	3, 5, 8, 9, 10, 18, 129, 130, 131, 132, 133, 134, 135, 139, 140, 156, 171, 225, 226, 230, 232, 234, 253, 254, 255, 256, 258, 259, 263, 264, 265, 267, 268, 269, 273, 274, 276, 279, 280, 281, 282, 283, 304, 305, 318, 324, 325, 339, 345, 346, 347, 350, 353, 354, 356
Heiskell, Wayland	227
Heiskell, William Alexander (General)	2, 3, 4, 5, 6, 7, 8, 15, 65, 82, 84, 88, 90, 91, 96, 101, 103, 106, 112, 113, 115, 127, 131, 138, 143, 145, 171, 180, 183, 207, 208, 209, 224, 225, 231, 233, 234, 249, 318, 345, 349, 353
Hempstead County, Arkansas	321
Henning, R. S.	372
Henrico County, Virginia	353
Herald of Freedom (newspaper)	109
Hersperger, J. C.	318
Hickman Mills, Missouri	196
Hill, Esther Clark	287
Hill, Jennie	138
Hillsborough County, New Hampshire	274, 353
Hines, Celinda E.	76

Home Guard	207, 269
Hoover, Archie B.	318
Hoover, Clatta	318
Hoover, Julia	318
Hoover, Mary Lykins	134
Hoover, Samuel	318
Hoover, W. D.	142, 143, 155, 156, 160, 161, 162
Hoover, Woodson D.	5, 160, 318
Hopper, Ann	122, 146
Hostetter, Hortense	332, 348, 355
Hostetter, Sam	332
Hotel Roslin	186
House of Ewing	32
House on the Hill	289
Hoyt, George	vii
Hughes, Alphonse	194
Hunter, David	199
Hustad, Marcus	315
Hutchinson, Kansas	258, 347
Huxman, Walter	297
Huxman, Walter (Governor)	297

I

Illinois (Native American nation)	12
Independence, Missouri	58, 73, 80, 81, 82, 93, 138, 143, 180, 181, 196, 214, 250, 336, 349, 363
Indian Territory (Kansas)	3, 13, 16, 21, 25, 31, 33, 37, 40, 47, 49, 57, 59, 63, 72, 73, 80, 157, 279, 380
Indian Territory (Oklahoma)	7, 9, 155, 225, 226, 241, 319, 325, 326, 328, 331, 362, 377
Indian traders	32
Indian Wars	155, 167
Indianapolis, Indiana	164
Indianola, Kansas	121
Industrial Home for the Orphans and Indigent Children of Missouri	*See* Confederate Widows' and Orphans' Home
Ingham County, Michigan	353
intoxication	36
Iola Daily Register (newspaper)	284, 285

J

Jackson County, Missouri	iii, 47, 54, 58, 93, 95, 147, 156, 161, 196, 198, 210, 216, 220, 249, 311, 312, 313, 316, 317, 318, 322, 323, 324, 329, 330, 331, 332, 336, 337, 345, 346, 348, 349, 350, 355
Jackson, Mr. and Mrs.	19
Jacobs, Isaac	91, 157
Jayhawkers	vi, vii, 137, 138, 139, 140, 141, 142, 149, 151, 155, 161, 162, 175, 176, 197, 203
Jeffers, Floyd F.	328
Jeffers, Harvey B.	328
Jeffers, Kenneth M.	328
Jefferson City, Missouri	57, 211, 213, 216, 247, 335, 336, 337, 339, 340, 342, 349, 350, 352
Jefferson County, Kentucky	312, 313, 317
Jennison, Charles (Colonel)	161, 162, 192, 193, 197
Jessamine County, Kentucky	318
Jewel, Kansas	323
Johns, William	211, 239, 250
Johnson County, Kansas	325
Johnson, A. H.	330
Johnson, Albert	329, 347, 354
Johnson, Andrew (President)	219
Johnson, Anna	330
Johnson, Elphie Dorothy	330
Johnson, Nancy	*See* Lykins, Nancy (Johnson)
Johnson, Richard (Colonel)	361
Johnson, Samuel	314
Johnson, Samuel A.	78, 95, 96
Johnson, Sara LeMaistre	*See* Wallace, Sara LeMaistre (Johnson)
Johnston, A. H.	72
Jones, (Sheriff)	109
Jones, Hiram	380
Joplin, Missouri	162, 180, 322, 329, 331
Journal of Commerce (newspaper)	237

K

Kankakee River 12
Kansas City Enterprise (newspaper) 237
Kansas City Star (newspaper) 9, 65, 94, 169, 186, 214, 215, 250, 280, 283, 285, 288, 290, 292, 298, 304, 305, 306, 307, 349, 356, 357, 364, 374, 393, 394, 397, 404
Kansas City Times (newspaper) 96, 143, 144, 214, 238, 250, 251, 285, 292
Kansas City, Missouri 2, 6, 12, 14, 23, 31, 53, 54, 55, 57, 58, 63, 65, 74, 76, 81, 82, 93, 94, 95, 105, 106, 142, 162, 191, 200, 205, 211, 214, 216, 220, 230, 235, 247, 248, 267, 299, 304, 318, 325, 330, 333, 334, 336, 337, 339, 342, 345, 346, 347, 348, 349, 350
Kansas Ledger (newspaper) 68
Kansas Legislature (Territorial) 3, 84, 108, 155
Kansas River 58, 80, 82
Kansas State University 289
Kansas statehood 4
Kansas Territory viii, 1, 2, 11, 18, 22, 23, 26, 34, 40, 47, 57, 63, 65, 67, 72, 83, 85, 90, 100, 101, 103, 105, 108, 116, 118, 119, 120, 123, 125, 129, 130, 131, 140, 145, 157, 160, 228, 233, 237, 267, 280, 316, 321, 334, 361
Kansas Valley Railroad Company 74
Kansas Weekly Capitol (newspaper) 284
Kansas-Nebraska Act 3, 49, 70, 73, 78, 79, 80, 84, 85, 157
Kaskaskia (Native American nation) 13, 73, 158, 226
Kaw River 74
Keller, Charles 4, 84, 90, 96, 101, 138, 147, 231
Keller, Ermina 4, 82
Keller, Florence 231
Keokuk (Chief) 25, 233
Kickapoo (Native American nation) 12
Kil-son-sak *See* Baptiste, Sam
Kimball, Philip Albert 272, 355
Kimball, Wallace O. 355

King, William J. 212, 315
Kleinfelter, Laura 332
Knox County, Indiana 312, 315
Knox County, Tennessee 313
Koehler, Fred 364

L

Labette County, Kansas 178, 211, 239, 250, 311, 314
Lafayette County, Missouri 312, 317
Lamar, Colorado 322, 328
Lane, Jim 120, 122, 129, 157, 159, 195, 196, 197, 200
Langston, Gemima 325
LaPorte County, Indiana 318
LaPorte, Indiana 18, 313
Larned, Kansas 51, 94, 286, 307, 341, 351, 357
Latimer, Cloyd 330, 342, 349, 352
Latimer, Ellis James 330, 348
Latimer, Philip E. 349, 352
Latimer, Philip F. 9, 268, 279, 282, 283, 324, 325, 346, 347
Latimer, Philip Heiskell 269, 325, 330, 347, 348, 352
Latimer, Robert 324, 346
Latimer, Sue Heiskell *See* Heiskell, Sue Austin
Lawrence, Amos 78, 79
Lawrence, Kansas vi, 3, 6, 74, 76, 78, 79, 80, 81, 82, 84, 87, 88, 97, 105, 107, 108, 109, 110, 118, 122, 123, 124, 126, 127, 129, 130, 139, 143, 144, 145, 152, 155, 162, 189, 190, 191, 192, 193, 194, 195, 196, 199, 200, 202, 207, 214, 219, 235, 236, 305, 306, 317, 324, 350, 356
Lawton, (Mr.) 106
Leavenworth Daily Commercial (newspaper) 235
Leavenworth Kansas Weekly Herald (newspaper) 119, 145
Leavenworth Times (newspaper) 284
Leavenworth, Kansas 133, 195
Lecompte, (Judge) 77
Lecompton, Kansas 122

LeCompton, Kansas 118
Lecompton, Titus (Colonel) 118
Lewis and Clark County, Montana 332, 348, 354
Lewis, C. E. 194
Lewis, Cora G. 289
Lewisburg, Kansas 24
Lincoln, Abraham 63, 149, 184, 196, 262, 362
Linder, Blanche M. 340, 342, 348, 352
Linder, Blanche Rife 325, 330
Linn County, Kansas 137
Little Sisters of the Poor 224
Livingston, Martha *See* Bingham, Martha A. "Mattie" (Livingston) Lykins
Livingston, Stepehen J. 3, 78, 95, 122, 146, 221
Livingston, William Jackson 3, 6, 183, 184, 189, 207, 213, 216, 247
Los Angeles County, California 317, 323, 328, 350
Los Angeles, California 323, 331
Louisburg, Kansas 267, 268, 269
Lovejoy, Charles 156
Lovejoy, Julia 156
Lowe, Schuyler 181, 183
Lykins Addition 188
Lykins County, Kansas 4, 11, 40, 41, 64, 90, 97, 117, 119, 131, 147, 152, 161, 167, 316, 334
Lykins Float 78
Lykins Institute 244, 245
Lykins, Abigail 2, 41, 44, 65
Lykins, Abigail (Webster) 2, 18, 67, 231, 316
Lykins, Abigail Ann (Webster) 40, 316
Lykins, Alexander Wayland 329, 331
Lykins, Amanda 314
Lykins, Andrew Chute 5, 29, 175, 179, 210, 211, 212, 315, 320, 338, 341
Lykins, Andrew Willis 230, 313
Lykins, Archibald 178
Lykins, Caliborne Bloomfield 1, 3, 5, 6, 7, 8, 39, 40, 73, 74, 86, 143, 161, 171, 175, 176, 178, 179, 207, 239, 242, 315

Lykins, Charles (Johnston's son) 27, 44, 312
Lykins, Charles C. S. (David's son) 316
Lykins, Charles G. (Wayland's son) 322
Lykins, Charles R. (Claiborne's son) 315, 335
Lykins, Charly 27
Lykins, Claiborne Bloomfield 311, 314
Lykins, Curtis E. 322
Lykins, Cynthia 18, 311, 313, 314
Lykins, Cynthia Ann 315
Lykins, David viii, 1, 2, 3, 4, 11, 13, 16, 17, 18, 39, 40, 41, 42, 47, 49, 51, 55, 61, 64, 67, 74, 81, 83, 84, 90, 91, 103, 115, 134, 135, 137, 142, 143, 151, 152, 153, 157, 160, 161, 226, 228, 231, 241, 311, 312, 313, 316, 336
Lykins, David A. 5, 7, 175, 180, 207, 315
Lykins, David L. 311
Lykins, David P. 322
Lykins, Delilah (McCoy) 1, 2, 17, 19, 26, 40, 49, 53, 228
Lykins, Delilah McCoy 317
Lykins, Edward W. W. 13, 14, 18, 152, 153, 155, 167, 226, 228, 241, 316, 322
Lykins, Eliza (dau. of Jonas and Sarah (Kelso) Lykins) 314
Lykins, Eliza (Ritchie) 1, 18, 65, 312, 315
Lykins, Elsie 322
Lykins, Emma V. 315
Lykins, Fred Carey 322, 328, 341
Lykins, Fred Gordon 331
Lykins, Grace (Tull) 16, 137, 149, 153, 316
Lykins, Hannah 11, 17, 18, 29, 67, 311, 313, 345
Lykins, Harry C. 248, 322, 328, 341
Lykins, Ivy 321
Lykins, James F. 5, 7, 40, 54, 88, 115, 134, 160, 161, 162, 233, 241, 313
Lykins, James Samuel 315
Lykins, Jane 314
Lykins, Jared 17, 18, 67, 311, 312
Lykins, Jemima (dau. of David and Jemima (Willis) Lykins) 312

Lykins, Jemima (Willis)   16, 18, 39, 67, 311
Lykins, Jessie   321, 328
Lykins, John Johnson   315, 335
Lykins, John Samuel   321
Lykins, Johnston   viii, 1, 2, 3, 5, 6, 7, 8, 14, 15, 16, 17, 18, 19, 21, 22, 25, 26, 28, 29, 30, 32, 33, 34, 36, 37, 39, 40, 41, 47, 49, 53, 54, 55, 57, 59, 61, 63, 64, 65, 74, 76, 78, 81, 83, 84, 86, 95, 103, 105, 106, 127, 128, 135, 136, 137, 143, 151, 152, 164, 171, 175, 177, 185, 186, 187, 188, 189, 194, 205, 206, 207, 214, 216, 224, 228, 235, 236, 237, 238, 239, 244, 245, 246, 247, 248, 250, 267, 279, 281, 311, 312, 333, 334, 335, 336, 337, 369, 370, 371, 372, 374
Lykins, Johnston Franklin   316
Lykins, Jonas Philip   2, 4, 18, 29, 39, 67, 74, 228, 311, 314
Lykins, Joseph Willis   3, 5, 7, 8, 17, 18, 39, 40, 54, 74, 88, 115, 134, 143, 160, 161, 228, 232, 240, 251, 311, 313, 334
Lykins, Julia A. (Claiborne's dau.)   29, 315
Lykins, Julia McCoy (Johnston's dau.)   313, 317
Lykins, Juliann (dau. of David and Jemima Lykins)   27, 53, 311, 314
Lykins, Lorene   322
Lykins, Mariah Browne Williams   7
Lykins, Marion   313
Lykins, Martha   322
Lykins, Mary Elizabeth   313, 318, 337
Lykins, Mary Jane   321
Lykins, Mary V.   315
Lykins, Mattie   *See* Bingham, Martha A. "Mattie" (Livingston) Lykins
Lykins, Merb*See* Lykins, Mariah Browne Williams
Lykins, Nancy (Johnson)   29, 40, 178, 240, 314, 315
Lykins, Orville Lee   331
Lykins, Prudence   40, 314
Lykins, Queenie   322, 328

Lykins, Ralph Wayland   328
Lykins, Ruth   311
Lykins, Samuel   242
Lykins, Sarah (Kelso)   29, 67, 314
Lykins, Sarah D. (Tull)   67, 83, 96, 149, 316
Lykins, Sarah E.   315
Lykins, Sarah J.   *See* Russell, Sarah J. (Lykins)
Lykins, Sophronia   312
Lykins, Susan Elizabeth   316
Lykins, Sylvia A.   180, 321, 328, 338, 341
Lykins, W. Leopold   314
Lykins, W. Ray   321
Lykins, Wayland Carey   11, 13, 47, 51, 55, 152, 154, 155, 226, 241, 316, 321, 322, 338, 341
Lykins, Webster M.   322
Lykins, William C.   242, 315
Lykins, William Hall Richardson   3, 28, 30, 31, 53, 55, 74, 76, 78, 81, 84, 85, 105, 135, 191, 192, 194, 235, 312, 316, 321, 336, 337, 339
Lykins, Willis   167, 226, 248, 322, 339
Lykins, Willy   27
Lykins' mansion   186
Lyons, Emory J.   31, 37, 51, 53, 54
Lyric West (journal)   292

M

Mac-o-se-tah   *See* Valley, Frank
Madeira, Addison Dashiell (Reverend)   5, 206, 208, 234, 346
Madeira, May   346, 350
Madeira, Price Heiskell   8
Madeira, Romaine   346, 349
Marais des Cygnes River   116, 132
Marais des Cygnes, Kansas   207
Marcy, Joshua   260
Marion County, Indiana   330, 348
Marion County, Missouri   183
Marshall, (General)   122
Martial Law   *See* Order No. 11 (painting)
Mastin, John   372
Mau-me-way (Mrs. Baptiste Peoria)   319

428

Maury, Dabney H. (Major) 182
McCall, Meck 332, 333, 348, 355
McCoy, Christiana 18
McCoy, Delilah 1, 2, 39, 53, 67, 312, 334, 336, 337, 339
McCoy, Eliza 15, 49
McCoy, Elizabeth 39
McCoy, Isaac viii, 1, 16, 18, 19, 21, 22, 25, 31, 33, 34, 36, 37, 40, 49, 51, 52, 53, 54, 55, 61, 92, 228, 281, 312
McCoy, John Calvin viii, 32, 204, 369
McCoy, Spencer Case 6, 204, 206
McGee Hotel 205
McIntosh, James 158
McLachlin, (Mr.) 140
McLachlin, H. M. 63
McLean County, Illinois 332
McNair, Sally 319, 338
McNaughton, Ann 333
McNaughton, Clara Bernice 331
McNaughton, Clara Pearl 326
McNaughton, Clarence Earl 326
McNaughton, Guy Peery 326, 331
McNaughton, J. Patrick ii, 326, 377, 379, 381
McNaughton, John Carter 333
McNaughton, John Lewis 331, 333
McNaughton, Ray 326
McNaughton, Willis 326
McPheeters, Samuel Brown 209
Me-Cha-Co-Me-Yah *See* Lykins, David
Mechanics Bank of Kansas City 76, 236, 237
Me-cho-zah-ke-mah *See* Black, Ed
Meeker, Jotham 33, 53, 70
Meridian, Mississippi 183
Merrimack County, New Hampshire 274, 275, 316, 324, 346, 353, 354, 355
Mesa County, Colorado 330
Me-shin-go-me-shia *See* Peery, David Lykins
Mexican War 184
Miami (Native American nation) 12, 13, 16, 22, 142, 155, 157, 162

Miami County, Kansas 4, 18, 24, 51, 52, 53, 54, 55, 93, 94, 97, 132, 140, 146, 147, 152, 156, 167, 168, 169, 248, 249, 251, 254, 269, 273, 274, 276, 277, 304, 305, 311, 313, 316, 318, 319, 322, 324, 325, 326, 329, 330, 334, 335, 336, 337, 338, 339, 340, 341, 342, 345, 346, 347, 348, 349, 350, 351, 352, 353, 354, 356
Miami Republican (newspaper) 132, 224, 225, 229, 231, 234, 248, 249, 254, 255, 256, 258, 273, 274, 297, 307, 334, 337
Miami, Oklahoma 241, 319, 322, 326, 328
Miamis (Native American nation) 361
Middaugh, Anna Abbie 241, 321
Middaugh, Charlton 321
Middle Town, Indiana 11, 313
Middleton, Doc 242, 243, 251
Middleton, Indiana 23
Miege, Bishop 42
Miller, George W. 161, 162
Milton County, New Hampshire 355
Milton, New Hampshire 272
Milwaukee, Wisconsin 318, 324
Mississineways (Native American nation) 23, 24
Mississippi River 23, 370
Missouri Compromise 80, 85
Missouri Pacific Railway 76
Missouri River 22, 23, 28, 58, 59, 69, 72, 85, 86, 101, 175, 188, 195, 212, 370
Missouri Statesman (newspaper) 70
Mitchell, David D. 68
Mitchler Spring 131
Monroe County, New York 321
Montgomery County, Kansas 330
Montgomery, James 137
Moore, Ely, Jr. 105
Moore, L. T. 372
Mormons 59
Mound Valley, Kansas 240, 241
Murray County, Minnesota 322

N

Nance, Bessie 327
Nance, Fern 327

Nance, Norma 327
Nance, Ross Augustus 327
Nance, Roy C. 327
Nance, Sevigna Edgar 327
National Kansas Committee 118
National Republican (newspaper) 260
Native American forced removal 32
Native American forced removals 22
Nebraska Territory 69, 312, 338
Neutralists 101
New Castle County, Delaware 329, 347, 354
New England Emigrant Aid Society 70, 76, 78, 79, 95, 96, 100, 106, 108
New Market, Missouri 178
New York Daily Times, The (newspaper) 30, 53, 144
New York Evening Post (newspaper) 71
New York Herald Tribune (newspaper) 296
New York Sun (newspaper) 281
New York Times (newspaper) 108
New York Tribune (newspaper) 70, 118, 136
New York, New York 9, 30, 52, 53, 93, 96, 144, 145, 146, 148, 167, 169, 211, 213, 215, 216, 250, 251, 273, 277, 284, 295, 296, 299, 330, 332, 334, 338, 348, 349, 355, 389
Newcombe, George W. 380
Newtonia, Missouri 315
Neylon, James (Mrs.) 133
Nez Perce (Native American nation) 227, 375, 376
Nixon, Margaret 67, 313, 334
Nodaway County, Missouri 332
Nolte, Jennie May 322
Norfolk, Virginia 333
Northampton, Massachusetts 355
Northern Pacific Railroad 236

O

Occidental Messenger (newspaper) 49, 73, 95
Ogle County, Illinois 51, 169, 316, 336

Ohio River 23, 130, 225, 370
Okay Creek 362
Oklahoma Constitutional Convention 9
Order No. 11 vii, 6, 195, 196, 197, 198, 200, 202, 208, 215
Order No. 11 (painting) 197
Osage (Native American nation) 13, 39, 160, 241
Osage River Agency 158
Osawatomie Congregational Church 106
Osawatomie, Kansas 39, 79, 100, 107, 112, 113, 161, 162, 314
Osgood, Sarah Ann 44, 65
Ossawatomie, Kansas 12, 65
Osterman, Elsye W. 272
Osterman, Rolf 272
Osterman, Rolf Alexander 354
Ottawa County, Kansas 381
Ottawa County, Oklahoma 316, 321, 331
Ottawa Creek Rangers 116
Ottawas (Native American nation) 361
Owen, Albin 235
Owen, Judson 5, 7, 173, 206, 235, 250
Owen, Robert D. 192

P

Pace, Florida 331, 333
Padgitt, Frank Lamont 322
Page, Elizabeth 354
Palmyra, Missouri 183
Panic of 1873 8, 234, 236
Paola Advertiser (newspaper) 231, 249
Paola Free Library 8, 9, 147, 148, 265, 267, 268, 276, 280
Paola Town Company 132
Paola, Kansas vii, 2, 3, 4, 13, 14, 18, 23, 40, 41, 51, 52, 53, 54, 55, 63, 64, 65, 74, 84, 88, 91, 93, 94, 95, 97, 106, 115, 129, 132, 139, 142, 146, 147, 148, 149, 151, 152, 155, 161, 167, 168, 169, 195, 207, 227, 228, 229, 230, 233, 247, 248, 249, 251, 263, 267, 273, 274, 276, 277, 304, 305, 334, 335, 336, 337, 338, 339, 340, 341, 342, 349, 350, 351, 352, 356
Paradise, Missouri 331

430

Parsons, (General) 138
Paschall, Luther 48, 131
Pate, Henry Clay (Captain) 113
Pawhuska, Oklahoma 326
Pawnee (Native American nation) 24
Pawnee County, Kansas ii, 278, 288, 296, 306, 325, 329, 332, 341, 343, 346, 347, 348, 350, 354, 355, 357, 393, 394
Peery, Albert (son of Hannah and William Peery) 13, 313
Peery, Albert E. (son of Albert J. Peery) 325, 330
Peery, Albert Johnston (son of David L. Peery) 47, 319, 325
Peery, Alice Elizabeth 325
Peery, Charles Williams Lennox 326
Peery, Christine Elizabeth 326
Peery, Clara E. 319, 326, 377
Peery, Clyde Vest 326
Peery, Cynthia 67, 312
Peery, David L. (son of Albert E. Peery) 331
Peery, David Lykins 2, 4, 7, 9, 15, 47, 49, 64, 65, 73, 74, 88, 91, 92, 106, 115, 131, 134, 149, 155, 226, 230, 241, 248, 319, 340, 365, 377
Peery, David Lykins Baptiste 326
Peery, Elsie Ethel 319, 327
Peery, Emeline Jamima *See* Heiskell, Emeline Jamima (Peery)
Peery, Eva May 319
Peery, Evan David 327
Peery, Frances Albert 327
Peery, Frank Cleveland 319, 327
Peery, Hannah (Lykins) 11, 17, 18
Peery, John Philip 331
Peery, Maud Mabel 319, 326
Peery, Nell Naomi 326
Peery, Nellie Lucile 319
Peery, Samuel 312, 313
Peery, William 2, 11, 13, 17, 313, 326, 345
Peery, William Baptiste 319, 326
Pe-ke-nom-wah *See* Charley, John, *See* Charley, John
Peoria Mining Company 381
Peoria Reservation, Oklahoma 322, 328
Peoria Springs 64
Peoria, Baptiste viii, 1, 3, 4, 5, 7, 11, 12, 13, 24, 25, 73, 74, 88, 91, 101, 106, 113, 131, 133, 149, 152, 157, 158, 159, 160, 167, 168, 169, 225, 228, 231, 233, 319, 338, 365, 377, 378
Peoria, Elizabeth 319
Peoria, Illinois 26
Peorias (Native American nation) 11, 13, 47, 70, 73, 157, 158, 226, 228, 378
Periman, Pearl 321
Perry, David 57
Perry, William 258
Phillips, Alfred 324, 346
Phillips, Hiram Lafayette 8, 9, 263, 264, 276, 279, 324, 325, 340, 346, 347, 350
Phillips, Jessie 268, 325, 330, 347, 348
Phillips, Lenora 268, 325, 330, 347, 348
Phillips, Leslie Earle 264
Phillips, Nellie 268, 325, 347
Piankeshaw (Native American nation) 1, 13, 16, 55, 73, 83, 157, 158, 226, 228
Pickett, Mabel 329
Pierce, Franklin 103, 109
Pierce, Laveria A. 320
Pike, (General) 159
Pine Tavern, Kentucky 235
Piper, (Mr.) 244
Pittsburg (Kansas) Headlight (newspaper) 295
Placer County, California 328
plague of locusts/grasshoppers 234
Platte County Self-Defense Association 85
Platte County, Missouri 175, 200
Pleasant Hill, Missouri 196
poem
   Children 293
   Dream Days 397
   Loss 403
   Memories of the Dead 382
   Nocturne 402
   Prairie Grave 404
   Requiem 42, 43

Sonnet 400
Steel Mill 399
Sung to Youth (sonnet sequence) 293
Sunset Mound 46
The Editor's Guests 385
The Kansas Emigrants 71
The Last Indian 49, 55
Trees on the Plains 398
Untitled 401
Polk, Christiana 312
Polke, Charles 19
Pomeroy, (Mr.) 140
Porter, P. B. 22
Pottawatomie (Native American nation) 12, 13, 16, 18, 30, 32, 36, 361
Pottawatomie Baptist Indian Mission 2, 30, 61
Pottawatomie Creek 3, 111, 116, 117
Pottawatomie Massacre 100, 107, 111, 119
Potter farm 199
Potter, W. L. 141, 161, 162
Prairie Creek Baptist Church 16, 51
Prairie Creek Township (Indiana) 16
Prairie Flower (horse) 365, 366, 367
Prairieton, Indiana 18
Preston, Frank 272
Price, Connie 82, 96, 97, 138, 147
Price, Elisabeth 345, 346
Price, Evalina *See* Heiskell, Evalina (Price)
Price, Silas 82, 84, 96, 138, 345
Price, Sterling (General) 161, 180, 207
Price-Willet Cemetery 82
prison collapse (Kansas City) 189
Proctor, Henry A. (General) 361
Prophet, The (Tenskwatawa) 362, 364
proslavery forces 3, 63, 72, 81, 84, 88, 100, 103, 105, 107, 108, 109, 110, 111, 112, 113, 115, 116, 117, 118, 120, 121, 122, 123, 124, 125, 126, 127, 128, 129, 130, 135, 136, 137, 140, 141, 151, 156, 160, 161, 186
Putnam, Connecticut 355

Q

Quality Hill 185
Quantrill, William Clarke vi, viii, 3, 6, 131, 132, 140, 141, 142, 148, 156, 161, 162, 169, 189, 190, 192, 194, 195, 196, 199, 207, 214
Quapaw (Native American nation) 227

R

Ragan, Maude 325, 330, 348
Ravenwood, Missouri 240
Ray County, Missouri 200
Reader's Digest 296
Rector, Harvey M. 321
Red Legs vii, 197
Reed, Laura (Coates) 372
Reeder, Andrew (Governor) viii, 77, 89, 103, 105, 106, 144
Reno County, Kansas 332, 347, 348, 354, 355
Requiem (poem) 55
Revolutionary War 113
Reyher, Edward C. 327
Reyher, Grace 327, 334, 335, 338
Reyher, Jacob 327
Reyher, Mary Ella 327
Reyher, Robert Edmund 327
Reynolds, Lucile 331
Rhea, William A. 332, 348, 355
Rice County, Kansas 256
Rice, Charles 29
Rice, Martin 198, 215
Rich, Martha 314
Richmond, Virginia 6, 262
Robinson, charles (Governor) 120
Robinson, Charles (Governor) 108
Robinson, Sara 71, 87, 120
Robotaille, Robert 76
Rocker, Alice 325
Rocker, John 325
Rockingham County, New Hampshire 340, 350, 353, 355
Rogers, Tom 48
Rollins, James 245

Roosevelt, Theodore 282, 392
Royal Templar of Temperance 281
Russell, Cornelia Victoria 317, 323
Russell, Effie 7, 317
Russell, Egbert Freeland 5, 63, 171, 317
Russell, Julia 317, 323
Russell, Mattie 317
Russell, Sarah J. (Lykins) ii, 27, 61, 63, 216, 233, 249, 312, 317, 362, 363, 382
Russell, Theodora Case 317, 323
Russell, William Henry 62, 63, 362
Russell, William Lykins 7, 317
Russell, Zaenett 317, 322, 323

S

Sac (Native American nation) 25, 158
Salt Lake City, Utah 59
San Diego, California 322, 328
San Felipe, California 263, 353
San Francisco, California 13, 210, 215, 315, 332
Sanborn, F. B. 113, 145
Sanders, Rachel Babb 259, 260
Sanderson, J. P. 207
Santa Fe Trail 113, 291
Schofield, (General) 171, 173, 196
Schwitgebel, Henry C. 317
Scott, (candidate for representative) 90
Scott, Elvira 156
Scott, Jim 131
Sears, Benjamin 19
Sears, John 19
Sedgwick County, Kansas 325, 347
Seminole (Native American nation) 157
Sequoyah (proposed Indian state) 9
Shaw, Cyrus 65, 131
Shaw, Isaac 65
Shaw, Knowles 65, 131
Shaw, William 65
Shawnee (Native American nation) 1, 12, 22, 34
Shawnee Baptist Indian Mission 1, 2, 39, 40, 61, 90, 237
Shawnee County, Kansas 39, 40, 54, 311, 314, 335

Shawnee Sun, The (newspaper) 34, 54, 237
She-kon-saac-quah *See* Paschall, Luther
Shelby County, Kentucky 312
Shepherd, James 320, 338
Sherman, William Tecumseh (General) 375
Shore, Benjamin 332
Shore, Chester 293
Shore, Chester Klinefelter 332, 347, 354
Shore, David Anthony 332
Shore, Earle Michael 332
Shore, John Christopher 332
Shore, Ralph Wallace 332
Shore, Sara Leslie 332
Shorter County, Nebraska 320, 338
Shurz, Carl 380
Sidney, Nebraska 243
Simerwell, Robert (Reverend) 40
Simmons, Charles L. 315
Simpson, B. J. 65
Simpson, Basil 256
Simpson, Benjamin F. 256
Siwinowe Kesibwi (newspaper) *See* Shawnee Sun, The (newspaper)
slaves vii, ix, 60, 61, 63, 69, 70, 79, 80, 81, 82, 84, 85, 87, 90, 92, 93, 94, 96, 99, 100, 101, 105, 107, 108, 110, 111, 112, 114, 115, 120, 130, 136, 157, 191, 203, 205, 206, 216, 372
Smart, Robert 156
Smith, Cornelia Victoria 316
Smith, James 316
Snow, F. H. 324
Snow, Mary Margaret 324
Snyder, (Captain) 142, 151
Snyder, Eli (Captain) 4, 151
Southern sympathizers 4, 136, 151, 152, 155, 156, 175, 193, 199
Spalding, C. C. 188, 214
Spring River 380
Squatters' Sovereignty (newspaper) 72
St. Joseph Gazette (newspaper) 68, 70
St. Joseph, Missouri 1, 6, 29, 40, 70, 72, 73, 86, 87, 96, 101, 137, 175, 176, 177,

433

178, 184, 205, 207, 211, 240, 243, 244, 251, 315, 321, 334, 335, 338, 339
St. Louis, Missouri 4, 26, 57, 63, 68, 105, 136, 138, 147, 173, 184, 185, 186, 207, 213, 220, 369
St. Mary's Pottawatomie Catholic Mission   42
Stanton, Edwin   159
Stanton, Kansas   107, 117, 132, 140, 141, 142, 264
Starkey, Rhoda   320
Stewart, (Governor)   138
Strafford County, New Hampshire 274, 278, 324, 346, 353
Strange, Amos V.   321
Stringfellow, Ben   85
Stringfellow, J. W.   115
Strope, (Mr.)   373
Sullivan County, Indiana   169, 314, 319, 320
Sumner (Colonel)   36
Sumner County, Kansas   325, 347
Sumner, Charles   110, 142

T

Tabor, Iowa   118
Talbot, Myrtle Alta   328
Tammany Hall   x, 9, 284, 391, 392
Tamworth, New Hampshire   355
Tecumseh   62, 361, 362, 364
Tenskwatawa   See Prophet, The
Terre Haute, Indiana   16, 22, 23, 51, 94, 249, 333, 334, 335, 336, 338
Thames River   361
Thatcher, William Whitehead   317
Thomas, Daniel W.   330, 348
Thomas, Jessie May   330, 348
Thomas, Robert (Reverend)   370
Thompson, A. Scott   327
Thompson, Daniel   327
Thompson, John Stewart   327
Thompson, Joseph   327
Thompson, Virginia   327
Thorne, Joshua (doctor)   190

Tiller and Toiler, The (newspaper) 10, 51, 94, 286, 287, 288, 289, 291, 292, 293, 295, 296, 298, 299, 302, 304, 305, 306, 307, 308, 341, 343, 350, 351, 357, 393, 394, 401
Topeka Capital (newspaper)   297
Topeka Capitol, The (newspaper)   9
Topeka Daily Capital (newspaper)   284
Topeka Journal (newspaper)   282
Topeka State Journal (newspaper)   284
Topeka, Kansas   2, 9, 39, 51, 52, 53, 54, 74, 79, 95, 96, 97, 123, 143, 144, 145, 146, 147, 148, 162, 167, 211, 215, 250, 252, 274, 276, 304, 305, 306, 307, 308, 335, 339, 340, 341, 343, 350, 351, 356, 357, 408, 412
Torrey, (Colonel)   132, 162
Torrey, (Mrs.)   See Wagstaff, (Mrs.)
Town of Kansas   See Kansas City, Missouri
transportation
    air-Douglas Skysleeper Transport 299
    air-Midcontinent Airport (Kansas City)   299
    steamboat   57, 72
    steamboat-Clara   57
Travis, Sally   314
Truman, Harry S   200
Truman, Martha Ellen   200
Tulare County, California   330
Tull, Grace   See Lykins, Grace (Tull)
Tull, Sarah D. See Lykins, Sarah D. (Tull)

U

Underground Railroad   107
Union Cemetery   93, 96, 204, 211, 214, 216, 334, 339, 349
Union Hotel   142, 161
Union Pacific Railroad   242
Union Station Kansas City   362
Union, New Hampshire   354, 355
University of Iowa   ix
University of Kansas   vi, 78, 79, 97, 214, 292, 357

University of Missouri vi, 53, 55, 93, 95, 146, 167, 210, 213, 214, 216, 247, 248, 250, 273, 334, 336, 337, 339
Upton, L. R. (Mrs.) 373

V

Valley, Frank 48
Venable, John 330, 342, 348, 351
Venable, John T. 330, 341, 348, 351
Venable, Margaret 330, 348
Venable, Wilma 330, 348
Verdigris River 158
Vernon County, Missouri 196
Vernon, Lidia 328
Victor, Bob Lee 10, 296, 329, 347, 354
Victor, Robert 329, 347, 354
Vigo County, Indiana 25, 51, 65, 94, 311, 312, 313, 314, 315, 316, 318, 319, 333, 334, 335, 336, 338, 345

W

Wade, Florence 152
Wade, Virginia J. 320, 338
Wagstaff, (Mrs.) 141
Wakarusa War 122
Walker, Jacob 326
Walker, Lora 326
Walker, Lora Ellen 326
Walkinshaw, James Riccard 333
Wallace, Alice Josephine 354, 355
Wallace, Dana 5, 6, 259, 260, 261
Wallace, Elizabeth 333
Wallace, Elsye Maude 354
Wallace, Eunice Cora ii, 293, 329, 332, 343, 347, 351, 354, 357, 395, 402, 403, 404
Wallace, Jerome Bruce 332
Wallace, Josie L. 272, 354
Wallace, Leslie Earle vii, ix, 8, 9, 10, 51, 65, 94, 278, 279, 283, 292, 297, 298, 302, 303, 304, 305, 306, 307, 325, 329, 332, 341, 346, 347, 350, 354, 357, 393, 398
Wallace, Lew ix

Wallace, Ralph L. 293, 299, 400, 401
Wallace, Ralph Leslie 285, 330, 348, 355
Wallace, Sara LeMaistre (Johnson) 10, 285, 294, 329, 347, 354
Wallace, Sue Austin See Heiskell, Sue Austin
Wallace, Suzanne 333
Wallace, Virginia 333
Wallace, William F. 5, 8, 9, 253, 255, 256, 260, 262, 263, 269, 270, 271, 273, 274, 275, 277, 282, 304, 324, 325, 340, 346, 350, 353, 354, 356, 357
Wallace, William True i, 5, 259, 260, 262, 263, 274, 324, 346, 353, 355
Ward, May Williams 293
Washington Hotel 373
Washington, D. C. 52, 53, 54, 55, 69, 73, 97, 125, 143, 146, 168, 169, 196, 209, 210, 211, 212, 213, 247, 250, 262, 273, 274, 275, 277, 283, 284, 298, 304, 305, 338, 356, 357, 358
Waterloo, Iowa 315
Waterman, Amasa 263
Waterman, Lydia M. 259, 260, 274, 324, 346, 353, 356
Watie, Stand 158
Watts, Dale 119
Wayne County, Kentucky 324, 346
Wea (Native American nation) 1, 2, 11, 13, 15, 16, 18, 40, 41, 42, 47, 49, 55, 57, 64, 65, 66, 67, 73, 82, 83, 84, 91, 151, 152, 157, 158, 160, 226, 227, 228, 241, 268, 269, 276, 304, 316, 318, 321, 322, 345, 351
Wea Mission 14, 228
Wea Mission Cemetery 45
Webster, Abigail Ann See Lykins, Abigail Ann (Webster)
Webster, Charles 2
Western Spirit (newspaper) 167, 249, 258, 259, 263, 264, 267, 273, 274, 276, 304, 305, 307, 338, 339, 340, 349, 350, 356
Westport Historical Society 363
Westport Landing 58

Westport, Missouri   2, 23, 24, 27, 28, 47, 57, 59, 60, 62, 63, 64, 81, 82, 83, 84, 91, 93, 105, 112, 137, 138, 147, 205, 207, 215, 237, 249, 268, 281, 312, 316, 317, 323, 339, 342, 346
Wheat, Josiah (Reverend)   184
White, Martin   107, 117
White, Velna   332
White, William Allen   ix, 288, 302, 305
Whitefeather, Sara   155, 322
Whittier, John Greenleaf   71, 94
Wilhelm, Paul (Duke of Wuerttemberg)   58
Wilkinson, (candidate for representative)   90
Williams, Burton   191, 214
Williams, Mariah (Brown)   313
Williams, Sarah "Lena"   322
Williamsburg, Virginia   261
Wills, Anna E.   328
Wills, Beulah B.   328
Wills, Don Carl   322, 328, 341
Wills, Don L.   328
Wills, Ruth M.   328
Wilson County, Kansas   158
Wilson, (U.S. Land Commissioner)   77
Wilson, John   40
Wilson, Steve   377, 378, 379
Wingate, Mabel (French)   272
Wingate, William   272
Wood, Samuel N.   80
Woodring. Harry (Governor)   297
Woodson, (Acting Governor)   127
World War II   10, 197, 303, 342, 352
Wyandot (Native American nation)   76, 82
Wyandot, Calhoon (General)   118
Wyandots (Native American nation)   361

Y

Yankee settlement   *See* Free-staters
Young, Harriet Louisa   200
Young, Sallie   192
Younger, (candidate for representative)   90

Z

Zygmond, Jack   332

ABOUT THE AUTHOR

Rose Ann (Gard) Wallace-Findlen grew up in the Missouri-Kansas Borderland, blissfully unaware of her own history. Until she researched the material for this book, she had little or no understanding of the intensity of the Border Wars, or of their symbolic representation of humanitarian and political issues shaping the character of the United States from its beginning. In writing this book, she learned who she was as an American.

Until her graduation from Northwest Missouri State University, she lived on the family farm near Maryville, Missouri. While studying for her Master's Degree in English at the University of Kansas, she first became aware of the Border War and the grim conflict between the Missourians and Kansans, but the Civil Rights demonstrations and Vietnam War protests were at the forefront of her and other students' consciousness in those years. The history of the Borderland and ancestral origins did not appear to be relevant to their lives.

Living in France and the former Yugoslavia, teaching English to Native Americans in Colorado, providing courses to soldiers monitoring communiqués across the Iron Curtain, finishing a Ph.D., becoming a mother and a college English professor filled her mind and her years to the brim. Only after her career in college administration, in which she served as a dean, provost and president, did she turn seriously to writing and to this book.

Now living in Madison, Wisconsin, she better understands how their journeys across the Mississippi are interwoven with hers. The conflicting values of America's citizenry—Northerners and Southerners, Anglo-Americans and Native-Americans—came with the settlers crossing Missouri and Iowa into the Kansas Territory.

Emeline and William Heiskell, Johnston and Mattie Lykins, Baptiste Peoria, and William F. Wallace and all the people converging on the Borderland still live, in bits and pieces, in the Borderland and in the American psyche.

As emblems of America's early formation, they are part of who the Rose Ann Findlen is as well...a daughter of the Borderland.

www.ingramcontent.com/pod-product-compliance
Lightning Source LLC
Chambersburg PA
CBHW071959150426
43194CB00008B/927